Class and Religious Identity:

The Rhenish Center Party in Wilhelmine Germany

Thomas M. Bredohl

PRESS

2000

MARQUETTE STUDIES IN THEOLOGY No. 18
Andrew Tallon, Series Editor

Library of Congress Cataloguing in Publication Data

Bredohl, Thomas M. (Thomas Matthias), 1957-
 Class and religious identity : the Rhenish Center Party in Wilhelmine Germany / by Thomas M. Bredohl.
  p. cm. — (Marquette studies in theology ; no. 18)
 Includes bibliographical references and index.
 ISBN 0-87462-642-0
 1. Deutsche Zentrumspartei—History. 2. Rhine Province (Germany)—Politics and government. 3. Catholics—Germany—Political activity—History. 4. Church and state—Germany—History. 5. Catholic Church—Germany—History. I. Title. II. Series: Marquette studies in theology ; #18.
 JN3946.Z5 B74 1998
 324.243'05—ddc21
                                                98-25326
                                                    CIP

All rights reserved.
No part of this publication may be reproduced, stored in a retrieval system,
or transmitted in any form or by any means,
electronic, mechanical, photocopying, recording or otherwise,
without prior permission of the publisher,
except for quotation of brief passages in scholarly books, articles, and reviews.

Member, THE ASSOCIATION OF AMERICAN UNIVERSITY PRESSES

MARQUETTE UNIVERSITY PRESS
MILWAUKEE WISCONSIN USA
2000

MARQUETTE UNIVERSITY PRESS
MILWAUKEE

The Association of Jesuit University Presses

For my wife, Elizabeth A. Toporowski

ACKNOWLEDGMENTS

The book began as a University of Toronto dissertation directed by James Retallack. For his generous, continual support, encouragement, and critical reading I am very grateful. I want to thank Ronald Ross of the University of Wisconsin and Thomas Saunders of the University of Victoria for their helpful criticism. They both gave the penultimate version of this book a close reading and spared me quite a few blunders. This book was only made possible because of the help of friends in Canada and Germany. I am especially thankful to Günter Schnitker, Mechtild Thull, Ursula Hecht, Kerstin and Jürgen Tollkamp, and David Zimmerman. Finally, I owe more than I can express to my wife Elizabeth A. Toporowski to whom this book is dedicated.

CONTENTS

I. INTRODUCTION 7

II. THE SETTING 18
   A. Integration into Prussia 18
   B. Industrialization of the Rhineland 23
   C. Catholics in the Rhineland 31

III. THE WORLD OF CATHOLIC POLITICS 47
   A. The Founding of the Center Party 50
   B. The People's Association for Catholic Germany 60
   C. Ernst Lieber's Leadership 68

IV. KARL TRIMBORN'S CENTER 81
   A. Karl Trimborn's Organization of the Rhenish Center 92
   B. Organization of the Center Press 93

V. WORKERS, CENTER, AND SOCIALISTS 107
   A. Catholic Workers' Clubs and Christian Trade Unions ... 107
   B. Center and Socialists 126

VI. GEWERKSCHAFTSSTREIT AND ZENTRUMSSTREIT 149
   A. Gewerkschaftsstreit 151
   B. Zentrumsstreit 163

VII. THE RHENISH CENTER AND NATIONAL POLITICS ... 177
   A. The Center and Weltpolitik 185
   B. The Bülow Years, 1900-1909 198
   C. Bethmann Hollweg and the Center Party 216

VIII. CONCLUSION 234

TABLES & APPENDICES
   Reichstag Elections in the Prussian Rhine Province 1890-1902 242
   Chairmen of the Center in the German Reichstag 243
   Rhenish Members of the Center Party's Reichstag Caucus, 1871-1918 244
   Bishops of the Dioceses in the Rhine Province 248
   Glossary 249
Bibliography 251
Indices 271

Abbreviations
Used in the Footnotes

BAK	Bundesarchiv, Koblenz
BAP	Bundesarchiv, Abt. Potsdam
HAStK	Historisches Archiv der Stadt Köln
HStaD	Hauptstaatsarchiv Düsseldorf
KB	Bachem, Karl. *Vorgeschichte, Geschichte und Politik der deutschen Zentrumspartei.* 9 vols. Cologne: Verlag J. P. Bachem, 1927-1932.
KV	*Kölnische Volkszeitung*
Nl.	Nachlaß
SBR	*Stenographische Berichte über die Verhandlungen des Reichstages*
StaMG	Stadtarchiv Mönchengladbach
WK	Wahlkreis

I.

INTRODUCTION

A RELIGIOUS animosity divided the state created by Prussia's armies and its most brilliant statesman, Otto von Bismarck. Germany's Catholic minority was frequently viewed by the Protestant majority as backward; by the Protestant clergy as heretical; by court and government officials as seditious and tied to a foreign power. Catholics viewed Bismarck's creation with equal misgivings; they complained that the institutions which controlled the state—court, army and government—systematically discriminated against them. To defend the rights of their co-religionists, Catholic politicians created a political party, the Center. Ironically most post-Bismarckian governments could only achieve a majority in the Reichstag with Center support. While Catholics were engaged in their struggle against Protestant adversaries, they also had to find ways to adapt to the changes that industrialization had brought to their lives. This study examines how Catholics of the Rhineland dealt with these threats to their religious and political culture.

Chronologically, this study will range from the early 1890s to the outbreak of the First World War. The early 1890s are a suitable point of departure, for they mark a turning point in the history of German political Catholicism. The church-state confrontation of the 1870s, known as the Kulturkampf, had died down by that time allowing the Center Party to pay attention to pressing political, social and economic questions rather than to fighting the state. Wilhelm II ascended the throne in 1888, and Bismarck's chancellorship survived the young Kaiser's investiture by less than two years. Lastly, the Center itself underwent a generational change after the death of Ludwig Windthorst, the party's legendary leader and perhaps Bismarck's staunchest and most skilled opponent in the Reichstag. As younger men succeeded as leaders, the party gradually moved away from the traditional politics of notables to a modern organization that took account of the large middle-class following of the Center and the political demands of Catholic workers. The year 1914 seems to be a logical terminal date: the war disrupted party politics and ultimately destroyed much of the political pattern of the Kaiserreich.

Geographically, this history is confined to the five *Regierungsbezirke*, or districts, (Aachen, Cologne, Düsseldorf, Krefeld, and Trier) of the Prussian Rhine Province.[1] There are a number of reasons why the Rhineland lends itself to the study of political Catholicism. A regional study promises some degree of coherence and unity of the area under scrutiny and, by definition emphasizes the differences that existed among the regions that made up the Second Empire. Germany was, after all, a federal state composed of economically and politically diverse regions with their own cultural characteristics.

The Center was a regional party. For it, Berlin in many ways was less relevant than Stuttgart, Munich, or Cologne. The Center was also a hybrid between political ideology and faith. Catholics were concentrated in a few regions of the Kaiserreich, and so was the political strength of the Center. The great majority of its supporters and activists came from Bavaria, Silesia, Westphalia, and the Rhineland. The Rhineland was not only a predominantly Catholic area but also the most influential region of political Catholicism in Imperial Germany. In 1871, of the thirty-five Reichstag seats in the Rhineland, twenty-one were held by the Center. Nearly half of the eighty-eight Center deputies elected to the Prussian Landtag came from the Rhine Province. Moreover, the Rhineland was the center of Christian trade unions. The Church as well as the Center were powerful institutions which helped facilitate the conversion of a largely agrarian population into an efficient industrial work force. In that regard, the Rhineland was different from Bavaria or Württemberg or Silesia; on the whole it was more industrialized, with a relatively large number of Catholic workers.

Political parties are usually conceived to protect and further the interests of a particular socio-economic group. The Center is an outstanding exception to this pattern; its composition followed religious rather than social or class lines. Apart from religious and ecclesiastical concerns, the members and supporters shared little in common. However, in Germany religion was a powerful political force. In German electoral politics religion had a stronger influence on voters than class. This relationship between confessional allegiance and electoral behavior has been a significant factor in party politics even in the

---

[1] For the purpose of this study I shall use the terms Rhine Province and Rhineland interchangeably.

Federal Republic of Germany.[2] Among other things, the founding of the Center marks the beginning of a political movement which in time offered an alternative to Socialdemocratic and Liberal recipes for coping with economic and social change.

The Center was a hermaphrodite equipped with characteristics inherited from its religious and political origins. Contrary to the claims of its opponents, Center and curia did *not* work hand-and-glove in strengthening the position of Catholics in the German empire. In fact, more often than not, their policies contradicted each other, and rarely if ever was the Pope in a position to force upon the Center's leaders a position they opposed. If the Pope could not determine Center Party policies, the party could not function without help from the clergy. Priests were usually capable and occasionally gifted advocates of the Center cause; virtually all were fierce opponents of Socialism. Despite government attempts to silence priests, the sermon remained an effective instrument for Catholic political propaganda and the parish a fertile recruiting ground for Center voters and supporters. In the Rhineland, as in other Catholic regions, the Church provided various institutions, notably schools, hospitals, orphanages and charitable societies for the poor, that were crucial ingredients for the success of a Catholic political movement. Gradually, the Center and its associations provided some of these services. Thus for Catholics who clearly saw that the Church failed in many ways to adapt to the modern world, the Center offered an alternative. Center politicians took over some of the educational tasks of the Church, particularly the education of workers; although the Church maintained a foothold through priests active in the People's Association. It is note worthy that it was not a clerical institution but a secular one which provided these services; this can be seen to be a part of secularization, or laicization of German society. As the support among workers waned, or threatened to disappear, Centrists became concerned about the party's future. To play a significant role in German politics, the party depended on popular support in the country's industrialized regions. To preserve such support it had to offer more than a haven for Catholic beliefs. It had to offer an alternative to the promises of Socialism. In the end the Center failed in this ambition.

Historians of the Center have had to resist the seductive temptation to see political Catholicism in the terms established by party rivalries and political rifts created during the Kaiserreich. Certainly

---

[2] Karl Rohe, ed. *Elections, Parties and Political Traditions: Social Foundations of German Parties and Party Systems, 1867-1987* (New York: Berg Publishers, 1990), pp. 3-4.

all contemporary writers perceived the Center as born out of and sustained by the struggle between Protestants and Catholics, between Bismarck and the National Liberals on one side and the Center on the other. Two diametrically opposed interpretations appeared in the literature. On the one hand the Center was portrayed as the "ultramontane" enemy of the state whose allegiance was not to the Kaiser in Potsdam but to the Pope in Rome. In this view the Center was an alien element in Hohenzollern Germany. On the other hand, the Center and the Catholic population it represented emerged as a beleaguered but loyal minority defending its legal and moral rights.

The works of Heinrich von Treitschke and Heinrich von Sybel are the most accomplished examples of what Winfried Becker has called the Prusso-National Liberal interpretation (*kleindeutschnationalliberale These*).[3] Treitschke and Sybel saw the Center as a clerical, purely Catholic party. The former charged that the ultramontane Center was a subversive force which recognized the new state only to use it toward its own, clerical ends.[4] This interpretation is, of course, colored very much by Treitschke's admiration for Otto von Bismarck. Already suspicious of Catholic anti-Prussian sentiments in southwest Germany and the Rhineland before he had founded the Reich, Bismarck openly questioned the Center's allegiance to the Kaiserreich when he was in search of a like-minded political ally in the early 1870s. Bismarck alleged that Centrists were enemies of the state who, in fact, supported the subversive tendencies of the Socialists, the enemies of all legitimate authority.[5]

Germany's liberal parties were all too willing to combine a coalition with the government with the persecution of a political and ideological enemy. Among them the National Liberals were the most ardent opponents of the Center and the most enthusiastic champions of anti-Catholic legislation. Heinrich von Sybel belonged to the right wing of the National Liberal Party; his historical analysis reflects his party affiliation. To the modern historian of the Center, Sybel's almost exclusively political and narrative account, dominated by personal antagonism and unashamedly partisan, is primarily use-

---

[3] Winfried Becker, "Die Deutsche Zentrumspartei im Bismarckreich," in *Die Minderheit als Mitte—Die Deutsche Zentrumspartei in der Innenpolitik des Reiches 1871-1933*, ed. *idem* (Paderborn: Ferdinand Schöningh, 1986), p. 11. Sybel was born in Düsseldorf and represented Krefeld in the Prussian Landtag.

[4] Heinrich von Treitschke, *Der Sozialismus und der Meuchelmord*, 1878, quoted in Becker, "Zentrumspartei," p. 13.

[5] Lothar Gall, *Bismarck. Der weiße Revolutionär* (Frankfurt: Ullstein Verlag, 1980), p. 473.

ful as a particularly forceful example of liberal indictments of political Catholicism.

More useful, though hardly less partisan, is Karl Bachem's thorough and detailed defense of political Catholicism. The largest and most important study written by a Center politician, Bachem's nine-volume work argues that "nothing was further from the minds of its [the Center's] founders than the creation of a fundamental opposition to the government...the new German empire...and its emperor." Bachem stressed the loyalty of German Catholics and the Center to Bismarck's creation, if not to the man. To Bachem the Center was a political party dedicated "to the defense of Christian principles." That in the end it turned out to be the "political and parliamentarian representative of the Catholic population" was a consequence not of its founders' intentions, but of the need (brought about by the Kulturkampf) to defend "the religious freedom of the Catholic Church."[6] Winfried Becker has noted that Bachem was not just partisan but in addition represented a particular group within the Center. He was a proponent of the so-called Cologne wing (*Kölner Richtung*): a segment of the party eager to turn it into an interdenominational rather than a Catholic organization. Thus Bachem's study is partisan in two ways: it portrays the Center as a party loyal to Reich and Kaiser, anxious to integrate Catholics into the new Germany, but, paradoxically, also a party capable of attracting non-Catholics.

Whether sympathetic or antagonistic, the tendencies which have been sketched here were written from the standpoint of party politics, inspired by contemporary battle cries, not historical analysis. To expect the men who witnessed and were part of the past to assess its importance accurately or even to describe it fully, would be unrealistic. One of their biases—their concentration on the period of the Kulturkampf—was particularly difficult for early historians to shed. In recent decades, though, historians have been able to provide a more detached view and explore new questions about the Center. Much of the argument, however, remains largely unchanged. The central question continues to be: How Catholic, how clerical, how political, how secularized was the Center, and how did it fit into the Kaiserreich's spectrum of political parties?

In 1947 Karl Buchheim asserted that "political Catholicism was a civil liberties movement predicated on the existence of excessive

---

[6] KB, 3:157, 166, 168.

demands of state powers coupled with the danger of a state church."[7] He argued that Ultramontanism should be understood as a precursor to Christian democracy. To his mind Catholicism was not a reactionary, anti-modern view of the world but an integral part of modern, democratic societies.[8] Ultramontanism was part of the nineteenth-century revolutions, "the industrial, social and political revolutions, which had to concern the Church."[9] Like Bachem, Buchheim stressed the political rather than religious aspects of the Center.[10] The Center was seen as a democratic mass party, not unlike the Social Democratic Party (SPD), but with an ideology based on Roman Catholicism not Marxism.[11] During the 1890s, Buchheim argued, the party underwent an "inner democratization" which he regards as evidence of the Center's role as a pioneer of democracy in Germany.[12] Center efforts bore, however, no immediate fruits. Christian democracy was achieved only after the catastrophe of the Third Reich. Buchheim's interpretation has been roundly criticized for lacking evidence to substantiate his claims.[13]

More convincing, though in some ways not dissimilar from that of Buchheim, is the interpretation offered by Rudolf Morsey, the most important historian of the Center after the Second World War. To Morsey, Center policies after the end of the Kulturkampf were determined by the need to satisfy a constituency composed of all social groups and regional interests. Rhenish Centrists, for example, had to cater to the interests of Catholic farmers but also to those of industrial workers in order to secure support at the polls. Socialist success in attracting Catholic workers, in part, explains the Center's social politics and the defense by Center politicians of civic rights and democratic emancipation.[14] Morsey's work, which concentrated

---

[7] Karl Buchheim, "Grundlagen und Anfänge des politischen Katholizismus," *Frankfurter Hefte*, December 1947, 1225, quoted in Michael Klöcker, "Der politische Katholizismus. Versuch einer Neudefinierung," *Zeitschrift für Politik* 18 (1971), p. 124.

[8] Karl Buchheim, *Ultramontanismus und Demokratie. Der Weg der deutschen Katholiken im 19. Jahrhundert* (Munich: Kösel-Verlag, 1963), p. 9.

[9] Ibid., p. 517.

[10] Becker, "Zentrumspartei," p. 16.

[11] Buchheim, *Ultramontanismus*, p. 532.

[12] Karl Buchheim, *Geschichte der christlichen Parteien in Deutschland* (Munich: Kösel-Verlag, 1953), p. 221.

[13] Wilfried Loth, *Katholiken im Kaiserreich. Der politische Katholizismus in der Krise des wilhelmischen Deutschlands* (Düsseldorf: Droste Verlag, 1984), p. 27.

[14] Rudolf Morsey, *Die Deutsche Zentrumspartei 1917-1923* (Düsseldorf: Droste Verlag, 1966), pp. 44-7.

on the years after 1917, spurred interest in the Center Party during the Weimar Republic and the Third Reich. As historians turned toward the Kaiserreich, the role of the Center during that period became the subject of a number of first-rate studies.

Two American and one German historian published important studies of the Wilhelmine Center in the mid-1970s. John K. Zeender's political history concentrates on the relationship between the Center and the Imperial government between 1890-1906, the years when the party could tip the scales in the Reichstag. Ronald J. Ross's Center is a party "undermined from within" by the insoluble internal conflict between secularism and sectarianism and "besieged" from without by a hostile Protestant majority. The central issue for Catholics was the quest for parity with their Protestant counterparts in the central institutions of the empire: the army, the civil service, the professions (particularly in education).[15] In comparing the SPD and Center factions, Ursula Mittmann draws the picture of an opportunistic Center. As opposed to the Social Democrats (a party motivated by its ideology and its principles), the Center emerges as a party loyal to the state (*staatstragend*), offering (unlike the Socialists) no alternative to the existing society, and primarily concerned with the satisfaction of the various interests of its constituency.[16]

Regionalism and provincial patriotism were powerful forces in Imperial Germany. Until fairly recently, however, these aspects of German society have been neglected by professional historians.[17] Exceptions to this tradition are Karl Möckl's excellent account of Bavarian politics before the First World War and David Blackbourn's detailed analysis of the workings of the Württemberg Center. Although a local study, Blackbourn's investigation of Württemberg's political microcosm never loses sight of national issues. Indeed, Blackbourn chose Württemberg because Center politics there "mirrored the politics of the national party."[18] Contrasting his work to

---

[15] John K. Zeender, *The German Center Party 1890-1906* (Philadelphia: Transactions of the American Philosophical Society, 1976); Ronald J. Ross, *Beleaguered Tower: The Dilemma of Political Catholicism in Wilhelmine Germany* (Notre Dame, Ind.: University of Notre Dame Press, 1976).

[16] Ursula Mittmann, *Fraktion und Partei: Ein Vergleich von Zentrum und Sozialdemokratie im Kaiserreich* (Düsseldorf: Droste Verlag, 1976), p. 381.

[17] One of the very few studies to address these concepts is Celia Applegate's *A Nation of Provincials: The German Idea of Heimat* (Berkeley: University of California Press, 1990).

[18] David Blackbourn, *Class, Religion, and Local Politics in Wilhelmine Germany. The Centre Party in Württemberg before 1914* (New Haven, Conn.: Yale University Press, 1980), p. 21.

that of Eckart Kehr, Blackbourn sets out to show that Center politicians were not motivated by purely political, unscrupulously tactical considerations. At the root of their decisions were, as in other political parties, "a combination of economic, social and political" motives.[19] Center policies and leadership, he contends, underwent "a marked de-clericalisation" beginning in the 1890s.[20] The Kulturkampf party of old was replaced by a party that had "cast off the more obvious clerical and confessional attributes," to become at last the political party its founders had intended it to be. Its new leadership was not the traditional mixture of priests and aristocrats but a "thoroughly bourgeois" assortment of businessmen, academics, officials, publishers and "those quintessential political brokers of bourgeois parliamentary" politics: lawyers.[21] In later work, Blackbourn refined his initial judgment, paying greater attention to the role religion played in Center politics. How far, Blackbourn asks, did the party embody "a specifically Catholic faith and piety in its politics?" He concludes that their "common faith informed the everyday reality of Center politics."[22] The annual assemblies of German Catholics (instead of party congresses), their political language, the frequent combination of religious observance and Center meetings all show "how necessary it is to see the Centre firmly located within a distinctively Catholic milieu."[23] The Center emerges as a party similar in many ways to other German political parties. For instance, the relationship between the Center party and interest groups and the role economic policies played in the formulation of policies and strategies, were not unlike those in German liberalism. The Center's position as a political pariah, on the other hand, was akin to that of Social Democracy. What made the Center different from other parties was, according to Blackbourn, the fact that their "material grievances...were embedded in a sense of discrimination and exclusion which embraced the religious, the social and the political."[24]

Perhaps the most impressive single example of scholarship on the Center is the great Windthorst biography by Margaret Lavinia Anderson. Ludwig Windthorst, arguably Imperial Germany's greatest parliamentarian, was leader of the Center for more than two de-

[19] Ibid., p. 20.
[20] Ibid.
[21] Ibid., pp. 231-3.
[22] David Blackbourn, *Populists and Patricians: Essays in Modern German History* (London: Allen & Unwin, 1987), p. 199.
[23] Ibid., p. 200.
[24] Ibid., p. 210.

INTRODUCTION   15

cades: in Anderson's words, the "uncrowned king of Catholic Germany."²⁵ According to her, Windthorst's conception of his party's place within the constitution changed him from a "monarchist of the old school" in 1870 to a party leader who, by the end of his life, had made the Center essentially a liberal party with a Catholic twist.²⁶ In subsequent work, Anderson argues that before 1866 there existed "no necessary relationship between Catholic confession and conservative politics."²⁷ It was the Kulturkampf that "effected a massive political realignment of Catholics"; prior to this (i. e., between 1862-66) Catholics had voted liberal more often than clerical.²⁸ Motivated "by advantage and conviction in about equal measure," Windthorst supported "every element of the liberal constitution" both during and after the Kulturkampf interlude.²⁹

Historians have been slow to do justice to the Center Party. Justice, though belatedly, seems to have come. One of the most important contributions of the last decade has been Wilfried Loth's *Katholiken im Kaiserreich. Der politische Katholizismus in der Krise des wilhelmischen Deutschlands* (1984). Loth's book presents the first sustained criticism of the existing literature on the Center Party and the first adequate realization of the importance of the Center Party for the development of Germany's political culture. Loth's *tour de force* takes account of virtually all published works on the topic and subjects them to unrelenting criticism—one reviewer refers to his "almost obsessive corrections of his predecessors' work."³⁰ Loth's most significant contribution is the fact that he has moved the discussion of political Catholicism from the sidelines of the historiography of Imperial Germany to the very center. The Center Party, in Loth's view, played a crucial role in preventing a stabilization of governmental power in the early years of the Kaiserreich. Later it contributed to a permanent crisis of government and, despite advancing the process of parliamentarization of German politics, blocked the country's democratization.³¹ But with all its virtues and width of view, Loth's study does not compare in originality with the work of

[25] Margaret Lavinia Anderson, *Windthorst: A Political Biography* (London: Oxford University Press, 1981), p. 3.
[26] Ibid., pp. 401-2.
[27] Margaret Lavinia Anderson, "The Kulturkampf and the Course of German History," *Central European History* 19 (1986), p. 87.
[28] Ibid., pp. 82, 85.
[29] Anderson, *Windthorst*, p. 402.
[30] Margaret Lavinia Anderson, "Piety and Politics: Recent Work on German Catholicism," *Journal of Modern History* 63 (1991), p. 71.
[31] Loth, Katholiken, pp. 386-7.

Anderson and Blackbourn; it lacks the distinctive, clear line of argument of the former and the innovative methodology of the latter.

Finally, there has been a greatly increased interest in political biographies. Until Margaret Anderson's seminal study of Windthorst, virtually no Center leader had found a scholarly biographer; during the last decade or so, we have seen the appearance of several important studies. Already in 1977 Manfred Bierganz wrote a doctoral dissertation on Hermann Cardauns, editor of the influential *Kölnische Volkszeitung*. The *Kommission für Zeitgeschichte* has also published a number of biographies, including the first volume of Winfried Becker's study of Georg von Hertling, covering his youth and political career until the Kulturkampf; there are also biographies of Karl Bachem and the leader of the Silesian Center leader Felix Porsch.[32] Nevertheless, scholarly biographies of important Rhenish Centrists such as Karl Trimborn and Julius Bachem are still desiderata.

Even this brief synopsis of scholarship on the Center Party and political Catholicism must end on a note of optimism. Between the state of the art in the 1950s and that of today, the gulf is enormous. The effect of this growing scholarship has been to demote considerably the Kulturkampf from the central position it previously occupied. In place of Kulturkampf studies we are now offered a wide array of studies: establishing the early 1890s as a watershed in the history of the Center and the Kaiserreich; providing information on the crucial decade before 1914; complementing the national picture with regional sketches; and giving us biographies of a number of Center leaders. There has also been an effort to place the Center and its problems during the Kaiserreich more integrally than before in the context of German party politics, to stress the extent to which the tensions which existed in the Center Party and among its constituency found their parallel in other political parties. The Center, in this view, was not so much an aberration of German politics as one of the manifestations of the Bismarckian unification of Germany and the peculiar structure of German society.

This study, then, is primarily concerned with the question of how the general influences of industrialization and integration into the Second Empire made themselves felt within the context of Catholic

---

[32] Winfried Becker, *Georg von Hertling 1843-1919* (Mainz: Matthias-Grünewald-Verlag, 1981); Rolf Kiefer, *Karl Bachem: 1858-1945; Politiker und Historiker des Zentrums* (Mainz: Matthias-Grünewald-Verlag, 1989); August Hermann Leugers-Scherzberg, *Felix Porsch: 1853-1930. Politik für katholische Interessen in Kaiserreich und Republik* (Mainz: Matthias-Grünewald Verlag, 1990).

politics in the Rhineland. Therefore its purpose is fourfold. First, it will shed light on the organizational workings of the Rhenish Center. In particular, this study will focus on the reorganization of the Cologne and Rhenish chapters of the party by Karl Trimborn. The Catholic milieu was also rich in religious and political voluntary associations (such as the People's Association, the Pius-Vereine and the many workers and journeymen clubs). An analysis of their organizational structure and their relationship with the Rhenish Center is crucial to an understanding of the workings of political Catholicism. Secondly, this study suggests that Rhenish Center leaders vigorously courted Catholic workers in an attempt to maintain the level of support they had achieved during the Kulturkampf years. The Rhineland with its heavily industrialized areas is well-suited to an investigation of the political, economic, and religious behavior of Catholic workers. Furthermore, the Center's failure to attract large numbers of workers (as well as Protestants) was central to the controversies that rocked the party in the decade after the turn of the century. Thirdly this book argues that the Center's drive for democracy, which was strongly supported by many of the most prominent Rhenish party leaders, was incompatible with the *Weltanschauung* of the Center. The double heritage of patriarchical traditions of the Roman Catholic Church and the political traditions of a party of notables hindered efforts to democratize the party. And fourthly, I will raise some questions about the place of the Center in German party politics and about continuities in German politics in general. The Center, I will argue, was neither an exception nor an oddity in the landscape of German politics. Center politicians, often accused of being opportunist, understood that a modern political party had at times to make uncomfortable coalitions or favor practical considerations over lofty political principles. Although Centrists were unable to create a party attractive to Protestants as well as Catholics, their ideal here provided a model for the post-1945 Christian Democratic Union (CDU).

II.

THE SETTING

THREE CIRCUMSTANCES more than any others shaped the history of the nineteenth-century Rhineland: The integration of the Rhineland into Prussia at the Congress of Vienna; the changes brought about by industrialization together with the growth of Rhenish cities and towns that resulted from it; and lastly the emergence of a potent political Catholicism.

A. Integration into Prussia

"*Do hirohde mer in'n ärm Familije*," (There we are, marrying into a poor family!) is how the Cologne banker Abraham Schaaffhausen sarcastically commented on the marriage of the Rhineland and Prussia which was arranged at the Congress of Vienna. The Rhineland had been under French control during the Revolutionary and Napoleonic periods and only reluctantly joined the unloved Prussians, who in turn favored the acquisition of Saxony.[1] These reservations aside, the Prussian government swiftly and efficiently introduced its administrative institutions to the new territories.

The diplomats at the Congress of Vienna created a bewildering patchwork of secular and ecclesiastical boundaries. The arrangements regarding the Rhine Province nowhere reflected the boundaries drawn by French administrators. To the north the border with the Prussian province of Westphalia was drawn, in general, along the lines of the pre-revolutionary territorial boundaries; the western border with the Netherlands did not follow old borderlines. There were oddities such as Neutral-Morsenet, a small (1.26 square miles) zinc-rich patch of land a few miles west of Aachen over which the Congress could reach

---

[1] Schaaffhausen's quip cited in Bernhard Poll, "Das Hineinwachsen der Rheinländer in den Preußischen Staatsverband," in *150 Jahre Regierung und Regierungsbezirk Aachen. Beiträge zu ihrer Geschichte*, ed. Regierungspräsident (Aachen: Regierungspräsident, 1967), p. 17. For Prussian attitudes see Rudolf Vierhaus, "Preußen und die Rheinlande," *Rheinische Vierteljahrsblätter* 30 (1965), pp. 154-5.

no agreement. Administered jointly if not harmoniously by Prussia and the Netherlands (and by Belgium after 1830), the de-militarized enclave became a haven for unwilling conscripts and remained a bone of contention for over a century.[2] At times the Rhine Province reached beyond the old border, at times it receded; at no point did it reach the Maas river.[3] In 1822 the initial six districts of the Lower Rhine Province and the Province of Jülich-Kleve-Berg were consolidated into the Rhine Province, consisting of five districts: Düsseldorf, Aachen, Cologne, Trier, and Koblenz. This administrative organization survived until 1945.

Even more complicated than redrawing the political map was defining new ecclesiastical borders. A large part of the archdiocese of Cologne, for instance, reached into Westphalia. The rest of the archdiocese extended over the entire Rhenish portion of the region, except for the northern half of the Düsseldorf district, which was part of the diocese of Münster. The bishopric of Aachen, established by Napoleon, covered much of the left bank of the Rhine, but some of its parishes now belonged to the Netherlands; the ecclesiastical territory of the bishopric of Liège, on the other hand, reached into the Rhine Province. None of these territorial conflicts were resolved at the Congress of Vienna. Furthermore, the hope that the Congress would create a uniform church law for all German states was not realized; and on the left bank of the Rhine French ecclesiastical law continued to be in force.[4]

Pius VII, who had been strong-armed to consecrate Napoleon as emperor and was later driven out of Rome by him, reorganized the ecclesiastical borders in the Rhine Province with the papal bull "De salute animarum" (1821). The Napoleonic bishopric of Aachen was dissolved and its territory became part of the archbishopric of Cologne, now consisting of the Prussian districts of Cologne, Aachen, and Düsseldorf. Although the new archbishopric grew in population

[2] Klaus Pabst, "Neutral-Morsenet. Ein Dorf ohne Staatszugehörigkeit (1815-1915)," in *150 Jahre Regierung und Regierungsbezirk Aachen. Beiträge zu ihrer Geschichte*, ed. Regierungspräsident (Aachen: Regierungspräsident, 1967), pp. 45-6.
[3] For details on the integration of the Rhineland into Prussia, see Bernhard Poll, "Preußen und die Rheinlande," *Zeitschrift des Aachener Geschichtsvereins* 76 (1964), pp. 5-44 and more recently, Gerhard Brunn, "Zentrale und Provinz in der preußischen Geschichte vom Wiener Kongreß bis zur Revolution von 1848," in *Die Rheinlande und Preußen: Parlamentarismus, Parteien und Wirtschaft*, ed. Landschaftsverband Rheinland (Cologne: Rheinland-Verlag, 1990), pp. 27-39.
[4] Eduard Hegel, *Geschichte des Erzbistums Köln* (Cologne: Verlag J. P. Bachem, 1987), p. 29.

and the reestablishment of the bishopric of Aachen was often proposed to make the administration more manageable, Aachen only became an independent bishopric again in 1930, as part of the Prussian Concordat. The same papal bull that reorganized Cologne, also drew new borders for the bishopric of Trier which encompassed the administrative districts of Trier and Koblenz.[5] The territory of the Prussian Rhine Province was now congruent with that of the bishoprics of Trier and Cologne.

During the French Revolution the Church had lost more than just control over ecclesiastical borders; much of its wealth in land and tax income had been seized, first by Napoleon and then by the king of Prussia. Catholics bemoaned this "robbery," but they also realized that "the loss of its riches gave back to the Church its inner freedom and its religious vitality."[6] Educational institutions belonging to the Church had also all but disappeared. Of the eighteen Catholic universities, only three (Münster, Würzburg and Freiburg) survived Napoleon's secularization. And they, like the Catholic schools run by abbeys, monasteries and religious orders which had also been closed down, never reached their former numbers and influence. In retrospect, some Catholics thought the Revolution and secularization an unexpected benefit, since they cleared the way for the "strong, well-organized, efficient and purified"[7] Church of late-nineteenth-century Germany.[8] On the other hand, secularization and integration into the Prussian state were among the main reasons for Catholic backwardness. They weakened the cultural influence of Catholicism, created a typical diaspora constellation and led to a wide-spread feeling of inferiority among Catholics.[9] This sense of isolation, combined with opposition to militant Protestantism and a determination to fight discrimination, later provided the popular foundation for political Catholicism.

[5] For details on the history of the bishoprics of Aachen, Cologne, and Trier see Erwin Gatz, ed. *Geschichte des kirchlichen Lebens in den deutschsprachigen Ländern seit dem Ende des 18. Jahrhunderts. Die Katholische Kirche* (Freiburg/Br.: Herder, 1991), pp. 160-7, 389-401, 615-23.
[6] KB, 1:41-2.
[7] KB, 1:43.
[8] Wilfried Evertz, "Das Zusammenwachsen des Klerus unter Erzbischof Spiegel im neugegründeten Erzbistum Köln 1825-1835," *Annalen des Historischen Vereins für den Niederrhein* 197 (1994), pp. 157-8.
[9] Heribert Raab, "Auswirkungen der Säkularisation auf Bildungswesen, Geistesleben und Kunst im katholischen Deutschland," in *Säkularisation und Säkulisierung im 19. Jahrhundert,* ed. Albrecht Langner (Paderborn: Ferdinand Schöningh, 1978), p. 63.

The Setting

The Rhine Province, like all Prussian provinces, was headed by a provincial governor (*Oberpräsident*).[10] The office was political rather than administrative; its importance lay in its supervisory functions and its role as coordinator of government policies in the two lower levels of provincial government: the district and the county. The provincial governor was primarily the province's representative in relations with Berlin. The almost complete absence of Catholics among the ranks of provincial governors and other high administrative offices was a source of bitter discontent and friction between the government and the Catholic population.

Still, Prussian reorganization of the Rhine Province was much more considerate than the same process in Saxony or Posen, taking into account Rhenish traditions and to some degree Rhenish wishes.[11] Heinrich von Treitschke referred to the Rhineland as the "the darling of the Prussian Crown, as Silesia had been under Frederick the Great."[12] Nevertheless, Rhinelanders complained. Much to the disappointment of Rhenish notables, the Prussian government chose Koblenz rather than Cologne as the seat of the provincial government. Cologne was slighted in other ways, too. Anxious about creating a "Roman Catholic Berlin," the Prussian government decentralized the new province's administrative and cultural institutions. In addition to the provincial government, Koblenz received the military command; Bonn was granted a university with a Catholic theological faculty; the Land Captaincy and the Art Academy went to Düsseldorf.[13] Some Rhinelanders objected to the predominance of "Old Prussians" in the civil administration. In Koblenz, for example, the Pomeranian Baron von Ingersleben replaced the local candidate Johann August Sack, much to the chagrin of Koblenzers and of Sack

---

[10] The provincial governors between 1872 and 1918 were: Dr. Moritz von Bardeleben (1872-1890), Berthold Nasse (1890-1905), Klemens Freiherr von Schorlemer-Lieser (1905-1910), Freiherr von Rheinbaben (1910-1918). For the role of *Oberpräsidenten* in the Prussian administration see Max Bär, *Die Behördenverfassung der Rheinprovinz seit 1815* (Bonn: P. Hansteins Verlag, 1919), pp. 139-53.

[11] For details see Karl-Georg Faber, "Die kommunale Selbstverwaltung in der Rheinprovinz im 19. Jahrhundert," *Rheinische Vierteljahrsblätter* 30 (1965), esp. pp. 146-51.

[12] Cited in Brunn, "Zentrale und Provinz," pp. 30-1.

[13] Ross, *Beleaguered Tower*, p. 9.

himself.¹⁴ Rhinelanders also resented the long delays they had to endure before Berlin granted Rhenish (and Westphalian) municipalities the right to self-government already given to the eastern provinces. Ever since the province's incorporation into Prussia, Rhinelanders had urged the government to grant them the same privileges to make administrative appointments, and give them the same control over local police and other municipal affairs. Demands for reform were led by notables from Aachen; the most prominent among them was the liberal banker David Hansemann. Hansemann requested that the Prussian king grant Rhenish municipalities "enough elbow-room for free and independent decisions."¹⁵ Despite promises and assurances from Berlin, municipal self-government was not conceded until 1886.¹⁶ Resentment toward the Prussian and imperial governments hardly diminished after these changes. Indeed, resentment toward the government in Berlin is one of the main features of Rhenish politics and social life; such attitudes are not found solely among Catholics, of course, but they were more ardent in their resentment of Prussian influence because they faced the added frustration of being religious outsiders. On the whole, however, integration into Prussia worked. Some sore spots and grudges remained but not more than in most of the other territories integrated into Prussia during the course of the century; by the time of Germany's unification, the Rhineland had already been part of Prussia for fifty-five years and much of the early resentment had worn off. Catholics had a strong political voice in the Prussian Landtag if not adequate say in municipal administration with its three-class voting system and the skewed census controlled by liberal city councils and the Prussian government. Arguably more difficult and more long-lasting than the effects of political integration into Prussia were the effects of industrialization the Rhineland underwent in the nineteenth century.

¹⁴ Walter Gerschler, "Aachen als Sitz staatlicher Verwaltungsbehörden in der Zeit vom Ende der freien Reichsstadt Aachen im Jahre 1794 bis zum Amtsantritt der Aachener Regierung am 22. April 1816," in *150 Jahre Regierung und Regierungsbezirk Aachen. Beiträge zu ihrer Geschichte*, ed. Regierungspräsident (Aachen: Regierungspräsident, 1967), p. 12.

¹⁵ Cited in Margret de Roy, "Die Kommunalverwaltung im Regierungsbezirk Aachen seit 1816," in *150 Jahre Regierung und Regierungsbezirk Aachen. Beiträge zu ihrer Geschichte*, ed. Regierungspräsident (Aachen: Regierungspräsident, 1967), p. 35.

¹⁶ For details on the Rhineland's long struggle see, Rüdiger Schütz, "Ultramontanismus und preußische Verwaltungsreform: Die Auseinandersetzung um die westfälische und rheinische Kreis- und Provinzialordnung von 1886/87," in *Rheinland-Westfalen im Industriezeitalter*, ed. Kurt Düwell and Wolfgang Köllmann (Wuppertal: Peter Hammer Verlag, 1984), pp. 25-39.

B. Industrialization of the Rhineland

If we can believe the story of the Elbersfeld merchant Johann Gottfried Brügelmann, the industrial revolution in the Rhineland began with a theft.[17] Brügelmann claimed to have come by the secret of Richard Arkwright's (1732-92) spinning frame while working at a Nottingham mill in 1780. With the help of an English master weaver, Brügelmann assured his sovereign, the elector Karl Theodor, that a modern cotton mill could be set up in the dukedom. Ironically, Karl Theodor granted the thieving merchant a twelve-year monopoly on the "invention" and even threatened to punish anyone who attempted to lure away Brügelmann's employees in order to obtain the secret of the spinning frame. Brügelmann's travels to England, his copying of English machines, his hiring of English technicians and workers, and his subsequent founding of an industry at home, mark the typical steps of early industrialization in western Germany and, indeed, in Germany as a whole.[18] Industrial espionage was eventually conducted systematically and with governmental support. In 1818 a section of the Prussian Ministry of Finance was devoted to obtaining the blueprints of new machines and new technologies which were then passed on to Prussian entrepreneurs.[19]

The Rhineland, with its good river transportation and rich coal resources, had an invaluable geographical advantage that would eventually make it one of Europe's most advanced industrial regions. Its principal industries were the manufacturing of textiles and the industries associated with iron, coal, and steel. Typically, as the textile industry grew, manufacturers produced increasingly more complicated and more expensive products. During the eighteenth century linen was the main product, but Rhenish textile manufacturers also made ferret silk, half silk, and smaller amounts of silk; they made pack-thread, shoestring and lace-work. Some regions, particularly those around Cologne, Aachen, and Krefeld, already showed signs of

---

[17] For J. G. Brügelmann's story see, Wolfgang Köllmann, "Von Rheinisch-Westfälischer Wirtschaft," in *Rheinisch-Westfälische Rückblende*, ed. Walter Först (Cologne: Grote, 1967), pp. 134-5.

[18] Gernot Wittling, "Zum Verhältnis von früher Industrialisierung und Technologietransfer im Rheinland und Westfalen nach 1815," in *Die Rheinlande und Preußen: Parlamentarismus, Parteien und Wirtschaft*, ed. Landschaftsverband Rheinland (Cologne: Rheinland-Verlag, 1990), pp. 84-5.

[19] Beuth to Graf Mittrovsky, 21 Dec. 1839, excerpted in Walter Steitz, ed. *Quellen zur deutschen Wirtschafts- und Sozialgeschichte im 19. Jahrhundert bis zur Reichsgründung* (Darmstadt: Wissenschaftliche Buchgesellschaft, 1980), pp. 157-9.

industrialization during the closing decade of the eighteenth century. The growth of new commerce occurred primarily outside the traditional manufacturing towns, and usually outside the larger cities. In the process, new urban centers such as Krefeld and Hagen emerged.[20]

Some credit for economic growth must be given to efforts of the Prussian government to promote commerce and industry. But such efforts were not always successful. The attempt to introduce silk worms to the Kleve area in order to free the Krefeld silk mills from their dependence on imported raw materials, is one example of a failed enterprise.[21] In 1835, almost half a century later, the mayor of Kleve still complained that his town and its surroundings did not have one single factory and that trading consisted exclusively of small retailers who served the local population.[22] Other attempts, such as the introduction of small-scale iron works to the county of Mark, met more success.

The failure to supply Krefeld with domestically produced silk did not prevent the city from becoming the first textile center on the left bank of the Rhine. By the early nineteenth century it had moved from linen weaving to the production of silk. Rheydt and Mönchengladbach attracted cotton manufacturers from the Wuppertal area, since these towns were located within French territory and thus enjoyed protection from French customs. In Aachen, on the other hand, the textile industry shrunk in the early nineteenth century. Limited in their entrepreneurial freedom by the guilds, factory owners moved their facilities. Nearby Burtscheid and Monschau and other places free of guild regulations profited.[23] Often economic growth was a very slow process; the first industrial loom operating in the Rhineland was installed by a weaving mill in Elberfeld in 1844— long after it had been introduced to England. Mechanization of the textile industry, too, proceeded slowly. Rhenish cities (e.g. Aachen and Monschau) were, however, among the few centers of factory manufacture. Most such "factories" were small, equipped with a jenny

---

[20] Köllmann, "Wirtschaft," pp. 129-31.

[21] Ibid., p. 131.

[22] Mayor of Kleve to district governor of the Düsseldorf district, Graf zu Stolberg-Wernigerode, 8 Nov. 1835, reprinted in Steitz, *Quellen zur Wirtschafts- und Sozialgeschichte*, pp. 128-9.

[23] David S. Landes, *The Unbound Prometheus: Technological change and industrial development in Western Europe from 1750 to the present* (1969; reprint, Cambridge: Cambridge University Press, 1987), p. 134; Köllmann, "Wirtschaft," p. 133.

The Setting

or two. The largest producers were in Aachen, with around 1,000 spindles in 1843 (the average spindage in Prussia in 1837 was 103).[24] As a result of the efforts of entrepreneurs like Brügelmann and of the Prussian government, the Rhineland experienced significant economic and social changes even during the early years of Germany's industrialization. Not all of these changes were beneficial. The integration into Prussia meant that the area on the left bank of the Rhine lost the advantage of having access to the markets in the west. Limited access to markets abroad and tough competition on domestic markets had catastrophic consequences during the difficult years of the 1840s. Industrialization also meant a significant increase in population. At first workers were recruited from neighboring regions. When this source was exhausted, around the middle of the century, immigrants came from further afield; the majority came from Prussia's eastern provinces and Poland. Protestant employers preferred Protestant workers from East Prussia, whereas Catholic entrepreneurs looked to the Catholic regions of West Prussia and to Poland for much needed industrial labor. In the process, the Rhine Province became one of the most densely populated regions of Europe and housing for workers one of the most pressing social issues.[25]

Like the manufacture of textiles the production of metal goods had a long tradition in the Rhineland. Aachen, for instance, was well known for its needle manufacturers. Just before the Rhineland fell to Prussia, there were 16 needle factories in Aachen and Burtscheid with some 160 employees, many of them children. Needles from Aachen have been found in English merchant ships that sunk of the east coast of Mexico. The rich copper and zinc mines of the region favored the production of brass. The furnaces were fired by coal mined in the Eifel region and in the coal mines near Aachen.[26] Until the middle of the nineteenth century, metal products were made "wher-

[24] Ibid., p. 172.
[25] For details on population growth see, Hermann Kellenbenz, "Wirtschafts- und Sozialentwicklung der nördlichen Rheinlande seit 1815," in *Wirtschaft und Kultur*, ed. Franz Petri and Georg Droege (Düsseldorf: Schwann, 1979), pp. 17-9; and Gertrud Milkereit, "Wirtschafts- und Sozialentwicklung der südlichen Rheinlande seit 1815," in *Wirtschaft und Kultur*, ed. Franz Petri and Georg Droege (Düsseldorf: Schwann, 1979), pp. 203-12; housing conditions of industrial workers are analyzed in Lutz Niethammer und Franz Brüggemeier, "Wie wohnten Arbeiter im Kaiserreich?," *Archiv für Sozialgeschichte* 16 (1976), esp. pp. 68-92.
[26] Bernhard Poll, "Zur neueren Wirtschaftsgeschichte des Aachener Landes," in *150 Jahre Regierung und Regierungsbezirk Aachen. Beiträge zu ihrer Geschichte*, ed. Regierungspräsident (Aachen: Regierungspräsident, 1967), pp. 59, 65.

ever iron ore joined water transportation,"[27] i. e., along the southern bank of the Ruhr and along the Rhine and its tributaries. After a slow beginning, steel production and machine building became cornerstones of Rhenish industry. The Ruhr region (roughly consisting of the Westphalian district of Arnsberg and the district of Düsseldorf) soon eclipsed the older centers involved in the metal industry, overshadowing all other areas after 1861.[28] It emerged as a separate social and economic region during its phenomenal growth from the 1850s to the 1880s; the district of Düsseldorf, although it did not develop as rapidly as Arnsberg, after 1861 grew faster than the other Rhenish districts and became the province's most industrialized region.

In contrast to the iron and steel mills in France, Great Britain and the United States, German mills produced much of their product for the domestic market, namely for the building of railways. By the late 1850s Germany was independent of imports.[29] In Prussia the construction of railways and rolling stock was a combined effort of private entrepreneurs and the state. The state's involvement meant that capital was available; yet businessmen had to make concessions to state interests. The military often demanded that the railway follow a particular route. In Cologne, a city of strategic importance, the construction of a railway line was delayed when the military objected to the building of some of the necessary bridges.[30]

Industrialization, obviously, did not affect all parts of the Rhineland in the same way, and some areas hardly at all. Roughly speaking, the northern part of the Rhine Province experienced industrialization in full force from the 1840s onwards; the southern part, on the other hand, remained largely agricultural. In the southern districts of Trier and Koblenz political circumstances had hampered pre-industrial development and these districts were never able to make up for the disadvantages of the early phase of industrialization.[31] Even in the north, there was no uniform and universal industrial development. The Aachen district may serve as an example of the coexistence of various forms of industrialization and agriculture.

[27] Frank B. Jr. Tipton, *Regional Variations in the Economic Development of Germany During the Nineteenth Century* (Middletown, Conn.: Wesleyan University Press, 1976), p. 64.
[28] Ibid.
[29] Alf Lüdtke, "Eisenbahnfahren und Eisenbahnbau," in *Bürgerliche Gesellschaft in Deutschland,* ed. Lutz Niethammer (Frankfurt a. M.: Fischer Verlag, 1990), p. 104.
[30] Ibid., p. 107.
[31] Lademacher, "Rheinlande," p. 485.

The Setting

Rural counties in the north and east of the district (counties Geilenkirchen, Heinsberg, Erkelenz, and Jülich) were almost exclusively agrarian. The Eifel region (counties Schleiden and Monschau) featured a mixture of farming, small factories and artisans. Schleiden, place of origin of the family of Alexandre Gustave Bönickhausen, whom the world knows as Gustave Eiffel, prospered during the sixteenth and seventeenth centuries from iron working brought to the region by enterprising and industrious Lutherans who made their mark in this predominantly Catholic region. After its incorporation into Prussia the town enjoyed another period of prosperity but the spread of railways in the late nineteenth century ended the North Eifel iron industry and somewhat reduced Schleiden's status. Sandwiched between the Eifel region and the agricultural northeast of the district was a heavily industrialized zone comprised of the counties Aachen-Stadt, Aachen-Land and Düren. Agricultural regions were not homogeneous either. The majority of the farms in the counties of Monschau and Heinsberg were small and had poor soil. Here most farmers could barely eke out a living for their families. Only in the counties Jülich, Düren, Erkelenz and in parts of Geilenkirchen was farming profitable. There the quality of the soil was good enough so that even small to mid-size farms were viable.[32]

Hard times set in even for productive farmers between 1847 and 1857, when the Rhineland suffered greatly from poor harvests. Though the following decade proved to be better, in mid-century the agricultural crisis, rapid increase in population, as well as the troubles of artisans caused by the abolition of the guild system, left a majority of Rhinelanders living in misery.[33] The poor suffered most, as Ludolf Camphausen noted in his 1846 report to the Cologne Chamber of Commerce. Others, too, were affected. Bankruptcies of Cologne businesses in 1846, for instance, were up by more than 300 percent from the previous year. The production of goods declined sharply (with the notable exception of metal products), the prices for real estate plummeted, as did many of the stocks of local enterprises.[34] Rhinelanders reacted in several ways to these economic hardships. After 1850 rural-urban immigration increased dramatically. Rather

---

[32] Günter Plum, *Gesellschaftsstruktur und politisches Bewußtsein in einer katholischen Region, 1928-1933. Untersuchung am Beispiel des Regierungsbezirks Aachen* (Stuttgart: Deutsche Verlags-Anstalt, 1972), p. 16.

[33] Lademacher, "Rheinlande," p. 487.

[34] Ludolf Camphausen, "Jahresbericht der Handelskammer zu Köln für das Jahr 1846," excerpted in Steitz, *Quellen zur Wirtschafts- und Sozialgeschichte*, pp. 224-5.

than choosing North America, as impoverished farmers of southwestern Germany had done, emigrants from the northern Rhineland preferred to move to the close-by industrial cities of the Rhine Valley and Ruhr basin. To name only one example, Aachen, a city with a population of some 50,000 in 1849, gained over 10,000 new inhabitants through immigration between 1850 and 1867.[35]

Another way of coping with hard times was to turn to religion. Indeed, Jonathan Sperber in his seminal study of popular Catholicism argues that "Catholic religious revival was, inter alia, a common response to the mid-century socioeconomic crisis."[36] This renewed interest in religion was not an attempt to turn back the clock; rather, its focus was on finding ways of coping with and of adapting to an industrial-capitalist economy and society.[37] Part and parcel of this religious revival was the emergence of Christian social reformers, such as the Rhenish Center politician Peter Reichensperger who called the factory "a breeding ground of corruption and prostitution" but at the same time realized that machines could free man "from the most arduous and injurious work."[38] And Johann Hinrich Wichern, founder of *Innere Mission*, or Adolph Kolping, a Rhenish priest who founded Catholic journeymen's associations to give free vocational training to working men. They were among the first to try to come to grips with the social consequences of industrialization, criticizing these developments and suggesting measures such as state factory legislation which might alleviate or even solve what was termed the "social question."

While Catholics were early in recognizing the social consequences of industrialization, they played a much smaller part in the making of the industrial revolution. Many observers have commented on the conspicuous absence of Catholic entrepreneurs in the Rhineland. The textile industry of Krefeld, Elberfeld and other cities were largely founded and run by Calvinists.[39] In Rheydt and Mönchengladbach, two cities with predominantly Catholic populations, almost all owners of factories were Protestants, many of them related to each other.

---

[35] Jonathan Sperber, *Popular Catholicism in Nineteenth-Century Germany* (Princeton, N.J.: Princeton University Press, 1984), p. 41.

[36] Ibid., p. 284.

[37] Ibid., p. 282.

[38] Quotation from Joseph Höffner, "Die Stellung des deutschen Katholizismus in den sozialen Entscheidungen des 19. Jahrhunderts," *Geschichte in Wissenschaft und Unterricht* 4 (1953), pp. 604-5. For a biographical sketch see Winfried Becker, "Peter Reichensperger," in *Zeitgeschichte in Lebensbildern*, ed. Jürgen Aretz, et al. (Mainz: Matthias-Grünewald Verlag, 1982), pp. 41-54.

[39] Landes, *Prometheus*, p. 134.

There were about ten Catholic entrepreneurial families, yet none rivaled the Protestants in economic importance or social prestige.[40] The few members of the Silesian aristocracy (Ballestrem, Henckel-Donersmark, Hohenlohe and a few others) who, based on their landed wealth, became industrialists are the exception rather than the rule. Rarer still are Catholic tycoons in the Rhineland and Westphalia; only August Thyssen and Peter Klöckner break this pattern.[41] Throughout the Kaiserreich Catholics remained underrepresented among wealthy German families. The fact that during the periods of high and late industrialization the business world recruited its members from its own ranks made it even more difficult for Catholics to reach the top positions of industrial and commercial enterprises.[42]

Initially, the creation of the German empire in 1870/71 hardly changed the economy of the Rhineland.[43] Prussia had prospered during the unusually long economic boom of 1850 to 1857 and, after a short recession, continued to grow—in particular during the years after 1866. Virtually all sections of industry and commerce continued to thrive. The number of steam engines, only 651 in the Rhineland and Westphalia in 1849, had risen to nearly 12,000 by 1875; they produced almost as much energy as all of France's steam engines. Iron production doubled in the decade after 1865, steel production increased by an astonishing 54-fold in 24 years (1850-74). In a parallel development, coal production grew sixteen-fold between 1850 and 1875. Similar growth rates exist for the production of the textile industry, and the construction of railway lines and roads. We must not overlook, however, that other regions in western Europe experienced similar or even more rapid industrialization.[44] But in the German context the Rhineland was exceptional. Particularly dur-

---

[40] Throughout the nineteenth century about 80 percent of Mönchengladbach's population was Catholic. In Rheydt the proportions were almost reversed at the beginning of the century, however, the Catholic proportion grew steadily to 40 percent in 1880, 50.1 percent in 1895 and 55.2 percent in 1910. See Löhr, "Honorationsgruppen," pp. 10-1.

[41] For a recent appreciation of the role the Thyssen family played in the Rhineland see Horst A. Wessel, ed. *Thyssen & Co. Mühlheim a. d. Ruhr. Die Geschichte einer Familie und ihrer Unternehmung* (Stuttgart: Franz Steiner Verlag, 1991), esp. the chapter by Lutz Hatzfeld, pp. 53-178.

[42] On the social origins of Germany's business élite see Dolores L. Augustine, *Patricians and Parvenus. Wealth and High Society in Wilhelmine Germany* (Oxford: Berg Publishers, 1994), pp. 51-5.

[43] For the following see Lademacher, "Rheinlande," pp. 570-8.

[44] Hartmut Kaelble, "Der Mythos von der rapiden Industrialisierung in Deutschland," *Geschichte und Gesellschaft* 9, no. 1 (1983), pp. 107-8; Poll, "Zur neueren Wirtschaftsgeschichte," p. 66.

ing the two decades after 1860, the Rhineland's economic and population growth "diverged sharply from the national average."[45]

It is important to keep in mind that industrialization did not occur uniformly and concurrently. There were some advanced areas, such as the northern Rhineland, which prefigured the rapid industrialization, but until well into the second half of the century the bulk of Catholic Germany retained its pre-industrial social structures.[46] Most of the Catholic population remained a rather long way from industrialization. The Rhineland was an exception to this pattern; this is a major reason why it is so important to study this region. Here we have a predominantly Catholic region where industrialization occurred early and with great force. This circumstance gives us an opportunity to explore the role Catholicism played in the unfolding of a process often referred to as modernization.

Modernization is a slippery concept, defying precise definition. It seems impossible to explain with one coherent, all-encompassing theory the particular way in which German society changed during the crucial three decades that followed the take-off of Germany's industrial revolution in the 1840s. In the following decades, Germany was transformed into an industrialized society, an often painful process bringing with it fundamental social change and economic hardship. In the past, the lives of those working in factories were "barely distinguishable from the omnipresent agricultural life which ran alongside it and sometimes submerged it."[47] During the eighteenth and early nineteenth century the divide between rural and urban areas, between peasants and town dwellers, had begun to open. These growing differences between village and town were heightened by the massive migrations of the years after 1850. Besides coping with these economic and social transformations Rhenish Catholics were faced with the wide-ranging political changes. In the nineteenth century Germans experienced two political revolutions: the revolutions of 1848/49 were in significant ways failed attempts to accommodate the consequences of modernization; the political revolution brought about by Bismarck's unification also had wide implications for the direction and limitations of political modernization of Germany. It was within the framework of the Second Empire that modern politics developed in Germany. Within this framework occurred the for-

---

[45] Tipton, *Economic Development*, p. 63.

[46] Clemens Bauer, *Deutscher Katholizismus. Entwicklungslinien und Profile* (Frankfurt a. M.: Josef Knecht, 1964), pp. 35-6.

[47] Fernand Braudel, *The Wheels of Commerce*, trans. Siân Reynolds (New York: Harper & Row, 1982), p. 304.

mation of political Catholicism led by the founding of the Center Party in 1870 and the political mobilization of the masses by highly organized political parties and special interest groups. For the Roman Catholic Church and for Catholic politicians and citizens alike, coming to terms with these upheavals was the most difficult challenge of the nineteenth century. For Rhenish Catholics, industrialization, urbanization and unification changed not only the material but also the spiritual conditions of their lives; these processes affected virtually all aspects of their existence and nobody could escape the consequences of these events. In short, the history of Rhenish Catholicism in both its religious and political incarnations is dominated by this sharp dualism between two forces: modernization, with its enormous impetus for change; and the Roman Catholic belief system, with its reverence for tradition and hierarchy, its internationalism and its high theological culture.

C. Catholics in the Rhineland

During the nineteenth century Rhenish Catholics experienced profound crises, economically, socially, politically and, especially, spiritually. Despite such volatility Roman Catholicism maintained persistent strength among Rhinelanders; and one cannot understand the Rhineland during that period unless one recognizes this strength. In certain circumstances belief in Catholicism waned, in some segments of Rhenish society it did not exist, but as an influence on Rhenish society there was nothing to set beside it.

More than three quarters of the population were Catholics; the district of Düsseldorf had the lowest percentage of Catholics, some 58 percent, while in the Aachen district more than 95 percent of the inhabitants were Roman Catholics. Although the spiritual hold of the Catholic Church over its flock lessened under the impact of industrialization and urbanization, the parish remained the focus of most social and political activities, and priests continued to exercise great influence over their parishioners. As we will see, for many Catholic workers, the conditions of factory work and urban life did not lead to estrangement from the Church and still less from the Catholic milieu.

In some ways, Catholics were a relatively new group in Prussia. After the Reformation they practically disappeared from Hohenzollern lands. Not until the conquest of Silesia (1740) did the number of Catholics in Prussia increase significantly; the divisions of Poland (1772, 1793 and 1795) added yet more Catholics to the kingdom.

In the process Prussia had lost its confessional homogeneity. In 1815 the predominantly Catholic Rhineland also became part of Prussia, but not without a dispute about the consequences of the incorporation of so many more Catholics into a Protestant state.[48] When the Second Empire was founded in 1871, Catholics represented about a third of the population. They differed in this respect from Catholics in France and Italy where they were a majority. The German Catholic minority also differed from its English counterpart in that it was heavily concentrated in a few regions. More importantly, only in Germany did a potent Catholic party emerge before World War I: Don Sturzo's *Partito popolare* challenged the Socialists only after the Great War; French Catholicism has traditionally been equated with conservatism, and the Christian democratic *Mouvement républicain populaire* was a child of the Fourth Republic. The early appearance of a strong Catholic political party in Germany must, to a large degree, be understood as the result of the conflict of interest between the Protestant state and its Catholic subjects. This antagonism between Protestants and Catholics, and the disadvantaged social and political position of Catholics, is one of the keys to explaining the early emergence of political Catholicism in Germany. Catholics saw themselves as a disadvantaged minority in Germany and the Prussian state did nothing to alleviate these apprehensions. Catholics such as the Bonn professor and Center politician Count Georg von Hertling, who praised Catholicism "as the religion of authority, dogma, and religious duty," were generally viewed with suspicion by Protestants.[49] Particularly Prussian Protestants in high administrative positions regarded Catholic allegiance to the authority of the pontiff, even if confined to purely religious matters, as seditious and dangerous.

As a consequence, Catholics were almost completely absent from Prussia's high ministerial and administrative offices. There was only a handful of Catholic ministers in Prussia in the entire nineteenth century. Among Prussian provincial governors (*Oberpräsident*)—the pinnacle of Prussian provincial administration created by the reforms of Stein and Hardenberg—Catholics were scarcer still. There was between 1815 and 1918 only one Catholic provincial governor: Klemens Freiherr von Schorlemer-Lieser, who held the post in the Rhine Province from 1905 to 1910. He went on to become Prussian minister of agriculture, one of the few Catholic ministers in Prussia. Never was there more than one Catholic provincial governor or minister in

---

[48] Ross, *Beleaguered Tower*, p. 9.
[49] BAK Nl. 36 Hertling Nr. 28 f. 64.

The Setting 33

Prussia's administration.[50] Catholic district governors (*Regierungspräsidenten*) are equally rare in the administrative annals of the Rhine Province. With the exception of a few weeks during the revolutionary disturbances of 1848, the district of Trier never had a Catholic district governor, nor did the Cologne district. In 1910, only four (Koblenz, Aachen, Münster, Sigmaringen) of Prussia's thirty-six district governors were Catholics.[51] *Landräte* (district magistrates) were the cornerstones of Prussian administration. Entrusted with the administration of the *Kreis* (local district), the local police, and the military garrison, they were often described as the "king" of the district.[52] "At the steps of the Landrat office," one commentator lamented, "general equal civil rights cease to exist in Prussia."[53] Of the 487 Prussian local districts 176 were predominantly Catholic but in 1911 just 65 had Catholic *Landräte*. In the Rhine Province the situation was only slightly better, 51 of the province's 60 local districts had Catholic majorities, 35 of those had a Catholic *Landrat*.[54] Discrimination against Catholics did not stop there. Municipal professional employees in the gas and electricity works, in abattoirs, hospitals, school administrators, police chiefs, in short the vast majority of higher municipal civil servants were overproportionately Protestant. This was even true, although to a lesser degree, for cities, such as Cologne, Aachen, and Trier, where the Center Party had a majority in municipal councils.[55]

The crucial event shaping the relationship between Church and state, and between the government and its Catholic subjects before 1848, was an incident known as the Cologne Conflict (*Kölner Wirren*). This incident, in the words of the (Catholic) Prussian general and statesman Josef Maria von Radowitz, brought "fear and hatred" to the province, in its wake the conciliation of "truly well-intentioned men in the new territories with the Prussian government was bru-

---

[50] Schorlemer's predecessor Nasse (1890-1905) was the first Rhinelander to occupy the office. For the representation of Catholics in Prussia's civil service see Johannes Rost, *Die wirtschaftliche und kulturelle Lage der deutschen Katholiken* (Cologne: J. P. Bachem, 1911), esp. pp. 163-69; Ross, *Beleaguered Tower*, pp. 9-10.

[51] Rost, *Wirtschaftliche und kulturelle Lage*, p. 163.

[52] On the election and function of the Prussian *Landrat* see Bär, *Behördenverfassung*, pp. 219-22; Gerhard A. Ritter, ed. *Das Deutsche Kaiserreich 1871-1914: Ein historisches Lesebuch* (Göttingen: Vandenhoeck & Ruprecht, 1981), pp. 74-7.

[53] Rost, *Wirtschaftliche und kulturelle Lage*, p. 163.

[54] Ibid., p. 166.

[55] Blackbourn, *Class*, p. 32; Rost, *Wirtschaftliche und kulturelle Lage*, p. 170.

tally torn apart."[56] It all started rather simply, if not innocently, with a decree by Friedrich Wilhelm III in 1803 concerning the religious education of children in mixed marriages. In an effort to make the Prussian state's policy uniform and to curtail Catholic proselytizing, the order was extended to the Rhineland in 1825,[57] prohibiting Catholic clergy from making these marriages dependent on a promise by bride and groom to bring up future children in the Catholic faith. Catholic priests were caught between the king's instruction and the canon law which stipulated that mixed marriages were only allowed if they guaranteed the unencumbered religious freedom of the Catholic spouse, assured the education of children in the Catholic faith, and allowed only a Catholic priest to administer the sacrament. In a move that foreshadowed the measures of the Kulturkampf half a century later, the government also intruded into the Church's prerogative to make ecclesiastical appointments. By declaring only a single candidate *persona regi grata*, the ministry of culture determined who became bishop. The Church's only option was to comply; failure to do so meant that the bishopric remained vacant. In Cologne and Paderborn the cathedral chapters were forced to elect candidates whose names they had not heard of before.[58] As of 1834 even the ordination of ordinary priests required ministerial approval. In June 1834, under pressure from government the archbishop of Cologne Ferdinand August Graf Spiegel[59] and the bishops of Trier, Münster and Paderborn agreed to a secret "convention," in accordance with which they instructed their clergy to refrain from insisting on the Catholic education of children in mixed marriages.

Archbishop Spiegel died of cancer in August 1835, leaving the archbishopric of Cologne vacant. Immediately, the wrangling over Spiegel's succession began. Eventually the chapter of the cathedral elected the Westphalian aristocrat Clemens August Freiherr Droste zu Vischering [60], the favorite candidate of Crown Prince Friedrich Wilhelm. Droste's investiture was as much a political as a spiritual act; the Crown Prince hoped that the new metropolitan could help improve the attitude of Rhenish and Westphalian Catholics toward

---

[56] Cited in Poll, "Das Hineinwachsen," p. 19.

[57] Hegel, *Erzbistum Köln*, p. 461.

[58] Julius Bachem and Karl Bachem, *Die kirchenpolitischen Kämpfe in Preußen gegen die katholische Kirche insbesondere der "grosse Kulturkampf" der Jahre 1871-1887. Sonderabdruck der Artikel aus der dritten Auflage des Staatslexikons der Görres-Gesellschaft* (Freiburg i. Br.: Herdersche Verlagsbuchhandlung, 1910), p. 11.

[59] For a biographical sketch see, Hegel, *Erzbistum Köln*, pp. 48-57.

[60] For biographical information see, ibid. pp. 57-66.

the Prussian state.⁶¹ Droste stubbornly refused to oblige. Not only was he much less conciliatory on marital matters than his predecessor, he also took a dogmatic stand toward Hermesian theologians whom he regarded to be in violation of Catholic dogma and whose removal from several universities he demanded. The conflict came to a head in September 1837 when archbishop Droste declared unequivocally that canon law could not be bent and thus publicly withdrew from the secret agreement his predecessor had reached with Berlin. The government was determined to force Droste's resignation, but the archbishop would not go voluntarily. In the end, two battalions of infantry surrounded the episcopal residence, uniformed officials (led by the provincial governor of the Rhine Province, the district governor of Cologne, and the city's mayor) entered the house and arrested the archbishop who was then taken to Minden and put under house arrest.⁶²

Initially, Catholics in Cologne and the archdiocese hardly reacted to the incarceration of their archbishop; even the German episcopacy remained silent. Karl Schorn, a student at the University of Bonn heard rumors that the archbishop's arrest had led to civil unrest. Eager to witness a "revolution," he set out to Cologne, only to find that the streets were disappointingly quiet.⁶³ It was Joseph Görres's treatise *Athanasius* that triggered public uproar. Görres saw the imprisonment as a "fortunate incident" that galvanized Catholic resistance to Prussian anti-Catholicism. He urged Rhenish Catholics to protect their regional character and to reject everything "alien, that with hostile intentions infiltrates" one of Germany's tribes.⁶⁴ Görres's famous pamphlet also provided the quintessential position Catholic politicians would later assume in questions of church-state relations. The Catholic goal is, Görres concluded:

---

⁶¹ Ibid., p. 59.

⁶² A passionate description of von Droste's arrest that still echoes the indignation of Rhenish Catholics can be found in Rudolf Amelunxen, *Das Kölner Ereignis* (Essen: Ruhrländische Verlagsgesellschaft, 1952), pp. 61-72; more detached and reliable is Heinz Hürten, *Kurze Geschichte des deutschen Katholizismus, 1800-1960* (Mainz: Matthias-Grünewald-Verlag, 1986), pp. 62-68; for the significance of the event in Germany at large see Thomas Nipperdey, *Deutsche Geschichte: 1800-1866* (Munich: C.H. Beck, 1983), pp. 418-20.

⁶³ Karl Schorn, *Lebenserinnerungen. Ein Beitrag zur Geschichte des Rheinlandes im 19. Jahrhundert* (Bonn: Verlag von P. Hanstein, 1898), pp. 79-80.

⁶⁴ Joseph Görres "Athanasius" (1838), *Ausgewählte Werke*, ed. Wolfgang Frühwald (Freiburg: Herder, 1978), 2:716.

the complete and full realization of the solemnly granted religious freedom and of the promise to all denominations that political and civil equality [be guaranteed] in their entirety without prejudice and reservations.[65]

To Centrists the *Kölner Wirren* were to acquire special meaning. Ludwig Windthorst, the matchless Center parliamentarian and strong opponent of Bismarck, was inspired to enter public life by the state's attack on Catholic rights and by Görres's spirited response.[66] Even much younger men, such as Martin Spahn, who were born long after the events, saw them as the "first illumination" of the religious divide that determined much of their political behavior throughout the century.[67] The tradition of "Catholic self-confidence" in battling politicians which received its final boost during the Kulturkampf had its origins in the 1837 clash with the Prussian state.[68] Indeed, the roots of Rhenish political Catholicism can be traced to these events. In Aachen priests and devout laymen met at the house of Louis Fey, a local owner of a spinning mill. After his death, Fey's son Andreas invited like-minded friends to his late father's house, where they discussed ways to renew piety and to ensure the church's freedom. A police report described Andreas Fey as "young, fanatical, educated."[69] Among the members of the Aachen circle were Franz Xaver Scholl, later a professor and Domkapitular at Trier, and Leonhard Alois Nellessen, a parish priest in Aachen who advocated social activities of the church.[70] The most important member of this circle was Johann Theodor Laurent, at the time a priest in the nearby Belgian village of Gemmenich. As apostolic vicar of Luxemburg, Laurent continued his advocacy for a reform of state-church relations and the revival of Catholic piety. Because of his influence on Rhenish clergymen he

---

[65] Görres "Athanasius," 2:719.

[66] Wilhelm Spael, *Ludwig Windthorst. Bismarcks kleiner großer Gegner. Ein Lebensbild* (Osnabrück: Verlag A. Fromm, 1962), p. 23.

[67] Martin Spahn, *Das deutsche Zentrum* (Mainz: Kirchheim'sche Verlagsbuchhandlung, 1907), pp. 9-10.

[68] Höffner, "Stellung," p. 601.

[69] Cited in Heinrich Schrörs, "Die Geheimpolizei am Rhein zur Zeit der Kölner Wirren (1837-1838) mit besonderer Rücksicht auf Aachen," *Zeitschrift des Aachener Geschichtsvereins* 48/49 (1928), p. 42.

[70] For details see August Brecher, "Oberpfarrer L. A. Nellessen (1783-1859) und der Aachener Priesterkreis," *Zeitschrift des Aachener Geschichtsvereins* 76 (1964), esp. pp. 70-90.

The Setting

has been viewed by some as the "founder of political Catholicism" in the Rhineland.[71]

In Koblenz a similar circle existed. As in Aachen, the group often met in the home of a prominent layman, the merchant and city councilor Hermann Josef Dietz. Joseph Görres, who had founded the circle in 1817, and the romantic poet Clemens von Brentano were participants, as was Abundius Mähler the future mayor of Koblenz, as well as Jakob Clemens who went on to become a professor of philosophy at Münster. Concern for the poor and religious enthusiasm also attracted the brothers August and Peter Reichensperger; 1810-1892). As founding members of the Center Party they provide a direct personal link between the circle's social and religious activities and the political work of the Center. The Koblenz circle was different from the one in Aachen in that it consisted primarily of laymen and concentrated its efforts on charitable work.[72] The theological position of the circle in Aachen was characterized by dogmatic rigor and an unwavering loyalty to the Church and a piety that centered around the veneration of Mary. Their political goals were limited to the independence of the Church and its institutions from state interference; they were not the nucleus of the Center Party and had no political ambitions. Although Laurent was held responsible by the Luxemburg government for inciting unrest in 1848, he and his friends were monarchists, opposed to the notion of revolutionary change.[73]

The arrest of the Archbishop of Cologne also had an effect on the piety of Rhenish Catholics, shown in the increased number of pilgrims and church-goers.[74] In a letter to a friend Johann Theodor Laurent reported that churches in Aachen had never been so full; thousands had participated in procession. More than half a million people made the pilgrimage to Trier in 1844; such a mass demonstration of faith strengthened the position of the Church and pointed to the potency of political Catholicism. During the 1840s, the government eased its restrictions on the Church and seemed to become

---

[71] Eduard Hegel, "Die katholische Kirche in den Rheinlanden 1815-1945," in *Wirtschaft und Kultur im 19. und 20. Jahrhundert*, ed. Franz Petri and Georg Droege (Düsseldorf: Schwann, 1979), pp. 342-3; Gatz, *Bistümer*, pp. 443-4; Brecher, "Oberpfarrer Nellessen," p. 80.

[72] Hortense Martin, "Soziale Anschauungen und Bemühungen der Gebrüder Reichensperger und des Freihern von Thimus um die Mitte des 19. Jahrhunderts," *Archiv für mittelrheinische Kirchengeschichte* 7 (1955), p. 220; Brecher, "Oberpfarrer Nellessen," pp. 84-5.

[73] Brecher, "Oberpfarrer Nellessen," pp. 89-90.

[74] Sperber, *Popular Catholicism*, p. 70.

less hostile toward Catholics. In Aachen, for example, Klara Fey, daughter of the industrialist, began to work for poor and homeless children of her hometown. In 1848, more than a decade after she had begun her work, she obtained royal permission to open a Sisterhood of the Poor Child Jesus (*Genossenschaft der Schwestern vom armen Kind Jesus*), which grew to be the largest and most influential order of its kind in the archdiocese of Cologne.[75] Klara Fey's order is notable not only as part of the renewed piety, but also because her sisterhood, as well as other charitable organizations founded at the time, addressed the problems of poverty and misery among the working class which were to become central issues for the Center and the People's Association. The political organization of Catholic women, however, was disadvantaged by the existence of these orders. Women who might have been pioneers of a political Catholic women's movement instead focused on philanthropic work.[76] Karl Trimborn's wife, Jeanne, for example, turned her household into a "charitable headquarters of a kind", she devoted much of her time to three organizations concerned with the welfare of Catholic working women.[77]

Lastly, the *Kölner Wirren* led to the founding of Catholic newspapers in the Rhineland which can be interpreted as early attempts to create a voice for the political concerns of Rhenish Catholics. Commentary on the events in Cologne, let alone criticism of the government's actions was curtailed by Prussian censors; the issue was simply not mentioned in existing newspapers. Attempts like that of the Aachen circle to establish a Catholic paper in January 1837 were prohibited by the provincial governor Ernst Freiherr von Bodelshwingh-Velmede. To circumnavigate Prussian restrictions the priests in Aachen arranged for a paper to be printed in bordering Belgium and than smuggled and distributed throughout the Rhine Province. The police tried but were unable to restrict distribution of such newspapers.[78]

---

[75] Rudolf Morsey, ed. *Zeitgeschichte in Lebensbildern. Aus dem deutschen Katholizismus des 20. Jahrhunderts* (Mainz: Matthias-Grünewald-Verlag, 1973-1976), pp. 60-61; Hegel, *Erzbistum Köln*, p. 313; August Schumacher, "Zur Familiengeschichte der Ordensgründerin Klara Fey," *Mitteilungen der Westdeutschen Gesellschaft für Familienkunde* 8 (1934), pp. 62-63.

[76] Alfred Kall, *Katholische Frauenbewegung in Deutschland: Eine Untersuchung zur Gründung katholischer Frauenvereine im 19. Jahrhundert* (Paderborn: Ferdinand Schöning, 1983), pp. 323-4.

[77] Cardauns, *Trimborn*, p. 60.

[78] Brecher, "Oberpfarrer Nellessen," pp. 142-4.

There is little doubt that formal religious observances declined during the nineteenth century.[79] During the first half of the century there were signs of decreasing popular piety in the Rhineland. Contemporary observers saw that the Catholic bourgeoisie sympathized with the ideas of the French Revolution; Masonic lodges flourished in the major cities of the Rhineland. The lower classes, too, were attracted to the ideas of the Revolution.[80] Peasants, urban laborers, factory workers and craftsmen left Sunday church early or stayed away altogether, preferring the tavern to the sermon. The pub, a place beyond the immediate control of the clergy, became a meeting place for lower-class organizations and, after 1848, the recruiting ground for liberal and democratic agitators.[81] Nevertheless, secularization appears to have been slower in Catholic than in Protestant areas; this was also true in regions with similar social and economic structures.[82] Behind the veil of secularization, a religious awareness continued to exist and in some areas—including the Rhineland—a new religious fervor appeared after mid-century.[83] A sign of such renewed piety was the more frequent occurrence of processions, pilgrimages, and apparitions. The showing of relics at Charlemagne's cathedral in Aachen attracted growing numbers of believers.[84] At Kevelaer, the annual number of pilgrims almost tripled from an average of some 36,000 between 1816 and 1824 to approximately 100,000 in 1861. If Catholic sources are accurate, that number jumped to 400,000 by 1872. The largest German pilgrimage of the century took place in Trier during the late summer months of 1844. Half a million pil-

---

[79] For an introduction to the phenomenon of secularization in Germany Thomas Nipperdey, *Religion im Umbruch: Deutschland 1870 - 1918* (Munich: Verlag C. H. Beck, 1988), esp. pp. 14-23; the best introduction to secularization in Europe at large is still Owen Chadwick, *The Secularization of the European Mind in the Nineteenth Century* (1975; reprint, Cambridge University Press, 1990), esp. pp. 88-106.
[80] Sperber, *Popular Catholicism*, pp. 13-4.
[81] Ibid., pp. 17-8.
[82] Richard J. Evans, "Religion and Society in Modern Germany," *European Studies Review* 12 (1982), p. 274; Werner K. Blessing, "Reform, Restauration, Rezession. Kirchenreligion und Volksreligiosität zwischen Aufklärung und Industrialisierung," in *Volksreligiosität in der modernen Sozialgeschichte*, ed. Wolfgang Schieder (Göttingen: Vandenhoeck & Ruprecht, 1986), pp. 108-10.
[83] For an excellent review of recent works on this topic see Caroline Ford, "Religion and Popular Culture in Modern Europe," *Journal of Modern History* 65 (1993), pp. 152-75.
[84] Dieter P. J. Wynands, "Die Aachenfahrt während der französischen Herrschaft im Rheinland (1792/94-1814). Ein Beitrag zur Auslagerung des Aachener Münsterschatzes nach Paderborn," *Annalen des Historischen Vereins für den Niederrhein* 197 (1994), 145.

grims (mostly peasants, artisans, and impoverished vintners from the Mosel region and the bishoprics adjacent to Trier) followed the call of bishop Wilhelm Arnoldi to worship Trier's most treasured relic— a garment believed by Catholics to be worn by Jesus when he died and brought to Trier in the fourth century by the Roman empress Helena who, according to local folklore, discovered the robe during a visit to Jerusalem.[85]

The second half of the nineteenth century also saw a large number of apparitions. The Marian vision of Bernadette Soubirous in Lourdes is only the most famous of many hundreds of such apparitions—a surprising number of which occurred in German-speaking Europe. The German counterpart to Lourdes was Marpingen, an obscure village in the northern Saarland (Trier district) where, on 3 July 1876, the Virgin Mary allegedly appeared to three local girls.[86] David Blackbourn's brilliant study reveals the visions of Marpingen as a fascinating example of the entanglement of religion and politics, regional identity and state authority that characterized Imperial Germany. When state authorities declared that the Marpingen visions and Catholic reactions to them constituted a challenge to the authority of the state, a metaphysical event became the cause (or pretense) of a political contest. Matters became violent after an infantry company was dispatched to Marpingen. As it turned out, the actions of the Prussian state achieved the very opposite of their intended purpose. Instead of controlling the situation and calming tensions between populace and local authorities, the state "unwittingly inflated the importance of Marpingen" and "added new force to the religious vigour of the Catholic population."[87]

---

[85] Contemporaries estimated the number of pilgrims at over one million; Wolfgang Schieder's calculations, however, appear to correspond closer to the actual number of pilgrims. For details see his "Kirche und Revolution. Sozialgeschichtliche Aspekte der Trierer Wallfahrt von 1844," *Archiv für Sozialgeschichte* 24 (1974), pp. 419-54 and Rudolf Lill's reply in the same journal 18 (1978), pp. 565-75. There have also been three displays of the Holy Shroud in our century: 1933, 1959 and 1996 (the first time the Protestant church took part in the exhibition).

[86] David Blackbourn, *Marpingen: Apparitions of the Virgin Mary in Bismarckian Germany* (Oxford: Clarendon Press, 1993), pp. 17-57 provides an introduction to the phenomenon of Marian apparitions in Germany. For a discussion of the phenomenon in Europe at large see Mary Lee Nolan and Sidney Nolan, *Christian Pilgrimage in Modern Western Europe* (Chapel Hill: University of North Carolina Press, 1989), esp. pp. 36-78.

[87] Blackbourn, *Marpingen*, pp. 402, 268.

In the volatile climate of the Kulturkampf, confrontations between Catholics and the government erupted even without manifestations of the supernatural. The refusal of a Catholic priest in the village of Rheinbrohl to peal the church bells for the funeral of the two-year old son of a Protestant worker led to a feud between the parish and Prussian authorities that lasted more than seven years. When the local mayor demanded that the bells be rung the parishioners refused to hand over the church keys. The *Landrat* received the same answer and when police threatened to open the church by force they were confronted by a large hostile crowd. Only a company of armed soldiers dispatched by special train from Koblenz was able to disperse the crowds, break into the church and ring the bells for the child's funeral. Angered Center Landtag deputies used the Rheinbrohl incident to charge the government with discrimination and abuse of power. The matter was eventually settled in the courts where Julius Bachem successfully pleaded the Catholic case, as he had done in the Marpingen affair.[88] Like Marpingen, Rheinbrohl demonstrates with convincing clarity that there was no tidy separation of religious, political and judicial matters. What began as a local dispute between an obdurate Catholic parish and a rash Protestant mayor acquired larger significance when Center politicians used the event to their political ends. It also revealed the limits of the Prussian government, which could send in the troops but not control the courts. As in Marpingen it was again the Catholic side that scored a victory. Incidents such as these deepened the suspicion and mistrust many Catholics felt towards the Prussian state. Such incidents also contained dangers for the Center Party. An alienated Catholic population might not welcome closer relations between the Center and other political parties. These tensions and perceptions also were a factor in relations within the camp of political Catholicism: the very definition of the Center Party was fought over in the notorious *Zentrumsstreit* (which will be the subject of chapter V). Marpingen is also an example of the ambivalent relation between Catholic workers (who in the thousands went to Marpingen to protest their economic hardship) and the church hierarchy (who perceived such demonstrations as challenges to cleri-

---

[88] Julius Bachem, *Erinnerungen eines alten Publizisten und Politikers* (Cologne: J. P. Bachem, 1913), pp. 141-9; "Der Rheinbrohler Glockenstreit," *Germania* no. 297, 25 December 1889.

cal authority).[89] Historians have noted that the character and form of pilgrimages and apparitions changed. Pilgrimages were now highly organized affairs. Government officials noted the disciplined and orderly conduct in pilgrimages as well as the increased male participation.[90] David Blackbourn also stresses the importance women played in pilgrimages to Marpingen, interpreting this as "another sign of the 'feminization' of nineteenth-century Catholicism."[91]

The church hierarchy played a large role in organizing pilgrimages such as the one to the Holy Shroud of Trier in 1844 and 1891.[92] Wolfgang Schieder sees such involvement as a move of church leaders to contain the revolutionary ambitions of their flock, as an attempt of a "reactionary stabilization of the system."[93] Moreover, pilgrimages served to restore the bond between the Church and Catholics who had grown indifferent to their religion. As one Jesuit put it the pilgrimages would lead "the lost back to the Holy Church." The public display of Catholic worship, the same Jesuit argued, might even make converts of bystanders.

Fervent Rhenish Catholics built new churches or re-opened those which had been closed during French rule. The reopening of churches usually was initiated by parishioners who also bore the cost. More often than not parishes in which old churches were opened again were small. New parish churches were generally constructed in the diaspora, on the initiative of and paid for by the diocese.[94] The local clergy also went through a series of transformations. The most important change in the Roman Catholic Church during the nineteenth century was the disappearance of monks and friars as parish priests. In the areas on the left bank of the Rhine the French had forced into exile virtually all religious orders by 1802. By 1840, their influence in Germany at large had become negligible.[95]

---

[89] Klaus-Michael Mallmann, "'Aus des Tages Last machen sie ein Kreuz des Herrn...'? Bergarbeiter, Religion und sozialer Protest im Saarrevier des 19. Jahrhunderts," in *Volksreligiosität in der modernen Sozialgeschichte*, ed. Wolfgang Schieder (Göttingen: Vandenhoeck & Ruprecht, 1986), pp. 160-1.
[90] Sperber, *Popular Catholicism*, pp. 64-6.
[91] Blackbourn, *Marpingen*, p. 401.
[92] Michael N. Ebertz, "Die Organisierung von Massenreligiosität im 19. Jahrhundert. Soziologische Aspekte zur Frömmigkeitsforschung," *Jahrbuch für Volkskunde* 2 (1979), p. 65; Gottfried Korff, "Formierung der Frömmigkeit: Zur sozialpolitischen Intention der Trierer Rockwallfahrten 1891," *Geschichte und Gesellschaft* 3 (1977), pp. 354-5.
[93] Schieder, "Kirche und Revolution," p. 454.
[94] Gatz, *Bistümer*, p. 75.
[95] Ibid., p. 82.

In towns as well as in villages the parish was still the center of religious and in many ways of social life. Here people attended church services, their children received their education in *Volksschulen* supervised by the parish priest. The most important rituals in their lives—baptism, confirmation, marriage, funeral—were administered by their priest. Parish priests also addressed social problems: poverty, housing, occupational training. Through the backdoor of the social question priests and the Church entered the political stage; a religiously motivated act of charity could acquire a political dimension. And religious behavior became political. There were also new Catholic institutions that broke out of the confines of the parish. The first were the journeymen's associations founded by Adolph Kolping in 1846 later followed by workers' clubs and Christian trade unions. As will be seen in the Chapter V, the organization of the Rhenish Center Party was based on the parish, too. The religiosity of the industrialized Rhineland and of the Center was often less concerned with church attendance and traditional religious observances and more with the social responsibility of individual Catholics and their institutions. Religious affiliation was not expressed exclusively through the Church and its institutions any longer but through political bodies, such as the Center Party, and through social and economic associations such as the People's Association for Catholic Germany. The Catholic Church was unrivaled—even by the Socialists—for its ability to mobilize and organize its followers.

Something must be said about the notions of religion and politics that are implicit in my view of political Catholicism. This book argues that political Catholicism was both a political and a religious movement. Although many Centrists would have bridled at this idea, it seems that their actions belie their programmatic assertions that a strict division existed between religion and politics. As we shall see, as long as the Center addressed questions that were clearly confined to the realm of day-to-day political business, it acted very much like any other party. However, when faced with questions that touched upon aspects of faith or the rights of the Church it acted in a unique way. Again and again Centrists proclaimed that, ideally, the beliefs of a Catholic politician were coterminous with the ultimate standards of individual and social behavior in a Christian, if not a Catholic, society. The Cologne Centrist Karl Bachem understood his party's role as part of the antagonism between state and church that followed the political restructuring of Germany at the Congress of Vienna and, even more important, after unification in 1870/71. Bachem also understood the Center Party's role as part of the "process of the resuscitation and inner healing of European Catholicism."[96] This dualism of political and religious functions is the key to an understanding of the role the Center Party played in German politics and of the controversies that plagued political Catholicism for decades. To a large extent, this dualism of purpose that characterized political Catholicism can be explained by two opposite tendencies that violently tore at the fabric of German Catholic life. One was the result of the anti-Catholic sentiments harbored by many Protestants, most violently expressed during the Kulturkampf.[97] Among the allegations was the charge that practicing Catholics (and in particular those who supported the Center) could not be loyal Germans since their allegiance was to the Church not to the state. These attacks forced Center politicians to emphasize the political aspects of their party program and play down the religious ones. The other tendency was the atheist threat of Socialism. Their numbers growing steadily, armed with seductive arguments of Marxism, German Socialists successfully courted industrial workers—Catholic and Protestant. To fight off the intrusions of the Prussian state and to ward off the temptations of Socialism, spokesmen of political Catholicism emphasized the religious aspects of life which they thought to be under attack. The pace and the extent of this process go a long way in explaining why the Center was able to maintain much of its support until the party was dissolved in 1933.

Part of this notion of political Catholicism is the concept of a Catholic milieu. The concept of milieu is more useful than that of class in explaining the ability to maintain the Center's electoral support and the cohesion of Rhineland Catholics. M. Rainer Lepsius defines milieu as a social unit, which by the coincidental combination of several structural dimensions (such as religion, regional traditions, economic circumstances, and cultural outlook) was formed into a specific amalgam of its intermediary groups. Thus milieu is a socio-cultural entity that is determined by the classification of a particular group of people by assigning the above criteria.[98] For the purpose of this study, the Catholic milieu of the Rhineland is understood as a shared way of life that, besides a regional identity and a common religious faith, featured an institutional framework (church

---

[96] KB, 1:12.

[97] The Kulturkampf in the Rhineland will be discussed briefly in the following chapter.

[98] M. Rainer Lepsius, "Parteiensystem und Sozialstruktur: zum Problem der Demokratisierung der deutschen Gesellschaft," in *Die deutschen Parteien vor 1918*, ed. Gerhard A. Ritter (Cologne: Kiepenheuer & Witsch, 1973), p. 68.

hierarchy, Center Party, Catholic voluntary associations etc.) that enabled Catholics to bridge diverse economic interests.[99] Among German parties, the Center was the least homogeneous. Its supporters came from all classes, but farmers, artisans, and the middle classes (*Kleinbürgertum*) constituted the largest segments. This heterogeneous composition has made class analysis a blunt tool when it comes to explaining the Center and the Catholic milieu from which it drew its strength. The concept of milieu, ascribing the reasons for political behavior to a combination of regional, religious, social and economic factors, is much better suited to help understand the complexities of political Catholicism.

However difficult it might be to define the notion of milieu and its specific characteristics in one region, the milieu of Rhenish political Catholicism "showed an astonishing cohesion, inner unity, and attractive force."[100] This cohesion and force was not based on Catholic beliefs and regional identity alone, it was also built on a solid organizational foundation. By establishing various associations, Catholic activists gave material form to their demands for the right of workers to improve their economic and spiritual condition as well as to assert their civic rights.[101] Politically speaking, a "confessional bloc" was founded during the early years of the Kaiserreich which lasted until its forced dissolution by Hitler.[102] The creation of a web of Catholic associations can also be interpreted in negative terms. Konrad Repgen, for instance, views it as the "organizational expression of what a cultural historian might call the path into the ghetto."[103] By referring to Carl Amery's line of argument, Lepsius, too, emphasizes the negative effects of close-knit milieux on the political structure of a society. The close association of a party with a social milieu, Lepsius argues, might pose a danger to the party system at large. The purpose of such a party is primarily to protect the autonomy of its milieu; the integration of its members into the larger society is not just a secondary concern, but actually a threat to the very identity of its members.[104]

---

[99] This definition of milieu is based on Karl Rohe, *Wahlen und Wählertraditionen in Deutschland. Kulturelle Grundlagen deutscher Parteien und Parteiensysteme im 19. und 20. Jahrhundert* (Frankfurt a. M.: Suhrkamp, 1992), pp. 19-28.

[100] Sperber, *Popular Catholicism*, p. 297.

[101] Franz Hitze, "Die Quintessenz der sozialen Frage," (1880) excerpted in Rüther, *Geschichte*, 2:210-2.

[102] Anderson, "Kulturkampf," p. 89.

[103] Repgen, "Entwicklungslinien," p. 23.

[104] Lepsius, "Parteiensystem," p. 68.

While such concerns should not be underestimated, it is important to realize that this "Catholic ghetto" was a potent weapon in fending off the state's attack on German Catholics during the Kulturkampf. For the historian, the milieu of Rhenish Catholics provides one of Germany's most instructive examples of the intricate process by which different social and religious groups are interwoven in the formation of a regional political culture. The notion of a political and cultural Catholic milieu not only helps us understand the strength of the Center in German politics; it also permits us to extend the idea of political Catholicism beyond the limits of party politics.

Catholics devised various strategies to provide some protection from religious intolerance. Maintaining the delicate balance of religion, politics and social work was a tricky business in a complex environment driven by the interests of the Church, the Center Party and the Catholic populace. The lines between these different interests were not clearly drawn, of course: clergy, laymen, and politicians were divided into changing and overlapping coalitions which as a whole represented political Catholicism. In addition to the existing elements making up the Catholic milieu new groups emerged. The integration of Catholic industrial workers and their institutions into the Catholic milieu is among the most fascinating chapters of the history of political Catholicism. The traditional "organic" Catholic milieu of the village could not be moved to the growing industrial cities, a new kind of milieu had to be created.

III.

THE WORLD OF CATHOLIC POLITICS

THE WORLD of Catholic politics revolved around the Center Party. The Center was a Catholic party, founded in 1870 to represent the interests of the Catholic minority in the new German Empire. Its founding members believed they had to create a political party dedicated to defending "the civil rights and interests"[1] of Germany's Catholic minority. Beyond the defense of civil rights went the demands for the sanctity of the Christian marriage, for the protection of denominational schools, and the independence of ecclesiastical institutions.[2] The origins of political Catholicism reach back to the Cologne conflict, though the beginnings were minuscule. Konrad Repgen estimates that at that time only a few hundred of Germany's ten-million-strong Catholic community belonged to the salons and private circles that concerned themselves with the political rights of Catholics.[3] The revolution of 1848/49 changed little.[4] While the resentment of Rhineland Catholics toward Prussian law, military service, administrative decrees and the Hohenzollern monarchy "emerged with great clarity" during the revolution,[5] political Catholicism still was no more than a minor move-

---

[1] Peter Reichensperger to KV, 11 June 1870. Reprinted in Ludwig Bergsträsser, ed. *Der politische Katholizismus. Dokumente seiner Entwicklung* (1921-1922; reprint, Hildesheim: Georg Olms Verlag, 1976), 2:5.

[2] Soester Programm, 28 Oct. 1870, reprinted in Bergsträsser, *Katholizismus*, 2:27-8.

[3] Konrad Repgen, "Entwicklungslinien von Kirche und Katholizismus in historischer Sicht" in *Entwicklungslinien des deutschen Katholizismus*, ed. Anton Rauscher (Munich: Verlag Ferdinand Schöningh, 1973), pp. 20-1.

[4] For the involvement of Rhineland Catholics in the 1848 Revolution see Jonathan Sperber, *Rhineland Radicals: The Democratic Movement and the Revolutions of 1848-1849* (Princeton, N. J.: Princeton University Press, 1991), esp. pp. 337-41.

[5] Sperber, *Rhineland Radicals*, p. 469.

ment without any political structures or organized following. Although bishops and priests had considerable influence on newly enfranchised voters in their congregations, they channeled this influence into religious and confessional demands rather than laying the groundwork for a proper political party. Still, two developments are noteworthy: the founding of *Pius-Vereine* and the establishment of *Katholikentage*. *Pius-Vereine* were Catholic electoral associations, named after the current Pope; the liberalization of Prussian association laws had made this possible. The first *Pius-Verein* was founded in Mainz, among the earliest ones in the Rhine Province was that of Aachen. Its statutes declared it "a society for religious and civic [*bürgerlich*] freedom." Membership was restricted to Catholics but its goals went beyond religious concerns. From their inception, the Pius Associations pursued social as well as political goals.[6] The annual assembly of these associations (*Generalversammlung der Katholischen Vereine Deutschlands*) was the forerunner of the *Katholikentage*.[7] These yearly meetings were eventually dominated by Center politicians. The first "political" *Katholikentag* was held in Aachen in 1879. Presiding over the local organizing committee was Joseph Lingens, a member of the Reichstag; Ludwig Windthorst led a group of forty-two Center politicians who largely determined the agenda of the *Katholikentag*.[8] The general assembly of German *Pius-Vereine* met also at Aachen and it, too, was used as a political platform. The president of the Aachen *Pius-Verein*, Leonhard Timmermanns, invited Center politicians to address the political and social questions of the day. One spoke about the "unholy" consequences of free trade, others condemned the "work of modern Liberalism," and demanded confessional primary schools, and one Centrist launched the election campaign for the forthcoming elections to the Landtag.[9] As can be seen, political and religious activities did not contradict or exclude each other. Political Catholicism, as the term implies, had a dual character. Believing the fate of their faith as well as their civil rights at stake, Catholics fought a struggle in which every public act had both a religious and political purpose.

[6] Hubert Immelen, *Der Piusverein zu Aachen, 1848-1898. Gedenkblatt* (Aachen: n. d. [1898]), pp. 9-12.

[7] Friedrich Hohmann, "Die Soester Konferenzen 1864-1866. Zur Vorgeschichte der Zentrumspartei in Westfalen," *Westfälische Zeitschrift* 114 (1967), p. 293.

[8] Herbert Lepper, "Die Generalversammlung der Katholiken Deutschlands vom 8. bis 11. September 1879 in Aachen," *Zeitschrift des Aachener Geschichtsvereins* 80 (1970), pp. 235-6.

[9] Ibid., pp. 236-7.

The two decades following the revolution of 1848/49 were characterized by the formation of Catholic voluntary associations (*Verbandskatholizismus*). Konrad Repgen sees this as a critical step toward the formation of a political party, but also as "the organizational manifestation of what in terms of cultural history is termed the way into the ghetto."[10] However, this assessment has a positive side, too. The creation of a tightly-knit milieu was the precondition of the Center as a cohesive, powerful party based not on socio-economic or class interests but on the acceptance of the principles of Roman Catholicism. While the creation of a particularly Catholic environment tended to exclude Catholic Rhinelanders from Protestant Prussia, "the Church's counter-revolutionary activities helped to foster a rapprochement with the Prussian state"[11] which was to become a crucial element in the acceptance, however reluctant, of the Bismarckian *kleindeutsch* state.

In 1852, sixty-three deputies of the Prussian Landtag came together; this formation, consisting essentially of two opposing wings (liberal Rhenish and Westphalian conservative Catholics), lacked a common political program, and lasted only until 1859. The following year it reconstituted itself under the name "*Fraktion des Zentrums (Katholische Fraktion)*."[12] Repgen rightly points out that it is all too tempting to perceive a continuity between the early formations and the founding of the Center Party in 1871. During these years parties came and went, and there was certainly no inevitable mechanism that would lead to the creation of a Catholic party strong enough to play a pivotal role in imperial Germany's politics. Even the Catholic associations, which, unlike the *Katholische Fraktion*, existed without interruption, shifted their attention away from social and political issues toward confessional and religious ones.[13] Thus one must not overlook the long absence of a Catholic party during the 1860s. Political parties in Germany still lived a shadowy existence, and much depended on the dedication and determination of rather small groups. Prussian party politics were still the domain of notables; mass public meetings were rare and organization was loose even during election campaigns.

---

[10] Repgen, "Entwicklungslinien," p. 23.
[11] Sperber, *Popular Catholicism*, p. 47.
[12] Hohmann, "Soester Konferenzen," p. 294.
[13] Repgen, "Entwicklungslinien," p. 24.

A. The Founding of the Center Party

Already before the Franco-Prussian war efforts were under way to resurrect the Center. The defeat of Austria in 1866 had destroyed the hopes of many Catholics for a *großdeutsch* unification of Germany. Compelled by the necessity of their situation, men such as the bishop of Mainz Wilhelm Emmanuel Baron von Ketteler[14] urged German Catholics to embrace the new Prussian state and work within it for the religious rights and civil liberties of Catholics. An important impetus for this political revival came from a number of bishops who believed that the Church had to be actively involved in politics. Most Catholic politicians in the Rhineland agreed with bishop Ketteler's evaluation. Opposition to this came above all from Bavarian Catholics and Edmund Jörg, editor of the *Historisch-Politische Blätter* and until 1867 the most vehement Bavarian particularist. In order to make the Catholic voice heard, the archbishop of Cologne Paul Melchers "withdrew the prohibition against clerical participation in elections."[15] This declaration had considerable weight since Melchers was not only the metropolitan of an important diocese but also president of the *Fuldaer Bischofskonferenz*. Melchers, who had come to the diocese of Cologne from the much smaller diocese of Osnabrück[16], was struck by the problems industrialization had brought to the Rhineland[17]; his political initiative is best explained in terms of the social problems he encountered in his new diocese. The bishops of Münster, Trier and Kulm joined Melchers in his demand for more clerical involvement in politics. Consequently, clergy were prominent among the Center caucus; twelve of the Center's first deputies were priests.[18]

Rhinelanders figured prominently in the inception of the party. Among the Center's early leaders, who were later revered as founding fathers, were Karl von Savigny, Hermann von Mallinckrodt who "shared Windthorst's unhappiness at the new order"[19], and the brothers August and Peter Reichensperger. Savigny and Peter

---

[14] Bishop of Mainz 1850-1877.

[15] Anderson, *Windthorst*, p. 134; for a biographical sketch of Melchers see Hegel, *Erzbistum Köln*, pp. 80-5.

[16] Although very similar in physical size to the diocese of Osnabrück, that of Cologne contained almost ten times as many Catholics (ca. 1.5 million) and nine times as many parishes (800).

[17] Hegel, *Erzbistum Köln*, p. 82.

[18] Anderson, *Windthorst*, p. 134.

[19] Ibid., p. 137.

Reichensperger had particularly close ties to the Prussian state. Savigny, a childhood friend of Bismarck and his representative at the constituent Reichstag had been an active proponent of the *kleindeutsch* solution.[20] Peter Reichensperger, too, had put aside his initial enthusiasm for a *großdeutsch* unification and in 1870 "voiced his pleasure at German unification in terms scarcely distinguishable from those of the National Liberals."[21] He was convinced that the Prussian constitutional traditions would protect the interests of Catholics in a *kleindeutsch* empire.[22] His brother August, like the majority of Catholic politicians, was less optimistic; they believed that confessional peace was in danger. They agreed, however, with Peter Reichensperger that Catholics needed a parliamentary representative in the form of a political party.[23]

Conscious of anti-Catholic sentiments among the Protestant majority, the founders of the Center stressed that their party's goals were purely political. Nonetheless, the party program featured prominently ecclesiastical and religious aspects. There was also clearly articulated interest in the social question; Peter Reichensperger, after all, had been among the earliest advocates. The fundamental structure of society was not put into question but they understood the problems industrial workers were facing. Many among the founders were inclined to accept German unification, some were outright enthusiastic about it. This, however, was not Windthorst's Center. The Hanoverian parliamentarian, not surprisingly, hesitated to join the new party and it took Savigny and Reichensperger much time and effort to convince Windthorst to enter their ranks. He finally agreed and his signature was on the first electoral appeal of 11 January 1871.[24] The number of clergy among the signatories of the program was remarkably high; twenty-one out of fifty-one can be identified as priests. Of the others fourteen were landowners, three lawyers, five merchants, there were also three farmers, and three teachers.[25]

[20] Ibid.
[21] Ibid., p. 138.
[22] Winfried Becker, "Peter Reichensperger," in *Zeitgeschichte in Lebensbildern*, ed. Jürgen Aretz, Rudolf Morsey, and Anton Rauscher (Mainz: Matthias-Grünewald Verlag, 1982), 5:51.
[23] Ludwig Pastor, *August Reichensperger 1808-1895. Sein Leben und sein Wirken auf dem Gebiet der Politik, der Kunst und der Wissenschaft* (Freiburg i. Br.: Herder'sche Verlagsbuchhandlung, 1899), 2:4-5.
[24] For Windthorst's attitude toward the Center in 1870/71 see Anderson, *Windthorst*, pp. 138-40.
[25] Karl Egon Lönne, *Politischer Katholizismus im 19. und 20. Jahrhundert* (Frankfurt a. M.: Suhrkamp, 1986), p. 153.

From the beginning the Center was a considerable force in the Reichstag. In the new empire's first Reichstag election it won 63 of the 382 seats. This remarkable success was not just the result of the recent founding of the Center Party. Rather it was the culmination of a long process. In 1871, as Jonathan Sperber has observed:

> all the elements needed for a clerical electoral victory came together: universal and equal suffrage, the potent electoral slogan of endangered religion, active participation of the clergy in the election campaign, and an effective local, regional, and national political organization.... The sudden emergence [of political Catholicism] ought not to blind us to the decades of pastoral work, social changes, and political organizing which had preceded it.[26]

Sperber's analysis also explains, at least in part, the continued strength of the Center. The strength obtained by the Center during the 1870s was retained until 1918; the party always held about a quarter of all Reichstag seats.

The uncomfortable peace many Catholics had reached with the Prussian state during the late 1860s did not last long. Within a year of the founding of the Second Empire, the Prussian government transformed the spasmodic antagonism which had characterized the relations between itself, its Catholic citizens and the Catholic Church into a prolonged, elaborate anti-Church campaign known as the Kulturkampf. Liberals whose traditional suspicion of Roman Catholicism had already been heightened by Pius IX's infamous *Syllabus Errorum* (1864) were further enraged by the First Vatican Council's proclamation of the doctrine of papal infallibility. The reaction to these pronunciations exposed a deep-seated anti-Roman sentiment among the mass of German liberals and many conservatives whose notion of a Protestant empire was threatened by the demands of Roman Ultramontanism and what they believed to be its German political ancillary: the Center.[27] The greatly successful novelist and playwright Gustav Freytag saw the dogma as an attempt by the ultramontane party in Rome "to put the curse of the old Church on our souls, our state, our education [*Geistesbildung*], on much that we all consider national honour, pride, and virtue." Few, however, shared Freytag's confidence "that the condemnation, that their high priest

---

[26] Sperber, *Popular Catholicism*, pp. 190-1.
[27] Fritz Fischer, "Der deutsche Protestantismus und die Politk im 19. Jahrhundert," *Historische Zeitschrift* 171 (1951), p. 495.

hurls against us shall not disturb the peaceful coexistence with the majority of [Catholics]."[28] Protestant indignation towards Catholic Germans was heightened by other events, too. Many viewed the founding of the Center as a threat to the new empire. This threat appeared to be increased by the curia's involvement in the strengthening of Polish nationalism which threatened to create tension in the eastern territories of the young empire.

Catholics, too, felt threatened and they reacted vehemently to liberal attacks on their religion. As some liberals, some Catholics perceived the Kulturkampf in terms of an ideological contest. The Catholic counterpart to the liberal conspiracy theory of ultramontane forces was a ploy by revolutionary freemasons to destroy the Church. Most clergy and pious Catholics were, however, less concerned with conspiratorial schemes by freemasons or fanatic anti-Catholics. To them the Kulturkampf was above all a call to defense of their religious beliefs and rights against the encroachments of a hostile state.[29]

In this atmosphere Reich Chancellor Otto von Bismarck could easily exploit anti-Catholic feelings to eliminate a political foe (the Center) and try to accommodate a needed political ally (the National Liberals). Publicly he defended the anti-Catholic measures of his government as purely defensive actions. He had gone as far as he could, Bismarck argued, in dealing with confessional questions, but in the face of an opponent bent upon destroying the very foundations of the state he had to defend the Prussian state.[30] It was Bismarck whom Catholics blamed above all for turning this conflict into "the longest and most difficult confrontation the Catholic Church had to weather" during the nineteenth century.[31]

The motives for this anti-Catholic campaign do not necessarily have to be interpreted as an aggressive act from above. Margaret Anderson has suggested that legislation to reduce the influence of the Catholic Church "began as a defensive reaction of local elites to the challenge of subordinate groups of their local dominance." In Anderson's scenario the Kulturkampf was triggered less by Catholic religious revival or Bismarck's Machiavellian schemes or the "needs of a modern

---

[28] Gustav Freytag, "Die politische Lage" (May 1870), *Politische Aufsätze*, vol. 7, 1st series of *Gesammelte Werke* (Leipzig and Berlin-Grunewald: G. Hirzel und Verlagsanstalt für Literatur und Kunst Hermann Klemm, n. d.), 356-7.

[29] KB, 3:272.

[30] Reich Chancellor von Bismarck's speech to the Prussian Chamber of Peers, 24 April 1873 in Otto von Bismarck, *Die gesammelten Werke* (1972; reprint, Berlin: 1924 ff.), 11:296.

[31] KB, 3:209.

state," but by the "anxiety of Germany's elites faced with the sudden emergence of mass politics," facilitated in part by the introduction of the democratic franchise. For Anderson, the Pulpit Law of November 1871, which prohibited priests from using the pulpit as a vehicle for political agitation, is evidence of this defensive reaction toward mass politics.[32]

Among the very first steps the government took against the church was the law on supervision of schools *(Schulaufsichtsgesetz)*.[33] Liberals hailed the law as a victory of reason over the Church's authoritarian obscurantism. German bishops condemned it as a violation of the "organic union between school [*Volksschule*] and Church which had existed for more than a millennium."[34] The most drastic measures, requiring changes to the constitution, were introduced by the so-called May Laws.[35] Among the restrictions these laws introduced were the state supervision of Catholic seminaries, far-reaching changes in the curriculum of the study of theology, a state veto in clerical appointments, and the curtailing of the Church's disciplinary powers.

Karl Bachem loudly complained that the link between bishops and their clergy had been willfully severed and that this abscission was followed by the government's intrusion into episcopal prerogatives.[36] The reaction to these laws naturally was strongest in Poland, Silesia and the Rhineland, the regions of Prussia with the largest Catholic populations. With the Jesuit Law of 4 July 1872, the Reichstag prohibited and expelled the Jesuit order which had experienced a resurgence since the 1850s and traditionally dominated the higher education of the Catholic élite. In the archdiocese of Cologne, Jesuit hauses in Aachen, Bonn, Cologne, and Essen were forced to close. A Prussian law of 31 May 1875 went even further, forbidding virtually all Catholic orders; ultimately twenty-four monasteries and seventy nunneries were closed in the archdiocese.[37] Among the victims of such purges was Klara Fey's order in Aachen. Since its founding in 1848 the sisterhood had opened over twenty-five new houses. The order was primarily concerned with the education of and care

---

[32] Anderson, "Kulturkampf," p. 89.

[33] The law was promulgated on 11 March 1872.

[34] Catholic bishops of Prussia to [Staatsministerium?], 11 April 1872 reprinted in Hans Fenske, ed. *Im Bismarckschen Reich 1871-1890* (Darmstadt: Wissenschaftliche Buchgesellschaft, 1978), p. 74.

[35] Promulgated 11 to 14 May 1872.

[36] KB, 3:269.

[37] Hegel, *Erzbistum Köln*, p. 556.

for poor women, but it also maintained three orphanages and taught some twelve thousand pupils in its schools. In the district of Aachen alone Fey's order ran eighty-four elementary schools.[38] First the government prohibited the sisters from working as teachers in the schools run by the order. Despite the city council's petitions to parliament and Emperor and Klara Fey's appeal to the Empress Augusta, the schools were closed. The mother house in Aachen was swamped with "unemployed" nuns. Since there was no hope of finding work for them in Germany many went abroad, most to Austria where the order had already established a foothold, but also to Hungary, Luxemburg and Belgium. Gradually the government restricted the order's activities further, and by September 1878 the mother house in Aachen had closed; the last house, that in Burtscheid, had to be vacated in May 1879, only a few nuns too ill to be moved were permitted to remain.[39]

Almost all areas of religious life were affected by the Kulturkampf. Seminaries were closed, and the education of priests regulated by laws drafted in Adalbert Falk's Ministry of Religion and Education. To take a single but typical example, the seminary of Trier was informed by telegram that its doors had to be closed and its training priests had to vacate the premises within two days. In the face of determined clerical and lay resistance it took several months and the detachment of local police officers, a small troop of Hussars and half an infantry company to enforce the order.[40] Bishoprics remained vacant after bishops had died or been removed by the government. Bishops, Paul Melchers of Cologne and Matthias Eberhard of Trier among them, were arrested and incarcerated, others were forced to leave the country. Eventually most Prussian bishops were either in prison or in exile. A few years after the introduction of the May Laws legislation only three of Prussia's twelve bishoprics were occupied. Many parishes were left without priests. Of Aachen's eight parishes, for example, five were without a parish priest as late as 1885.[41] Priests who refused to comply with the May Laws were left without salary, Catholic seminaries were dissolved, and the training of clergy practically ceased in Prussia.

[38] Otto Pfülf, *M. Clara Fey vom armen Kinde Jesus und ihre Stiftung. 1815-1894* (Freiburg i. Br.: Herdersche Verlagsbuchhandlung, 1913), pp. 402-3.

[39] Morsey, *Zeitgeschichte*, pp. 62-3; Pfülf, *Clara Fey*, pp. 407-21.

[40] Franz Rudolf Reichert, "Das Trierer Priesterseminar im Kulturkampf (1873-1886)," *Archiv für mittelrheinische Kirchengeschichte* 25 (1973), pp. 84-91.

[41] The exceptions were Ermland, Kulm, and Hildesheim, for details see Erich Schmidt-Volkmar, *Der Kulturkampf in Deutschland 1871-1890* (Göttingen: Musterschmidt-Verlag, 1962), pp. 168-9; Poll, "Das Hineinwachsen," p. 26.

The campaign went beyond attacking the legal autonomy of the Catholic church; it "was also a means of germanizing the Prussian Catholic population."[42] The Kulturkampf purge of Prussia's administration was unique since it was the only purge carried out in imperial Germany that was "at least partly in response to pressure from public opinion."[43] The National Liberals demanded and achieved the removal of "Ultramontanes" and those in the Prussian bureaucracy who took a "lukewarm stance toward [them]."[44] *Landrat* Janssen of Heinsberg, for instance, was refused the mayorship of Aachen and was later forced to give up his position because of his "unreliable attitudes toward ultramontanes." In Aachen the district governor convinced two civil servants (*Geheimer Medizinalrat* Dr. Schervier and *Landgerichtsobersekretär* Thissen) to quit Constantia, the local Catholic election association. Constantia's president, a Dr. Förster, was not as easily intimidated. Despite instructions from the Minister of Religion and Education Adalbert Falk to discipline the suspicious Förster, he refused to resign as city councilor, clung to the presidency of Constantia, and continued to teach at the *Realschule* in Aachen. Occasionally, government schemes backfired. Mayors were instructed by Aachen's district government to keep a close eye on the population. One of them who had gained notoriety as an eager denouncer of "Ultramontanes" ran afoul of his superiors when he was sentenced to five months in prison for accepting bribes.[45]

Despite these severe measures the Kulturkampf failed in the end. Bismarck and the Liberals had made the mistake of underestimating the power of religion and the resilience of the Church. Pious Catholics felt compelled by moral imperative to support their beleaguered Church.[46] Their response to Kulturkampf legislation—a combination of passive resistance, open defiance and occasional violence—was strong enough to render government measures, if not powerless, at least ineffective. Government representatives were unable to control vacant bishoprics because they had little control over the ecclesiastical machinery. Although bishoprics and ecclesiastical corporations including charitable and educational ones had lost whatever state

---

[42] Margaret Lavinia Anderson and Kenneth Barkin, "The Myth of the Puttkammer Purge and the Reality of the Kulturkampf: Some Reflections on the Historiography of Imperial Germany," *Journal of Modern History* 54 (1982), p. 657.

[43] Ibid.

[44] Ibid., pp. 657, 660.

[45] Heinrich Schiffers, *Der Kulturkampf in Stadt und Regierungsbezirk Aachen* (Aachen: Verlag Kaatzers Erben, 1929), pp. 121-2; Poll, "Das Hineinwachsen," pp. 25-6.

subsidies they used to receive, the Church found unconventional ways of raising money. The *Paulus-Verein* of Cologne, for example, collected and distributed a million marks to the Church's coffers.[47] When the government stopped paying priests, Archbishop Melchers ordered quarterly collections in the parishes to provide some income. Participation in everyday religious observances became a political matter, participation in extraordinary religious events became a symbol of defiance and resistance. An example of the politicization of religious events was the special pilgrimages organized in the years 1871-1873.[48] Men like the Cologne farmer Engelbert Schwäbig, a leader of the annual procession to Kevelaer, who was imprisoned for this act of defiance, became Catholic heroes.[49] Public holidays became occasions to demonstrate dissatisfaction with the government. On the Kaiser's birthday and on Sedan Day, Catholics were demonstratively absent from public affirmations of the monarchy and the state. They refused to flag their houses, kept their children away from municipal parades, local Catholic councils refused official recognition of these holidays, and bishops declined the celebration of masses. Instead Catholics celebrated the anniversary of the election of Pius IX as Pope.[50]

The Catholic press was arguably the most effective tool the Catholics had to fight the Kulturkampf. Nationally, *Germania*, the unofficial organ of the Center, under its editor Paul Majunke, was the most efficient critic of the anti-Catholic campaign. In the Rhine Province it was the *Kölnische Volkszeitung* which played that role. Catholic newspapers mushroomed particularly in the Rhineland and Westphalia. By the end of 1873, one hundred twenty new Catholic dailies had joined the journalistic war against the government.[51] Catholic editors and publishers paid a heavy price for their resistance. It has been estimated that they "spent a total of fifteen years and two months in jail and accumulated a total of 40,000 marks in fines."[52] Since priests were muzzled by the *Kanzelparagraph*, other

---

[46] KB, 3:341.
[47] Ronald J. Ross, "Enforcing the Kulturkampf: The Bismarckian State and the Limits of Coercion in Imperial Germany," *Journal of Modern History* 56 (1984), pp. 477-8.
[48] Sperber, *Popular Catholicism*, p. 224.
[49] Julius Bachem, *Erinnerungen eines alten Publizisten und Politikers* (Cologne: J. P. Bachem, 1913), p. 61.
[50] Anderson, *Windthorst*, pp. 179-80; Sperber, *Popular Catholicism*, p. 225.
[51] J. Bachem, *Erinnerungen*, p. 32; KB, 3:279.
[52] Ross, "Enforcing the Kulturkampf," 473.

organs of political Catholicism took their place. One of the most active was the Cologne *Katholische Volksverein,* founded by a group of Cologne burghers in 1867. Speakers were sent throughout the Rhineland and beyond to agitate against the Kulturkampf. The young Julius Bachem was among those who had their early political experience in public speaking during that campaign.[53] Thus the government, while attempting to curtail the political influence of the clergy, unintentionally drove Catholics to search for new avenues to spread their political message.

By launching an anti-Catholic crusade the government compelled Catholic citizens to declare themselves for or against the new order. Rudolf Morsey argues that forcing them to make this decision was a "serious political mistake" since Catholics had been "without reservation loyal to state and monarch,"[54] a loyalty which was left badly bruised after the Kulturkampf ended. Even if one disagrees with Morsey's assessment of the Catholic population's commitment to the Second Empire, there is little doubt that the Kulturkampf created among Catholics the rebellious oppositional identity of a besieged minority. How could they unconditionally support a state determined to destroy the institutions which safeguarded the continuance of their faith? This was obviously not only a question of religious freedom since the Church, Catholic lay associations, and the Center provided protection against spiritual and material hardship as well as a cultural and social framework in which Catholics found the certainties necessary to cope with revolutionary change. Among most Catholics there was little enthusiasm for Bismarck's new state. The marked unwillingness of Catholic theorists to allow the National Liberal veneration of the Hegelian *Machtstaat* or conservative-Prussian anti-parliamentarian statism in their own political culture separated them from Protestant Germany. As an alternative to the Hegelian concept of an omnipotent state they offered a state concerned with the "natural rights" of its citizens; as an alternative to laissez-faire capitalism they offered a Christian welfare state.[55] No wonder, then, that "far from weakening the political power of the clergy, state persecution

---

[53] J. Bachem, *Erinnerungen*, pp. 44-5.

[54] Rudolf Morsey, "Die deutschen Katholiken und der Nationalstaat zwischen Kulturkampf und Erstem Weltkrieg," in *Die deutschen Parteien vor 1918*, ed. Gerhard Ritter (Cologne: Kiepenheuer & Witsch, 1973), p. 272.

[55] Horst Gründer, "Nation und Katholizismus im Kaiserreich," in *Katholizismus, nationaler Gedanke und Europa seit 1800*, ed. Albrecht Langner (Paderborn: Ferdinand Schöningh, 1985), p. 67.

added the nimbus of martyrdom to a group whose remarkable influence was already apparent in 1870/71."[56]

At the polls, too, the Center seemed to benefit from the Kulturkampf. The number of deputies the party could send to the Prussian Landtag grew from fifty-two to ninety after the 1873 election. A few months later similar successes were made in the Reichstag election; the Center increased its representation from fifty-nine to ninety-one seats. Most of these gains came at the expense of the National Liberals and the Free Conservatives. In the Rhineland the Center increased its number of seats from twenty-two (1871) to twenty-seven (1874). It gained one seat in each of the five Rhineland districts. The party was also able to attract a large number of former SPD voters in the industrial region of the Rhineland. Far from espousing the SPD's atheist propaganda, Catholic workers retained considerable loyalty to their church. Even Catholic workers who had previously voted for Social Democratic candidates rallied to the defense of their Church by casting their vote for the only political party committed to the protection of their religious beliefs. A comparison of election returns before and during the Kulturkampf clearly shows that the Center had taken away many SPD votes. In his study of the Düsseldorf area, J. D. Hunley demonstrates that after 1871 support for the Socialists "coincides precisely with the division between Protestant and Catholic election districts."[57] Furthermore, it seems that the Kulturkampf widened the appeal of the Center to workers who had formerly voted for the SPD; "predominantly Catholic areas in Germany were not fruitful recruiting grounds for socialism, even where working-class parties had had considerable success prior to 1871, as they had in the Ruhr, Krefeld, and even Gladbach."[58] The Center emerged from the Kulturkampf as a stronger party, more powerfully organized, with more representatives in both the Reichstag and the Prussian Landtag, and with massive popular support from its growing constituency.

---

[56] Sperber, *Popular Catholicism*, p. 208.
[57] J. D. Hunley, "The Working Classes, Religion and Social Democracy in the Düsseldorf Area, 1867-78," *Societas—a Review of Social History* 4 (1974), pp. 144-5.
[58] Hunley, "Working Classes," p. 148.

B. The People's Association for Catholic Germany

Karl Trimborn's political career began in earnest in 1890, when he became deputy-chairman of the newly founded People's Association for Catholic Germany. Trimborn was charged with creating an efficient structure for this new organization. Already as a student Trimborn had displayed his organizational and political talents, and at university he met some of the men who became friends and political allies for life. In Leipzig, Trimborn and a fellow student, the future Center politician Adolf Gröber, founded Teutonia, a Catholic fraternity. During a social meeting of a fraternity in Cologne, Trimborn also met Karl Bachem.[59] Apparently an outgoing man in the Rhenish tradition, Trimborn moved easily among the workers, artisans and merchants of his home town. These two characteristics, organizational talent and rapport with workers, were the very attributes required of a man in charge of building up the People's Association.

Ludwig Windthorst created the People's Association with the goal of constraining the conservatives within his party and hope of maintaining Catholic workers' support of the movement after the fading of the Kulturkampf had removed an important incentive to vote for the Center. He had advocated the creation of the People's Association as a conduit for increased participation in politics by ordinary Catholics.[60] The Association was conceived in explicit opposition to intentions of the conservative wing of the Center and the episcopate, namely the bishop of Trier Michael Felix Korum, to found a Catholic counterpart to the Evangelical League.[61] The Center leader had argued that pursuing confessional polemics as suggested by the Center notables would only embitter the political discourse but not solve any practical problems. In place of an anti-Protestant organization he advocated the People's Association as a tool designed to contribute to the solution of the pressing "social question."

Ludwig Windthorst chose the industrial city of Mönchengladbach as the seat of the new organization. Located in the Rhineland, where bourgeoisie and industrialists dominated politics, Mönchengladbach was safe from the influence of aristocratic Center leaders. As for the threat Socialism posed, for many years Center leaders had been concerned about its growing influence. The founders of the People's As-

---

[59] Cardauns, *Trimborn*, p. 19.
[60] August Pieper to Julius Bachem, 8 March 1904, BAP 74VO1 no. 2 f. 138.
[61] Franz Brandts to Fritzen, 2 May 1907, StAMG Nl. Hohn 15/2/195.

sociation viewed the Social Democratic Party as a "powerful enemy" who threatened "the foundation of Christian society and civilizaion."[62] They feared that thousands of "prophets of atheism clad in smocks"[63] as one propagandist put it, came in contact with Christian workers; therefore it was necessary to provide adequate protection against the dangers of Socialism.

Among the founders of the People's Association were three men whose influence on the development of the new association during the next decades was to be profound. One of these was Franz Brandts, a member of a prominent Mönchengladbach family and a pioneer of Rhenish industrialization. Another was Franz Hitze a theologian and professor of Christian sociology who provided much of the People's Association's theoretical foundation. The youngest member of this triumvirate was Karl Trimborn, who had been hand-picked by Windthorst as the right hand of Franz Brandts and "architect" of the new organization.[64]

Franz Brandts was the first chairman of the People's Association.[65] Although he agreed to take the position only under the condition that he would serve just one year, he actually remained chairman from the fall of 1890 until his death in 1914. Brandts, who had brought the first mechanical half-wool weaving-mill to Mönchengladbach, was not only a pioneer in the mechanization of the Rhenish textile industry, he also was at the forefront of social reform. He was among the six factory owners of the Mönchengladbach chambers of trade and industry who promoted the introduction of a maximum workday of twelve hours in 1867. Between 1872 and 1880 he introduced health insurance to his factories, eliminated Sunday and nighttime work, provided inexpensive meals for out-of-town workers, improved safety conditions, and opened a kindergarten. Workers worked only 10 ¼ hours daily at his factories and he paid the

[62] "Deutsche Katholiken," proclamation of the Volksverein's founding, HStAD Regierung Aachen/910, f. 42.
[63] Franz Hitze, speech at the *Katholikentag*, Amberg (1884), reprinted in Günther Rüther, ed. *Geschichte der christlich-demokratischen und christlich-sozialen Bewegungen in Deutschland* (Cologne: Verlag Wissenschaft und Politik, 1986), 2:218-19.
[64] August Pieper to Julius Bachem, 8 March 1904, BAP 74VO1 no. 2 f. 138; Cardauns, *Trimborn*, p. 70.
[65] Protocol of the constituent meeting of the Volksverein für das katholische Deutschland, 24. Oct. 1890, HAStK Nl. Bachem 1006/59. For a short biographical sketch see Wolfgang Löhr's essay in Morsey, Zeitgeschichte, pp. 91-105; for Brandts's involvement in the early Christian labor movement see Eric Dorn Brose, *Christian Labor and the Politics of Frustration in Imperial Germany* (Washington, D.C.: Catholic University of America Press, 1985), pp. 62-5.

highest wages in town. Assisted by the chaplain Dr. Peter Norrenberg, Brandts made a mark with the so-called Brandt Factory Regulation, which established moral and behavioral rules for his employees.[66] Brandts saw the Church and its teachings as a bulwark against social disorder. Attitudes such as Brandts's and Norrenberg's seem to support the argument that Catholicism was not necessarily an obstacle in the way of industrialization. Instead, it could be employed to legitimize the new economic system and provide the ideological justification for orderly behavior, not only for the subjects of the king but also for the employees of the factory owner. The Catholic Church, its priests, and Catholic capitalists such as Brandts, may be said to have played a significant role in producing the stable, disciplined labor force required by modern industry.

Franz Hitze was the theoretician of the People's Association. Already as a theology student in Würzburg, he had concerned himself with the "social question"; he lectured to his fellow students at the Catholic fraternity *Unitas* about socialism and about the position of workers in modern society.[67] Hitze's ideal world was a modified medieval guild system (*Ständestaat*). His Utopia had a democratic foundation and sought to come to terms with industrialization and the existence of a working class. Workers' associations were to survey working conditions and try to improve them. As a last resort, he thought even strikes were legitimate.[68] When addressing workers celebrating the first anniversary of their association in Cologne, he declared that their goal was the struggle "against liberal capitalism and against the revolutionary fanatics of Social Democracy." He promised his audience victory if they put their trust "in the might of the Church, the Holy Father...and the benevolence of his majesty the Emperor."[69] Although of a naturally reflective, analytical turn of mind, Hitze was determined to apply his theoretical considerations to practical problems. But he was no orator: his voice was weak, and he was uncomfortable in front of crowds, so he shunned the limelight, preferring to work behind the scenes.[70]

---

[66] Wolfgang Löhr, "Die Fabrikordnung der Firma Franz Brandts in Mönchengladbach," *Annalen des Historischen Vereins für den Niederrhein* 178 (1976), pp. 145-57.

[67] Morsey, *Zeitgeschichte*, 1:54.

[68] Michael Schneider, "Religion and Labour Organization: The Christian Trade Unions in the Wilhelmine Empire," *European Studies Review* 12 (1982), p. 348.

[69] "Katholischer Arbeiterverein Köln-Süd," *KV*, no. 282, 11 Oct. 1886.

[70] K. Trimborn to his wife, 9 August 1908, quoted in Hermann Cardauns, *Karl Trimborn* (M. Gladbach: Volksvereins-Verlag, 1922), p. 72.

Hitze believed that the Center's most dangerous enemy was secularization, more pervasive than the Kulturkampf and more serious than the divisions within political Catholicism. This struggle took place not only on the battlefield of material and political interests; it was a fundamental conflict encompassing all aspects of life. Already in 1880 Brandts and Hitze had founded the "*Verband Arbeiterwohl,*" a forerunner of the People's Association. It was an attempt to immunize workers against the "socialist disease" and to bring them closer to the Church. Hitze had realized that the romantic vision of renewing medieval society he had developed in his early writings was unworkable. He now advocated a two-pronged solution to the social question: improvements of conditions in factories, along the lines of Brandts's efforts, and state efforts, such as regulating conditions or work by law and social insurance.[71] Hitze was a deputy in both the Prussian Landtag and the Reichstag but not a member of the inner circle of the Center leadership; nonetheless, he belonged to a group of priests who had considerable influence on the party, not least because he was one of Karl Trimborn's closest personal friends.[72]

A close relationship existed between the People's Association and the Center. Although they both claimed to work independently of each other, they cooperated closely in creating Catholic organizations and in furthering the political influence of the Center. During an organizational conference of Center men, August Pieper pointed out that the People's Association was *the* Catholic mass organization which dealt with the Catholic population on a daily basis; thus the Center should support the association wherever possible.[73]

During its first year the People's Association experienced some difficulties attracting members, mainly, the board of directors complained, because too many Catholics did not appreciate "its extraordinary significance for the public affairs of German Catholics." Nevertheless, more than 100,000 Catholics had joined by the end of 1891 and the People's Association had distributed over a million pamphlets and brochures.[74] Success varied greatly from region to region and from community to community. When we consider the Reich as a whole, the Rhineland stands out as the most fertile ground for the

---

[71] Horstwalter Heitzer, *Der Volksverein für das katholische Deutschland im Kaiserreich 1890-1918* (Mainz: Matthias-Grünewald-Verlag, 1979), p. 17.
[72] Loth, *Katholiken,* p. 53.
[73] "Protokoll der Organisationskonferenz westdeutscher Parteifreunde," 4 Oct. 1904, BAK Nl. 176 Herold Nr. 1.
[74] "Bericht über den Stand des Volksvereins für das katholische Deutschland im Jahre 1901," StAMG Nl. Hohn 15/2/165.

People's Association's message, but Rhinelanders varied in the strength of their response. In Aachen, for instance, the People's Association established a chapter in March 1891, only a few months after its founding. In Burtscheid and Düren the People's Association also had early successes; by 1894 it had 242 and some 1600 members respectively and was busy agitating against the Social Democrats. In nearby Eschweiler, on the other hand, no branch had been established by 1894.[75] The Prussian Ministry of the Interior was soon concerned enough about the People's Association's influence to instruct local authorities to monitor it and to report on its activities.[76] Even Social Democrats grudgingly acknowledged it as a "tenacious and purposeful" opponent.[77]

The organization of the Association was, above all, the work of Karl Trimborn. He had insisted on structuring the People's Association from the top down. Accordingly, it was the responsibility of the appointed local secretary (*Geschäftsführer*) to enlist stewards (*Vertrauensmänner*) who in turn recruited new members. The local clergy played a central role in organizing and administering People's Association chapters. They were the Association's first contact when going to a new town. Clergy often became local secretaries and they provided the names of possible stewards.[78] Mönchengladbach urged the local secretaries of a district to meet at least once a year and report to headquarters about the activities and progress of the People's Association in their area.[79]

The first step of a membership drive was a public meeting, announced in the local press and on posters provided by headquarters or by priests from the pulpit. The local priest usually presided over

---

[75] Police President of Aachen to District Governor of Aachen (von Hartmann), 15 March 1894, HStAD Regierung Aachen/910, f. 39-40; Mayor of Burtscheid (Mitteldorf) to District Governor of Aachen, 17 March 1894, HStAD Regierung Aachen/910, f. 36-7; Landrat of Düren (Bruening) to District Governor of Aachen, 22 March 1894, HStAD Regierung Aachen/910, f. 70; Mayor of Eschweiler (Fischer) to District Governor of Aachen, 19 March 1894, HStAD Regierung Aachen/910, f. 38.

[76] Minister of Interior (signed Braunbehrens) to District Governor of Aachen (von Hartmann), 24 Feb. 1894, HStAD Regierung Aachen/910, f. 30.

[77] Jean Meerfeld, *Die Deutsche Zentrumspartei* (Berlin: Verlag für Sozialwissenschaft, 1918), p. 62.

[78] Karl Trimborn „Welche Mittel sind für eine erfolgreiche Ausbreitung und Erhaltung des Vereins anzuwenden?" Versammlung der Geschäftsführer des Volksvereins für das katholische Deutschland, 13 March 1894, BAP 74VO 1 no. 1 f. 12-3.

[79] Sitzung des Gesamtvorstandes des Volksvereins, 25 August [1897], BAP 74VO 1 no. 1 f. 207.

such meetings; local Catholic dignitaries joined him at the head table. Trimborn believed that mass meetings by themselves would not suffice to attract members. After meetings the local press was to report on them in "the most impressive way possible."[80] These reports of the meetings and People's Association activities were also spread to neighboring towns and villages in the hope of extending the organization. The most important part of gaining and maintaining membership were personal visits by stewards. Every six weeks they distributed the official journal of the People's Association. On these occasions stewards could answer questions, announce upcoming events and gauge the mood of the membership. Trimborn even encouraged them to find out "which newspapers and literature were read," particularly in the households of workers. If need be the steward could provide "guidance and advice" on proper reading material.[81] In larger towns and cities, Trimborn said, much depended on attracting workers and their representatives to the People's Association; but stewards had to be cautious only to recruit those who could afford the annual membership dues of one mark.[82] Bishop Korum of Trier and a number of aristocratic Center men who had lobbied hard for an anti-Protestant league had argued for a fee as high as ten marks per year but, Brandts, Hitze and eventually Windthorst decided on the affordable rate.[83]

Workers were the most sought-after members. Trimborn hoped to attract some by passing on literature to them—not only through "official" channels, but also by ordinary People's Association members, who were encouraged to pass on their copies to friends and colleagues.[84] Attacks on Social Democracy, descriptions of the moral and economic damage caused by atheism contrasted with the beneficial social policies pursued by the Center were part of such propaganda. Lectures on the history and activities of the Center figured largely in public meetings of the People's Association. The involvement of many Center politicians and the prominence of political topics and concerns in meetings belies the programmatic statement that the People's Association was not political. Lists of speakers and speeches made available by Mönchengladbach almost always contain

---

[80] Trimborn, "Mittel," BAP 74VO 1 no. 1 f. 12.
[81] Ibid.
[82] Ibid.
[83] August Pieper to Julius Bachem, 8 March 1904, BAP 74VO1 no. 2 f. 138.
[84] Trimborn, "Mittel," BAP 74VO 1 no. 1 f. 12.

the names of Center politicians and include lectures on the history and activities of the Party.[85]

By 1898 the People's Association was the leading organization of Catholic public education. This commitment to *Volksbildung*, advocated by August Pieper, was seen as the first step in the solution of the social question. The dedication and enthusiasm of Center politicians and clergy was incessantly employed in the service of public education. Education went beyond lectures and libraries. People's Association leaders feared for the moral and aesthetic well-being of Catholic workers. Afraid that working people fall victim to unscrupulous salesmen "who peddle the most vulgar art at high prices" they offered for sale paintings "particularly suited for working-class homes."[86] Concern over the education of workers drove some Catholic priests to the absurd. J. Peter Oberdörffer used the following criteria to prepare a catalogue of suitable plays and books. As a matter of course, all works had to be of ethical value, and naturally not offend Catholic moral beliefs. In order to be useful they must not be over the workers' heads. To exclude any chance of confusion or contamination even useful plays requiring only a few revisions, could not be included since one never knew whether people would indeed carry out the necessary changes, or whether they would get them right. Oberdörffer also saw dangers lurking in collections of plays. Among the "good" plays he warned there might be some of doubtful value, and one could be certain that workers would be attracted to risqué pieces. Oberdörffer excluded all plays with characters of both sexes, "for the circles in question," workers that is, would surely fall victim to carnal temptations. During rehearsals even the most watchful Präses could not prevent "hanky panky." Changing into costumes back stage, indecent gestures, or the stressing of words which might "introduce something unseemly into the play" were irrepressible. The thought of women playing men's parts or of men in women's clothing made Oberdörffer shiver with "revulsion and repugnance." The only exceptions to these rules were, of course, religious plays.[87] Not surprisingly Oberdörffer's catalogue was short, dull and widely ignored. Besides lectures, pamphlets and books (distributed through

---

[85] A few examples are: Redner-Liste für die Versammlungen des Volksvereins im Kreise Geldern, BAP 74VO1 no. 1 f. 290; Redner-Liste für die Versammlungen des Volksvereins (Oberrhein und angrenzende Bezirke), BAP 74VO 1 no. 1 f. 296.
[86] Brochure entitled "Schmücke Dein Heim!,"n. d., StAMG Nl. Hohn 15/2/132.
[87] Johann Peter Oberdörffer, *Verzeichnis geeigneter Bücher und Bühnenstücke für katholische Vereins-Bibliotheken* (Cologne: J. P. Bachem, 1893), pp. iii-iv.

its own libraries), the People's Association in later years provided slide lectures and distributed "morally unobjectionable" films to movie theaters and schools. The aim was to provide an alternative to movies distributed by commercial distributors, which, the directorate added, revealing its anti-semitism, allegedly were "primarily in the hands of unscrupulous Jews."[88] In addition to moral health, hygiene was also a concern of the People's Association; it provided information on the cleanliness of food, clothes, and house.[89]

In time the success of the People's Association was also noted abroad as a model for similar organizations in other countries. Pope Pius X strongly recommended the organizational structure of the People's Association when the Italian Catholic Action was reorganized.[90] Although this imitation of the German model ultimately failed, the very fact that the People's Association was perceived as a model is notable. More significant for our purposes, however, is that the People's Association, despite its assurances to the contrary, was an auxiliary of the Center. There was a close personal union between the two organizations; many of the People's Association's leaders, for instance, were Center deputies in the Reichstag. Moreover, the annual congresses of the People's Association were held as part of the *Katholikentag*, and the principal speeches were always delivered by leaders of the Center who also orchestrated the decision on the People's Association's future tasks and strategies. With the People's Association the Center had acquired an effective instrument to attract workers to political Catholicism. Moreover, the Association played a role in the conversion of the Center from a party of notables to a mass party. But the impetus for change provided by the People's Association was not sufficient to reform the party, it required a leadership struggle between the conservative, aristocratic wing of the party and "Popular Centrists"[91] to prepare the Center for the challenges of the future.

[88] Memorandum "'Lichtilderei GmbH. M.-Gladbach' 1913: Bedeutung und Verbreitung des Kinowesens," presented to the directorate [Vorstand] of the Volksverein, 27 April 1913, StAMG Nl. Hohn 15/2/157. For a discussion of the extent and nature of anti-semitism in the Center Party see David Blackbourn, "Catholics, the Centre Party and Anti-Semitism," in *Populists and Patricians: Essays in Modern German History*, (London: Allen & Unwin, 1987), pp. 68-87; Loth, *Katholiken*, pp. 47-8.

[89] Protokoll der Sitzung des Gesamtvorstandes des Volksvereins für das katholische Deutschland," 2 Oct. 1911, StAMG Nl. Hohn 15/2/157.

[90] Sándor Agócs, "'*Germania Doceat!*' The *Volksverein*, the Model for Italian Catholic Action, 1905-1914," *Catholic Historical Review* 61 (1975), p. 46.

[91] This expression is borrowed from Zeender, *Center Party*.

C. Ernst Lieber's Leadership

Ludwig Windthorst had been among the founders of the Center, and as its leader he had skillfully steered the Center ship through the stormy days of the Kulturkampf. His enemies maligned him as a cunning demagogue determined to undermine the authority of the state; his supporters revered him as a demigod under whose leadership the Center had grown into a formidable political force in an empire largely hostile to its aspirations. Already during the last years of his life, Windthorst had faced a strong conservative challenge to his concept of the Center's character. As Margaret Anderson has observed, conservatives in the party, many of them noble landowners who had derived their political position from their social standing within their community, resented the emergence of professional politicians.[92] Notables such as Baron Burghard von Schorlemer-Alst, Prince Franz von Arenberg and Count Franz von Ballestrem, felt "deeply threatened by the growing influence of democratic elements" within the party.

When Ludwig Windthorst died on 14 March 1891, he left the Center without an obvious successor. By far the most serious challenge the Center faced after the death of its leader was the threat of a split in the party.[93] It was Windthorst who possessed "the skill and authority almost always to bring under one roof the various factions within the caucus when important questions were concerned." But now that unity was acutely threatened.[94] Although the powerful Prince Bishop of Breslau, Georg Kopp, vowed in his eulogy to Windthorst that "we shall remain united, together we shall protect our unity as a precious legacy that you left behind"[95] a serious rift divided the Center. Like Bishop Kopp, Count Ballestrem, a very ordinary politician from the school of *noblesse oblige*, and Silesia's most prominent and perhaps richest[96] Centrist, implored the party to remain united, urging that without unity the Catholic minority would not be able to

---

[92] Anderson, *Windthorst*, p. 368.

[93] Zeender, *Center Party*, p. 20.

[94] Graf Ballestrem to Freiherr von Hertling, 10. April 1891, reprinted in Bergsträsser, *Katholizismus*, 2:248-9.

[95] Spael, *Windthorst*, p. 208.

[96] For tax purposes Ballestrem declared his personal wealth to be fifty-six million marks; Michael Traut, *Der Reichsregent. Ernst Liebers Weg vom Männer-Casino Camberg an das Ruder kaiserlicher Großmachtpolitik* (Bad Camberg: Camberger Verlag, 1984), p. 109.

fend off the incursions of its enemies.⁹⁷ The struggle between Windthorst and the Right had culminated in the conservatives' attempt to create an anti-Protestant organization. Only by the weight of his personal authority and by threatening to retire from all political offices was he able to prevent conservative aristocrats within the party (among them Felix von Loë-Terporten, Prince Karl zu Löwenstein, Franz von Wamboldt and probably Friedrich Carl von Fechenbach from founding an anti-Protestant organization in order to counter the Evangelical League.⁹⁸ Windthorst had won this round against the conservatives, but it was only a first round. The controversy over the kind of party the Center should be was to rage for nearly three decades. Immediately after Windthorst's death the conservatives entered the second round of this long fight for the leadership of the party. The conservatives were in tune with governmental policies but these Center aristocrats hardly understood the social changes occurring in the Reichstag and the country at large—a new guard of young Center politicians was about to take the places of the aristocrats who had until then dominated the party.⁹⁹

Young Centrists such as Felix Porsch from Silesia, Ernst Lieber from Camberg and Julius and Karl Bachem from Cologne represented a new breed of politician that challenged the notables who had dominated Center politics. Thus the struggle for the succession was also a struggle between the conservative wing of the party, represented by Count Ballestrem and Baron Karl Huene von Hoiningen, and the democratic wing, represented by Ernst Lieber and the Bachems. When Ballestrem suggested to Count Georg von Hertling that he (Hertling) should succeed Windthorst, Ballestrem argued that unless "we attract to parliament talented members of the upper classes who understand politics as well as rhetoric" the Center will die not because of its enemies but of old age.¹⁰⁰ The new guard, on the other hand, was primarily concerned with maintaining electoral support for their party; of particular concern was continued support of artisans and industrial workers. Lieber foresaw that diverse economic

---

⁹⁷ Graf Ballestrem to Freiherr von Hertling, 10 April 1891, reprinted in Bergsträsser, *Katholizismus*, 2:249.

⁹⁸ Horstwalter Heitzer, *Der Volksverein für das katholische Deutschland im Kaiserreich 1890-1918* (Mainz: Matthias-Grünewald-Verlag, 1979), p. 1; Loth, *Katholiken*, p. 40.

⁹⁹ For a detailed account of the changes in Center leadership in the early 1890s see Zeender, *Center Party*, pp. 19-34.

¹⁰⁰ Graf Ballestrem to Freiherr von Hertling, 10 April 1891, reprinted in Bergsträsser, *Katholizismus*, 2:250.

interest among the Center voters might threaten the very existence of the party.[101]

Only thirty-two years old in 1871, Ernst Lieber was the youngest member of the Reichstag and the youngest member of the Center caucus in the Prussian Landtag. An astute politician, he "carried himself from the beginning with the assurance of a skilled parliamentarian," a quality which, according to Martin Spahn, originated in the "traditional self-confidence of a respected, accomplished patrician family."[102] Ernst Lieber's father, Moritz Lieber, gained national prominence through his many articles in Catholic newspapers and magazines and his vehement repudiation of the imprisonment of the archbishop of Cologne in the wake of the Cologne Troubles. Like his father, Lieber would become a lawyer; after studying at the universities of Würzburg, Munich, Bonn and Heidelberg, he received a doctorate in law in 1861. For years after the completion of his university studies, Lieber contemplated becoming a Jesuit. Not until 1867 did he abandon this idea in favor of a political career. He wrote to a friend: "I still sympathize with the Jesuits, I am ultramontane and close to the Roman Catholic Church, yet I myself shall not become a Jesuit."[103]

A certain pompousness in the style of his letters suggested to the more clear-sighted among his relatives and friends that young Lieber might grow up to be a prig; later observations by his colleagues confirmed this suspicion. Hermann Cardauns, managing editor of the *Kölnische Volkszeitung* and author of a Lieber biography, noted vanity, arrogance and obstinacy as life-long character traits of his subject.[104] Martin Spahn testified that his colleague lacked a sense of humor, and instead tended to treat subjects with irony; when Lieber was challenged he resorted to calculated, biting criticism.[105] These characteristics and a reluctance to participate in the dull parliamentary work in Berlin explain why Ludwig Windthorst resented Lieber and relegated him to the back benches.[106] Ernst Lieber's "sour attitude" toward Windthorst was described by a friend of both as "some-

[101] KB, 5:32.

[102] Martin Spahn, *Ernst Lieber als Parlamentarier* (Gotha: Friedrich Andreas Perthes, 1906), p. 4.

[103] Letter to Henri Wallon, 5 July 1867 quoted in Hermann Cardauns, *Ernst Lieber. Der Werdegang eines Politikers bis zu seinem Eintritt in das Parlament (1838-1871)* (Wiesbaden: Verlag Hermann Rauch, 1927), p. 105.

[104] Cardauns, *Lieber*, p. 34.

[105] Spahn, *Lieber*, p. 4; KB, 5:331.

[106] Karl Bachem, "Ballestrem und Lieber," (MS 17 pp.), HAStK Nl. Bachem 1006/357; Anderson, *Windthorst*, p. 239.

thing unalterable."[107] Lieber had become openly critical of Windthorst's move from sharp opposition to the government to "a positive participation in parliamentary work." On one occasion, Lieber later boasted, he told Windthorst: "Your Excellency, in the past you made the party great, with your current policies you will make it small again."[108]

At first it appeared as if the aristocratic bloc would gain the upper hand after Windthorst's death. The claim of Ballestrem and Huene was backed by leading aristocrats in the Center and by Germany's most influential clergyman, Bishop Kopp. In his bid for party leadership, Ballestrem managed to secure Windthorst's seat in the Landtag for himself and the late leader's Reichstag seat for Georg von Hertling, thus excluding middle-class Centrists who were claiming at least one of the two seats.[109] Yet not all was well in the conservative camp. For some time, Catholic aristocrats had faced the decline of their influence in the Reichstag caucus. In 1889 aristocrats held just forty-one of the Center's ninety-eight seats. And while the party gained more seats (106) in the 1890 election, only thirty noblemen were elected; the percentage of Catholic aristocrats in the Reichstag was cut roughly into half, from forty-two to less than nineteen per cent of the Center caucus. John K. Zeender argues that they either became "bored with the dullness of parliamentary routine and life in Berlin" and retired to their estates, or were not nominated again by local election committees who preferred bourgeois candidates to aristocratic Kulturkämpfer.[110]

Initially, the Rhineland also fielded a strong candidate for the party leadership. Julius Bachem divided his time between publishing the Görres Society's *Staatslexikon*, writing for the *Kölnische Volkszeitung*, and representing his party on the Cologne city council (since 1875) and in the Prussian Landtag (since 1876). His colleagues recognized in him the "intellectual" leader of the Rhineland Center.[111] Notwithstanding his continued influence as a political journalist, Bachem's parliamentary career came to a sudden end when, just two months after Windthorst's death he admitted his responsibility in a paternity case and had to give up his mandate.[112] His role as representative of the Catholic bourgeoisie among the leaders of

---

[107] Anderson, *Windthorst*, p. 245.
[108] K. Bachem, "Ballestrem und Lieber," HAStK Nl. Bachem 1006/357.
[109] Zeender, *Center Party*, p. 20.
[110] Ibid., p. 21.
[111] KB, 3:154.
[112] Note in E. Lieber's diary, 30 May 1891 quoted in Zeender, *Center Party*, p. 22.

the Rhineland Center was taken by his cousin Karl Bachem and by Aloys Fritzen, a *Landrat* and Center parliamentarian from Düsseldorf.[113] Hermann Cardauns, a colleague of Julius Bachem at the *Kölnische Volkszeitung*, supported Lieber and his "democratic wing" and wrote articles defending Lieber's position in his influential paper.[114]

Lieber's undisputed leadership was challenged by two groups. The less dangerous challenge came from some Rhineland Centrists, among them Julius and Karl Bachem. Lieber, however, categorically rejected their attempt to establish a "directorate" and by 1894 his position as the uncontested head of the party was accepted by the Cologne group.[115] The most determined opposition to Lieber came from Westphalian and Rhenish farmers and their aristocratic spokesmen. Aristocratic-conservative notables who favored an alliance between Catholics and pro-government forces (*Thron und Altar*) were clearly looking for an arrangement of all truly conservative forces in the empire. The abolition of most Kulturkampf measures had removed the prime reason for Center conservatives to oppose the government. A sign of this willingness to cooperate with non-Catholic conservatives was the support many Center notables gave to Leo XIII's urgent request in 1887 to accept Bismarck's *Septennat* bill in order to clear the way for a reconciliation between the Church and the Reich.[116]

The Center's support of Bismarck's trade and tariff policies during the 1870s and 1880s had made it popular among farmers and the landed aristocracy who welcomed state protection from foreign competitors. Responding to the growing need to open markets for German industrial products, Chancellor Leo von Caprivi reversed this policy (Caprivi, unlike Bismarck was not a landowner). The easing of trade restrictions was welcomed by Rhenish industrialist and factory owners. Textile manufacturers, for instance those in Karl Bachem's riding, urged their member of parliament to do his best to ensure that the trade agreement with Russia would be signed. A re-

---

[113] He was a member of the Reichstag (1881-87 and 1889-1911), and of the Prussian Landtag (1889-1903).

[114] Manfred Bierganz, "Hermann Cardauns (1847-1925). Politiker, Publizist und Wissenschaftler in den Spannungen des politischen und religiösen Katholizismus seiner Zeit" (Ph. D. diss., Rheinisch-Westfälische Technische Hochschule Aachen, 1977), pp. 193-4.

[115] Friedrich Klein, "Reichsfinanzpolitik und 'Nationalisierung' des Zentrums unter Ernst Maria Lieber 1891-1900," *Historisches Jahrbuch der Görres-Gesellschaft* 108 (1988), p. 122.

[116] Loth, *Katholiken*, p. 39.

duction in Russian tariffs, they argued, would "open up a new, large and rich market" for Krefeld's velvet industry. Beyond that, other industries located in the area would profit from the increased exports of velvet.[117] When the Reichstag voted on the Russian trade treaty the Center was divided: forty-five of the ninety-nine Center delegates voted for, thirty-nine against the treaty; fifteen members were absent. The twenty-four Rhenish Center representatives maintained a more united front: only Peter Spahn was absent, nineteen voted "yes," only four did not support the treaty.[118]

In the past, Catholic voters, faced with Kulturkampf measures, had willingly rallied to the party's cause. Center politicians were confident that a large majority of Catholics, be they farmers, merchants, civil servants or workers, gave their support to the party that defended and safeguarded their religious interest.[119] The end of the Kulturkampf and the changed economic situation of the early 1890s removed much of this incentive for cohesion. Already in the Reichstag elections after 1877 the percentage of Catholics who went to the polls as well as those who voted for the Center had leveled off. The Center had to begin taking into account seriously the various social and economic groups which made up its constituency and demanded representation of their material interests as well as protection of the rights of Catholics. These colliding economic interests had troubled the party before, but Windthorst's skills had kept them together. After his death it became more difficult to contain the demands of the party's conservative-agrarian wing.

The leadership struggle between Ballestrem, Huene and Lieber came to a head in 1893. Lieber used the division within his party over a controversial army bill to secure the leadership. Adroitly he claimed that Center opposition to the bill was a matter of principle. Indeed, he urged, the very existence of the party hinged upon a unanimous rejection of the bill. Lieber was keenly aware of rank and file support of his stance and saw an opportunity to outmaneuver those influential conservatives in his party who supported a larger army. He had also built up substantial support for his position by incessantly delivering public speeches. Throughout the debate of the 1892

---

[117] Krefeld Chamber of Commerce to Karl Bachem, 18 Januar 1894, HAStK 1006/335.
[118] Klaus Müller, "Zentrumspartei und agrarische Bewegung im Rheinland, 1882-1903," in *Spiegel der Geschichte; Festgabe für Max Braubach zum 10. April 1964*, ed. Konrad Repgen and Stephan Skalweit (Münster: Verlag Aschendorff, 1964), p. 835.
[119] Cardauns, *Trimborn*, p. 92.

Army Bill he had traveled every Saturday evening from Berlin to be able to appear at some venue on Sunday morning. Most often he addressed gatherings of the People's Association, thus, according to Karl Bachem, contributing to the growth of this organization. Lieber's speeches—full of pathos, "exaggerations, and glittering, not necessarily factual, images"—gained him the scorn of the anti-Center press; but they were popular among large circles of the Catholic population.[120]

On 6 May 1893 the Reichstag voted on the Army Bill. With the help of the Center the bill was defeated, the Kaiser dissolved parliament and new elections were scheduled for 15 June. Only twelve Center parliamentarians had voted for the bill, ninety-three opposed it and three did not cast a vote. Of the twenty-nine Center men from the Rhineland only two voted for the bill, both representing rural ridings.[121] Although they realized that Lieber was using the Army Bill as a pretext for his claim to the leadership of the party,[122] the conservatives found no arguments that could convince the majority of the Catholic population or the other members of the Center faction of their point of view. Nevertheless, they detested Lieber's "democratization of the Center and raised their voices to warn against Lieber's poliics which were contaminated by demagogy"—only grudgingly did they "surrender" to his leadership.[123] A few weeks after the Reichstag had rejected the Army Bill, a number of Catholic notables, mainly landowners and mayors in rural areas, sent an open letter to the *Rheinisch-Westfälische Zeitung*, accusing the "democrats" in the Center of giving "into the hands of their enemies weapons which one day they will use to attack" German Catholics. Perhaps worse, the Center caucus had failed to "demonstrate any understanding for the need of the government's demands" and had moved away from the party's "traditional conservative foundation on which Catholic efforts should rest."[124]

The conservatives, already weakened by their defeat on the Army Bill and the leadership debate, demanded a stronger representation of agrarian candidates for the upcoming election. Baron Burghard

---

[120] K. Bachem, "Ballestrem und Lieber," HAStK Nl. Bachem 1006/357.

[121] "Die Abstimmung über die Heeresvorlage," *Germania*, no. 117, 24 May 1893.

[122] "Die Hüter des Friedens," *Kölnische Zeitung*, no. 867, 9 June 1893.

[123] [Fechenbach, L.], "Herr Dr. Lieber, die Centrumspartei und ihre Zukunft," *Der neue Kurs*, 6 May 1893, 1024.

[124] "Eine Erklärung rheinischer Katholiken zur Militärvorlage," *Rheinisch-Westfälische Zeitung*, no. 158, 9 June 1893.

von Schorlemer-Alst, chairman of the Westphalian Farmer's Association, demanded that four of the nine Westphalian ridings be represented by agrarian candidates. Cardauns, among others, charged that Schorlemer's demands constituted a narrow representation of special interests ignoring the wider interests of the Catholic population.[125] After the party rebuked Schorlemer-Alst, he and his followers fielded their own candidates in three Westphalian constituencies—all of whom were defeated.[126]

The agrarian challenge in the Rhineland was a more serious affair. Hermann Cardauns considered it the "most difficult struggle over the political character of the Center Party" he had participated in.[127] The charge was led by the Rhenish Farmer's Association (*Rheinischer Bauernverein*) and its chairman Baron Felix von Loë — a more determined "opponent" than his Westphalian colleague. Von Loë, owner of the Terporten estate in the *Kreis* of Kleve (in the Düsseldorf district), had frequently been at loggerheads with his party. He had disagreed with Windthorst over the organization of the People's Association.[128] Notwithstanding his contributions to the party and and his popularity among Catholic farmers, Loë was considered something of a loose cannon. His stubbornness and willfulness seemed to have disqualified him from high political office. His colleagues thought that he put too much emphasis on agrarian demands, probably in an effort to curb the influence of the Agrarian League (*Bund der Landwirte*).

The Rhenish Farmers' Association was founded in 1881 and modeled on the Westphalian Farmer's Association, with Franz Schreiner's *Rheinische Volksstimme* as its most militant and markedly anti-Semitic voice. Peasant associations were a "hybrid in the peculiar soil of the Wilhelmine political terrain."[129] Unlike the Agrarian League they sought no mass following and insisted on representing a "healthy *Mittelstand*," not just the narrow interests of an occupationally defined group. Robert G. Moeller has likened them to "post-1945 agrarian pressure groups [rather] than to the mass electoral or-

[125] Bierganz, "Cardauns," p. 198.
[126] Ibid., p. 197.
[127] Hermann Cardauns, *Fünfzig Jahre Kölnische Volkszeitung. Ein Rückblick zum goldenen Jubiläum der Zeitung am 1. April 1910* (Cologne: J. P. Bachem, 1910), p. 71.
[128] KB, 5:292f.
[129] Robert G. Moeller, *German Peasants and Agrarian Politics, 1914-1924: The Rhineland and Westphalia* (Chapel Hill, N.C.: The University of North Carolina Press, 1986), p. 30.

ganization of the Agrarian League."[130] The Rhenish Farmer's Association represented the economic interests of landowners, insisting that religion and politics could not be discussed in its meetings.[131] However, the participation of many Center politicians in its founding belied this intention. Despite assurances to the contrary it became an important rural "vote catcher" (*Wahlhilfsorganisation*).[132] Like the Center, it welcomed Protestant members; a few did indeed join, but essentially the Rhenish Farmer's Association was a Catholic organization. Von Loë, who was a member of the Prussian Landtag, believed that the Center was a Catholic party which only had to take a united stance when religious matters were concerned. On all other questions Center politicians were free to follow the economic or social interests of their constituency.[133] Among conservatives who feared the "distinct democratic and anti-agrarian" attitudes of the new leadership there was great resentment of Lieber's insistence on caucus discipline.[134] This view, of course, was not supported by men like the Bachems and Karl Trimborn.

The agrarian challenge in Westphalia had been a warning to Rhenish Centrists. They were eager to avoid a split in their ranks and to maintain a united party as they embarked on the Reichstag election campaign. To this end, the provincial executive (*Provinzialausschuß*), following the demands of the congress of delegates (*Delegiertentag*) held in Cologne on 23 May 1893, decided to publish a Rhenish election proclamation in addition to the one published by the Reichstag caucus. The issue that dominated the proclamation was a defense of the Center's rejection of the Army Bill. The additional money required for the Army Bill, it argued, prevented "the execution of social reforms needed for the necessary reconciliation of social antagonism."[135] Aimed squarely at the agrarian dissenters, the proclamation urged Center voters to vote only for Center politicians who supported the party's stance on the Army Bill. Karl Bachem had sent a draft of the proclamation to all members of the *Provinzialausschuß*, including Loë and Hoensbroech, who did not answer. When Bachem sent a telegram, asking them to sign, von

---

[130] Moeller, *German Peasants*, p. 30.
[131] Von Loë founded the daily *Rheinische Volksstimme* in Cologne on 1 Oct. 1894; in 1896 its offices moved to Kempen.
[132] Müller, "Zentrumspartei," p. 830.
[133] KB, 5:353.
[134] Friedrich Carl Reichsfreiherr von Fechenbach-Laudenbach, "Die Familie Bachem-Lieber," *Die Zukunft*, vol. 14 (1896), p. 155.
[135] Bierganz, "Cardauns," pp. 199-200.

Loë answered abruptly "I shall not sign! Felix von Loë." Hoensbroech sent a longer and more polite letter that none the less conveyed the same message. Despite their refusal to endorse the proclamation, it was published with all signatures on it; and even the notables who so vehemently criticized the Center for its rejection of the Army Bill publicly supported the proclamation.[136] Somewhat prematurely, the liberal *Berliner Tageblatt* celebrated the destruction of the Center: the division in the Center's ranks would achieve what Bismarck's repression could not. In debates on the Army Bill, the *Tageblatt* added, Huene and Schorlemer-Alst had revealed the Center's true face as the "reactionary" representative of "agrarian interests."[137] The true face of the Center, however, was two-sided. The party was not merely the representative of agrarian interests, or that of any other interest group. The Center can only be understood if viewed as a complex amalgam of economic, political and religious interest. As it turned out it was Lieber and not the agrarian nobles who had carried the day and who shaped Center politics for the coming decade. The short time left before the election made it impossible for von Loë to field separate agrarian candidates. He was content to let the matter rest—at least for the time being. Lieber's victory over the conservatives had settled the immediate struggle for leadership but did not end internal arguments. The feud between conservative and democratic forces in the Center resurfaced with the publication of the socio-political program of the Cologne priest Peter Oberdörffer in June 1894. Oberdörffer's article belongs to a long line of conservative efforts to restore the "natural organic society" destroyed by the French Revolution.[138] Oberdörffer's ideas and programmatic distinction between four estates (*Berufsstände*)—agriculture, industry, trade, free professions—appealed to von Loë and his adherents in the Farmer's Association and the Center. Seventeen members of the Reichstag caucus subsequently signed Oberdörffer's program; with the exception of von Loë, no prominent Center man was among them. Of the Rhenish members only eight put their names on the document: Baron von Loë; his right hand man, Count Hoensbroech; Peter Hauptmann, publisher of the *Deutsche Reichszeitung* in Bonn; Louis Pleß and Jakob Euler, leaders of the artisans' movement; Hermann Roeren, Hermann de Witt, and Hugo am Zehnhoff.[139]

---

[136] "Erklärung," *Rheinisch-Westfälische Zeitung*, no. 158, 9 June 1893.

[137] "Matuschka, Schorlemer und Huene," *Berliner Tageblatt*, no. 277, 3 June 1893.

[138] Müller, "Zentrumspartei," p. 837.

[139] Ibid., p. 839.

Like Oberdörffer, von Loë was determined to jettison the "political character" of the Center. Their notion of society envisioned no role for modern parliamentary parties. The Center was to be confined to addressing religious questions such as marriage laws or the independence of the Church from state interference. In their view, the party was to follow closely the instructions of the clergy and the Pope, the ultimate arbiter in religious questions. On political and economic issues the party would have no uniform stance and its parliamentary representatives would be free to vote according to their individual convictions. Moreover, their vision of a Catholic party was deeply rooted in the conventions of the politics of a landed aristocracy. The *Historisch-politische Blätter* probably best summarized the contrary visions of the Rhenish Farmer's Association and the Center:

> For a general understanding of agrarian particularism within the Center it must be emphasized that it has a political background. Its real leaders, namely those in the Rhineland, are aristocrats, who were faithful to Church and Center, and earned great honors. Now that the Kulturkampf is virtually over, they intend to move the Center closer to the Prussian Conservative Party. They dislike our modern constitution and would not be disinclined to a change of the Reichstag franchise.[140]

These ideological disputes gained urgency in 1895, when low grain prices (in Cologne wheat prices were at their lowest since 1847) and trade treaties again dominated political discussion.[141] In February, as a response to these developments and as a countermove to the Agrarian League's demands for the nationalization of grain imports (Kanitz bill), von Loë launched a new attack on the Rhenish Center. He called an extraordinary meeting of the Farmer's Association which took place at the Fränkische Hof in Cologne on 13 February. According to the *Rheinische Volkszeitung* the mood among the nearly two thousand farmers who had come to Cologne from all regions of the Rhineland was "somber, proof of our deep embitterment over

---

[140] "Centrum und Interessenpolitik," *Historisch-politische Blätter für das katholische Deutschland* 116 (1895), pp. 350-65, 559-60, quoted in Müller, "Zentrumspartei," pp. 841-2.

[141] Franz S. Pichler, "Centrum und Landwirtschaft," *Sociale und politische Zeitfragen*, (1898), pp. 278-9.

[the government's] agrarian policies."[142] The *Germania* condemned the heckling of "moderate" Center politicians at Cologne as "repulsive terrorism," and assured its readers that voters in Rhenish cites as well as in the countryside would remain faithful to the Center.[143] This prediction turned out to be correct. The Center, dependent on the working class vote and worried about SPD encroachment was in no position to let the Farmer's Association's narrow pursuit of agrarian interests go unchallenged. The *Kölnische Volkszeitung*, encouraged and supported by Karl Bachem, Karl Trimborn and other Rhenish Centrists, intensified its campaign against the agrarians, publishing dozens of articles that underlined the Center's role as "the arbiter of divergent material interests."[144] Eventually, von Loë lost his seat on the executive committee of the Landtag caucus. His failure to understand the workings of a modern mass party had become untenable.

Why did the Center leadership of the Rhineland refuse to cater to the demands of the Farmer's Association? Three reasons, it seems, were foremost in the minds of Centrists. The first, mentioned by most students of the Center, is that the Center catered to the interest of middle-class voters—the owners of small enterprises and merchants who benefited from lower export tariffs. Secondly, the conservative-agrarian hold on rural areas was not as formidable as it initially appeared. Aristocrats like Huene, Schorlemer and Loë could not count on the rural lower classes to support their bid for a conservative renewal, for such groups had begun to develop into an independent political force with a political agenda that differed from that of farmers and landed aristocrats.[145] Thirdly, the Center leadership was acutely aware of the shifting balance of voters. Farmers were not their largest or most important constituency anymore. The largest Center constituency in the Rhineland, and the one most vigorously and successfully wooed by the Social Democrats, were industrial workers. The Center leaders sacrificed the interests of Rhenish farmers to those of the worker. In Württemberg, where farmers played a greater role and workers a smaller one among Center voters, the Center steered a more cautious course; it defended its support for protective tariffs in

---

[142] "Die große Versammlung rheinischer Landwirthe im Fränkischen Hof," *Rheinische Volksstimme*, no. 37, 14 February 1895.
[143] "Die Versammlung rheinischer Landwirthe," *Germania*, no. 41, 19 February 1895.
[144] Cardauns, *Fünfzig*, 72; KB, 5:353-4.
[145] Loth, *Katholiken*, p. 41.

the countryside as well as in the towns.[146] The Rhenish working class benefited in two ways from the reverses in trade policies. As a result of lower grain tariffs the price of foodstuffs decreased. Secondly, increased markets for Rhenish industries as a result of lower export tariffs meant more jobs, more security, and eventually better pay. Only at the risk of losing the support of the working-class vote could Center leaders ignore these facts.

During Lieber's struggle for power and the challenge of the agrarian movement, the Rhenish Center had emerged as the most important regional group of the party. The Rhineland group represented about a quarter of the Reichstag caucus, and the *Kölnische Volkszeitung* had become the most influential press organ of German political Catholicism, eclipsing the influence of the semi-official *Germania*, which had to be rescued by Lieber from bankruptcy.[147] The close relationship between the Rhenish Center and the People's Association provided Rhenish Centrists with unique access to the views and moods of Catholic workers, an increasingly important segment of the Center in the Rhine Province but also in Germany at large. Lastly, the "élan" that distinguished the Rhineland Center from other regional organizations and the determination of its leaders to form "the intellectual Center of modern German Catholicism"[148] made it the most important theoretical component within the Center.

---

[146] Joseph Andre, "Zentrum und Landwirtschaft. Stoff für Vorträge in Ortsversammlungen der württembergischen Zentrumspartei," *Politische Zeitfragen in Württemberg. Zwanglos erscheinende Hefte*, vol. 26 (1918), p. 3.

[147] Zeender, *Center Party*, p. 36.

[148] Ibid.

IV.

KARL TRIMBORN'S CENTER

AT THE SAME TIME as Lieber established himself as the national leader of the Center, Karl Trimborn grew into the leader of the Rhineland Center. Like most of the other leading Centrists, Trimborn came from a respectable middle-class family; his father was a successful Cologne lawyer and Center representative to the Reichstag. His mother also belonged to an old Cologne family with political ambitions—one brother was a member of the Reichstag of the North German Confederation, another was a Cologne city councilor for many years.[1] Trimborn belonged to a generation of Center politicians whose political career began after unification of 1870/71. Since 1890, when Trimborn had become deputy-chairman of the People's Association, he had expanded his political activities considerably. In 1893, at age thirty-eight, he had won a highly contested seat in the Cologne city council (one anecdote has Trimborn minding a haberdashery so that the owner could cast his vote without having to close his store).[2] He was also elected into the city commissions responsible for studying social questions and local administration.[3] Soon afterwards, he succeeded Eduard Fuchs as leader of the Cologne Center, and also became chairman of the Rhineland Center in 1894. Karl Trimborn was now the leader of the largest regional chapter of the German Center Party and its most important Rhenish spokesman.

As his reputation as a gifted public speaker and skillful politician grew, Trimborn was offered more important positions in his party. In 1896 he entered both the Reichstag and the Prussian Landtag as member for Cologne. During his first years as a member of parlia-

---

[1] Josef Jörg, "Organisator Rhenaniae," *Mitteilungen der Zentralstelle der Rheinischen Zentrumspartei*, vol. 4 (2 December 1914), p. 30.

[2] Ibid., p. 32.

[3] He remained a city councilor until 1903, because of his other obligations he rarely attended its sessions after 1896.

ment, Trimborn concentrated on legal issues, such as reforms of criminal and civil law. Later he focused on social legislation, occasionally running afoul of the Catholic middle class when the craftsmen and merchants of Cologne attacked him for his advocacy of the Rhenish working class.[4] He made even more enemies when, together with his political mentor, Julius Bachem, and his friend Franz Hitze, Trimborn became one of the more outspoken proponents of Christian, that is to say interdenominational, trade unions.[5] In the sphere of theoretical and political thinking Trimborn followed, rather than led; however, as an organizer, his talents were unrivaled.

A. Karl Trimborn's Organization of the Rhenish Center

It was a fundamental feature of the German Center Party that it lacked a real center of power. Apart from institutions of a parliamentary character, such as the Landtag and Reichstag caucuses and their executive committees, the party had no framework; there existed no permanent, uniform organizational structure. The connections among the various regional organizations, caucuses in the Reichstag, the Landtag, as well as Catholic voluntary associations remained loose and informal.

Germany's religious geography was partly to blame; Catholics were dispersed around the perimeter of the Reich rather than being equally distributed throughout the country. The Prussian Association Law of 1851 was a substantial obstacle to political organization. Designed to monitor and repress politically active individuals, the law required all political organizations to inform the police of the statutes, their membership and all their meetings. Under the terms of this law, political associations were broadly defined as any organization that in any way attempted to influence public affairs. An early victim of this repressive legislation was Düsseldorf's local gymnastic society. But the searching gaze of the police also fell on taverns, dances, *Kirmes* celebrations, and religious gatherings which all might have served as occasions for political discussions and breeding grounds for opposition.[6] Supplemented by the Prussian Press Law,[7] the

[4] Cardauns, *Trimborn*, p. 103.
[5] Ibid., pp. 11, 48, 117.
[6] Elaine G. Spencer, *Police and the Social Order in German Cities: The Düsseldorf District, 1848-1914* (DeKalb: Northern Illinois University Press, 1992), pp. 39-41.
[7] Promulgated on 12 May 1851.

Kulturkampf legislation (and, of course, anti-Socialist Laws) the Prussian Association Law was a formidable impediment to political organization. Despite such legislative weapons and police efforts to curtail political organization, the government failed to prevent the formation of political opposition in the long run. Eventually even socialist meetings became common events, hardly worth commenting on by the local authorities.[8] As a consequence of the restrictions of the Association Law and the concentration of Catholics in particular regions, virtually the only organizational components of the Center Party outside of parliament were election committees, formed only for local elections. Such election committees were usually headed by a priest. There was no formal party membership and the only political activity carried out by most of these committees was election propaganda.

A glance at one of the oldest and most successful electoral associations (*Wahlverein*) shows how local notables dominated Center politics. Founded in 1845 by Catholics from Aachen's "most distinguished and most influential"[9] families, Constantia became the city's focal point of Catholic life. Initially much time was devoted to religious and church activities: money was collected to carry out repairs on Charlemagne's cathedral, a new church was built, the association took a prominent part in the septennial pilgrimage to Aachen's holy relics and participated in virtually all of Aachen's frequent religious processions and festivities.[10] The influence Constantia and other election associations had on voters "was dependent on the existence of a lively religious sentiment among the Catholic lower classes. Popular morality was a means to successful clerical politics for Constantia, and an important goal of its clerical politics was the improvement of popular morality."[11] Constantia's staunch and determined opposition to the 1848 revolution was its first significant political act. Later it saw its primary function in disseminating its "conservative ideology" by assisting the Center in communal, provincial and federal elections.[12] Indeed, Constantia was the backbone of Center election campaigns in Aachen, helping to ensure the party's domination of the town council and the city's seats in Landtag and Reichstag.

[8] Verwaltungsbericht für das IV. Vierteljahr 1900, Düsseldorf, 31 Januar 1901. HStaD Regierung Düsseldorf Präsidialbüro Nr. 26 f. 20.
[9] Gedenkblatt zur goldenen Jubelfeier des Katholischen Bürger- und Wahlvereins 'Constantia' in Aachen, 1894, HStaD Regierung Aachen/780, f. 115.
[10] Ibid., f. 115-6.
[11] Sperber, *Popular Catholicism*, pp. 71-2.

Constantia prided itself in being able to ensure that not just any Center politicians represented their city, but that the "right" candidates were chosen. In Landtag elections, for example, only twice in the first five decades of its existence (in 1863 and 1869) was Constantia forced to tolerate a "leftist" candidate; all the other Landtag deputies from Aachen had been candidates advanced by Constantia.[13]

A closer look at the composition of Constantia will help us understand the association's importance for city politics. According to its intentions Constantia represented Aachen's better Catholic families. Among the association's 342 members in 1888, not a single one was a worker. The largest group was that of merchants (128); of the rest, ninety were artisans and forty-six pensioners. Twenty-four members were entrepreneurs, who owned factories or large companies. The number of clergy is surprisingly low, merely five, the same number as government officials (three of whom were mayors).[14] It seems safe to argue that the economic and political élites of Aachen's Catholic population were identical. Apart from minor variations in social composition and size, associations such as Constantia dominated local political life in Catholic Rhineland. However, some Center men felt that this patriarchal structure had run its course once the Kulturkampf had ended and new ways to bind Catholics together had to be found; the organization of the party had to be reformed.[15] This reorganization was only in part aimed at an external foe it was also an assault on opponents within the ranks of the party; Trimborn's "democratic" and organizational reforms were directed against and occurred at the expense of the patriarchal rule of notables who dominated the Center.[16] Trimborn argued that the only way the Center would not "be overrun and crushed by the enemy's legions" was to build a party that could match the "great organization" of the SPD; organization was the "magic word" of "our modern times."[17] Yet to regard Trimborn

---

[12] Gedenkblatt, HStaD Regierung Aachen/780, f. 117.
[13] Ibid., f. 118.
[14] Mitglieder der Constantia-Gesellschaft, Dezember 1888, HStaD Regierung Aachen/780, f. 102-9. This list gives the members' professions. I have tried to create meaningful categories. Of course, there are difficult decisions to be made. Two categories were particularly difficult, that of the merchants and that of the pensioners. Merchants are all those who declared themselves "Kaufmann," shopkeepers, accountants, managers and directors. Sixty members declared themselves to be "Rentner," pensioners. Using the address book of the previous year I was able to determine the occupation of 14 of them and to distribute them accordingly.
[15] Cardauns, *Trimborn*, p. 92.
[16] Morsey, *Zeitgeschichte*, 1:85.
[17] Jörg, "Organisator," p. 30.

and his political friends simply as pupils in a Socialist masterclass is to miss the point. The Center Party followed a distinctive path to creating a new, modern party structure, this path began in Cologne. By virtue of its historical, economic and religious preeminence, Cologne was the nerve center of the Rhenish Center Party. Its local party organization eventually served as a model for the entire Rhine Province. When Trimborn joined the city council in 1893, the smallest unit of Cologne's party organization was the parish.[18] Each parish in the city and its suburbs had a parish committee chaired by a parish foreman who was assisted by a varying number of volunteers. The foremen, supplemented by Center councilmen, members of the Reichstag and the Prussian Landtag, formed the so-called central electoral committee; in 1891 the central committee had 213 members, and was chaired by the "enthusiastic and fiery" Eduard Fuchs, a Cologne merchant who "worked tirelessly for the Center cause."[19] The immediate purpose of the central committee was to appoint the members of the managing committee of the Cologne Center, which in 1891 consisted of nineteen members (twelve from Cologne proper, the others from the suburbs). The managing committee presented to the plenary meeting a slate of candidates for the various elections. Although most active during election campaigns, the central committee also met frequently when no election was being fought. Among other things it managed the party's finances and oversaw the expenditures of the parish committees.

This parish system was essentially patriarchal in character, dominated by a close-knit group of notables and supported by unpaid volunteers. Such a design was well suited to the particular needs of a party as geographically dispersed and sociologically diversified as the Center. The organization of the party took into account the crucial role of parish and parish priest and reflected the realities of political power in the early decades of the Kaiserreich. The parish was the foundation on which the rest of the party organization was built. It is as hard to imagine that such meetings did not have a Catholic "feel" to them, for participants understood each other in ways only members of a coherent, homogeneous community share. Thus the very structure of the party was at once an advantage and a disadvantage

---

[18] This section is based on Karl Bachem. "Organisation der Kölner Zentrumspartei 1891/92, unpublished newspaper article, HAStK 1006/62; Rudolf Morsey, "Die Zentrumspartei in Rheinland und Westfalen," in *Politik und Landschaft*, ed. Walter Först (Cologne: Grote, 1969), pp. 11-50.

[19] Cardauns, *Trimborn*, p. 92.

for the Center. Its advantage was that the parish was as close to its grassroots as possible, providing a natural organization to which voters and supporters had easy access. Many Center leaders who were involved in their parishes, such as Julius Bachem, could regularly talk to ordinary supporters who would not necessarily have access to the party leadership. On the other hand, it is hard to see what attraction the ardently Catholic atmosphere of parish meetings might have exercised on non-Catholics. Besides the few Protestants who "converted" to the Center, the party failed to attract any significant number of non-Catholic voters or supporters.

Trimborn, who had brought his organizational talents to the People's Association and the Cologne Center was to do the same for the Rhenish Center. Its leader since 1894, Trimborn set out to reorganize his party, a task made the more difficult because of the resistance of the "old guard" to the young lawyer who was frequently attacked by middle-class representatives for his sympathies for the concerns of the working-class.[20] Eventually the Rhenish Center was given a uniform organizational structure and a measure of internal democracy. Trimborn's creation recognized the various elements that made up the support system of the party: the clergy, representatives of trade and occupational associations, members of the People's Association, parliamentarians, and the Catholic press.[21]

Trimborn first focused on the local election committees; he sought to tighten and to democratize them. Under his leadership, the permanent council of notables, parliamentarians, artisans and representatives of the various regions which had led the party throughout the 1880s was replaced by an organization that was not limited to occasional meetings in Cologne but had offices and representatives as well as formal, regular meetings throughout the Rhineland. The first step in this reform was the selection of chairmen for electoral districts and later for rural areas (*landrätliche Kreise*). With chairmen in place, the recruitment of supporters and the arrangement of regular party meetings could begin.[22] Of course, it took time before this new organization could be established everywhere. It was a slow process, opposed by party notables weary of change; it took literally years before all Rhenish districts were reformed. The Center in Aachen, for instance, did not introduce the "Cologne model" until 1906. For

[20] Ibid., pp. 94, 103.
[21] Satzungen betreffend die Organisation der rheinischen Centrumspartei, n. d. [1907], BAK Nl. 176 Herold, Nr. 2.
[22] Jörg, "Organisator," p. 33.

nearly a decade Constantia fought a dogged battle against the reformers. Their resistance was formidable, their methods ruthless, their influence insidious, and their opposition to their political bedfellows was neither softened by Catholic solidarity nor by threats of a split of the party. One of the last, the rural district of Schleiden-Malmedy-Montjoie, was not reorganized until 1908.[23] Local party secretariats were even slower in coming; as late as 1911 the Center could not match the number of such offices established by the SPD.[24] The "democratic" forces under Trimborn repelled and defeated their repeated, but ultimately doomed, attempts to maintain an organizational structure which had outlived its usefulness. Trimborn intervened personally. Only complete blindness he said, would allow the electoral society to deny the workers of Aachen the fully justified desire to be better represented in the electoral association.[25] Once the opposition of the "old guard" had been overcome, the city's parishes, trade and commerce associations and other Catholic interest groups were invited to send delegates to the local party organization (*Zentralwahlkomitee*). A look at the eventual composition of the local party organization demonstrates why the members of Constantia were so adamantly opposed to Trimborn's reforms. All in all, more than three hundred Aacheners joined the new election committee. In stark contrast to the membership of the Constantia, they came from all walks of life and from all electoral classes.[26]

The smallest unit of the Rhenish party organization created by Trimborn was the district committee (*Kreiskomitee*). In districts consisting of several communities, such as Schleiden-Malmedy-Montjoie, local councils (*Ortskomitees*) were the first rung of the organizational ladder. Members of the local council were elected at public meetings. Usually, Center supporters in a parish chose about one councilor for every ten voters; five to ten councilors per local council were considered the minimum.[27]

As a rule, each parish and its clergy were to be represented on the district committee. By taking into account local conditions, farmers,

---

[23] Organisations-Statut der Zentrumspartei der Kreise Schleiden-Malmedy-Montjoie, 1 January 1908, HStaD Regierung Aachen/780, f. 124-7.
[24] *Mitteilungen der Zentralstelle der Rheinischen Zentrumspartei* no. 1 (July 1911), 4.
[25] Herbert Lepper, "Vom Honoratiorenverein zur Parteiorganisation. Ein Beitrag zur 'Demokratisierung' des Zentrums im Rheinland 1898-1906," *Rheinische Vierteljahrsblätter* 46 (1984), p. 246.
[26] "Die Reorganisation der Aachener Zentrumspartei," *Echo der Gegenwart* no. 244, 21 Oct. 1906.
[27] Schleiden, HStaD Regierung Aachen/780, f. 125.

artisans, merchants and workers, too, sent spokesmen to the committee. Other conventions were also established: an important part of the district committee was the delegation of the People's Association; Center parliamentarians were natural members; and there was to be an appropriate contingent of Catholic journalists. The district committee also had to elect a chairman as well as other officers who constituted the executive. The number of executives depended on the number of eligible voters in a district. Schleiden had 10,947 voters, Malmedy 7,853, and Montjoie 4,609; they were entitled to eleven, eight and five executive officers respectively. The executive of a district committee represented the district at provincial meetings of the Rhenish Center. Its most important task, however, was the conduct of elections. For election campaigns, election committees (*Wahlkreiskomitees*) were formed. In constituencies encompassing several districts, representatives of each participated in the election committee; where district and constituency borders coincided the board members of the district committee constituted the election committee.

The statutes also made arrangements for a congress of delegates (*Delegiertentag*), usually to be held before each Reichstag and Landtag election. The Center organizations for the five districts of the Rhine Province held party conventions, too. Like the one that took place in Koblenz in October 1907, they dealt primarily with election tactics, and the faults and shortcomings of the previous campaigns were analyzed. Traditionally, Karl Trimborn, in his capacity as chairman of the Rhenish Center (1894-1914), or Wilhelm Marx, his deputy, addressed the delegates; also present were several members of parliament and representatives of the *Kreise*. A particular concern of the meeting in Koblenz was the need to field a variety of candidates in the upcoming Landtag election. The delegates were concerned that farmers, workers and the middle class were among the Center candidates in the district of Krefeld. They also urged that a teacher and an area magistrate (*Landbürgermeister*) were chosen to run for the Center. Above all they emphasized that it was up to the *Kreise* to select their candidates.[28]

The following week a party rally for the district of Trier was held at Saarlouis. Several thousand Center supporters participated in the convention which was chaired by Karl Trimborn. After a eulogy to the chaplain Georg Friedrich Dasbach, editor of the *Triererische Volk-*

[28] "Centrumsparteitag für den Regierungsbezirk Koblenz," *KV* no. 869, 8 Oct. 1907.

szeitung and member of the Reichstag for the ridings of Aachen (1898-1903) and Trier (1903-1907), the assembly "raised its flag in the fashion of soldiers and [vowed] to return to the battlefield with a war-song on their lips."[29] We find much of this martial rhetoric in Center assemblies: it was part of the party's eagerness to embrace the German nation in the hope of shedding Bismarck's accusation of being "enemies of the state" and of gaining "unhampered religious freedom and complete social recognition."[30] Again the assembly discussed the last elections and considered tactics for the upcoming Landtag election. The delegates argued against multiple candidacies and, taking into account local conditions, suggested the inclusion of representatives of the railway workers association (*Eisenbahnhandwerkerverband*), of civil servants and particularly of farmers on the Center roster.[31]

The delegates at Saarlouis also considered the *Windthorstbund* as part of the Center organization. Initially the *Windthorstbund* was a youth organization independent of the Center, dedicated to dissemination of religious ideals and apologetics among young Catholic men. By the turn of the century it had been transformed into the youth wing of the Center. By 1906, questions around this transformation had developed into an internal debate. Karl Trimborn argued that the *Windthorstbund* should abandon apologetics altogether, leaving this kind of work to other youth groups.[32] The general secretary of the Trier Center district, a Dr. Scharmitzel, concurred with Trimborn. During the meeting at Saarlouis he argued that the Center needed an aggressive youth organization to counter the efforts of the Socialists and Liberals. It was imperative, Scharmitzel went on, to establish chapters of the *Windthorstbund* in those parts of the Trier district where they did not yet exist. Without the *Windthorstbund* it would be impossible to instill in Catholic youths "an understanding of Center policies" and of "the importance of the preservation of denominational and social peace," the cornerstones of the Center's *Weltanschauung*.[33]

---

[29] "Centrumsparteitag für den Regierungsbezirk Trier," *KV* no. 890, 14 Oct. 1907.

[30] Ernst Deuerlein, "Die Bekehrung des Zentrums zur nationalen Idee," *Hochland*, (1970), p. 449.

[31] "Centrumsparteitag für den Regierungsbezirk Trier," *KV* no. 892, 15 Oct. 1907.

[32] Cardauns, *Trimborn*, p. 97.

[33] "Centrumsparteitag für den Regierungsbezirk Trier," *KV* no. 892, 15 Oct. 1907.

At the top of the Rhenish party organization was the provincial executive (*Provinzialauschuß*) incorporating natural and elected members. Natural members were the chairmen of the Reichstag election committees or their deputies; elected members were chosen at a congress of delegates which preceded a Reichstag election. The number of elected members was not to exceed forty-six. Again the provincial executive elected a chairman, a deputy chairman, a secretary and a treasurer.

In 1903 a general secretariat was established in Cologne, headed by Josef Jörg. The general-secretariat carried out the day-to-day work of the party. It conducted the correspondence between the provincial executive and the election committees, coordinated the election propaganda and lectures in the various districts, and kept up-to-date lists of committee members. Soon after the establishment of the Cologne office, similar offices were established in other Rhenish cities; by 1914 there were ten of them.[34] Two years after the establishment of the general secretariat in Cologne, regular party congresses began to be held in various parts of the Rhineland. The general secretary also oversaw the party archive and was responsible for the printing and distribution of pamphlets and brochures. An essential task was the collection of material on current political, ecclesiastical, and economic affairs which party activists, and above all Center deputies, would use for their work in the parliaments and in public. Keeping in touch with the press, friendly and antagonistic, was another of the general secretary's responsibilities. To fulfill this task he was a member of the Augustine League[35], the powerful Catholic press association. Through the *Windthorstbund*, the Center's youth organization with headquarters in Cologne, the general secretary stayed in contact with the Catholic youth and in a similar manner kept abreast of developments in the province's trade and commerce associations. In all these matters the general secretary reported to the provincial executive, to whom he was ultimately responsible.

Party finances were handled by the treasury. The main sources of funds were voluntary donations from "capable gentlemen" (*leistungsfähigere Herren*) and contributions by the district committees. The annual contribution of district committees was between 30 and 500 marks. A third way of fundraising was copied from SPD practices, whereby publishers of Rhenish Center newspapers occa-

---

[34] Morsey, "Rheinland," p. 18.
[35] The Augustine League will be discussed in detail later in this chapter.
[36] "Protokoll der Organisationskonferenz westdeutscher Parteifreunde," 4 Oct. 1904, BAK Nl. 176 Herold, Nr. 1.

sionally made contributions to the party coffers.[37] During election campaigns the Center elicited supplementary financial support from the press. For the Landtag election of 1913, Trimborn recorded contributions from thirteen newspapers, totaling almost 1800 marks. The largest contribution came from the *Kölnische Volkszeitung* (1,275.10 marks), the smallest, in the token amount of one mark, from the *Jülicher Kreisblatt*.[37] The Rhenish Center was the wealthiest of the Prussian provincial chapters (*Landesverbände*). In 1911 it contributed 4000 marks to the Prussian Center; the Westphalian chapter gave 3000 marks, and all the other chapters combined (Silesia, Hesse-Nassau and Hanover) contributed 3300 marks.[38]

The organization of the Rhineland Center became the model for other regions. Center politicians in Westphalia, Hesse-Nassau and the Grand Duchy of Hesse followed the lead of Trimborn and organized their regional chapters according to the Rhenish example. On 4 October 1904, representatives from these provincial chapters met with their Rhenish counterparts to discuss a uniform party organization for Prussia. Although participants agreed in principle to the creation of a single Center organization for all of Prussia and to the establishment of a central bureau in Berlin, it took almost four years before their plans were realized.[39] Based on this agreement, the Executive Committee of the Prussian Center (*Landesausschuß der preußischen Zentrumspartei*) was established in Berlin in December 1908.[40] The executive council's first chairman was the Silesian Center leader Felix Porsch, first and second vice-chairmen were Karl Herold and Karl Trimborn, leaders of the Westphalian and Rhineland Center respectively. These three men represented the largest regional chapters of the Prussian Center. The executive council's function was twofold: to improve the organizational structure of the Prussian Center and to coordinate election tactics of the various provincial councils, paying particular attention to alliances with other parties during election campaigns and run-off elections. The thirty-member-strong executive committee consisted of the directorates of the Reichstag and Landtag caucuses, and the chairmen of the provincial councils. Up to seven more members could be elected to the executive council in

---

[37] Ergebnis der Sammlung für den Wahlfonds, n. d. [September 1913], HAStK, Nl. Trimborn 1256/121 f. 11.
[38] Morsey, "Rheinland," p. 19.
[39] "Protokoll der Organisationskonferenz westdeutscher Parteifreunde," 4 Oct. 1904, BAK Nl. 176 Herold, Nr. 1.
[40] What follows is based on "Konstituierung des Landesausschusses der preußischen Centrumspartei," *Germania* no. 282, 5 December 1908.

Berlin. Among those chosen in 1908 were Karl and Julius Bachem, Otto Krefeld (chairman of the Augustine League), and Franz Brandts (chairman of the People's Association).[41] The inclusion of Krefeld and Brandts in the executive council underlines the close relationship between the party and allegedly independent organizations such as the Augustine League and the People's Association. Perhaps more important still is the absence of any statutory representation of the Church. There were priests among the members of the executive council, but they held their positions because of their political, not their religious function—the Center was a Catholic, not a clerical party.

Trimborn's reorganization of the Center and his introduction of democratic procedures at the district level, however, must not be interpreted as a democratization of the party at large. Party leaders were not elected, and candidates for the Reichstag and the Landtag, although usually chosen by the electoral district, required the approval of the party hierarchy. Jokingly, Trimborn once remarked that he was the Rhenish Center's "bishop, his deputy a auxiliary bishop (*Weihbischof*), the general secretary was akin to a vicar general; his travels to party conventions a kind of political visitation."[42] One is struck by such a comparison from a leader of a political party that went to some length to distance itself from suggestions that the clergy exercised undue influence over it. All the same, such a remark must qualify any notion that Trimborn intended to "democratize" the Center. Trimborn's remark also throws some light on the language used by Center politicians. Historians have pointed to the political language of the Center as an indicator of its religious roots. In contrast to Liberals and Social Democrats, who addressed their supporters as citizens or comrades, Center supporters were often seen as "the Catholic people," or even as the "Catholic flock."[43] In his remark, Trimborn reveals how he perceived his relationship between the leadership of the party and their followers. It is the corollary to the perception of voters and supporters as the "flock." It also underlines how important it is to view the Center within the context of the Catholic milieu.

---

[41] The other three members were: Stephan Beuthen, Matthias Werden, and Dr. Blumenberg.
[42] Jörg, "Organisator," p. 34.
[43] Blackbourn, "Catholics and Politics," p. 200.

B. Organization of the Center Press

"Where would Agamemnon be without Homer? Where would German Catholics be without the press?" Karl Trimborn's grandiloquent analogy, made during the opening speech of the Osnabrück *Katholikentag* (1901), grossly exaggerated the importance of the Catholic press. But it also made an important point understood by everyone in the audience.[44] Without the daily contact with their supporters through the newsprint, without a forceful voice to counter the press of their political opponents in government and rival parties, the Center could hardly have survived the Kulturkampf or maintained its support at the polls once the struggle was over. Newspapers were not just the party's mouthpiece, they were indispensable for election propaganda and often the source of financial support for local party chapters.[45] The importance of a Catholic press had already become evident during the clash of government and Church during the Cologne Troubles (1837) and in confrontations between state and church in Baden during the 1850s and 1860s.[46] Indeed, most Catholic newspapers, founded in the wake of the 1848 revolution, were older than the party they supported. This, and the fact that most were privately owned, not party property, distinguished them from the other great party press, that of the Social Democrats.[47]

Karl Trimborn's own contributions to the fifth estate were few, but his general secretary Jörg suggested that he considerably affected Catholic journalism, providing information and material to the press.[48] In the late 1870s, Trimborn was a frequent visitor in the offices of the *Kölnische Volkszeitung*; there he discussed politics with his friends Julius Bachem and Hermann Cardauns and, one might say, laid the foundation for his political career.[49]

The *Kölnische Volkszeitung* was clearly the most important Catholic newspaper in the Rhineland, and perhaps in all of Germany. Its history is tied to the fortunes of the Bachem family. The Bachem firm was founded by Johann Peter Bachem in 1818. In the early days

---

[44] K. Trimborn quoted in Jörg, "Organisator," p. 32.
[45] Wilhelm Kisky, *Der Augustinus-Verein zur Pflege der Katholischen Presse von 1878 bis 1928* (Düsseldorf: Verlag des Augustinusvereins, 1928), p. 175.
[46] Otto B. Roegele, "Presse und Publizistik des deutschen Katholizismus 1803-1963," in *Der soziale und politische Katholizismus. Entwicklungslinien in Deutschland 1803-1963*, ed. Anton Rauscher (Munich: Günter Olzog Verlag, 1982), p. 416.
[47] Mittmann, *Fraktion und Partei*, pp. 211-2.
[48] Jörg, "Organisator," p. 32.
[49] Cardauns, *Trimborn*, p. 48.

it was a book and print shop. Newspapers became part of the enterprise only after Lambert Bachem had taken over the business following his brother's death. After a failed attempt to acquire a newspaper in Cologne, Lambert Bachem bought the *Rheinische Provinzialblätter*, an "unpolitical" and, as it turned out, unprofitable monthly in Aachen, dedicated to the "intellectual and material advancement of Rhinelanders."[50] Karl Bachem, in his history of the early Catholic press, bemoans his grandfather's reluctance to take advantage of the Prussian government's permission to deal with political issues, "one looks in vain," he notes "for any mention of the Cologne Troubles" in the *Provinzialblätter*, "despite the "emotional outburst of Rhenish Catholics."[51] This is all the more surprising since Lambert Bachem's well-known personal views and the risks he took selling pamphlets attacking the Prussian government made him a local champion of "the cause of the Archbishop and the freedom of the Catholic Church."[52]

The demise of the *Rheinische Provinzialblätter* in 1839 was soon followed by the bankruptcy of Bachem's company. Karl Bachem blames a lack of business acumen for the failure of the family firm; his grandfather belonged to that class of Germans who admired "all things beautiful and good, had... high moral standards but little talent for making money." Lambert Bachem suffered the indignity of debtor's prison (*Schuldarrest*), and lost his house and much of his personal property to his creditors.[53] It took him almost thirteen years to repay his debts, and it was his son Joseph Bachem, the father of Karl, who eventually founded the *Kölnische Volkszeitung*. Before the *Kölnische Blätter* (renamed *Kölnische Volkszeitung* in 1869) was established in 1860, Joseph Bachem and some Cologne friends, among them August Reichensperger, had founded—like many others in the heady days of 1848—another newspaper: the *Deutsche Volkshalle*.[54] The *Volkshalle* did not survive for long; it fell victim to Prussia's cen-

---

[50] Karl Bachem, *Josef Bachem, seine Familie und die Firma J. P. Bachem in Köln, die Rheinische und Deutsche Volkshalle, die Kölnischen Blätter und die Kölnische Volkszeitung: Zugleich ein Versuch der Geschichte der katholischen Presse und ein Beitrag zur Entwicklung der katholischen Bewegung in Deutschland* (Cologne: Verlag und Druck J. P. Bachem, 1912), 1:85; Cardauns, *Fünfzig*, p. 6.

[51] Bachem, *Josef Bachem*, 1:91.

[52] Ibid., 1:92-3.

[53] Ibid., 1:107-12.

[54] For a brief account of Catholic press undertakings in 1848 see Roegele, "Presse," 409-13; or the exhaustive treatment in Bachem, *Josef Bachem*, 2:34-204.

sors and was closed down by the Cologne police in 1855 because of its support of "anti-Prussian schemes."[55] Not to be deterred by censors, Bachem started the *Kölnische Blätter* less than five years after the suspension of *Deutsche Volkshalle*. Editor of the new daily was Fridolin Hoffmann, a theology student at Bonn university; a Bonn theology professor, Franz Heinrich Reusch, set down its program. Like its predecessor it was to be a Catholic paper—a political one, that is, not a mouthpiece of the hierarchy. Reusch emphasized its conservative character and assured the censors of its patriotic convictions.[56]

As was also true of other Catholic newspapers, the *Kölnische Volkszeitung* was not really part of a party press; even the creation of the *Katholische Fraktion* had not changed that. Only with the birth of the Center Party did the Catholic press become a decidedly political press associated with a political party.[57] Until the Kulturkampf the number of Catholic newspapers remained small. At the *Katholikentag* in Linz(1856), one concerned Catholic pointed out that of Germany's 450 newspapers of significance, 400 were anticlerical and only six were Catholic.[58] On the eve of the Kaiserreich there were only two Catholic dailies in the Rhine Province: the *Kölnische Volkszeitung* and the *Echo der Gegenwart*, the Rhineland's oldest Catholic paper published in Aachen since 1848.[59] Karl Bachem estimates that all Catholic newspapers together had hardly 60,000 subscribers in 1864.[60] The relative scarcity of Catholic newspapers was not lamented by all Catholics. Some priests and church officials were suspicious of the influence an independent press might gain over Catholics. Clergy often scorned journalists and their work. In addition to the general contempt many German bourgeois held for journalists, they believed that "many an important question of the day would be better resolved if one strove for a thorough grounding in religious knowledge and in the Catechism rather than searching for all wisdom and rules of conduct (*Lebensregeln*) in the dubious

---

[55] Cardauns, *Fünfzig*, pp. 15-6.
[56] Ibid., pp. 18-9.
[57] KB, 3:151.
[58] Roegele, "Presse," pp. 413-4.
[59] Karl Bachem lists the following papers as important Catholic publications outside the Rhineland: *Westfälischer Merkur*, Münster, *Schlesische Volkszeitung*, Breslau, *Augsburger Postzeitung*, *Mainzer Journal*, *Badischer Beobachter*, Karlsruhe, *Deutsches Volksblatt*, Stuttgart, KB, 3:153-4.
[60] KB, 3:155.

doctrines espoused in newspapers."[61] Catholic journalists like their conservative counterparts had to overcome a particular ambivalence of their task. James Retallack has argued that conservative journalists, though they "sought to defend existing institutions,... were attacked for hastening change. Though empowered to cry out and tell all, they were expected to write cautiously and reveal nothing."[62] Catholic journalists faced a similar dilemma. They, too, had to walk a fine line between the demands for change by social reformers in the camp of political Catholicism and the staunch defenders of tradition and conservative Catholic values. One significant difference between Catholic and Protestant journalists was that Catholics were not expected to defend Bismarck's creation and the new nineteenth-century liberal-Protestant notion of nationalism. All this, however, hardly impeded the success of the Catholic press.

The main impetus for the extraordinary growth of the Catholic press, as for the Center, was Bismarck's persecution of Catholics. A whole crop of Catholic newspapers grew from this conflict. In the Rhineland their number grew steadily from thirty in 1871 to sixty-six in 1881 and 122 in 1912; the number of subscribers increased from seventy thousand to over a million during the same four decades—only the Catholic press of Bavaria rivaled that of the Rhineland in number of newspapers and readers.[63] Many priests clung to the notion that reading was bad for their flock. Some argued that ignorance is not at all detrimental, after all, "one can be a very good Catholic without reading newspapers." Such opinions were increasingly challenged. The priest and journalist, Albert Förster, for example, warned that "in our times, people, if they do not read can gradually be weakened in their religious faith. The Church which is part of this world and has to reckon with and fight against the powers of this world, will suffer if its members do not read."[64] Along with influential newspapers some Catholic publishing houses became important. The Bachem enterprise, founded earlier in the century

---

[61] Andreas Niedermayer, *Die katholische Presse Deutschlands* (Freiburg i. Br.) cited in Feldenkirchen, "Deutsche Reichszeitung," p. 13. On general attitudes towards journalists see James N. Retallack, "From Pariah to Professional? The Journalist in German Society and Politics, from the Late Enlightenment to the Rise of Hitler," *German Studies Review* 16 (1993), esp. pp. 175-83.

[62] Retallack, "Pariah," p. 195.

[63] Statistic of the Augustine League (1914), quoted in KB, 3:155; similar figures (1869, 22 newspapers; 1900, 119) can be found in Kisky, *Augustinus-Verein*, p. 55.

[64] Quoted in Michael Schmolke, *Die schlechte Presse. Katholiken und Publizistik zwischen "Katholik" und "Publik" 1821-1968* (Münster: Verlag Regensburg, 1971), p. 193.

has already been mentioned. The Bonifacius-Druckerei in Paderborn was founded in 1875 and the Paulinus-Druckerei a year later, a creation of the tireless Georg Friedrich Dasbach.[65] The Kulturkampf alone cannot explain the sudden rise of Catholic newspapers and publishing houses since it was not only the Catholic press that grew. The abundant capital and the willingness to risk it during the economic boom after unification explains why so many newspapers, not just Catholic ones were founded.[66] Thus the emergence of a substantial Catholic press was part of a larger phenomenon.

Germania was the quasi-official organ of the Center Reichstag caucus. Situated in Berlin, it was founded on 1 January 1871.[67] *Germania*, too, was not formally a party organ until the Weimar Republic, when Center politicians tried to buy it.[68] Although it was a national paper it did not achieve the same influence as the *Kölnische Volkszeitung*. Its first editor was the Rhenish convert Friedrich Pilgram, its most notorious editor was the Silesian journalist Paul Majunke who had learned his trade at the *Kölnische Volkszeitung*.[69] Under Majunke's editorship, *Germania* fought Kulturkampf battles like no other Catholic newspaper. No Berlin paper, not even the Socialist ones, was temporarily banned as often as *Germania*. Five of its journalists were once imprisoned during the same week; Majunke, despite parliamentary immunity was arrested in December 1874 and spent over a year in Plötzensee, a Berlin prison.[70]

Newspaper pages provided the battleground for struggles against enemies believed to threaten Catholic interests from within and without the Catholic world. Conceived and founded by Catholic businessmen, aristocrats and Jesuits and spearheaded by the retired publisher Peter Hauptmann[71], the *Deutsche Reichszeitung* launched a two-pronged attack on such internal and external foes from its editorial

---

[65] Roegele, "Presse," p. 419.

[66] Ibid., 416; Toni Feldenkirchen, "Die Bonner Deutsche Reichszeitung im Kulturkampf" (Ph. D. diss., Ludwig-Maximilians-Universität, München, 1933), p. 14; Retallack, "Pariah," pp. 178-9.

[67] For details see Kisky, *Augustinus-Verein*, pp. 36-40; KB, 3:133-5.

[68] In 1920 Matthias Erzberger gained controlling influence; after his murder, Franz von Papen and a group of Catholic aristocrats had a majority of shares; in 1927 *Germania* reached an agreement with the *Kölnische Volkszeitung* to cooperate in representing Center policies and the interest of German Catholics.

[69] Between 1874 and 1884 Majunke represented Trier at the Reichstag, in 1878 he became a deputy of the Prussian Landtag.

[70] Roegele, "Presse," p. 421; Kisky, *Augustinus-Verein*, p. 38.

[71] In 1885 Hauptmann was elected deputy for the Prussian Landtag, he was also one of the founders of the Augustinusverein.

offices in Bonn. The enemy within were the *Altkatholiken* who, opposed to the dogma of infallibility and supported by the faculty of theology at the University of Bonn—some of whom had been excommunicated—threatened to divide German Catholicism. In their effort to silence *Altkatholiken*, the *Reichszeitung* was supported by the *Katholischer Verein* and the Jesuits who had houses in Bonn and close by in Kreuzberg. More dangerous still were liberal antagonists who threatened Catholic interests from without. The *Deutsche Reichszeitung* was the most ardent Kulturkampf opponent in the Rhineland.[72] The main targets of the *Reichszeitung's* zealous attacks were, of course, Bismarck and the liberal press, the latter responded in kind, the former had journalists fined or locked up. The vitriolic tone of the *Reichszeitung* can be explained in at least two ways: first it was the result of the charged atmosphere of the Kulturkampf; second it was part and parcel of the "sharp polemic tone of political journalism in Germany.[73] Due to its feistiness, the *Reichszeitung* quickly attracted a readership larger in size than that of the *Germania* and the influential *Schlesische Volkszeitung* and was distributed far beyond the Bonn city limits.[74]

The name *Deutsche Reichszeitung* was chosen by its first editor Winand Virnich to demonstrate the paper's and its readership's loyalty to the Reich which had so often been put into question. Winand Virnich's career was typical for that of many journalists in nineteenth-century Germany. His checkered education included a few years at a Gymnasium in his hometown of Düren, followed by stays at a commercial school (*Handelsschule*) and a Jesuit college and yet another Gymnasium in Aachen. He eventually studied mining and worked for a Prussian mining office (*Bergamt*) in Düren. His journalistic career began at the *Kölnische Volkszeitung* (1867-1869); he worked briefly for the *Essener Volkszeitung* before he became editor-in-chief (*Chefredakteur*) at the *Schlesische Volkszeitung* in Breslau. He stayed there only until July 1870, returned to Düren and in January of the following year joined the Bonn *Deutsche Reichszeitung* where he became co-editor, joining the Silesian priest Franz Leopold Matzner.

---

[72] This account of the founding of the paper is based primarily on Feldenkirchen, "Deutsche Reichszeitung," pp. 17-29.

[73] Retallack, "Pariah," p. 193.

[74] Circulation: 1874, 3500; 1877, 5400; 1878, 6100; 1880, 6500; 1882, 7000; there were subscribers in all cities of the Rhineprovince, in most other large German cities and in a number of European capitals; cf. Feldenkirchen, "Deutsche Reichszeitung," pp. 28, 164-5n 29.

From the outset the *Reichszeitung*, with its reputation for radical solutions, was in outspoken opposition to *Kölnische Volkszeitung*. During the Kulturkampf the two papers buried their differences in the name of Catholic solidarity, the fundamental philosophical differences, however, never disappeared. These differences were crucial to political Catholicism and took center stage during the *Zentrumsstreit*. Although after the Kulturkampf the *Reichszeitung* lost readers and influence and only played a marginal role, the paper remains significant to the historian since its rivalry with the *Kölnische Volkszeitung* underlined the differences within the Catholic camp, differences that continued to plague political Catholicism long after the Kulturkampf had ended and which dominated political discussion as part of the Zentrumsstreit.[75]

Despite the attacks of the *Reichszeitung*, the most important Catholic newspaper in the Rhineland remained the *Kölnische Volkszeitung*. Two men shaped and dominated the *Kölnische Volkszeitung*'s stance on domestic policy for more than three decades. Julius Bachem who had joined the newspaper in 1868 dealt primarily with legal issues and social and political concerns. Hermann Cardauns, managing editor since 1876, concentrated his efforts on historical questions as well as religious and ecclesiastical concerns.[76] With Cardauns's entry into the newspaper a period of frequent change came to an end. Fridolin Hoffmann, Cardauns's predecessor, was forced to resign as editor because he had opposed the dogma of papal infallibility. Out of solidarity with Hoffmann, a number of other journalists also left the *Kölnische Volkszeitung*. Cardauns, Bachem, and the also newly hired journalist Karl Heinrich Brückmeyer moved into the vacated offices and assumed the day-to-day running of the newspaper.[77] This tumultuous start of the journalistic careers of Cardauns and Bachem was the beginning of a long period of editorial stability which helps to explain the success of the *Kölnische Volkszeitung*.

During the Kulturkampf years the *Kölnische Volkszeitung* made no profits. The newspaper survived this period only because the Bachem family subsidized it with profits from its printing and publishing concerns.[78] The newspaper's fortunes changed in 1891 when it made a profit of about 38,000 marks.[79] This profitability can be

[75] Feldenkirchen, "Deutsche Reichszeitung," p. 8.
[76] Bachem, *Erinnerungen*, pp. 31-5.
[77] Cardauns, *Fünfzig*, pp. 26-7.
[78] Ibid., p. 42.
[79] KB, 3:130.

explained by a number of developments. The owners invested in their paper in order to finance a change in layout which made the *Kölnische Volkszeitung* look similar to other national newspapers. The addition of a business section had attracted new subscribers and advertisers. At a time when Joseph Bachem invested in his newspaper, other Rhenish dailies were struggling to maintain their readership. Indeed, many could not adjust to the changed conditions after the end of the Kulturkampf had eliminated their *raison d'être*. Not the least reason of the newspaper's success was the journalistic work of Julius Bachem and Cardauns. They were generally regarded as the most effective Catholic journalists during the Kulturkampf.[80]

The inner workings of the *Kölnische Volkszeitung* also reveal some of the personal rivalries that existed among the leaders of political Catholicism. It had been Karl Bachem's ambition to become a journalist and his father had groomed him for this career.[81] Much to his chagrin, however, it was his cousin Julius who became editor at the family newspaper. It seems that there had been no room for Karl Bachem alongside Julius Bachem and Hermann Cardauns. Although Karl Bachem did not fail to notice the successful cooperation of his cousin and Cardauns which spanned a period of more than three decades, he was openly critical of Cardauns's fastidious treatment of young journalists. Moreover, he deeply resented being shut out from the paper. In his memoirs Bachem bitterly complained that Julius and Cardauns "obviously see me as a rival, even as a possible replacer, who therefore must not become too important and who had to be held back.... They unnecessarily edited my articles, often in the most nonsensical fashion so that nothing but skin and bone was left."[82]

The rivalry between the cousins intensified after Julius Bachem left politics in 1891. He employed the pages of the *Kölnische Volkszeitung* to criticize the policies of the Center Reichstag caucus. Karl Bachem perceived his cousin's criticism as deliberate attempts to torpedo his efforts to coordinate political opinions expressed by party and press.[83] This animosity is a reminder, too, that the Center, despite the claims of its opponents, was not a monolithic bloc. It also serves as a reminder that the Catholic press and the Center were not journalistic and political extensions of the Church, as the foes of political Catholicism never tired of claiming and its defendants in-

[80] Cardauns, *Fünfzig*, p. 42; KB: 3, 130; Bierganz, "Cardauns," pp. 67-8.
[81] HAStK Nl. Bachem 1005/2, p. 133 quoted in Kiefer, B*achem*, p. 88.
[82] Ibid., p. 88.
[83] Kiefer, B*achem*, p. 90.

cessantly denied.[84] Despite a common faith and a common political purpose, substantive political differences existed even among close allies within the Center Party.

Besides the *Kölnische Volkszeitung* there were, of course, lesser if not less ambitious Catholic papers. The political (and theological) differences that existed between them are further evidence for the varied and often antagonistic relationship among the various components of the Catholic milieu. The writings of Georg Friedrich Dasbach, who owned several newspapers in Trier, were assiduously critical of *Germania* and Berlin politicians, accusing them of being blind to regional issues and assuring his readers that the regional press would not similarly fail in its obligations.[85]

The *Westdeutsche Arbeiterzeitung* is a special case that deserves mentioning. Its predecessors were Catholic working-class newspapers such as the *Arbeiterfreund* in Krefeld, the *Paulusblatt* in Duisburg or the *Christlicher Arbeiterfreund* in Ehrenfeld (near Cologne). These were Sunday papers, above all concerned with local issues. They all went under after August Pieper and Otto Müller began publishing the *Westdeutsche Arbeiterzeitung* in the spring of 1899.[86] The *Westdeutsche Arbeiterzeitung* turned out to be one of the few genuinely democratic voices of political Catholicism. During the debate over the reform of the Prussian franchise, its editor, Joseph Joos, was an outspoken advocate of the introduction of the universal franchise. The *Westdeutsche Arbeiterzeitung* also demanded the participation of workers in the leadership of the Center as well as the introduction of a truly democratic party organization. It also criticized the Center's alliance with conservative forces.[87] These attitudes made the *Westdeutsche Arbeiterzeitung* a decided opponent of the political option for the Center that Karl Bachem and the *Kölnische Volkszeitung* advocated.

The first editor of the new newspaper was Johannes Giesberts. Giesberts, who later (1903-1914) functioned as liaison between Christian labour and the Peoples' Association, was one of the few influential Center men who came from the working class. He learned his

[84] "Die Vermengung von Politik und Religion im Zentrum," *Reichsbote* no. 3, 3 January 1909.
[85] Dasbach to Dieden, 8 Feb. 1883 quoted in Mittmann, *Fraktion und Partei*, pp. 222-3.
[86] Wilhelm Spael, *Das katholische Deutschland im 20. Jahrhundert. Seine Pionier- und Krisenzeiten 1890-1945* (Würzburg: Echter-Verlag, 1964), p. 30.
[87] Oswald Wachtling, *Joseph Joos. Journalist, Arbeiterführer, Zentrumspolitiker. Politische Biographie 1878-1933* (Mainz: Matthias-Grünewald-Verlag, 1974), pp. 31-2.

father's trade, but he could not make a living as a baker in his hometown of Straelen (located in the Lower Rhine on the border with the Netherlands). He worked in a brickworks, an oil-mill and a brewery before he left the area to search for work in Cologne. Even there it was not easy to find employment; he eventually found work in a railroad shop in Nippes (Cologne). His first direct contact with journalism came when he worked as a stoker in the Bachem publishing house, where the *Kölnische Volkszeitung* was printed. Soon he was reading drafts of articles he found in the trash bins.[88] Eventually Giesberts made a name for himself as an enthusiastic and effective speaker for the Workers' Associations and was noted by the leaders of the People's Association. In 1899 he moved from Cologne to Mönchengladbach, where under the guidance of August Pieper he edited the *Westdeutsche Arbeiterzeitung*.

According to his own account, it was a coincidence that he joined the Christian and not the Social Democratic workers' movement. Giesberts and a friend were already on the way to a SPD union meeting when they passed a church where mass was being celebrated. Giesberts was attracted by the light of the candles on the altar and drawn in to the church by the familiar *Lied zur Marienkönigin*. He missed the meeting and did not, as his friend did, join the SPD union. Later he confessed that had it not been for this coincidence he would surely have joined the Socialists.[89] Whether Giesberts actually was prevented by such a "divine sign" from joining the Socialists is not as important as the fact that he chose to tell the story. This act is typical of the attitude of many Catholics: to vote for the Center, to join a Catholic club or association of one description or another often was not a conscious or well thought-out decision. The attraction of familiar surroundings, familiar language or music, the very presence of clergy continued to have considerable attraction for many Catholics.

Karl Trimborn was a member and ardent supporter of the Augustine League (*Augustinus-Verein*), the "most influential and important" Catholic press organization founded in 1878 by his friend Hermann Joseph Schmitz (then a parish priest in Düsseldorf, later suffragan bishop [*Weihbischof*] of Cologne) and Eduard Hüsgen, editor of *Düsseldorfer Volksblatt*.[90] The Augustine League was conceived as a professional organization for Germany's Catholic journal-

---

[88] Ibid., pp. 13-4; Paul Misner, *Social Catholicism in Europe: From the Onset of Industrialization to the First World War* (New York: Crossroads, 1991), p. 273.
[89] Spael, *Deutschland*, p. 31.
[90] KB, 3:152.

ists, providing financial assistance for journalists who had fallen ill or for the widows and children of those who had died.[91] However, it soon became an organization representing the Center press whose main concern was a "uniform political stance" of all its members.[92] The engine driving the Augustine League was Heinrich Otto, editor and publisher of the *Niederrheinische Volkszeitung* (Krefeld), who was the League's president from 1889 to 1909.[93] In 1893 Paul Weilbächer was hired as general secretary and a savings bank (*Sparkasse*) was established which, in later years, became the pension fund of the Catholic press. The *Augustinusblatt*, the League's internal monthly publication, was founded in 1897. From the start the Augustine League was clearly associated with the Center and the People's Association. The relationship between the Augustine League and the People's Association was formalized in 1903 by making the general secretary of the People's Association (i. e. August Pieper) a permanent adviser (*ständiger Beirat*) to the meetings of the board of directors of the League.[94]

Heinrich Otto declared at the *Katholikentag* in Cologne (1903) that the League was dedicated to the teachings of the Church and devoted to its leaders. It strove to be in unison with the Center on all important political questions, seeing itself as a "mediator between Center and people."[95] As the League turned increasingly to coordinating the presentation of Center policies in parliament and their publication by the press it was necessary to create a liaison office. For this purpose, the *Centrums-Parlaments-Correspondenz* (CPC) was established in 1883. Nevertheless, during the early years, political issues were of secondary importance. A discussion of the "political situation" did not appear on an agenda for the annual congress of delegates until 1889.[96] Political considerations, however, became increasingly important and eventually the Augustine League took sides in all major disputes of the Center. Leaders of the League and the party regularly met every spring in Berlin and eventually even de-

[91] "Die Gründung des Augustinusvereins," Verhandlungen der XXV. Generalversammlung der Katholiken Deutschlands, 10-13 Sept. 1877, reprinted in Ernst Heinen, *Staatliche Macht und Katholizismus in Deutschland* (Paderborn: Ferdinand Schöningh, 1969,1979), 2:167-8.
[92] KB, 3:152.
[93] Otto resigned on 1 January 1909. He was succeeded by vice-president Eduard Hüsgen (1909-12).
[94] Kisky, *Augustinus-Verein*, p. 83.
[95] Bachem, *Erinnerungen*, pp. 125-6; quotation from Kisky, *Augustinus-Verein*, p. 167.
[96] Kisky, *Augustinus-Verein*, p. 167.

cided on the line of argument the Center press was to take on specific issues.⁹⁷ After the election of 1907, for instance, Center politicians and representatives of the press met and agreed upon a common strategy toward Reich Chancellor Bernhard von Bülow.⁹⁸ Ursula Mittmann has aptly summarized the dilemma of the Center press in suggesting that it offered an uncommonly broad target for its attackers. Its opponents made little or no distinction among Catholic papers, and they were as likely to object to apologetic essays as to political commentaries. The fact that papers such as *Germania*, *Kölnische Volkszeitung* and others frequently published articles written by clergy or pieces presenting the view of Rome on a particular issue, made attacks by rival newspapers that much easier. Mittmann correctly observes the influence of the clergy on the formulation of ideology when she asserts that "Catholic ideology was formulated outside the political party"; here political Catholicism differed from Socialism where ideological debates were carried out *within* the party.⁹⁹ In political matters, however, the Center claimed independence. It reserved not only the right to determine its own policies, but on occasion acted contrary to papal advice, as was the case in 1887 when the curia attempted to pressure the Center to support the Army Bill in order to gain concessions on anti-Catholic legislation. On several occasions, the curia questioned the loyalty of the Center press—for example, on the occasion of a meeting between Lieber and Mariano Rampolla del Tindaro . Rampolla, then papal Secretary of State, severely criticized the reporting of the *Kölnische Volkszeitung*.¹⁰⁰ On other occasions, the clergy praised the Catholic press for its commentary on political and religious affairs; clerics also clearly recognized the importance of the Augustine League for the defense of Catholic interests.¹⁰¹ Catholic newspapers and the Augustine League were among the most important weapons in the arsenal of political Catholicism. With their help Center politicians had daily access to their supporters.

⁹⁷ Bachem, *Erinnerungen*, p. 126.
⁹⁸ Protocol of a conference of Center parliamentarians and press representatives, 22-23 July 1907 (copy, dated 19 Aug. 1908), HAStK Nl. Bachem 1006/ 268b. Present were: Brandts (representing the People's Association), Fehrenbach,Fritzen-Düsseldorf, Gröber, Herold, Hitze, Pichler, Spahn, Trimborn (representing the Center), J. Bachem, F. X. Bachem, Otto, Spahn, Pieper (representing the press).
⁹⁹ Mittmann, *Fraktion und Partei*, p. 240.
¹⁰⁰ K. Bachem to Hitze, 12 Feb. 1900, BAP 74VO1 Nr. 143 f. 15-16.
¹⁰¹ J. Bachem, *Erinnerungen*, p. 131.

On balance it seems fair to conclude that Rhenish Center supporters justifiably believed that their regional party organization and their press were the most sophisticated, efficient and influential of all regional groups within the German Center. The building of an intricate and efficient party organization, and the growing of a press closely associated with the Center, however, were only two aspects of the changes the Rhineland Center Party, and to a lesser extent the Center in other parts of Germany, underwent during the 1890s.

Besides being better organized the party had also become more "democratic." Historians have noted a change in the social composition of the Center's leadership and a democratization of the party's elite structure. The party of old, led by an disproportionate number of aristocrats, farmers and clergy had a new kind of leadership made up overwhelmingly of lawyers and members of the middle class.[102] David Blackbourn has analyzed the composition of the Center faction in the Württemberg Landtag. The leadership of the Württemberg faction was in the hands of a few men, all of them lawyers or judges and some state officials in high legal positions. The bulk of the group consisted of professionals, teachers, artisans, peasants, small businessmen and four priests. But unlike the Rhineland Center, the Württemberg party had no strong aristocratic leadership. David Blackbourn attributes this peculiarity to the fact that the party emerged locally only in the 1890s—after the nobility had lost much of its political influence within the Center. The Württemberg Center also had "no upthrust of Catholic industrialists and commercial men." The Catholic working class in the state, too, "received no representation commensurate with its size.[103] The Rhineland Center was similar in that it, too, had a group of Landtag representatives composed disproportionately of lawyers. Aristocrats still played a role, although a sharply diminished one, in Rhenish politics after the turn of the century. Baron von Heeremann was elected chair of the Center faction of the Prussian Landtag in 1899. But when von Heeremann resigned the following year he was succeeded by the commoner Aloys Fritzen, a former *Landrat* and member of the Landtag for Düsseldorf. After 1893 Catholic aristocrats lost much of the political influence they had enjoyed during the Windthorst era. Under Ernst Lieber's leadership the Center also became an important supporter of gov-

---

[102] Anderson, "Kulturkampf," p. 109; Morsey, "Katholiken," p. 272; Loth, *Katholiken*, p. 76.
[103] Blackbourn, *Class*, pp. 101-2.

ernment policies. As part of the "national rehabilitation"[104] many Catholics aspired to during the 1890s, the Center Party, eager to demonstrate their loyalty to Kaiser and fatherland, supported much of the empire's foreign policy and its attempts to build a navy. As the conflict with the government abated another opponent grew in strength. Socialists replaced Liberals as the most potent political rival to the Center Party.

---

[104] Morsey, "Katholiken," p. 274.

V.

WORKERS, CENTER, AND SOCIALISTS

THE CENTER'S FUNDAMENTAL DILEMMA was that it expected its supporters and voters to put their religious and ideological interests before class interests. Ironically, this dilemma stemmed in part from the Center's very success during the Kulturkampf years. The persecution of the Catholic church and its representatives, who suffered for their religious beliefs, or at least for the integrity of their convictions, was a subject of indignation and outrage to most German Catholics; they publicly testified to their discontent by voting for the Center. After 1890, however, without the need to unite against government attacks on their church, fewer Catholics felt compelled to vote for Center candidates. Two other developments compounded the party's difficulties: the rising importance of the blue collar vote (particularly in Reichstag elections) combined with the success of the Social Democratic Party in attracting Catholic workers; and the unresolved question of the political and religious nature of the Center. All these dilemmas and developments were particularly pronounced in the Rhineland.

A. Catholic Workers' Clubs and Christian Trade Unions

Catholics had a long tradition of working-class activism and concern for social issues. Much more elaborate than those of the Liberals, at times rivaling those of the Socialists, Catholic voluntary associations unfolded a range of activities that on occasion made even the German episcopate nervous.[1] Among these associations, Catholic workers' clubs (*Arbeitervereine*) deserve special mention, for they were one of the vital social institutions which formed a link between Catholic industrial workers, Christian trade unions, and the Center leader-

---

[1] For examples of early Catholic workers' associations see Sperber, *Popular Catholicism*, pp. 280-2; Blackbourn, *Volksfrömmigkeit*, p. 34.

ship. Most significantly, a close investigation of these workers' clubs shows that rank-and-file members remained closely tied to the clergy, even if priests were not represented as prominently among Center parliamentarians. In many ways, economic policies and political decisions were motivated by their religious beliefs or by their perception of the religiosity of their constituency. Karl Bachem, for instance, was convinced that the "majority of our voters, despite all political education, are first and foremost of a religious and clerical disposition, only afterwards do they begin to think politically."[2] The Center, again and again, emerges as a deeply Catholic party, whose actions cannot be explained merely by political opportunism or the need to cater to a variety of special interests. Attitudes of Rhenish Centrists toward workers, workers' clubs and later the Christian trade unions, can only be understood if one realizes that religious as well as political motives lay behind them.

Catholic workers' clubs—founded as "a bastion against Socialist propaganda"[3] and conceived as a weapon in a struggle of ideologies—had one of their origins in Adolph Kolping's journeymen's associations (*Gesellenvereine*) of the 1850s. The goals of journeymen's associations mirrored the biography of their founder.[4] The son of a shepherd, Kolping grew up to be a shoemaker. According to his own testimony, his appetite for learning and his determination to escape the misery of a journeyman's life in early nineteenth-century Cologne compelled him to return to school. In April 1845, ten years after he had decided to leave his occupation, Kolping was ordained a priest by the bishop of Cologne. A few months later he became a chaplain of a parish in Elberfeld, an industrial town near Cologne where only about a quarter of the population was Catholic. Dismayed by the squalor in which factory workers and craftsmen lived, he established his first workers' association in Elberfeld. Soon there were chapters in Cologne and Düsseldorf. In 1858 there were already 191 chapters and by 1865 Kolping's idea had spread to the USA, Switzerland, Hungary, Poland and Belgium, with a total of some 460 journeymen's associations.

---

[2] Karl Bachem to Julius Bachem, 27 July 1910 (copy), HAStK Nl. Bachem 1006/293a.
[3] Rivinius, "Dasbach," pp. 259-60.
[4] What follows is based on Michael Schmolke, "Adolph Kolping (1813-1865)," in *Zeitgeschichte in Lebensbildern. Aus dem deutschen Katholizismus des 19. und 20. Jahrhunderts*, ed. Jürgen Aretz, Rudolf Morsey and Anton Rauscher (Mainz: Matthias-Grünewald-Verlag, 1979), 3:36-49.

Of an idealistic and pragmatic mind, Kolping was chiefly concerned with giving moral and educational support to young craftsmen. To him the social question was primarily a religious and educational one, to be solved by charitable work and moral and religious improvement. To this end, journeymen's associations arranged for "a friendly and spacious hall" where journeymen could meet regularly and where their "spirit and soul received truly uplifting and invigorating entertainment and amusement of the kind available neither at home nor in a public house." Of course, religious education was part and parcel of Kolping's program.[5]

As Germany experienced industrialization in full force the social question became ever more pressing. By the time the empire was founded Catholics on a variety of fronts searched for answers. Discussions during the early 1870s already touched on some of the questions that would dominate the bitter debates among Christian trade unions and the Center Party after the turn of the century: Were unions to be exclusively Catholic or open to Protestant workers? Was strike a legitimate weapon in the arsenal of Catholic workers' associations or was a cooperative approach better? What role should priests and the Church play in the formulation of policies and the leadership of workers' organizations? What was the relationship between political leaders from the Center Party, workers' leaders and the clergy? Priests, politicians and entrepreneurs proposed divergent solutions. Local priests sought for ways to ameliorate the hardships of industrial workers; some of these determined young men, broke with the past, advocating a confrontational, aggressive stance which did not spare the entrenched interests of Catholic notables and factory owners. Catholic industrialists, weary of the distasteful consequences of economic and political emancipation of workers, envisioned patriarchal schemes to improve the lot of Catholic workers.

The pope, too, was looking for an answer to the social question. In Rome, Christoph Moufang, canon (*Domkapitular*) of the Mainz cathedral, formulated a papal response to the social question. Moufang based his recommendations on bishop Ketteler's ideas but fell short of embracing Ketteler's latest demands made at the *Fuldaer Bischofskonferenz* (September 1869). The bishop of Mainz had argued that traditional methods of the ministry could not cope with the social question; he called on the state to provide legislation protecting industrial workers and to address the difficulties brought about

---

[5] Adolph Kolping, "Der Gesellenverein. Zur Beherzigung für alle, die es mit dem wahren Volkswohl gut meinen" (1849), in Rüther, *Geschichte*, 2:199-200.

by industrialization. In contrast, Moufang, afraid that the state might encroach on church rights, stressed the importance of the Church in solving the social question. He and other high clergy saw the pauperization of the working class but were also concerned with questions of ecclesiastical rights and privileges.[6] This stance was still more open to dealing with social problems than that of the Evangelical Church which condemned "social parsons" and their "thoughtless advocacy of the demands of a single class." The Church, the argument went, had no business interfering in political and social disputes; its mission was "the creation of blessedness for the soul."[7]

Center politicians who discussed the program of their newly founded party, too, had little concrete to offer to the working class. An election platform written by Peter Reichensperger in the name of "Catholic men from the country's various regions" published in the *Kölnische Volkszeitung* (11 June 1870) did not mention social policies. The so-called Cologne Program (29 June 1870) made vague demands for "healthy Christian legislation" in order to "eradicate social ills and promote the interests of the working class." The most significant of all early Center pronouncements on policy, the Soest Program, also offered nothing beyond general demands for legislation which protected workers against "moral and physical ruin."[8] None of these recommendations, however, were translated into policy. Center politicians, too, did not address these questions in the form of attempts to introduce legislation until the late 1870s. The first concrete efforts to improve the squalid lives of Catholic workers were made by local priests.

Father Peter Joseph Schings, publisher of the first Catholic publication concerned solely with the social question, the *Christlich-Soziale Blätter*, organized an initiative to help workers.[9] Schings's desire to work towards a more just Christian society sprang from a combination of personal experience (his brother had died young as a result of most difficult living and working conditions) and religious convictions.[10] His readers were those among the Catholic bourgeoisie and

[6] Erwin Gatz, "Das erste Vatikanische Konzil und die soziale Frage," *Annarium Historiae Conciliorum* 3 (1971), pp. 161-6.

[7] Cited in Gordon A. Craig, *Germany 1866 - 1945* (New York: Oxford University Press, 1978), p. 184.

[8] Emil Ritter, *Die katholisch-soziale Bewegung Deutschlands im neunzehnten Jahrhundert und der Volksverein* (Cologne: Verlag J. P. Bachem, 1954), pp. 108-9.

[9] For details on Schings and his publication see Herbert Lepper, "Peter Joseph Schings (1837-1876) und die 'Christlich-Socialen Blätter'," *Annalen des Historischen Vereins für den Niederrhein* Heft 191 (1988), esp. pp. 52-88.

[10] Lepper, "Schings," p. 37.

higher clergy who were interested in the social question, workers showed no interest in subscribing to the *Christlich-Soziale Blätter*.[11] Like Moufang, Schings was a follower of Bishop Ketteler. In Aachen he was joined in his charitable and political work by Johan Breuer, a schoolteacher who had worked with Kolping in Elberfeld.[12] Their plans for a Christian-social party, however, came to nothing. Catholic leaders at the Düsseldorf *Katholikentag* (1869) rejected their ideas for a political party because they feared that "a party formed mainly to pursue social reforms would alienate middle-class and upper-class Catholics."[13] Most Catholic political leaders preferred to integrate the demands of the working class and Catholic labor organizations "into the broader, more comprehensive political movement" formulated in the Soest program.[14] Their efforts, like those of most Catholic associations of the time, amounted to little more than an acknowledgment of the problems faced by industrial workers. Herbert Lepper has characterized their activities as a kind of "*Situationsanalyse*," a "critical stock-taking" limited to a moralistic critique of capitalism.[15] Few were prepared to follow bishop Ketteler's demand for "*Totalreform*,"[16] fewer still were willing to support the work of activists such as Franz Eduard Cronenberg and the Christian social-associations.

Like Kolping's journeymen's associations, Christian-social associations (which were founded around 1870) have also been regarded as forerunners of Catholic workers' clubs. In their hey-day they attracted some 30,000 members. For the most part, however, they did not survive the Kulturkampf.[17] Unlike workers' clubs, they tolerated Protestant members, and this interconfessional work later made the founding of Christian trade unions easier.[18] The clergy, particularly

[11] Alphons Thun, "Industrie am Niederrhein und ihre Arbeiter. Die linksrheinische Textilindustrie," *Staats- und sozialwissenschaftliche Forschungen* 2 (1879), 1:201.
[12] Brose, *Christian Labor*, p. 38.
[13] Ibid.
[14] Ibid., pp. 38-9.
[15] Lepper, "Schings," p. 39.
[16] Cited in Lepper, "Schings," p. 41.
[17] Josef Mooser, "Arbeiter, Bürger und Priester in den konfessionellen Arbeitervereinen im deutschen Kaiserreich, 1880-1914," in *Arbeiter und Bürger im 19. Jahrhundert: Varianten ihres Verhältnisses im europäischen Vergleich*, ed. Jürgen Kocka (Munich: R. Oldenbourg Verlag, 1986), p. 81; Höffner, "Stellung," p. 611.
[18] Ernst-Detlef Broch, *Katholische Arbeitervereine in der Stadt Köln 1890-1901* (Wentorf/Hamburg: Einhorn-Presse Verlag, 1977), p. 3*; Friedrich Lenger, *Zwischen Kleinbürgertum und Proletariat. Studien zur Sozialgeschichte der Düsseldorfer Handwerker 1816-1878* (Göttingen: Vandenhoeck & Ruprecht, 1986), pp. 225-6.

the higher clergy, and the Center establishment were very uncomfortable with this new movement. They thought it radical, too political and overly concerned with the distress of workers. They feared that workers would be politicized, aspiring to a role not becoming their station. Christian-Social associations were also a thorn in the side of Karl Marx. In a letter to Engels describing a journey through Aachen and the Lower Rhineland, Marx declared that he had become convinced that the International needed to deal energetically with Christian-Social associations and in particular with Catholic priests (*Pfaffen*). "These dogs," the philosopher said, "are flirting…with the workers' question wherever they see an opportunity."[19]

We do not know whether Marx ever met Franz Eduard Cronenberg, but if he did he would surely have identified him as one of "those dogs" who were courting industrial workers. Cronenberg, a young priest at the parish of St. Adalbert in a working-class district of Aachen, had founded the most important Christian-social association. The feisty priest who became its first chairman (*Präses*), named the association he founded after St. Paul, and it grew by 1875 to the impressive strength of 5,000 members.[20] The region around Aachen was fertile ground for Cronenberg's work. It had been an early stronghold for Catholic workers' clubs. Chapters were founded in Lendersdorf (near Düren, 1860), in Düren (1861), in Eschweiler (1864 and again in 1870), in Würselen (1868, second founding 1871).[21]

Cronenberg focused his attention on the most pressing problem workers and their families faced: housing. Aachen and Burtscheid were notorious for the poor condition of their housing for workers. Between 1800 and 1870 Aachen's population tripled and there was little construction of new housing. Only one of the city's Catholic entrepreneurs had built some apartments for his workers.[22] In particular Burtscheid and the eastern districts of Aachen, where many of the poorest workers lived, were awful. According to a report (1876) by the mayor of Aachen, the city had the worst housing conditions

---

[19] Marx to Engels, 25 September 1869 cited in Höffner, "Stellung," p. 611.

[20] Broch, *Arbeitervereine*, p. 3*. On Cronenberg see Herbert Lepper, "Kaplan Franz Eduard Cronenberg und die christlich-soziale Bewegung in Aachen 1868-1878," *Zeitschrift des Aachener Geschichtsvereins* 79 (1968), pp. 57-148.

[21] Günter Bers, *Katholische Arbeitervereine im Raum Aachen 1903-1914. Aufbau und Organisation des Aachener Bezirksverbandes im Spiegel seiner Delegiertenversammlung* (Wentdorf: Einhorn-Presse Verlag, 1979), p. 9.

[22] Thun, "Industrie," 1:56.

of all cities in the Rhine Province.²³ The living conditions of many of Aachen's industrial workers were abhorrent. Alphons Thun thought a visit of Aachen's working class districts "was like a voyage to dubious parts about which one would not talk in polite society."²⁴ Thun saw poverty, hunger—in one apartment he encountered a mother breast feeding her child although she was so starved that the feeding provided neither comfort nor nourishment for the infant. Above all Thun was struck by the filthy and crowded conditions of many working-class homes. At times two families shared one room in which they lived, cooked, slept and sometimes worked. A baneful stench filled houses, children spent the entire day on the streets, playing in dirty puddles on the poorly maintained roads which were in stark contrast to Aachen's "fashionable" neighborhoods.²⁵ In working-class streets houses had twenty to forty inhabitants (in better-off neighborhoods the number was between six and ten).²⁶ To make matters worse, rents were disproportionately high, in general rent per square meter was higher for working class apartments.²⁷ There were also new dependencies on the landlord or his agent; often rent was collected by a shopkeeper who had sub-rented the building from the owner. A silent yet important agreement was that renters who were at the mercy of the shopkeeper would also buy all their groceries from him, often at inflated prices. Often the shopkeeper could sell his lowest quality goods to the workers.²⁸ Hygienic conditions were awful because of the lack of canalization and sewage; two brooks served as sources for washing and drinking water as well as repositories for raw sewage. As a result of these unhygienic conditions Burtscheid was the hardest hit by the cholera epidemic of 1866.²⁹

In order to improve the living conditions of Aachen's working class, Cronenberg established a building society, to provide apartments for workers. The first building constructed by Cronenberg's building society was the *Paulushaus* where members of the *Paulusverein* met. Its hall which could accommodate 4,000 persons was also the venue for theater and opera performances attended above all by the

²³ Cited in Thun, "Industrie," 1:60.
²⁴ Thun, "Industrie," 1:59.
²⁵ Ibid., 1:56-9.
²⁶ Ibid., 1:59.
²⁷ Nipperdey, *Deutsche Geschichte*, 1:137.
²⁸ Thun, "Industrie," 1:61.
²⁹ Egon Schmitz-Cliever, "Die Choleraepidemien in Alt-Aachen und Burtscheid," *Zeitschrift des Aachener Geschichtsvereins* 64/65 (1951/52), pp. 152-5. There was another brief outbreak of cholera in Burtscheid in 1871/72; some thirty people fell ill.

city's bourgeoisie. Part of this project was the construction of apartments for unmarried workers and working-class families. In the same year, 1872, the building society also bought four acres land for the construction of more working class apartments.[30] Besides doing social work, organizing lectures, and staging spiritual uplifting evenings, Cronenberg's association had a political dimension. The by-laws declared that the members should campaign for the Party of Christian Socialists (*Partei der christlichen Sozialisten*[31]) during elections.[32]

His very success, however, turned Cronenberg into a threat for the established social and political élites. In 1870 and 1871 he still supported, though reluctantly, candidates for Reichstag elections put forward by Constantia and the Center Party. But already in 1873 a conflict over the candidature of Cronenberg for one of the three Landtag seats for Aachen (WK 282) and over the inclusion of a social program led to a permanent rupture between the Aachen notables represented by Constantia and the majority of workers in Aachen; Constantia turned down an attempted compromise by Cronenberg.[33] This outraged Aachen workers who felt that they were "good enough as voters" but that their desires went unheeded by Constantia; they summarized their feelings in a quotation from Schiller's "Conspiracy of the Fiescoes in Genoa": "*Der Mohr hat seine Schuldigkeit getan, der Mohr konnte gehen.*"[34] The National Liberals reveled in the dispute in the Catholic camp which led to a permanent rupture between Cronenberg and the Catholic establishment.[35]

Aachen's Catholic notables were deeply concerned because Franz Eduard Cronenberg and his association threatened to reshape the political landscape. The Socialists were "completely wiped out." Cronenberg and his confrater Johannes Laaf entered Socialist assemblies and with their combination of dazzling rhetoric and practical policies managed to undermine electoral support for the Social-

---

[30] Lepper, "Cronenberg," p. 72.
[31] Not to be confused with Adolf Stöcker's Christian-Social Party.
[32] "Statuten des Arbeitervereins zum hl. Paulus in Aachen und Burtscheid" (January 1870) excerpted in Herbert Lepper, ed. *Sozialer Katholizismus in Aachen. Quellen zur Geschichte des Arbeitervereins zum hl. Paulus für Aachen und Burtscheid 1869-1878 (88)* (Mönchengladbach: B. Kühlen Verlag, 1977), pp. 5-6.
[33] Lepper, "Cronenberg," pp. 82-84; Kühne, *Handbuch der Wahlen*, pp. 789-92. The three candidates supported by Constantia were Friedrich Baudri, a painter and brother of the Cologne suffragan bishop, the writer Dr. Joseph Krebs and Andreas von Grand-Ry, a landowner in Eupen.
[34] "An unsere Gesinnungsgenossen," *Echo der Gegenwart* no. 304 I, 5 Nov. 1873 reprinted in Lepper, *Sozialer Katholizismus in Aachen*, pp. 44-45.
[35] Lepper, "Cronenberg," p. 84.

ists who in 1874 fielded a candidate for the first time. In the election that followed the Socialists attracted just forty-seven votes.[36] Their enemies from within the Catholic camp, however, were not as easily defeated as the local Socialists. The 1874 Reichstag election further polarized the Catholic factions in Aachen. Cronenberg became the candidate for the newly-founded "*katholische Volkspartei*"[37] (Catholic People's Party) and received almost a third of the votes (32.4%) in those local election districts which were inhabited primarily by skilled and unskilled workers and by small artisans.[38] When all votes had been counted, however, Friedrich Baudri, the Center candidate, was elected.

Cronenberg's political opponents, unable to diminish his influence with the workers, shifted the battleground. The first attack was a "denunciation" of Cronenberg by his superiors; as a result Cronenberg was "admonished" by Archbishop Melchers of Cologne. The second attack was aimed at the financial foundation of the building society. The largest mortgage was called.[39] In April 1877 a former member of the building society, Nellessen, filed a complaint at the local senior prosecutor (*Oberprokurator*), alleging fraud. Charges of sodomy were brought against him. Based on the testimony of one Boffin, a man of "doubtful mental capacity"[40] and evidence of misappropriation of funds, Cronenberg was found guilty and sentenced to two years in prison and the loss of civic rights (*bürgerliche Ehrenrechte*) for five years.[41] Contemporaries questioned the validity of these charges and with the passing of time these suspicions have not been removed. Whether Cronenberg was the victim of trumped up charges or whether there was truth behind the allegations is of less importance to the historian than the fact that his conviction spelled the end of his political activities, and the end of the Christian-Social movement as a political movement of significance; it continued to exist but was a mere shadow of its former self. None the less, Cronenberg had made two significant contributions to the organization of Catholic workers and political Catholicism. He provided a model for successful working-class organization which at least in Catholic regions promised to successfully compete with Socialism.

[36] Thun, "Industrie," 1:202; Schiffers, *Kulturkampf,* p. 152.
[37] Renamed Christian-Social Party in 1876.
[36] Lepper, "Cronenberg," pp. 88-9.
[39] Thun, "Industrie," 1:207; Lepper, "Cronenberg," p. 99.
[40] The allegation was that Cronenberg had violated the notorious §175 of the Criminal Code, Lepper, "Cronenberg," pp. 128-9,145.
[41] Ibid., p. 145.

The crucial elements were workers' participation in decision-making and the abandonment of patriarchial attitudes. In addition, Cronenberg's political party showed that workers could be attracted to the message of political Catholicism if the party responded to their needs. Cronenberg's message was too "democratic" his detractors claimed, and it instilled hopes and desires in workers which could not be realized.[42] However, workers needed some form of representation and the social question had to be addressed in some form lest they, the workers, would be lost to the intriguing lure of Social Democracy. In the eyes of many Center politicians and most clergy, workers' clubs were the most important vehicle for this ambition.

The ties between workers' clubs and Church were close. The leadership of the clubs, comprised mostly of priests, was paternalistic in its attitudes towards the workers. Franz Hitze saw workers as naive and uneducated; like children they were incapable of making their own decisions. Even the souls of those workers who marched behind the banners of Social Democracy were "naturally Christian": their hearts, he believed, were still open to the ideals of Christianity and humanity. They had been led astray by the educated bourgeoisie who had spread irreligion among the lower classes.[43] These notions were widespread. The Catholic writer Leonz Niderberger, for instance, wrote a short book entitled *Der sozialdemokratische Schnaps*,[44] in which he promised to answer the following allegorical questions:

1. What is Social Democratic liquor made of?
2. Who has distilled it?
3. Who serves it?
4. Who shall drink it?
5. What effect does it have?

Workers who had imbibed Socialist ideology were, in the eyes of Niderberger and probably of Hitze, just intoxicated by Socialist liquor and, once sober again, would return to the fold.

Catholic as well as Protestant workers' clubs were first founded in the early 1880s. In contrast to journeymen's associations and other charitable institutions, they concentrated on "'ordinary, employed, church-going workers," rather than "the helpless, poor or irreligious workers."[45] Worker's clubs accepted capitalism as the basis of indus-

---

[42] Cited in Lepper, ibid., pp. 71-2.

[43] "Rede des Generalsekretärs, Landtags und Reichstags-Abgeordneten Hitze," *Echo der Gegenwart* no. 207, 9 Sept. 1887.

[44] Advertisement for Niderberger's book in Leonz Niderberger, *Der Sozialdemokrat* (M. Gladbach: A Riffarth, 1891), p. 63.

[45] Mooser, "Arbeiter, Bürger und Priester," p. 81.

trial society—a departure from Catholic social and economic theories of the early nineteenth century. Politics, however, was still explicitly excluded from their programs, and unlike the Center, these associations were exclusively Catholic. They provided services such as savings banks and burial funds. Like the People's Association a decade later, the primary purpose of workers' clubs was the defense against secularization and particularly against Socialism. Workers should see themselves as soldiers, Karl Bachem once wrote, ready to fight Socialism; the reward for their commitment would be a solution of the social question.[46] They had to be true Christians, Karl Trimborn said at a founding meeting in Cologne. With the condescending tone that virtually always colors Center statements on workers, Trimborn demanded that Catholic workers be "upright, loyal employees a master can count on."[47] The primary task of workers' clubs was to "assert Catholic faith and religious beliefs."[48] Members participated in processions, church services and religious feasts. One of the highlights was an audience with Pope Pius X where a delegation, which included one miner and two craftsmen but no factory workers, assured the pontiff of the organization's "subservience to the Church...and its laws and principles."[49] With the end of anti-Socialist legislation in 1890 and the subsequent increase in Social democratic activities, the fight against "Socialist errors" became the main occupation of Cologne's workers' clubs.[50]

The founding of workers' clubs was vigorously promoted by Workers' Welfare (*Arbeiterwohl*)[51], an organization of Catholic industrialists founded in 1880 by Franz Brandts and dedicated to creating harmonious relations between employers and workers. Eventually, Brandts, Hitze and other Workers' Welfare leaders agreed on a threefold program: (1) to educate compliant Catholic workers for their work in trade unions, which unlike Cronenberg's Christian-

[46] "Katholische Arbeitervereine Köln-Süd und Köln-Nord," *CAF* no. 5, 26. Oct. 1890, reprinted in Broch, *Arbeitervereine*, pp. 31-2.

[47] Ibid., p. 32.

[48] Copy of letter to Cardinal-Secretary of the Pope, 20 February 1904 [signed by Count Hompesch, Dr. Schädler, Dr. Porsch, Dr. Dittrich, Hitze, Dr. Pichler, Dr. Bachem, Dr. Spahn, A. Fritzen, Gröber, Franz Prince Arenberg, Trimborn], HAStK Nl. Bachem 1006/215.

[49] "Eine Huldigung des Verbandes der katholischen Arbeitervereine (Sitz Berlin) für Pius X.," *Germania* no. 68, 23 March 1904.

[50] Broch, *Arbeitervereine*, p. 13*.

[51] In 1905 the organization changed its name from *Arbeiterwohl - Verband katholischer Industrieller und Arbeiterfreunde* to *Verband für soziale Kultur und Wohlfahrtspflege (Arbeiterwohl)*.

social movement would not antagonize the Catholic employers; (2) to promote the establishment of factory committees and welfare institutions; and (3) to "mollify opposition to Workers' Welfare's social reform proposals in government and parliamentary circles."[52] Brandts's initiative, reinforced by Hitze's call at the *Katholikentag* in Amberg (1884) to field "a well-armed, well-educated army of Christian workers" to combat atheist Socialist organizations, led to a significant growth in the number of workers' clubs. By the turn of the century, this message, with the endorsement of German bishops and the Pope had attracted about 450,000 members.[53]

Although the organizational structure of Catholic workers' clubs in Germany was uniform (e.g. priests chaired all chapters), there existed considerable differences among the various regions. Unfortunately, with the exception of Bavaria, our knowledge of regional organizations is sparse. What is clear is that the West German Catholic Workers Association (*Verband katholischer Arbeitervereine Westdeutschlands*) grew to be the largest and most influential with 220,290 members in 1912.[54] The strongest areas of this association were the dioceses of Münster, Paderborn and Cologne. The industrial Rhine-Ruhr region was also the strongest region of the Christian trade unions and the People's Association, reflecting the high degree of industrialization and the large number of Catholic workers in these areas.[55] When a central office for the workers' clubs of South, East and West Germany was established in 1911, such Rhenish leaders as August Pieper and Otto Müller (chairman and deputy-chairman of the West German Catholic Workers Association) were instrumental in creating it, and they occupied important offices in the new organization. Franz Hitze became its honorary chairman.[56]

---

[52] Brose, *Christian Labor,* pp. 63-4.

[53] Franz Hitze speech at Katholikentag at Amberg (1884), quoted in Hürten, *Geschichte,* pp. 165-66; Höffner, "Stellung," p. 611; for details on the founding of workers' clubs see Jürgen Aretz, "Katholische Arbeiterbewegung und christliche Gewerkschaften—Zur Geschichte der christlich-sozialen Bewegung," in *Der soziale und politische Katholizismus. Entwicklungslinien in Deutschland 1803—1963,* ed. Anton Rauscher (Munich: Günter Olzog Verlag, 1982), pp. 163-5.

[54] Mooser, "Arbeiter, Bürger und Priester," p. 84; Aretz, "Katholische Arbeiterbewegung," pp. 166-8.

[55] Ibid., p. 85.

[56] Protokoll der Gründungssitzung des Kartellverbands kath. Arbeitervereine West-, Süd- und Ostdeutschlands, Mainz 7 Aug. 1911, BAP 74VO1 Nr. 1445 f. 2-3; for a brief biographical sketch of Müler see Jürgen Aretz, "Otto Müller (1870-1944)," in *Zeitgeschichte in Lebensbildern. Aus dem deutschen Katholizismus des 19. und 20. Jahrhunderts,* ed. Jürgen Aretz, et al. (Mainz: Matthias-Grünewald-Verlag, 1979), 3:191-203.

The leadership of workers' clubs was rarely in the hands of workers. Indeed, even a significant segment of the membership could not be described as industrial workers. Slightly more than one-fifth (21% in 1913) of the membership of the West German Catholic Workers Association did not come from the working class.[57] Following the journeymen's association model, workers' clubs were headed by a *Präses* (chairman), always a priest appointed by the bishop. The *Präses* had a decisive voice in the selection of the board of directors. He not only chaired all discussions but also had to approve any presentations made by members. His vote was decisive when there was a draw and he had the right of veto on all decisions made by the board of directors.[58] Social and political activities of priests were subject to church approval. The Church reserved the authority to determine the kind of political work a priest did, it could dictate a particular interpretation (*Richtung*), and, should a priest not conform, the Church could send him to a parish where he could not be politically active.[59]

Like church authorities, Catholic employers were concerned about the political independence of workers and the containment of Socialism and "radical workers." Factory owners pronounced with a tone of memorable patriarchal arrogance that "more important than increasing wages according to natural laws [i.e., supply and demand] is the instruction and care employers give their workers to use wages in an economically and morally orderly manner." Even as members of workers' clubs, workers were less important for the success of the Catholic workers' movement than "the nobility, doctors, civil servants, merchants, landowners, [and] teachers" for it was their membership that assured "the recognition of our efforts."[60] When the workers' club "Köln-Süd" celebrated its first anniversary, its chairman, a chaplain, opened the proceedings with a passionate speech against the Social Democrats, denouncing them as "a small troupe of immigrants." He proudly announced that his club now had 1,030 members, including about ninety honorary members.[61] Honorary members, usually such stalwarts of bourgeois values as factory owners, civil servants, academics, and clergy, had a decisive role to play in

[57] Mooser, "Arbeiter, Bürger und Priester," p. 85.
[58] Broch, *Arbeitervereine*, p. 15*.
[59] Aus den Vorlesungen von P. Biederlack S. J. (Rom) 1907. Vom Vortragenden selbst korrigiert im Dezember 1909 (Innsbruck). Abschrift, BAP 74VO1 Nr. 143 f. 39-44.
[60] Gründungsaufruf des Verbandes "Arbeiterwohl" (1881), excerpted in Rüther, *Geschichte,* 2:213-5.
[61] "Katholischer Arbeiterverein Köln-Süd," *KV* no. 282/2, 11 Oct. 1886 reprinted in Broch, *Arbeitervereine*, pp. 9-16.

the founding of workers' clubs. Workers' clubs, Hitze hoped would "bridge the social chasm between property owners and worker;... on the common ground of Christian love, coldness of the heart would thaw."[62]

In Cologne the first workers' clubs were established in 1885, one in the south of the city, a second one in Deutz. The *Kölnische Volkszeitung* soon reported that the drive for members was quite successful. During the first month of their life the two *Vereine* combined attracted some 450 members. In Nippes and Kalk, workers' clubs had been founded, too, and the formation of one in Mühlheim was imminent.[63] Their by-laws were modeled on Franz Hitze's maxims (*Leitsätze*). In the Aachen region, workers' clubs were founded only when the SPD threatened to cut into the Center's dominance at the polls.[64]

As chapters of the Cologne People's Association grew in strength, workers' clubs there shifted the emphasis of their work toward the development of occupational skills, and the creation of professional pride geared toward the social betterment of workers.[65] Thus they emphasized the very goal Kolping had envisioned for his journeymen's association: the engendering of bourgeois values. This concept of workers' clubs was criticized sharply by chaplain Oberdörffer, who argued that the clubs could only pursue religious tasks because they lacked a social program. Workers' clubs concentrated on the edification of workers, emphasizing harmonious relations with their employers and the responsibilities as Germans in the empire. Dr. Otto Müller, secretary general of workers' clubs in the archdiocese of Cologne, declared at the 1906 *Katholikentag* in Essen that workers' clubs went beyond safeguarding the economic and religious interests of their members, they "served the general interest of the Fatherland."[66] Despite such statements, the leadership of the workers' club movement could not prevent their clubs from pursuing political goals similar to those of trade unions. Although men such as Franz Brandts explicitly excluded political questions from workers' club statute, eventually it became impossible to deny workers' clubs a political

[62] Franz Hitze, *Bedeutung und Aufgabe katholischer Arbeiter-Vereine* (1884), quoted in Mooser, "Arbeiter, Bürger und Priester," p. 89.
[63] "Zur Gründung der Kölner Arbeitervereine," *KV* no. 299, 30 Oct. 1885.
[64] Albert Eßer, *Wilhelm Elfes, 1884-1969: Arbeiterführer und Politiker* (Mainz: Matthias-Grünewald-Verlag, 1990), p. 19.
[65] Broch, *Arbeitervereine*, p. 14*.
[66] Anträge der 53. Generalversammlung der Katholiken Deutschlands in Essen 1906. Ausschuß II. Soziale Fragen, BAP 74VO 1 Nr. 18 f. 69.

dimension. The Kulturkampf, the famous papal encyclical *Rerum Novarum* (which in 1891 approved of Catholic workers' clubs), and the end of anti-Socialist legislation in the same year, contributed to their growth. As workers' clubs grew and spread regional organizations were established.[67] Unlike individual chapters they were organized according to regions not according to the borders of church provinces. Growing membership and competition with Socialist unions forced Catholic workers' clubs to abandon at least some of their ties to the church hierarchy.[68]

In addition to workers' clubs, Christian trade unions were established during the final years of the 1880s. Although we lack precise data, it seems safe to argue that workers' clubs were an important recruiting ground for Christian trade unions. A report on the Krefeld unions, for example, estimates that approximately three out of five unionists were also members of workers' clubs—one quarter of the membership of Krefeld's workers' clubs joined the union.[69]

The year 1899 marked a turning point for the history of German trade unions and the relationship between Catholic workers and their political and religious representatives. Until the establishment of the Christian trade unions at the Mainz Congress (May 1899), only textile workers, miners, and metal workers had been organized in local or regional Christian trade unions. The delegates to the first joint congress of Christian unions decided on the Mainz program (*Mainzer Leitsätze*) which was to govern their trade union. August Brust's *Gewerkverein Christlicher Bergarbeiter* (Association of Christian Miners), founded in 1894 provided a model for subsequent trade unions such those founded by Aachen's weaver's and factory workers in Bielefeld.[70] The Mainz program adopted most of the principles established by the *Gewerkverein*; most significantly its interdenominational character and its independence of all political parties.

Thus Christian trade unions were organized as a coalition of nationwide unions for each branch of industry and headed by a national federation (*Gesamtverband*). A twelve-member central commission had its seat in Berlin. Among other things, the commission was to publish a newspaper, the *Mitteilungen des Gesamtverbandes der*

---

[67] Vereinigung der katholischen Arbeitervereine Süddeutschlands (1891), Verband katholischer Arbeitervereine Westdeutschlands, Verband der katholischen Arbeitervereine Sitz, Berlin (1913).
[68] Hürten, *Geschichte*, p. 166.
[69] Statistik über die christlichen Gewerkschaften, die dem Bezirkskartell Krefeld angehören [n.d. 1914], BAP 74VO1 Nr. 143 f. 113.
[70] Aretz, "Katholische Arbeiterbewegung," pp. 170-1.

christlichen Gewerkschaften Deutschlands, first brought out on 15 April 1901.[71] The unions were interdenominational, with no formal ties to the Center and concerned only with the economic interests of their members. Their demands and means were similar to those of the Socialist free trade unions (*Freie Gewerkschaften*), for they too acknowledged the right to strike as the ultimate means in disputes with employers. This attitude made them for a time and in some places serious rivals of Socialist unions; they distanced themselves from Socialist revolutionary goals by declaring that "reforms should be achieved by constitutional means within the existing framework of society."[72] In the Rhineland, Christian trade unions "regained much of the ground lost to the free unions since the late 1870s."[73]

Attitudes toward strikes were not uniform among Christian trade unions, since each union handled labor conflicts individually. Many unions preferred the social partnership approach of the *Gewerkverein*. Stressing the common interests of workers and employers, they argued "that all efforts of the trade unions should be pervaded and carried by the spirit of reconciliation.... A strike must be the last resort and should only be applied when it promises to be successful."[74] However, employers were not at all enamored of the notion of social partnership. Christian trade union leaders "must have noted with real bitterness that the employers, particularly in the mining industry of the Ruhr, but also in the textile industry," refused to cooperate.[75] One would expect Christian trade unions to have been less aggressive than their Socialist counterparts. Michael Schneider, however, argues convincingly that the very opposite was true. Notwithstanding the difficulty in determining whether a strike is aggressive or defensive, Schneider shows that between the years 1903-1913, "aggressive actions clearly represent a higher proportion of the total number of strikes" for Christian than for Socialist unions. The reason for this, Schneider speculates, might be found in the controversy

---

[71] In 1905 its title was changed to *Zentralblatt der christlichen Gewerkschaften Deutschlands*.

[72] Ludwig Altenhöfer, *Stegerwald: Ein Leben für den kleinen Mann. Die Adam-Stegerwald-Story* (Bad Kissingen: Verlag für Politische Schriften, 1965), p. 22.

[73] Brose, *Christian Labor*, p. 131.

[74] *Geschichte und Entwicklung der Christlichen Gewerkschaften Deutschlands nebst Protokoll des III. christlichen Gewerkschaftskongresses zu Krefeld (26.-29. Mai 1901)* (Mönchengladbach, 1901), excerpted in Michael Schneider, "The Christian Trade Unions and Strike Activity," in *The Development of Trade Unionism in Great Britain and Germany, 1880-1914*, ed. Wolfgang J. Mommsen and Hans-Gerhard Husung (London: George Allen & Unwin, 1985), p. 284.

[75] Schneider, "Christian Trade Unions," p. 284.

between Christian trade unions and the Catholic Church, known as the *Gewerkschaftsstreit*.[76] Their interdenominational character and their (at least theoretical) approval of strikes, however, antagonized some of their Catholic brethren in the workers' clubs as well as many clergy. The workers' clubs with their headquarters in Berlin demanded that Christian trade unions be replaced by so-called *Fachabteilungen*, trade union arms of the strictly Catholic workers' clubs that denounced the strike as an illegitimate weapon against employers. Prevailing ecclesiastical norms clearly favored workers' clubs over trade unions. For years Centrists in favor of the trade unions thought it necessary to justify their existence to the Church.[77]

The political organization of women was a particularly difficult issue in a region dominated by Catholic mores and the view that women should not involve themselves in politics. The Center Party and Catholic clubs for women workers (*Arbeiterinnenvereine*) actively opposed any efforts to secure the franchise for women. Politically active Catholic women such as Barbara Graß were rare. Graß—an early activist in the Catholic women's movement who married the editor of the *Westdeutsche Arbeiterzeitung* and Center politician Joseph Joos—publicly called for women's right to vote. Catholic politicians made light of her demands by labeling her a suffragette.[78] Initially, clubs for women workers were headed by a directorate whose *Präses* were *not* priests appointed by the bishop. Hitze argued that this "democratic" constitution was dangerous. He cautioned that once such a constitution was established there was no way to make sure that chapters were headed by nuns: the club might "become dependent on women workers who have little or no education."[79]

Workers' clubs were more closely associated with the Church than with the Center. Priests in their function as chairmen exercised direct control over the clubs. The relationship between the *Präses* and their superiors, however, was by no means always a peaceful or harmonious one, for the ecclesiastical concerns of the hierarchy often contradicted the political methods and the economic and social

---

[76] Ibid.

[77] Copy of letter to Cardinal-Secretary of the Pope, 20 February 1904 [signed by Count Hompesch, Dr. Schädler, Dr. Porsch, Dr. Dittrich, Hitze, Dr. Pichler, Dr. Bachem, Dr. Spahn, A. Fritzen, Gröber, Franz Prince Arenberg, Trimborn], HAStK Nl. Bachem 1006/215.

[78] Wachtling, *Joseph Joos*, p. 12.

[79] Hitze to Sister G. v. Schaffgotsch, 17 Dec. 1904, HAStK Nl. Bachem 1006/217.

aims of many of the young and eager clergymen who were attracted to the workers' clubs. Some Center leaders, among them Ernst Lieber and the clergy (particularly Cardinal Kopp), preferred the confessional homogeneity and the close control they exercised over the workers' clubs to the interconfessional Christian trade unions. They feared that neither the Center nor the clergy could "keep the unions in line." Trimborn, for his part, remained an ardent and outspoken proponent of Christian trade unions.[80] In view of the success of Catholic workers' clubs and Christian trade unions, one must agree with Michael Schneider that the notion that "the industrial working class inevitably became alienated from the church" needs to be qualified.[81]

Still, workers' clubs found it increasingly difficult to attract workers. A close look at the textile workers and their organizations in Krefeld and Mönchengladbach illustrates these difficulties. Throughout the closing decade of the nineteenth century, various unions and workers' associations competed for the loyalty of textile workers in the Rhineland. The largest one was the *Verband der christlichen Textilarbeiter* with some 3,500 members in Mönchengladbach in 1900 (nationwide the membership was about 6,500).[82] Founded in December 1899, Mönchengladbach's was the most recent chapter of the organization in the Rhineland; chapters had already been founded in Aachen and Eupen (1897) as well as in Düren and Wipperfürth (1898). Probably more important as an incentive to establish a chapter in neighboring towns was the success of rival unions. Social Democrats had founded a union in Krefeld in 1898 and they had fought a successful struggle for higher wages there.[83]

August Pieper reported that in Mönchengladbach unrest among workers was largely caused by rising prices for food and rent. At the same time there was a shortage of labor which gave clout to demands for higher wages.[84] It was these circumstances and the Socialist threat that induced textile workers to demand that their Catholic workers' clubs be transformed into Christian trade unions. The clergy followed this course only reluctantly; there was "no argument on principle against the right of Christian workers to defend their economic

---

[80] Pieper to Cardauns, 12 Feb. 1904, BAP 74VO1 Nr. 143 f. 30.

[81] Schneider, "Religion and Labour Organization," p. 365.

[82] August Pieper, "Bericht über die Entwicklung und Thätigkeit der christlichen Arbeiterorganisationen im M. Gladbacher Industriebezirk," 1900, BAP 74VO1 Nr. 146 f. 2.

[83] Ibid., f. 2-3.

[84] Ibid., f. 5.

interests with legal means," nor did these priests fail to see the "dangers of Socialist agitation." The two clerics who led Mönchengladbach's workers' clubs expressed the hope that by permitting the founding of trade unions, they would be able to exercise a "moderating influence," avoid strikes and facilitate "peaceful negotiations" between factory owners and workers.[85]

In their rhetoric the clergy emphasized the fundamental differences they perceived between Socialist and Christian unions: they disapproved of Socialist tactics, namely strikes, attacked them for being unchristian and accused them of being unpatriotic.[86] As a consequence, much of the clergy's work occurred behind the scenes. After the establishment of the textile union in Mönchengladbach, the two clergy did not participate in public meetings or in so-called *Fabrikversammlungen*, assemblies of workers of one factory where a strike was going on. Other clergy in Mönchengladbach followed this example and rarely participated in public trade union meetings.[87] Initially, however, the Socialist union in Krefeld recruited at most some 2,000 members. Only when they founded the "allegedly impartial weavers' association of the lower-Rhine region [*Niederrheinischer Weberverband*] in order to lure away Christian workers" did the Socialists attract some 12,000 members. To counter such Socialist activities, a Christian textile union was founded in Krefeld (1898), but initially did not attract more than 800 workers. Thus, noted Pieper, they played little role in the great strike of Krefeld textile workers in 1898, a strike which was dominated by Socialist unions.[88]

Despite these early difficulties the Christian unions of the Niederrhein organized over 9,000 workers by 1900; the Socialist union by then had shrunk to a membership of 8,000.[89] On a national level, too, Christian trade unions gained a permanent foothold, that steadily grew. After Adam Stegerwald took over the General Secretariat (the National Organization of the German Christian Trade Unions) in Cologne on 1 January 1903, this institution expanded so rapidly that one can say the Christian Unions had been consolidated on a local, regional and national level by 1906.[90] The possession of a

[85] Ibid., f. 3-4.
[86] Ibid., f. 4.
[87] Ibid., f. 8.
[88] Ibid., f. 3; Heidemarie Kempkes, *Der christliche Textilarbeiterverband in Krefeld* (Wentorf b. Hamburg: Einhorn-Presse Verlag, 1979), pp. 22-3.
[89] Pieper, "Bericht," BAP 74VO1 Nr. 146 f. 4.
[90] Schneider, "Religion and Labour Organization," pp. 358-60.

national press, the creation of a web of union functionaries, the extensive system of insurance benefits, the steady increase in membership—all this was solid evidence of the viability of a Christian alternative to Socialist unions.

The success of Christian trade unions had important repercussions for the Center Party. Many Center politicians, particularly those in the Rhineland, belonged to the leadership of the workers' clubs and the Christian trade unions. These were the most important ties the Center had with Catholic workers. Through the unions and workers' clubs, Catholic workers had access to politicians who could and did represent their interests in the world of politics. The organizational and personal ties between Christian trade unions, workers' clubs, and the Center Party assured that interests of a significant segment of the working class achieved some form of political representation. Through workers' clubs and unions, political Catholicism found a means to prevent Catholic workers from defecting to the Socialist camp.

B. Center and Socialists

The battlefields for Center and Socialist activists were the press, the labor movement, the parliaments and of course the election campaigns which determined the strength of parties in the parliaments. There were three levels of elections in Imperial Germany: municipal elections, elections to the Landtage and elections to the Reichstag, the federal parliament. Reichstag elections were based on universal male franchise, all German men who had reached the age of twenty-four were entitled to vote. There were only a few exceptions to this rule: paupers, prisoners, and men deprived of their civil rights and soldiers could not vote. Compared to Great Britain and the United States where tax requirements and voluntary registration withheld the suffrage from substantial numbers of men of voting age, the numbers of German males "without civil rights were minuscule."[91] It was a direct and secret voting system in which the candidate with the absolute majority of votes went to the Reichstag. If in the first election no candidate gained a majority a run-off ballot between the two candidates with the most votes became necessary; such run-off elections often led to coalitions and back-room deals. Germans took their voting seriously, draped in sober black clothing German men of all classes performed their public duty, for them "voting was less like a

[91] Suval, *Electoral Politics*, pp. 21-2.

public festival and more like a visit to the post office."[92] What German voters lacked in cheerfulness they made up in determination. In 1871 fifty percent of eligible voters made use of their new political right, in the last two imperial elections the figure had risen to an impressive eighty-five percent. The Center, like other parties, used "*Schlepper*", literally draggers, to bring their supporters to the election offices. Cologne Centrists, on one occasion attended the funeral of a local farmer with the declared purpose of "dragging" the already appropriately attired funeral party to city hall where they could cast their vote.[93] The German electoral system also excelled in carrying out accurate, fair, and undistorted election results. German bureaucracies efficiently administered one of the most complex electoral systems in the world which increased "the prestige of the electoral system" among voters.[94] On paper the Reichstag franchise was among the most liberal in Europe. In practice it had some important limits. The government manipulated or rather refused to reform constituency borders which favored conservative and liberal parties and disadvantaged the growing Social Democratic Party. Already in the early decades of the empire constituency borders did not reflect Germany's economic and demographic changes, throughout the existence of the Kaiserreich constituency borders drawn in 1869 were never reformed. This handicapped city voters and especially parties that drew their strength from urban areas; as time went by this handicap grew ever greater. According to Stanley Suval, by 1912 at least five times as many votes were required in the industrial Ruhr to elect a representative than in the agrarian east of Prussia.[95] In the Rhineland, this bias worked in favor of the Center Party who drew much of its support from rural districts.

Unlike the Reichstag franchise the Prussian Landtag franchise was based on the ability to pay taxes. The Prussian tax-based three-class voting system disadvantaged workers even more than unreformed constituency borders. The differences in voting systems explain to a large degree why the SPD despite ever growing support did not win a Landtag mandate in the Prussian Rhine Province and why the Center was able to maintain its number of seats in both the provincial and federal parliaments. Similarly most municipal governments were elected under some form of limited franchise. Under these circumstances Socialists also found it difficult to gain seats on city councils.

[92] Ibid., pp. 3-4.
[93] Bachem, *Erinnerungen*, p. 60.
[94] Suval, *Electoral Politics*, p. 36.
[95] Ibid., pp. 40-1.

During the Kaiserreich they never received the number of seats equal representation would have afforded them.[96] Until about 1890 Catholic workers in Westphalia and the Rhineland voted primarily according to their religious denomination.[97] Catholic workers in the Ruhr area generally voted for Center candidates, while Protestant workers preferred liberal or, increasingly, SPD candidates. Once the SPD had been freed from the shackles of Bismarck's anti-Socialist legislation it became more difficult for Catholic and liberal politicians to attract workers. Centrists felt and dreaded the inroads the SPD made into working-class constituencies.

The Socialist movement in the Rhineland had its origins in the Vormärz. Germany's first Socialist, Moses Heß, inspired a Socialist group in Cologne which maintained close contact with Karl Marx in Brussels. The most important Rhenish Socialist organization, and the only one which had more than local significance was the Cologne *Arbeiterverein* founded by the charity physician Andreas Gottschalk.[98] The first Socialist German daily was the *Trierersche Zeitung*, once a liberal and one of the oldest Rhenish newspapers which abandoned its liberalism to become "as radically socialist as possible under [Prussian] censorship," as Friedrich Engels put it.[99] Rhenish Socialists also formed an important part of the *Allgemeine Deutscher Arbeiterverein* (ADAV) founded by Ferdinand Lassalle in May 1863. Five of the eleven cities represented at the founding convention in Leipzig were from the Rhein Province. When the charismatic Lassalle died of wounds received in a duel with the fiancé of his lover, his organization had only about 4,600 members.[100] The growth of the movement was severely hampered by anti-Socialist government measures. Attempts on the emperor's life by a twenty year-old plumber named Hödel on 9 May 1878 and by a Dr. Nobiling in June provided the pretext to dissolve the Reichstag and to begin the

---

[96] Ibid., pp. 31-2.

[97] Ulrich von Hehl, "Zum politischen Katholizismus in Rheinland-Westfalen 1890-1918," in *Rheinland-Westfalen im Industriezeitalter*, ed. Kurt Düwell and Wolfgang Köllmann (Wuppertal: Peter Hammer Verlag, 1984), p. 57.

[98] Sperber, *Rhineland Radicals*, p. 119, Dieter Dowe, "Organisatorische Anfänge der Arbeiterbewegung in der Rheinprovinz und in Westfalen bis zum Sozialistengesetz," in *Arbeiterbewegung an Rhein und Ruhr. Beiträge zur Geschichte der Arbeiterbewegung in Rheinland-Westfalen*, ed. Jürgen Reulecke (Wuppertal: Hammer, 1974), pp. 54-5.

[99] Cited in Dieter Dowe, "Die erste sozialistische Tageszeitung in Deutschland. Der Weg der 'Trierschen Zeitung' vom Liberalismus über den 'wahren Sozialismus' zum Anarchismus (1840-1851)," *Archiv für Sozialgeschichte* 12 (1972), p. 55.

[100] Dowe, "Organisatorische Anfänge," p. 69; Sheehan, *German History*, p. 886.

repression of the Socialist movement. A coalition of government and industrialists assailed the working class with a two-pronged attack aimed at their economic well-being and their political freedom. The district governor of Aachen, Hoffmann, informed his superior in Berlin:

> Everywhere I met the same deep disgust of the frightening monstrosities of Social Democratic teachings. I also found complete willingness and iron determination to fight the machinations of the Social Democrats in cooperation with the government, in the spirit of the decisions… made at the Düsseldorf congress of Rhenish and Westphalian industrialists and manufacturers.[101]

For a dozen years Socialists were prevented from organizing, meeting, and publishing newspapers. The Socialist Law was an even harsher restriction on the activities of Socialists than the Kulturkampf measures had been on Catholics. Like Catholic priests and nuns, Socialists were forced into exile. But again like the Catholic Church, Social Democracy employed a myriad of ingenious schemes to escape state repression. In regions where the early organization of the ADAV had blossomed, such as Cologne and the Ruhr region, there existed a clandestine organization to sustain the movement.[102] Because of the Socialist Law, during the 1870s and 1880s the Socialists created little worry for the Center Party. The National Liberals and the Progressives with their Kulturkampf rhetoric and their strength in Rhenish cities were still the most powerful political opponents of the Center but Liberal strength waned as the Center successfully organized the support of the Catholic middle class and even attracted workers and academics who closed Catholic ranks under the impact of the Kulturkampf.[103]

None the less, the SPD achieved respectable results in the Reichstag elections of the 1870s and more importantly supported a wave of strikes that troubled employers and government.[104] The strikes were not just supported and initiated by the Socialists, Catholic priests played an important role, too. Even political alliances between Socialists and radical priests were possible, as shown by the Catholic metal worker Gerhard Stötzel who ran for the Christian Social Party

---

[101] Cited in Lademacher, "Rheinlande," p. 623.
[102] Lademacher, "Rheinlande," pp. 624-5.
[103] Cardauns, *Leben*, pp. 157-8.
[104] 1877: 9.1% of the vote and 12 seats; 1878 7.6% and 9 seats.

in the district Düsseldorf-Essen and was elected with the support of the Socialist in the run-off election.[105] Despite severe restrictions the Socialists managed to win a number of districts in the Rhineland. In Düsseldorf-Elberfeld the weaver Friedrich Harm was elected for the SPD as member of the Reichstag (the SPD held the mandate until 1907 and won it back from the Free Conservatives in 1912). Harm was also among the ninety-one Socialists who were prosecuted at the so-called Elberfelder *Geheimbund-Prozeß*, the last of the great court cases based on the Socialist Law. The parallels between the Kulturkampf and the Socialist Law are obvious, less clear is the relationship between Socialists and Centrists. On the surface there was no common ground between the proponents of two opposing ideologies. In daily political life, however, Catholic social advocates, such as the priest Eduard Cronenberg and Socialists shared many notions about the workers' question. It was the issue of the political allegiance of workers, and above all of Catholic workers that troubled the Center for the duration of the Kaiserreich.

When it came to the workers' question, the most difficult issue for Catholic politicians was that of strikes. Convinced of the preferability of mediation and harmonious relations between management and workers (an approach pursued with considerable success by the government of the former Centrist Konrad Adenauer after World War II), the Center, Catholic workers' clubs and the People's Association lost the support of workers who flocked to the combative Free Unions and who were backed by the SPD. A wave of strikes initiated by Social Democrats involving some 90,000 miners brought the mining industry of the Ruhr to a standstill in May 1889. In Silesia, Saxony and the Saar region miners went on strike to demonstrate sympathy for their fellow miners of the Ruhr. In the wake of these strikes Rhenish Socialists organized a successful Miners Union (*Bergmännischer Interessenverband*) which quickly acquired a large membership; the Catholic counterpart folded after only two years with a disappointing response by Catholic miners. The government's reply to the strikes had as little impact on workers as that of the Center. Against the advice of Bismarck, who counseled radical measures against workers, the young emperor steered a conciliatory course, arguing that strikes and confrontations can be avoided by compromises on wages and working conditions. The defeat of the Socialist Law and the Kaiser's promises to hold an international conference on

---

[105] Stötzel joined the Center caucus. He lost his seat to Friedrich Krupp in 1893 but won it back five years later.

workers' protection (*Februarerlasse*) could not prevent the soaring of Socialist fortunes in the next election. Reflecting on the strike wave and the actions of the government August Bebel, the Cologne-born leader of the SPD, believed that: "The main focus for the next Reichstag election is Rhineland and Westphalia. If I am not mistaken we shall get a substantial number of votes the next time around."[106] August Bebel's assessment proved correct. Nationally, the Socialists almost doubled their share of the popular vote (1887: 763,000; 1890: 1,427,000) and increased their number of seats from eleven to thirty-five. The results of the 1890 Reichstag election were genuinely alarming to the Center Party. The Kartell parties which had provided Bismarck with a majority for his policies in the Reichstag lost their majority (they were reduced from 220 to 135 seats).

Before the chancellor was driven out of the office he had held for almost three decades he attempted to destroy parliament by military force. In the end the emperor, the National Liberals and the Conservatives rejected Bismarck's coup d'état and preserved the Reichstag. Bismarck's last, desperate attempt to stay in power was a bid to construct a coalition with a long-standing adversary, the Center Party. In clandestine discussions with Ludwig Windthorst of which even Wilhelm II had not been informed, Bismarck tried to form a parliamentary majority. The conversation between the two archenemies could not bridge their differences and provided the Kaiser, who detested Windthorst and resented the chancellor's indiscretion, with one more reason to force Bismarck out of office.

Initially Socialist gains at the polls did not translate into lost Reichstag seats for the Center Party. Because constituency borders favored rural areas (Center strongholds) and disadvantaged urban, industrialized regions (Socialist strongholds), the Center could actually increase the number of seats it held from 98 to 106. It was now the largest party in parliament although it had suffered a hurtful loss in the popular vote (1887: 1,516,000; 1890: 1,342,000).[107] In the Rhineland, the Center did not actually lose any seats to the Socialists in the election of 1890, but Rhenish Center politicians were painfully aware of the threat to their constituencies. Trimborn attributed Reichstag election losses to industrialization, the accompanying in-

---

[106] August Bebel to Friedrich Engels, cited in Lademacher, "Rheinlande," p. 625.

[107] Unless noted otherwise election results have been taken from Gerhard A. Ritter, *Wahlgeschichtliches Arbeitsbuch: Materialien zur Statistik des Kaiserreichs 1871-1918* (Munich: Verlag C. H. Beck, 1980), p. 40.

flux of "alien elements," and the cooperation of National Liberals and Socialists during run-off ballots.[108]

Socialist agitation did not cease after the election campaign. The Düsseldorf government noted that the SPD increased its political activities. In Düsseldorf, Elberfeld and Krefeld the SPD founded industrial associations (*gewerbliche Vereinigungen*) and staged several mass rallies. At the same time the Prussian government noted that the SPD had toned down its revolutionary rhetoric. Its local newspapers as well as its public speakers seemed to follow the moderate policies agreed upon by their national leaders in the Erfurt Program of October 1890. Not all these activities were successful. The proclamation of a general "labor day" on 1 May found little resonance in the Düsseldorf district—almost nowhere was work interrupted. The Socialists' success at the polls and their increased activities also triggered new activities from their political opponents. The last Reichstag election led to several run-off ballots between Center and SPD candidates. That was a warning to the Center which responded by publishing a new Catholic paper *Der Arbeiter* (The Worker) which focused on the concerns of the Rhenish working class and also founded a new "*Verein der Zentrumspartei*" in Düsseldorf. [109] The Peoples' Association founded new branches in several cities of the Rhineland to join the fight against the SPD. All this activity added up to continuous campaigning (*Wahlagitation*), a significant change from the politics of notables carried out by Constantia.[110]

In contrast to their relative success in the cities of the Düsseldorf district, the SPD was unable to make any inroads in the countryside where "the influence of the clergy and the Center Party was still absolutely dominant." The larger farmers of the area—committed supporters of the Center—had enough influence to control the political behavior of their economically dependent farm hands. A demonstration of the SPD's difficulties to find support in the Rhineland's rural areas was a Socialist rally in the district of Kempen. There Socialist organizers brought some 250 non-residents to a local meeting to show their strength—they were joined by just two local rural workers. The SPD also organized meetings especially to address the problems of female workers which featured female speakers; they, too, found little

---

[108] Cardauns, *Trimborn*, p. 96.

[109] Verwaltungsbericht für das II. Vierteljahr 1890, Düsseldorf 15 Aug. 1890. HStaD Regierung Düsseldorf Präsidialbüro Nr. 23 f. 20-1.

[110] Verwaltungsbericht für das IV. Vierteljahr 1890, Düsseldorf 14 March 1891. HStaD Regierung Düsseldorf Präsidialbüro Nr. 23 f. 90.

resonance in the Catholic parts of the Rhineland.[111] However, the SPD was not put off by the initially disappointing response to their efforts to attract local woman workers. The party intensified its efforts and brought in more women speakers (*Wanderrednerinnen*) and eventually government reports spoke of undeniable successes.[112] The Evangelical workers' clubs were more successful than the Socialist in attracting women. They were particularly strong in Elberfeld, Barmen, Vohwinkel, Lennep, Radevormwald, Langenberg, Solingen. The government report noted with relief that they, too, helped to keep the Social Democrats in check.[113] After the election of 1890, political activities in the Rhineland markedly increased. In most urban and industrial constituencies a sharp rivalry between the SPD and the Center Party had developed which dominated future political battles.

The legislative period came to its natural end in 1898. The Center Party's election program hardly mentioned workers and their concerns; there was only a brief reference to the Center's regrets for the lack of progress concerning social reforms. Enemies of the Center were to be found on two fronts: Liberals and Conservatives whose enmity towards the Church and one-sided politics of interest threaten to resurrect the Kulturkampf measures, and the "hatred of religion [*Glaubenshaß*] and the delusions [*Wahnideen*]" of Social Democrats.[114]

When Karl Bachem reflected on the Center's situation after the elections it was the failing health of Center leaders and not the waning support of Catholic workers that was foremost on his mind.[115] He was somewhat justified in his focus on internal developments of the party since the Center had posted a six-seat gain and now held 102 Reichstag mandates. Two of these six seats were Rhenish mandates won back from the Free Conservatives (Essen) and the Conservative Party (Mörs-Rees). In Essen the industrialist and personal friend of the emperor Friedrich A. Krupp was defeated by the Catholic metal worker Gerhard Stölzel. Stölzel had lost his seat to Krupp at the previous election.

---

[111] Verwaltungsbericht für das IV. Vierteljahr 1890, Düsseldorf 14 March 1891. HStaD Regierung Düsseldorf Präsidialbüro Nr. 23 f. 89.
[112] Verwaltungsbericht für das I. Vierteljahr 1892, Düsseldorf 13 June 1892. HStaD Regierung Düsseldorf Präsidialbüro Nr. 23 f. 239.
[113] Verwaltungsbericht für das IV. Vierteljahr 1890, Düsseldorf 14 March 1891. HStaD Regierung Düsseldorf Präsidialbüro Nr. 23 f. 90.
[114] "Wahlaufruf 1898" reprinted in Bergsträsser, *Katholizismus*, 2:302-6.
[115] Bachem notes, 26 Oct. and 1 Dec. 1900, HAStK Nl. Bachem 1006/90.

Karl Trimborn won his seat in Cologne for the first full legislative period. He was first elected to the Reichstag in a by-election in 1896 after the death of his Center colleague *Landgerichtsrat* Adolf Greiß. But Karl Trimborn had faced a tougher competition than in the previous election. In the by-election 1896 he had still won an absolute majority of votes in the first election, in 1898 a run-off ballot against the Socialist candidate was necessary to secure his seat. According to Hermann Cardauns, editor of the *Kölnische Volkszeitung*, two developments favored the SPD. First, municipalities which had been incorporated into the city of Cologne remained for the purpose of Reichstag elections within the boundaries of the election district Köln-Land: these municipalities, located in the west of the city had been Center strongholds. Second, Cologne had experienced an enormous growth of heavy industry with a swelling of the Socialist ranks.[116]

The outcome of the election changed little in the Reichstag. The Center politician Graf von Ballestrem became the new president of the Reichstag, an office he occupied until December 1906. The Center again was the strongest faction (followed by the SPD caucus) and therefore could maintain its pivotal position in German politics. Without its support no legislation could pass, neither a majority on the left nor the right of parliament was possible without Center backing. In his personal notes and in his history of the party, Karl Bachem hardly mentions the gains the Socialists had made. To him the declining health of the leading Centrists and the Center's key role in forming parliamentary majorities were of greater importance than the competition of the Socialists.[117] The weakness of the Center in Rhenish working-class ridings again became apparent in a by-election in the district of Duisburg-Ruhrort-Mühlheim. The National Liberal member of parliament Theodor Möller had been appointed Minister of Trade and therefore had to vacate his seat. In an analysis of the Center defeat in the by-election the *Arbeiter-Zeitung* offered two explanations. The Center candidate, a railway worker named Molz, faced the opposition of determined anti-Catholic sentiment from the National Liberals and the Socialists, an "Ultramontane agitation" in Karl Bachem's words. In this climate of "infernal hatred [*infernaler Haß*]" the Socialists doubled their vote. The National Liberals, backed by employers who put pressure on dependent workers and salaried employees (*Angestellte*) carried the district in the end. The second reason for the Center's failure was its lack of effort and

---

[116] Cardauns, *Leben*, pp. 168-9.
[117] KB, 6:3-4; Bachem notes, 26 Oct. 1900, HAStK Nl. Bachem 1006/90.

organization. As in other industrial election districts, "better organization" and a "radical revamping" of campaign work was necessary. Crucial to reaching Christian workers was the People's Association, a fact ignored by many priests and politicians who paid no attention to the frequent "pleading" and the constant reminder of the consequences of the absence of local chapters of the Association.[118] Organization was an agnostic in the holy wars of party politics. Local party organizers, coordination between press and party, between voluntary associations, unions, interests groups and politicians were imperative for success at the polls, no matter which ideology they served. Karl Trimborn, of course, realized the importance of organization and his reforms went a long way to making the Center more competitive with the Socialists. Ironically, he lost his own Reichstag seat in 1912 to a coalition of National Liberals and Socialists in a run-off ballot.

After a bitterly fought campaign in the late spring of 1903, during which the Center again perceived itself to be simultaneously attacked by Liberals and Socialists, the SPD increased its number of seats from fifty-six (1898) to eighty-one.[119] The central issue on which the Socialists fought the campaign was the Tariff Bill the Reichstag had passed in December 1902 against the SPD's protracted and vehement opposition. From the very first reading of the bill in the Reichstag, Rhenish Centrists had realized that a successful Tariff Bill would pose a problem to their efforts to retain the working-class vote. Martin Spahn suggested that some of the revenue generated by the new tariff be used "to improve living conditions of the working class and to compensate them for higher food prices brought about by higher tariffs."[120] In the end, such Center suggestions did not find their way into the legislation and Center deputies voted for the bill—although those from Bavaria (concerned about the effects of high tariffs on barley for beer breweries) and the Rhineland (aware of the repercussions on Catholic workers) did so only reluctantly.[121] Karl Bachem felt uneasy about elections fought on economic issues. When the Canal Bill threatened to lead to the dissolution of the Reichstag in 1901, Bachem feared that an election with the Canal Bill as its main theme would soften Center support and divide the party.[122]

[118] "Die Reichstagswahl in Duisburg-Ruhrort-Mühlheim," *Arbeiter-Zeitung* no. 32, 10 August 1901.
[119] KB, 6:186-7.
[120] KB, 6:148.
[121] Zeender, *Center Party*, 88; KB, 6:150-3.
[122] K. Bachem notes, [June] 1899, HAStK Nl. Bachem 1006/105.

Better to fight an election on ideological, religious issues bound to unite Catholic voters and their representatives from the various regions and classes than risk the division of Center support by economic interest groups. When Center leaders discussed the 1903 election program, Bachem opposed Gröber's suggestion to make detailed economic demands. While such tactics were opportune in Gröber's small Württemberg "with its essentially homogeneous [economic] interests and attitudes," they would not fare well as a national election platform, which had to be designed to accommodate the Reich's "large disparities."[123] Local issues could nonetheless be addressed through supplementary means, as additions to the Center's Reichstag election program. Julius Bachem wrote a draft of the additions for the Rheinland which were presented to important Rhenish Centrists for approval.[124]

The election program bemoaned the "difficult economic conditions of the day"and the growing disparity between the various occupations and classes. Publicly, the Center tried to put as good a face as possible on its relatively poor showing in the 1903 election. Even before run-off ballots had decided the final composition of the Reichstag, it was obvious that the SPD had made "enormous gains." An article in the *Kölnische Volkszeitung* assured Catholic readers that Socialist gains had been achieved mainly at the expense of liberal candidates, concurring with the view of a liberal paper that the election results were the requital for the Tariff Bill. Given these circumstances, the article went on, the Rhenish Center had not fared badly. The Agrarian League had not been able to attract any significant number of Center voters. Similarly, the Socialists had made no inroads into Center ridings. Only two ridings were lost to the SPD: a seat in Silesia (Reichenbach-Neurode) which the Center had won by a small margin in the 1898 election, and Bielefeld-Wiedenbrück, a Westphalian riding with a Protestant majority. This loss was more than made up, the *Kölnische Volkszeitung* argued, by the Center victory over a National Liberal candidate in the Trier district of Ottweiler-St. Wendel.[125]

A few days before the run-off elections, *Germania* published a list of statistics from eighty-eight Reichstag ridings to demonstrate the "great increases in votes the Center had made." According to

---

[123] K. Bachem to J. Bachem, 15 Apr. 1903, HAStK Nl. Bachem 1006/193.

[124] K. Bachem to Prälat Hülskamp, 15 Apr. 1903, HAStK Nl. Bachem 1006/193.

[125] "Nach den Wahlen vom 16. Juni," *KV* no. 508, 18 June 1903.

these tabulations, nearly 240,000 more voters had opted for the Center in 1903 than in the previous election.[126] When investigated closely, however, *Germania's* claim actually turns the election results on their head. The newspaper article compared absolute numbers of voters without taking into account the increased number of eligible voters in 1903 and the significantly higher participation rate over 1898. For example, *Germania* statistics show that for the five ridings in the Aachen district, 81,649 votes were cast for the Center in 1903, roughly 18,000 more than in 1898. The Center share of the vote, however, slipped from 92.3 percent to 88 percent. Admittedly, such a decline in no way threatened Center dominance locally, but it indicated a trend which was much more serious in other ridings and which Catholic papers also attempted to veil.

A look at the district of Cologne shows that the Center had reason to be worried. Again the *Germania* statistics showed a healthy increase in Center voters. Yet a comparison of the Center's share of the vote indicates a decline of four percentage points. Moreover, it seems that the Center did have difficulty in attracting new voters. While the number of voters in the Cologne district grew by about 46,000 between 1898 and 1903, the Center could only attract about 50 percent of them, well below their share of the total vote. This trend continued. In 1907 the Center share shrank to 58.9 percent, in 1912 it fell further to 57.7 percent. As well, much to the surprise of Trimborn and his political friends in 1912, the Rhenish party leader lost his own seat in Cologne to the Socialist candidate. The party, said Hubert Sittard (the Center deputy for Aachen), was "struck dumb by this loss."[127] It is true that the Center did not lose its strong position in the Reichstag after the election of 1903, 1907 or even 1912. But it is also true that it was not the "unconquerable tower" Center propagandists made it out to be. The cracks in Center defenses had become visible.[128]

In Prussian Landtag elections the Center was helped by the three-class voting system which severely handicapped voters with lower incomes and parties which represented them. The principle governing elections to the Prussian House of Deputies (Landtag) and municipal elections was the notion that he who pays more taxes should have more political rights. This election system divided the elector-

---

[126] "Zunahme der Centrumsstimmen," *Germania* no. 141, 24 June 1903.
[127] Sittard to Trimborn, 22 Jan. 1912, HAStK Nl. Trimborn 1256/200 f. 37.
[128] Quotation from "Nach den Wahlen vom 16. Juni," *KV* no. 508, 18 June 1903.

ate into three groups each entitled to vote for the same number of electors or municipal councilors. The first class, composed of the richest citizens, was the one with the largest political influence and the highest participation rate in elections.[129] Because of Prussia's plutocratic franchise the SPD did not win any Landtag seats until 1908. In Prussia the Rhenish Center succeeded in maintaining its support at the polls throughout the Kaiserreich. After the Prussian Landtag election of 1879 the Center never held fewer than forty-three of the sixty-two seats from the Rhine Province. In 1908 they had forty-seven seats.[130] This seeming stability, however, hides the diminishing share of voters the Center was able to attract. In 1898 over sixty percent (61.3) of the votes were cast for the Center. By 1913 this share had shrunken to 52.1 percent. Center support from the first two classes remained relatively stable, fluctuating between a high of 57.7 in 1898 and a low of 52.9 percent in 1903. In the third class, however, which had grown dramatically because of tax reforms, the Center lost ground to the growing success of the SPD.[131] In 1898 the SPD was able to attract only 3.6 percent of voters in the third class; this had grown to 20.7 percent by 1913. But because of the three-class voting system these gains were never translated into mandates. Differences existed between rural and urban districts. In those predominately rural the Socialists made no or little headway. In Cologne-Land (WK 250), for instance, the SPD was able to gain 12.1 and 17.6 percent in the second and third class respectively in 1908, only to fall back to 0.5 and 4.4 percent in the next election. It appears that participation declined because Socialist voters were discouraged by the futility of voting in a district where Center victory was all but guaranteed.

In districts with a Protestant majority (e. g. Lennep-Solingen, WK 254), which traditionally had been dominated by the liberal parties the Socialists were able to make significant inroads into the second and third voting class. These gains of the SPD did not always come at the expense of the Center. In Cologne (WK 249), for example, the Socialists increased their share of the third class vote from 10 percent in 1903 to 33.7 percent in 1913. The Center share, on the other hand, only fell from 67.8 to 64.1 percent. The growth of

---

[129] Gunnar von Schuckmann, "Die politische Willensbildung in der Großstadt Köln seit der Reichsgründung im Jahre 1871" (Ph. D. thesis, Universität Köln, 1965), p. 118.

[130] The number of delegates from the Rhineprovince increased to 63 in 1908.

[131] In 1903 177,713 voters voted in the third class, the number swelled to 345,503 in 1908.

the Socialists in urban areas can most reasonably be explained by their ability to attract newly enfranchised voters. However, various coalitions of Left Liberals, National Liberals, Conservatives and the Center were formed to keep the Socialists from gaining a seat.[132]

Rhenish Centrists acknowledged, and even exaggerated, the importance of party organization in winning elections. Ironically, this mirrored SPD perceptions about their own party's organizational strength. Trimborn, who had realized the importance of thorough organization earlier than most Center politicians, had begun to remedy this fatal weakness of his party—but the Socialists seemed to be always a step ahead. The keys to Socialist election success were tight, uniform organization and the party's impressive financial resources. If we can believe Center estimates, Social Democrats outdid them by a large margin. Membership dues of the Cologne SPD alone were calculated to be nearly 33,000 marks in 1910; the district of Düsseldorf had contributed more than 188,000 marks to Socialist party coffers. In sharp contrast, the total funds raised by the Center in all five districts of the Rhine Province was about 13,000 marks. Thus Socialists could afford to mount impressive propaganda campaigns. In the lower-Rhine party district (which was almost congruent with the administrative district of Düsseldorf), Socialists staged some twenty-six hundred meetings and distributed well over two million pamphlets in 1909-10. National Liberals, the Center lamented, also raised more money than they did, relying largely on contributions from industrialists and by asking supporters to place advertisements in liberal newspapers.[133]

In order to stem the Socialist onslaught, Center politicians tried to convince workers that "satisfactory social conditions" could be achieved in the "state of the present [*Gegenwartstaat*]"; there was no need to wait "for a wild revolution and the coming of the "state of the future [*Zukunftsstaat*]."[134] While Socialist promises might not have tempted Karl Bachem, they did impress working-class voters. The Center tried to respond to the Socialist threat by fielding workers as candidates. But this was not always easy, as the 1908 Prussian Landtag election in Aachen illustrates. Because Viktor Rintelen, the eighty-three year old Center deputy of the riding of Aachen-Land, was not expected to run again for elected office, Centrists speculated about a possible successor at a party meeting in Aachen on 23 April

---

[132] Kühne, *Handbuch der Wahlen*, p. 719.
[133] "Welche finanziellen Opfer bringen unsere Gegner für ihre Parteizwecke?" *Mitteilungen der Zentralstelle der Rheinischen Zentrumspartei* no. 1 (July 1911), p. 5.
[134] KB, 5:92.

1908. The best successor for Rintelen, they agreed, was Franz Kaufmann, a parish priest in nearby Stolberg. A few members also mentioned the possibility of fielding a working-class candidate.[135] Kaufmann had alienated some Centrists by attaching a condition to his nomination. He would only run if his candidacy was backed by Cardinal Fischer's "expressed desire" for his candidacy. Some Centrists interpreted this announcement as a "grateful rejection" since they found it inconceivable that the Center, "a political party, which when purely political questions are concerned is independent of the Church," could bow to the cardinal's wishes.[136] At the same meeting it was agreed that the incumbents for the ridings of Aachen-Stadt (Alfons Klausener, mayor of Burtscheid) and Eupen (Hubert Sittard, teacher at a Volksschule) would run again.[137] When party officials met next, Rintelen had officially declared that he would retire from politics. But during this meeting the supporters of a working-class candidate voiced their opinions more forcefully. A stand-off was in the making between Kaufmann and their candidate, a trade unionist from Borbeck (Essen), named Hermann Imbusch.[138]

The central election committee met again in Aachen in order to decide on its candidates for the upcoming election. Sittard, Klausener, and Imbusch were chosen with 128, 118 and 105 votes respectively. The priest Dr. Kaufmann finished a distant fourth with only 36 votes. It seemed that the matter had been decided in favor of the working-class candidate from Essen. However, the Landtag election committee overturned the Aachen results. At its meeting in Karlsruhe Kaufmann received more votes than Sittard. A rift had developed between the delegates from the predominantly rural districts of Aachen-Land and Eupen, who favored the clergyman, and delegates from the city of Aachen who had cast their vote for the trade unionist and thus left Sittard just eleven votes short of defeating Kaufmann.[139]

The unexpected defeat of Sittard triggered an immediate protest in Aachen. The Center daily *Aachener Volksfreund* was flooded by

[135] Police President of Aachen (Hammacher) to District Governor of Aachen (von Sandt), 24 April 1908, HAStD Regierung Aachen/710, f. 225.

[136] "Die Kandidatenfrage im Aachener Wahlkreis," *Aachener Volksfreund* no. 117, 19 May 1908.

[137] Police President of Aachen (Hammacher) to District Governor of Aachen (von Sandt), 24 April 1908, HAStD Regierung Aachen/710, f. 225.

[138] Police President of Aachen (Hammacher) to District Governor of Aachen (von Sandt), 9 May 1908, HAStD Regierung Aachen/710, f. 261-2; Kühne, *Handbuch der Wahlen*, p. 791.

[139] Police President of Aachen (Hammacher) to District Governor of Aachen (von Sandt), 13 May 1908, HAStD Regierung Aachen/710, f. 263.

letters to the editor in favor of Sittard and published an article it had received from a Center veteran.[140] Despite efforts of provincial party leaders to keep the dissension within the party, supporters of Sittard charged publicly that "irregularities" in the voting process were responsible for Kaufmann's nomination. The election committee of the parish of St. Jakob in Aachen filed an official protest and demanded that a new vote take place.[141] Eventually Klausener, Imbusch, and Kaufmann were elected. Sittard, who also held a seat in the Reichstag, had voluntarily given up his candidacy in favor of the working-class candidate. There was no discussion about candidates in 1913 and the three incumbents ran again and were elected.[142]

This episode shows that Trimborn's new organization worked to a considerable degree. The very dispute over Kaufmann's candidacy indicates how the party had changed. No longer was this a decision made by a few notables in the backrooms of party power, but subject to open and vigorous debate. The fielding of candidates was decided by local and regional party organizations, not by the party leadership alone. However, this episode also illustrates that some problems cannot be solved by good organization alone. New party organs, such as the elections committees, offered no immediate solution to the tensions that existed among the many social and economic interests united under the umbrella of the Center Party. At the root of the dispute over Franz Kaufmann's nomination was the antagonism between rural and urban Center supporters. This antagonism was one of the fundamental dilemmas the Rhenish Center faced and remained basically unresolved during the Kaiserreich. Lastly, this episode also shows that the Center was capable of solving the dispute over the nomination, if not the underlying conflict between city and village. Sittard's withdrawal from the contest was a shrewd political maneuver that brought to an end a conflict that might have split the Center in the Aachen district.

Despite the success of the Rhineland Center in winning seats, the central fact of the history of Imperial Germany's elections remains the continuous growth of the Social Democratic Party. In the long run, the Center found it increasingly difficult to retain the alle-

[140] "Die Kandidatenfrage im Aachener Wahlkreis," *Aachener Volksfreund* no. 117, 19 May 1908.
[141] Police President of Aachen (Hammacher) to District Governor of Aachen (von Sandt), 10 June 1908, HAStD Regierung Aachen/710, f. 42.
[142] Police President of Aachen (Hammacher) to District Governor of Aachen (von Sandt), 21 April 1913, HAStD Regierung Aachen/711, f. 313; Kühne, *Handbuch der Wahlen*, p. 791.

giance of Catholic workers. Between 1903 and 1912 the Center share of votes in Reichstag elections decreased from nearly fifty percent of the Rhineland vote to thirty-four percent. Even more troublesome was the overall decline in the number of Catholics who were willing to vote for the Center. Roughly four out of five (80.5 percent) of all eligible Catholic voters in the Rhineland cast their vote for the Center in 1890. By 1912 this proportion had shrunk to three out of four (74.1 percent).[143] Comparing national election results of 1874 with those of 1907, Karl Rohe observes a similar trend: the Center's share of the vote had declined by about ten percentage points—a third of its original share of the vote.[144] But Rohe also cautions us to take into account that the absolute number of voters who chose the Center grew from 1.4 million (1874) to almost 2.2 million (1907), well in keeping with population growth and the increased number of eligible voters.[145] Thus the story of electoral success or failure and of Socialist inroads into Center support is not as straightforward as some statistics suggests. Indeed, the SPD was successful in attracting an increasing number of Catholic workers. At the same time, however, this success was not sufficient to dislodge the Center from most of its traditional strongholds. It stands to reason that religion played an important role in explaining the success of the Center Party in Germany at large, and particularly in the industrialized regions and cities of the Rhineland.

Commentators and politicians, even some theologians, were predicting the death of God. As society became more urban and more industrial it would become less religious; social and political behavior would be based on secular notions of the public good, not on divine decrees. Such predictions notwithstanding, religion continued to have a hold on large sections of German society. Even those who had turned their back on the Catholic Church in favor of the Socialist movement were troubled by questions of faith. Wilhelm Reimes, for example, a textile worker from a village near Kempen who later became a SPD member of the Reichstag thought the struggle to overcome his religious perturbations the greatest challenge of his conversion to Socialism. And even after he ceased to attend church services and severed his ties with the Church he did not embrace

---

[143] Johannes Schauff, *Das Wahlverhalten der deutschen Katholiken im Kaiserreich und in der Weimarer Republik: Untersuchungen aus dem Jahre 1928*, ed. Rudolf Morsey (Mainz: Matthias-Grünewald-Verlag, 1975), pp. 80, 88.
[144] Rohe, *Wahlen*, p. 99.
[145] Ibid.

atheism, still considering himself a religious man.[146] Indeed, Catholics were much less likely than Protestants to abandon their faith for agnosticism or atheism.[147] The great wave of apostasy allegedly generated by Socialist agitators during the years 1906 to 1914 affected mainly the Protestant church.[148] Ultimately responsible for this wave of atheism was not Socialism but Liberalism. Liberal Manchesterism had undermined the foundations of Christian society according to most Centrists.[149] Ernst Lieber accused Liberals of embracing false views of state and society which sanctioned secularization of society and the robbery of church property while at the same time vigorously defending the property rights of industrialists and stock speculators (*Großindustrie und Börsenkönige*).[150] As Winfried Becker convincingly argues, Catholic anti-liberalism was not directed against the bourgeoisie or bourgeois society per se. Catholics instead attacked liberal philosophy. The ideas of Enlightenment and *Gründerzeit* liberal capitalism had destroyed the Christian value system and paved the way for Socialism.[151] In the words of one commentator, the Catholic Church "traced a diabolical lineage from the Reformation, through the Enlightenment and the French revolution, to the rise of liberalism, socialism and communism."[152]

All the same, Catholic anti-Socialist propaganda in many aspects mirrored liberal anti-Socialist polemics. Schorlemer-Alst, for instance, responded to August Bebel's demands (1872) to bring about atheism, the republic and a Socialist economy by drawing the picture of a social democratic utopia with a disenfranchised family, irreligious

---

[146] William Reimes, "Wachsen und Werden (1920)," in Günter Bers, ed. *Arbeiterjugend im Rheinland: Erinnerungen von Wilhelm Reimes und Peter Trimborn* (Wentdorf b. Hamburg: Einhorn-Presse Verlag, 1978), pp. 34-9.

[147] Nipperdey, *Umbruch*, pp. 124-5.

[148] Jochen-Christoph Kaiser, "Sozialdemokratie und 'praktische' Religionskritik. Das Beispiel der Kirchenaustrittsbewegung 1878-1914," *Archiv für Sozialgeschichte* 22 (1982), p. 264.

[149] For a general discussion of the Church's reaction to the Enlightenment and the rise of liberalism see Joseph A. Komonchak's excellent "The Enlightenment and the Construction of Roman Catholicism," *Catholic Commission on Intellectual Affairs Annual* (1985), pp. 31-59.

[150] Ernst Lieber speech, Verhandlungen der 40. Generalversammlung deutscher Katholiken, Würzburg, 1893 quoted in Winfried Becker, "Die Zentrumspartei und die Enzyklika rerum novarum. Zur Wirkungsgeschichte der Sozialenzyklika auf den politischen Katholizismus in Deutschland," *Rheinische Vierteljahrsblätter* 56 (1992), p. 269.

[151] Becker, "Enzyklika rerum novarum," p. 269.

[152] Komonchak, "Enlightenment," p. 33.

state schools, and the unnatural equality of all professions, consumption and life styles.[153] It was important to make workers understand the function of the church in society and at the same time prevent the alienation of the masses from the Christian spirit.[154]

While Social Democrats divided society into antagonistic classes, Catholic thinkers "were fascinated by the idea of a society based on a corporate idea." Catholics constructed a model of society in explicit opposition to both the liberal the Socialist models. The Church found its model for a Christian society "not in the state-religion of the *ancien régime*, not in the Counter-Reformation, but in an idealized Middle Ages."[155] Not the working class should dominate society, but all classes of a Catholic society were united by the "the common ground of Church teachings." Initially, Hitze believed that the creation of a tightly knit network of Catholic clubs and voluntary associations encompassing various occupational groups and social groups was essential to creating a Catholic society. Later, after 1893, he grew disappointed because of the lack of social and political activities that came from occupational associations.[156] Never could the Center represent just the interests of a single social class; it always had to take into account the varied interests of its varied constituency. The Rhineland Center made concessions to workers, more so than in any other region of Catholic Germany, but it could still not afford to neglect the interests of Rhenish artisans and peasants whose support was indispensable. This is a further reason why the Center could not subscribe to an antagonistic view of society; instead, political Catholicism advocated the "peaceful cooperation of capital and labor." Frivolous confrontations or strikes had to be avoided, Trimborn argued. Society would function much better if it were based on a "healthy relationship between employers and workers according to Christian precepts."[157]

What role did the state play in all this? On this question Socialists and Centrists also held divergent views. Centrists basically subscribed to the view expressed by Leo XIII in his encyclical *Rerum novarum*. There was room for individual charity, and charitable work

---

[153] Verhandlungen der 38. Generalversammlung der Katholiken Deutschlands zu Danzig vom 30. August bis 3. September 1891, quoted in Becker, "Enzyklika rerum novarum," p. 270.

[154] Gröber, Verhandlungen der 40. Generalversammlung der Katholiken Deutschlands 1893, quoted in Becker, "Enzyklika rerum novarum," p. 271.

[155] Komonchak, "Enlightenment," p. 36.

[156] Becker, "Enzyklika rerum novarum," p. 271.

[157] Ibid.

by ecclesiastical institutions. But the state also had a role to play. In their view the state was more than the liberal concept of a "nightwatchman" who merely enforced basic conformity to the law. Catholic theorists argued that the state, within precisely defined limits, should intervene to assure just wages and support the working class, which, indeed, was the foundation upon which Germany's prosperity was based. The state had an obligation to protect all its citizens. The question whether a monarchy, a republic or another system of government was best suited to a Christian society was of secondary importance. The state had no right to interfere with private property, the sanctity of the family and the independence of clubs and associations.[158] Cooperation with the government, however, did not come easily to Catholic politicians. Most had a "strained relationship" to Bismarck's Germany. They never fully trusted the state that had persecuted them during the Kulturkampf and whose élites continued to discriminate against Catholic Germans.[159]

These theoretical considerations were among the reasons for the Center's opposition to Bismarck's social policies, which according to Centrists represented a first step toward state-sanctioned socialism and a dangerous limitation of individual responsibilities.[160] Ideological opposition to social legislation, however, did not prevent the Center from cooperating with the government in the long run. They were as pragmatic about social legislation as the chancellor who once prophesied that possibly "our political platform [*Politik*] will perish when I am dead but state-socialism will pull through [*paukt sich durch*]."[161] Center politicians realized, too, that a fundamental rejection of state involvement in shaping social policies was untenable in a modern industrialized society with a growing working class. Charity, from individuals or the church, could not solve the social problems of the day. With the support of Center votes the Reichstag passed legislation for health insurance (1883), accident insurance (1884), and pension and disability insurance (1889). Notable were also the Schorlemer-Galen Bill in 1877, the interpellation by Hertling of 1882,

---

[158] Based on Schädler's remarks at the Katholikentag 1891 and in *Germania*, quoted in Becker, "Enzyklika rerum novarum," p. 272.

[159] Bauer, *Katholizismus*, p. 53.

[160] Lönne, *Katholizismus*, p. 175.

[161] Notes of a converstaion with Otto von Bismarck, 26 June 1886, Moritz Busch, *Tagebuchblätter* (Leipzig, 1899), 3:43-4 excerpted in Florian Tennstedt and Heidi Winter, eds., *Quellensammlung zur Geschichte der Deutschen Sozialpolitik 1867 bis 1914. I. Abteilung. Von der Reichsgründung bis zur Kaiserlichen Sozialbotschaft (1867-1881)* (Stuttgart: Gustav Fischer Verlag, 1993), p. 621.

and the motions (*Anträge*) of Lieber and Hitze in 1885 and 1887. The Center contributed to the improvement of working conditions by its participation in drafting the Workers' Compensation Act (1890 and 1891), which regulated Sunday work, limited child work, as well as working hours for young workers and female workers. Rhenish and Westphalian Centrists were the driving force within the Center for the support of social legislation.

Socialists, too, shed ideological tenets in favor of practical politics. In the 1890s, when the SPD realized that their vehement campaign against Christianity had hampered their electoral success, they decided to accommodate the religious beliefs of their followers. They declared that "religion is a private matter."[162] This made the SPD an even more dangerous competitor for working-class votes, since voters could now switch to them with fewer qualms about their religious beliefs. The Center was much less flexible in its ability to accommodate disparate *Weltanschauungen*. Unlike the Socialists it was locked in tradition and tied to the ideological assumptions of a higher authority with a monopoly on dogmatic truth. Theoreticians of political Catholicism could not draw up a new constitution in the light of a fresh ideology and first principles. What Center leaders *could* do was to create organizations within the Catholic milieu that attracted workers, farmers and representatives of the lower middle-class into the party and allowed the party to embrace their demands.

Besides improvement of social conditions, the Center also hoped for improved political conditions. The discussion of social legislation, so the argument ran, would establish the Center in the eyes of any doubters as a truly political party, whose policies transcended narrow religious concerns.[163] Socialist successes in the 1903 Reichstag elections had frightened Center leaders, and strengthened Julius Bachem's conviction that the Center and the government could not afford to deal fitfully with social and labor questions.[164] The relationship between workers, Christian trade unions, the Catholic Church and the Center had to be put on a new footing. Julius Bachem eventually called for such a rethinking of the aims and methods of political Catholicism. Bachem, of course, was not alone. Many who shared his concerns came from the Rhineland, particularly from Cologne and Mönchengladbach. The two cities gave the name to a group

---

[162] Vernon L. Lidtke, *The Alternative Culture: Socialist Labor in Imperial Germany* (New York: Oxford University Press, 1985), p. 48.
[163] Becker, "Enzyklika rerum novarum," p. 262.
[164] Zeender, *Center Party*, p. 95.

of Center politicians and Catholic trade unionists which forced two divisive debates on party and unions that almost split them. These controversies were the *Gewerkschaftsstreit* and the *Zentrumsstreit*. The Center Party shared much of its social program with the SPD. Even as staunch an opponent of Socialism as Georg Friedrich Dasbach maintained that in some aspects the efforts of the two parties were not dissimilar.[165] What divided them was not so much their gradualist ideas for social legislation but Christian principles. In a speech to Catholic miners, Dasbach maintained that the fundamental principles of all Christian parties were the right to private property, the traditional family and a belief in God and life after death. "A party," he said "which undermines these three pillars of society will not amount to anything, and in its attempts to achieve its goals will bring nothing but unspeakable misery."[166] Many Centrists, among them Lieber and the mine owner von Ballestrem, had little sympathy for trade unions, but they were willing to participate in some of the Center labor legislation initiatives. Ballestrem had insisted on the chairmanship of the Reichstag committee on the worker protection program—though this instance was as much an assertion of Center presence in parliamentary committees as an expression of interest in social legislation.[167] Lieber liked to fashion himself as a "leading advocate of social reforms for the working classes," and in partnership with Hitze he championed the rights of workers in Reichstag debates.[168] Lieber's commitment to social legislation was probably not the result of an earnest concern for the working class, however, so much as a response to pressure from Rhenish Centrists who were more seriously concerned about workers.[169] As city councilor and member of Reichstag and Landtag, Trimborn also made a name for himself as a supporter of social and labor legislation.[170] Julius Bachem, too, promoted the interests of Catholic workers. He frequently was criticized for favoring workers at the expense of farmers.[171] Despite the efforts of men such as Karl Trimborn and Julius Bachem, the Center found it difficult to attract large numbers of workers into a

[165] Haupts, "Katholiken," p. 261.
[166] Quoted in Karl Josef Rivinius, "Sozialpolitische Wirksamkeit des Preßkaplans Georg Friedrich Dasbach (1846-1907)," *Jahrbuch für Christliche Sozialwissenschaften* 21 (1980), p. 261.
[167] KB, 5:134-5.
[168] Zeender, *Center Party*, p. 76.
[169] Ibid., p. 76.
[170] Cardauns, *Trimborn*, p. 81.
[171] *Deutsche Tageszeitung* no. 517, 4 November 1897.

party that often was more concerned with the economic interests of farmers and the middle class. The Center continued to lose ground to the Socialists. Only after World War II was the SPD pushed aside from its dominance over German workers by a Christian Democratic Party (CDU). Although it was led by Konrad Adenauer, an old Centrist and former mayor of Cologne and attracted many former Center politicians, it differed in significant ways from the Center. Perhaps the greatest difference between the CDU of the Federal Republic and the Wilhelmine Center was its attitudes towards Protestants. The question of the Center's relationship with Protestants and the role Catholicism played in Center politics was at the heart of the most divisive conflicts with political Catholicism: *Zentrumsstreit* and *Gewerkschaftsstreit*.

VI.

GEWERKSCHAFTSSTREIT AND ZENTRUMSTREIT

BEFORE ADDRESSING the controversies over Christian trade unions (*Gewerkschaftsstreit*) and the *Zentrumsstreit* (literally quarrel over the Center; controversy over the future nature of the party), it is necessary to explain why these two issues which threatened to split political Catholicism during the early years of the twentieth century are being dealt with in the same chapter. Among historians there has been some argument as to whether they are related to each other, and if so, how. Ernst Deuerlein sees two distinct but interrelated issues. The *Zentrumsstreit* was primarily concerned with the "political cooperation of Germany's [Christian] denominations." The *Gewerkschaftsstreit*, in contrast, was the debate over the question of Catholic workers' participation in interdenominational national trade unions.[1] Rolf Kiefer, the biographer of Karl Bachem, follows Rudolf Morsey's argument that the two debates are indivisible. Both dealt with the possibilities and limitations that interdenominationalism presented to political Catholicism; both considered the ways party and unions could influence state and society; and both were concerned with "the all-important question of the future of Catholics in Germany" and how Catholics could achieve parity with other segments of society.[2]

Margaret Anderson puts forward a somewhat strained argument for separating the two issues. In her view, care must be exercised not to equate the two debates because the *Gewerkschaftsstreit* was *not* essentially an argument over the dominance by Catholics of the organization itself. Since the majority of Protestant workers had already been attracted to Socialist Free Unions, "interdenominationalism in the Catholic-sponsored Christian Trade Union movement could only

---

[1] Ernst Deuerlein, "Der Gewerkschaftsstreit," *Tübinger Theologische Quartalsschrift* 139 (1959), p. 40.

[2] Morsey, "Rheinland," p. 22; Kiefer, *Bachem*, p. 129, quotation, p. 134.

add *clout* to Germany's Catholic minority." There were more than enough Protestants in the country, writes Anderson, "to dilute the ability of Catholics, qua Catholics, to articulate their interests."[3] This argument, however, ignores the fact that German Protestants were as unlikely to join or vote for the Center (no matter how far the party went in its interdenominationalist protestations) as Socialist workers were to sign up for an interdenominationalist Christian trade union.

A more convincing scenario brings the two issues back into close proximity, although in a new way. Though not wholly congruent, the *Gewerkschaftsstreit* and *Zentrumsstreit* share several important elements. Neither of them was confined to the inner circles of the Center or trade union leadership. Clergy, parliamentarians, and trade unionists, played a role in the *Gewerkschaftsstreit*. The debate over the nature of the Center, in the same fashion, was not carried out by Centrists alone but clergy, trade unionists and representatives of the Catholic associations, too. One only has to look at the participants of the Easter Tuesday Conference (see below) to realize that this debate was not confined to the party. Contemporaries believed that the debates overlapped and the opposing camps in both debates were remarkably similiar. The proponents of interdenominational trade unions were to be found in Cologne and Trier; the men of the People's Association and the Center who followed Julius Bachem's lead also found support from the Christian trade unions. The Cologne wing of the Center and the interdenominationalist trade unionists, also were attacked by the same bishops who argued that the realization of either model (Bachem's opening up of the Center as well as the interdenominational character of the unions) would dilute the Catholic character of these institutions and put into question their very existence. Both controversies were about independence from clerical supervision. In both disputes one side insisted on complete independence from the hierarchy in economic and political matters while the other side claimed that the hierarchy still should be the final arbiter. Both debates can also be seen as attempts to come to terms with the challenges of modern society. As such, these attempts were part of larger debates in the Catholic world.

The so-called Modernist controversy, which preoccupied European Catholic intellectuals at the turn of the century, was an effort by Catholic reform-minded thinkers to define the role Catholics and

[3] Margaret Lavinia Anderson, "Interdenominationalism, Clericalism, Pluralism: The *Zentrumsstreit* and the Dilemma of Catholicism in Wilhelmine Germany," *Central European History* 21 (1988), p. 358.

[4] For an introduction to this debate see Nipperdey, *Umbruch*, pp. 33-8.

their institutions (secular and religious) played in modern society. The papacy fought with all its canonical and doctrinal might attempts to renew and "modernize" Catholic theology by integrating into Catholic thought recent scientific discoveries.[4] Herman Schell, a theology professor at Würzburg and Germany's most influential proponent of Catholic reform (*Reformkatholizismus*),[5] warned that the "theoretical and practical conquest of science was the most urgent and pressing task of German Catholicism."[6] Among Schell's followers were also Center politicians. In 1906, the very year Julius Bachem's article ignited the *Zentrumsstreit*, a committee was founded to honour the recently deceased Catholic theologian with a monument. More than fifty Center politicians belonged to this committee, among them Julius Bachem, Hermann Cardauns and Martin Spahn.[7]

Parallel to the Modernist conflict ran the *Literaturstreit*, an effort to preserve and promote a particular Catholic literature. In Germany, Karl Muth used the pages of *Hochland*, a magazine devoted to Catholic culture, to liberate German Catholicism from its cultural isolation. Although the debates about the Catholic response to modern times and literature are not part of the following discussion, one most not forget that the political, social and economic arguments fought out in the Center and Christian trade unions were part of a larger debate about Catholic identity encompassing theological and cultural questions. Contemporaries linked the political and cultural debates when they attacked each other; thus integralist trade unionists denounced their interdenominational opponents as Modernists and demanded that the People's Association renounce their heretical ways.[8] Therefore during the first decade of the twentieth century political Catholicism faced the twin threat of division by internal debates and a stifling intervention of an integralist faction enjoying Pope Pius X's support and attempting to suppress efforts to escape the cultural isolation of German Catholics.

A. Gewerkschaftsstreit

The *Gewerkschaftsstreit* broke out in 1900 and did not end until more than a decade later. The debate was protracted because of the conten-

[5] The Catholic priest Josef Müller first used the term *Reformkatholizismus* in 1895.
[6] Herman Schell, *Der Katholizismus als Princip des Fortschritts* (Würzburg: Andreas Göbel's Verlagsbuchhandlung, 1897), p. 5.
[7] Nipperdey, *Umbruch*, p. 35.
[8] Brose, *Christian Labor*, pp. 256-7.

tiousness of the issues, the animosity between the opponents, and the Pope's aversion to Christian trade unions which was tempered only by resistance of a minority of cardinals, bishops, Jesuits and lay Catholic leaders. The immediate cause of the *Gewerkschaftsstreit* was the founding by Christian trade unionists of interdenominational trade unions (see previous chapter). This was above all an attempt to achieve an effective representation of the economic and social interests of Christian workers—a question of particular importance in the Rhineland, a region with a significant number of Catholic and Protestant workers. Workers' organization in Catholic trade unions had already been the subject of the encyclical *Rerum Novarum*, which had approved of Catholic workers' clubs but insisted on clerical supervision. It did not address the question of interdenominational trade unions.[9] The controversy was triggered by a series of articles written by Franz von Savigny, a member of the directorate of the Berlin Workers' Clubs. Savigny accused Christian trade unionists of fostering religious indifference. There was no need for Christian trade unions, Savigny argued, because the already existing Catholic workers' clubs were sufficient to protect and improve the material conditions of workers. Among those criticized by Savigny were not only trade unionists like Adam Stegerwald but also Center politicians such as Franz Hitze, Julius Bachem and Karl Trimborn.

Savigny believed that Christian trade unions posed a threat to the integrity of Catholic beliefs: interdenominationalism carried the "danger of religious dilution."[10] He and the Berlin-Trier group who rallied behind him argued that Center politicians and Catholic trade unionists were subject to papal authority not only in religious matters but also in questions of politics.[11] As we shall see, this line of argument was also used during the *Zentrumsstreit*. Neither the majority of Center politicians nor the Vatican supported these notions.[12] While the Pope refrained from demanding political allegiance, he also did not speak out unambiguously on the *Gewerkschaftsstreit*. His announcement left enough room for interpretation that for years both sides could and did claim that the Pope had supported their arguments.[13]

---

[9] Pope Leo XIII's encyclical was circulated in May 1891; it was an attempt to apply Thomistic philosophy to the social problems facing the modern world.
[10] Ritter, *Bewegung*, p. 314.
[11] Kiefer, *Bachem*, p. 141.
[12] Ibid., p. 142.
[13] Ibid., p. 143.

The "integralistic" representatives of the Berlin-Trier group vigorously opposed the notion of interdenominational trade unions by pointing to what they called secular and modern tendencies in the Christian trade unions. They opposed any workers' unions not guided and led by clergy. In their opinion trade unions without a religious (i.e., Catholic) affiliation as well as those that labeled themselves Christian trade unions were incompatible with the teachings of the Catholic Church. The advantage of creating interdenominational trade unions, and of combining Socialist tactics (namely the willingness to strike) with a commitment to Christian faith, might (in a unified political movement) justify the dangers inherent in widening the ideological framework of the representatives of a minority. In a movement as diverse and divided as political Catholicism, such a move was disastrous.

This insistence on purely Catholic unions and the notion that the People's Association and the Center were essentially extensions of the Catholic church, confirm some of the accusations that were hurled at Catholic politicians by their opponents. More important in the context of this study, however, is the fact that these rifts between trade unions, Center Party, People's Association and hierarchical authorities hampered the Center in its attempt to gain the support of Catholic workers. This bickering made it easier for Socialists to attract workers, because Catholic workers now had reason to doubt both the efficacy of Christian trade unions and the need to vote for the Center.

Savigny's views gained national currency when they were discussed at the congress of Christian trade unions in Frankfurt (3-4 June 1900) and at the Fulda bishops' conference two months later. At Fulda it was Cardinal Kopp who realized that the controversy sparked by Savigny's articles could be used to fight Christian trade unions which, in his view, did not provide effective protection against the Socialist threat.[14] Kopp drafted a pastoral letter (*Hirtenbrief*) which eventually became known as *Fuldaer Pastoral*. The *Fuldaer Pastoral* avoided addressing directly the question of Christian trade unions, but by extolling the virtues of workers' clubs it made its preference obvious.

The *Fachabteilungen* [confessional trade sections] within the *Arbeitervereine* [workers' clubs] will supply proof as they de-

---

[14] Hans-Georg Aschoff, *Kirchenfürst im Kaiserreich - Georg Kardinal Kopp* (Hildesheim: Bernward Verlag, 1987), pp. 115-6.

velop on a wide scale that no new, religious-neutral creations are required to defend and promote the material interests of Christian workers, rather that the Catholic *Arbeitervereine* are capable, and strong enough, to represent the material class interests as well as the spiritual well-being of their members.[15]

The pastoral letter urged priests to support local workers clubs. Moreover, it declared that the material interests of Catholic workers could be effectively represented by workers' clubs, which already cared for the spiritual needs of workers.

The bishops approved Kopp's draft, but were probably not aware of its political implications. In contradiction to tradition Kopp had not circulated a copy of the draft prior to the conference. Most of the bishops present were indeed surprised by the discussion of Christian trade unions and were at odds about the purpose of that pastoral letter.[16] Cardinal Kopp and his ally, the bishop of Trier Felix Korum, regarded the letter primarily as a fundamental critique of Christian trade unions. The majority of the German episcopacy, on the other hand, viewed the *Fuldaer Pastoral* as a rejection of religiously neutral unions, but believed that the pastoral letter was not a rejection of interdenominational unions based on a positive Christian *Weltanschauung*.[17]

The ambiguous stance of the German bishops fanned the fires of the union controversy. Integralists among the clergy, the Center, and the workers' clubs used the *Fuldaer Pastoral* as a weapon to denounce Christian trade unions, arguing that Germany's bishops, too, believed them to be incompatible with Catholic beliefs. Franz von Savigny and his integralist friends argued that Christian trade unions constituted a danger to the integrity of the Catholic milieu. More serious still they threatened the very fabric of society. By approving of strikes they were pitting one segment of society against the other, not unlike the Socialist notion of a class struggle. Such an adversarial view of society contradicted the Catholic tradition of the natural, divine order of the world as postulated by St. Thomas Aquinas and revived by the Neo-Thomists of the nineteenth century.

---

[15] The pastoral letter was published in *KV* no. 893, 3 October 1903. The letter is excerpted in Rüther, *Geschichte*, 2:223-4; this translation from Brose, *Christian Labor*, p. 149.

[16] Aschoff, *Kopp*, p. 116.

[17] Ibid.

Interdenominationalists rejected Catholic workers' clubs as conceived by Savigny and the Berlin-Trier group. Karl Bachem instead supported the workers' clubs as vehicles to educate workers and to spread Catholic ideas among them. A successful representation of working-class interests, however, was not possible by workers' clubs led by clergy, with no central organization and no commitment to use strikes as a means to achieve wage increases and the improvement of working conditions. To supporters of Christian trade unions such attitudes were unrealistic.[18]

Most Rhenish Center politicians were among the supporters of the Christian trade unions. They were joined by a number of bishops (e.g. Nörber, Simar, Fischer, Schneider, and Dinglstad), and by the leadership of the People's Association. During his two years as Archbishop of Cologne, Hubert Simar, was primarily concerned with the education of priests and the theological faculty at the University of Bonn, workers' organization, however, occupied him also. Not opposed to the labor movement and convinced that priests in his bishopric did not cooperate with Socialist workers, Simar sanctioned the work of the People's Association and recognized workers' natural right to organize.[19] Simar's successor, Antonius Fischer, took a decided stand in favour of Christian trade unions. For twenty five years he had observed the plight of workers in Essen, where he taught religion at a *Gymnasium*. As archbishop he backed up the People's Association when it was attacked by the Berliners, assuring August Pieper : "You can place full trust in me... And when I stand up for you, I won't stand alone."[20] His outspoken support of Christian trade unions put him into direct conflict with Cardinal Kopp.[21]

From the very beginning of the conflict Karl Bachem was an ardent supporter of the Cologne-Mönchengladbach group.[22] He vehemently opposed those "German Catholics who saw in the Center merely a representative of religious and clerical issues." These men had little understanding of politics and the role a political party played in a state. Many among them thought "that the Center was too 'democratic' because it favored the advancement of the working class and opposed all 'reactionary' sentiments" within its ranks.[23] The precise relationship between party and unions, however, was a matter of con-

[18] Kiefer, B*achem*, p. 134.
[19] Hegel, *Erzbistum Köln*, pp. 90-2; Brose, *Christian Labor*, p. 147.
[20] Quoted in Brose, *Christian Labor*, p. 260.
[21] Hegel, *Erzbistum Köln*, pp. 93-5; Misner, *Social Catholicism*, p. 279.
[22] Kiefer, B*achem*, p. 131.
[23] KB, 7:173-4.

tention even among Centrists who sympathized with Christian trade unions. In a conversation with Karl Bachem, Ernst Lieber expressed reluctance to recognize the legitimacy of Christian trade unions. He believed that a close association with the unions held real dangers; it might eventually lead to Social Democracy, Lieber cautioned, because neither the clergy nor the Center would be able "to keep on the right path." Lieber was also critical of Catholic labor leader August Brust, calling him a "dubious element" in the party. Bachem, on the other hand, believed Brust to be a man who "had made great sacrifices for his conviction" and surely deserved "to be trusted more."[24] As chairman of the miners' union, Brust was an early advocate and organizer of Christian trade unions which were confessionally and politically neutral. Already in the early 1890s, Brust had convinced Hitze of the need for interdenominational trade unions.[25] As a consequence the People's Association, as well as a number of Rhenish Centrists who shared the views of Hitze and Brust, became important supporters of the Mönchengladbach-Cologne side in the union controversy. Support in the Rhineland, however, was not unanimous. Hubert Immelen, for example, publisher of the *Aachener Volksfreund* and chairman of the Pius Association opposed Brust and spoke in favor of local and regional unions on a confessional basis and linked to the Center Party.[26]

Nevertheless, the majority of Rhenish Centrists shared Karl Bachem's conviction that only a strong organization of Christian workers could stand up to the Socialist unions. The strength required to challenge the Socialists could only come from interdenominationalist trade unions.[27] The defection of Catholic workers was the greatest threat to the Rhenish Center and to the voluntary associations which made up the milieu of political Catholicism. Bachem, realizing this, was flabbergasted by the shortsightedness and stubbornness of influential politicians and churchmen toward the establishment of Christian unions. "I never thought," Bachem wrote, "that it would be so difficult to obtain recognition and equal rights for the working class on a Christian foundation." He saw that there was enormous resistance in the ranks of the Center

[24] K. Bachem to Hitze, 12 Dec. 1900, BAP 74VO1 Nr. 143 f. 15-6.
[25] Hubert Mockenhaupt, "Franz Hitze (1851-1921)," in *Zeitgeschichte in Lebensbildern. Aus dem deutschen Katholizismus des 20. Jahrhunderts*, ed. Rudolf Morsey (Mainz: Matthias-Grünewald-Verlag, 1973), 1:59.
[26] Schneider, "Religion and Labour Organization," p. 353; Der Piusverein zu Aachen, 1908, HStaD Reg Ac/701, f. 43-7.
[27] Kiefer, *Bachem*, p. 133.

to his own social work and to the efforts of the People's Association. Everywhere he saw the party's old guard using the Catholic Church and its institutions as police instruments to keep the working class "obedient" and "satisfied."[28]

The People's Association, too, was drawn into the conflict between workers' clubs and Christian trade unions. As the conflict dragged on and became more bitter, the position of the Association grew more hostile toward the workers' clubs, with the notable exception of the Western League of Workers' Clubs (*Westdeutscher Arbeiterverein*), "where simultaneous membership in a union was almost required."[29] There had never been much enthusiasm among the leaders of the People's Association for exclusively Catholic trade unions. These leaders thought it their "duty to support Christian trade unions in order to stem the Socialist advance"; but for the sake of harmony among Catholic ranks they did not condemn outright workers' clubs and their confessional trade sections.[30] In 1902, at a meeting in Mannheim, the association's directorate decided to actively promote interdenominational Christian trade unions. But at the same time it stressed its tolerance of workers' clubs and declared that it shall not oppose *Fachabteilungen* in either "word or deed", particularly since many members of the workers' clubs also belonged to the People's Association.[31] Eager to avoid conflict with the German episcopacy it was also decided that Brandts, Trimborn, Porsch, and Hitze would inform the bishops of Freiburg, Cologne and Breslau about the People's Association's position, and, at the same time, sound out the bishops' concerns about Christian trade unions.[32]

The relationship between People's Association and Christian trade unions was again discussed at a meeting of the directorate in Mönchengladbach on 19 June 1906. The participants were concerned about the decline of the Association in Silesia and the Saar region, areas in which workers' clubs and their *Fachabteilungen* had made considerable headway at the expense of the People's Association. The directorate noted with chagrin that some chapters had left the association because of its support of interdenominational trade unions.

[28] Ibid., p. 134.
[29] Misner, *Social Catholicism*, p. 277.
[30] Beschlüsse des Vorstandes des Volksvereins betr. dessen Stellung zu den christlichen Gewerkschaften [n. d., 1911], BAP 74VO1 Nr. 147 f. 2.
[31] Brandts or Pieper to Pfarrer Stull, 13 May 1905 (copy), BAP 74VO1 Nr. 147 f. 20; Beschlüsse des Vorstandes des Volksvereins [n. d., 1911], BAP 74VO1 Nr. 147 f. 1.
[32] Beschlüsse des Vorstandes des Volksvereins [n. d., 1910], BAP 74VO1 Nr. 147 f. 1.

To prevent further erosion of their support the leadership of the People's Association turned to Cardinal Fischer of Cologne. With his help they sought support for their cause and Christian trade unions at the upcoming *Fuldaer Bischofskonferenz*. In principle the People's Association's stance toward the *Fachabteilungen* had remained unaltered from 1902, but the tone had changed. They still tolerated workers' clubs, but they found it impossible to actively support the confessional *Fachabteilungen* since their representatives "to this day have fundamental religious and ecclesiastical misgivings about… Christian trade unions."[33] In 1909 the directorate of the People's Association demanded that workers' clubs and particularly the *Fachabteilungen* stop "waging war against Christian trade unions." The People's Association's neutral attitude toward workers' clubs hinged upon "further consideration and the development of circumstances."[34]

Both sides, the Cologne-Mönchengladbach wing and the antitrade unionists from Trier and Berlin, sought to gain support from the clergy. They tried to outdo each other in publishing numerous brochures on the question, and they sent delegations to Rome to further their case. In February 1903, for instance, Karl Trimborn, Franz Brandts and Karl Bachem worked feverishly to publish a pamphlet before the opposition could make their case in Rome. Not willing to surrender the field, Pieper was sent to Rome once it was learned that Fournelle had arranged for a papal audience.[35] However, although a number of bishops declared themselves in support of one side or the other, neither the Pope nor the Fulda bishops' conference was willing to settle the issue in face of opposition. Rudolf Brack has argued that this indecision of the high clergy was one of the key reasons why the *Gewerkschaftsstreit* lasted so long: without an unequivocal statement of an endorsement or condemnation of trade unions from the Pope or the episcopate, the proponents of Christian trade unions were forced to claim that their unions were independent of the Church.[36]

The bishop of Trier, Felix Korum, was typical of the clerical opponents of Christian trade unions. In a letter to a Catholic priest he

[33] Beschlüsse des Vorstandes des Volksvereins [n. d., 1911], BAP 74VO1 Nr. 147 f. 3.
[34] Ibid., f. 6.
[35] Franz X. Bachem to K. Bachem, 11 Feb. 1903, HAStK Nl. Bachem 1006/217.
[36] Rudolf Brack, "Die Bemühungen Karl Bachems und führender Zentrumspolitiker um eine Beilegung des Gewerkschaftsstreites im Jahre 1904," *Annalen des Historischen Vereins für den Niederrhein* 177 (1975), p. 218.

argued that the People's Association was founded as a Catholic institution, representing the interests of the Catholic population and the Church. Its success was due in no small measure to the work of clergymen and the support of the hierarchy. This Catholic organization became "the standard-bearer of the Christian trade unions, a movement which openly or clandestinely defies pastoral letters and the advice of bishops."[37] Korum named August Pieper, secretary general of the People's Association, as one of the instigators of the association's support for Christian trade unions. From his headquarters in Mönchengladbach, Korum complained, Pieper flooded the country with articles and brochures extolling the virtues of Christian unions. The Augustine League, also influenced by Pieper, spread this agitation in the Catholic press. Not only did the People's Association betray its Catholic mandate, Felix fumed, it also abused its mandate by using Catholic money to support "non-Catholic" organizations. The publications of the People's Association were funded by money meant to support Catholic activities, and people like Giesberts were traveling around the province and giving speeches, all financed by funds provided to support Catholic, not interdenominational, interests. Such misappropriations and abuses, Bishop Korum believed, could not be tolerated by the episcopate. He warned that the Center would suffer if it supported Christian trade unions, and threatened that Pieper would have to resign if he continued to agitate for the trade unions.[38] The bishop of Trier and clerics like him were in a minority, but well-connected to likeminded integralists in the Vatican. Hohn argued that the majority of German bishops, Center parliamentarians as well as the Catholic press recognized the legitimacy of the People's Association's support of Christian trade unions, their right to strike and the right of Catholic workers to organize themselves in interconfessional unions.[39]

Among the German clergy, Cardinal Kopp had a special position. He was Germany's most influential clergyman with excellent connections to the court in Berlin and to the Vatican. Understandably, the Cologne-Mönchengladbach *Richtung* tried to neutralize him. Initially, Kopp was a determined opponent of Christian trade unions. Kopp, as most German bishops, argued that the papal encyclical *Rerum Novarum* permitted workers and clergy to promote the economic interests of workers but emphasized that this had to be done within a

---

[37] Bishop Felix Korum, 28 Oct. 1902, BAP 74VO1 Nr. 147 f. 10.
[38] Ibid., f. 10-1.
[39] Hohn to Hermann Biermann (copy), 23 Sept. 1908, BAP 74VO1 Nr. 147 f. 51-2.

Catholic framework.[40] He was immune to Cardinal Fischer's attempts to change his mind and Centrists thought it best in 1903 to tread carefully and treat him and his position with tact.[41]

But Centrists continued to woo Kopp. Hitze on several occasions tried to persuade him to support Christian trade unions, and so did Karl Bachem. In a conversation between Bachem and Kopp on the morning of 25 January 1904, Kopp seemed to soften his position. During the early days, he said, there was a real danger "that Christian trade unions would slide toward the left; this had to be prevented." But now this danger no longer existed, and Kopp believed it possible to alter his opposition to the unions. He was willing to consult Cardinal Fischer on this point, and if they could reach an agreement he would make a public statement that Catholic workers could join Christian trade unions. Bachem suggested that it was not at all necessary for the Church to embrace Christian trade unions in such a positive manner. It would suffice to state that: "The Church does not find fault with Catholic workers who seek to improve their economic condition by joining Christian trade unions as they currently exist. Therefore the Church does not object to Christian trade unions."[42] During a meeting of Center parliamentarians in early 1905 it was decided that the best way to deal with dissenters such as Savigny, who could not be silenced, was to gain Kopp's influence in order to change their minds. To that effect Gröber was delegated to write a memorandum which was to be sent to Kopp in order to convince the wavering cardinal of the need for Christian trade unions.[43]

Even bishops not fundamentally opposed to Christian trade unions (such as Archbishop Simar of Cologne) had serious reservations about the unions' affinity with Social Democracy, or, in their parlance, with the old unions. Simar thought that even the use of the word "neutrality" (an expression employed by Pieper, Hitze and others to describe the relationship between Christian and Social Democratic trade unions) was unacceptable because, in the hands of "less experienced priests," it might lead to "more concessions than are permissible."[44] Simar felt it was necessary to emphasize more strongly the religious aspect of Christian trade unions; he demanded that economic demands "must be in harmony with Christian beliefs." Bachem

[40] Kopp to Porsch (President of the Katholikentag), 19. Aug. 1904, HAStK Nl. Bachem 1006/217.
[41] K. Bachem note, 10 Dec. 1903, HAStK Nl. Bachem 1006/217.
[42] K. Bachem note, 25 Jan. 1904, HAStK Nl. Bachem 1006/217.
[43] K. Bachem note, 25 Jan. 1905, HAStK Nl. Bachem 1006/217.
[44] K. Bachem to Pieper, 3 Feb. 1900, BAP 74VO1 Nr. 143 f. 19.

was willing to concur with Simar's demands in order to avoid a dispute with the Church hierarchy "at a time when Catholics in Germany and Prussia are in a precarious position."[45]

Already in February 1904, Karl Bachem, in his innocence, tried to elicit an unequivocal statement from Pius X, who had become Pope in August 1903 and had not yet taken a stance on the subject. The new Cardinal of the archdiocese of Cologne, Antonius Fischer, too, had not made a definite statement regarding the Christian trade unions. Despite Fischer's earlier preference for the Catholic workers' clubs, Bachem had reason to believe that he now looked at Christian trade unions with more friendly eyes. Thus, it seemed to Bachem an opportune moment to intervene, solicit a definite response from Rome, and bring to an end a conflict damaging to his party and to Catholic workers.[46] In a letter to his friend Franz Hitze, Bachem outlined his plan. He suggested that a Center deputation, perhaps consisting of Spahn, Gröber, Trimborn and himself, go to Rome and seek a resolution of the dispute. He had hoped that a bishop would intervene on behalf of Christian trade unions, but realized that there was nobody in Rome to take such a position. Be that as it may, Bachem wrote, without a papal announcement on the question there was no hope of resolving this divisive issue.[47]

The *Gewerkschaftsstreit* came to a formal end on 24 October 1912. Pope Pius X's so-called union encyclical (*Singulari quadam*), allowed Catholics to join both workers' clubs and Christian trade unions. Though the Pope had at last accepted Christian trade unions, the debate was not over completely. The text of the encyclical still betrayed the pontiff's preference for Catholic workers' clubs. Thus residues of bitterness associated with the *Gewerkschaftsstreit* lingered on until the outbreak of the First World War.[48]

In a protocol of a meeting in Mönchengladbach of representatives of the workers' clubs of West, South and East Germany, the Center Party and the People's Association, the *Gewerkschaftsstreit* was declared to be over. The participants agreed that *Fachabteilungen* were to be ignored in future.[49] Thus Centrists did not allow Rome to

---

[45] Ibid., f. 20-1.
[46] Brack, "Bemühungen," pp. 218-21.
[47] K. Bachem to Hitze, 22 Dec. 1903, HAStK Nl. Bachem 1006/217; Brack, "Bemühungen," 220.
[48] Kiefer, *Bachem*, p. 145.
[49] Protokoll einer freien Aussprache von Mitgliedern des Ausschusses des Kartellverbandes kath. Arbeitervereine West-, Süd- und Osdeutschlands, 26 Nov. 1912, BAP 74VO1 Nr. 145 f. 7-8.

dictate policy or how to vote in the Reichstag, but they accepted Rome as the final arbiter (or at least the most authoritative voice) in a dispute. One did not have to follow political advice from Rome, but papal condemnation or approval of a position carried enormous weight. In short: the Center was a political party, but not a secular one; its constituency was Catholic. Political decisions were not dictated by the hierarchy, but the magisterial authroity of the pope and bishops was hardly ever challenged. Indeed, party disputes e appealed directly and unapologetically to this arbiter.

The *Gewerkschaftsstreit* disrupted the relationships between Center, Church, Christian trade unions, and Catholic workers for nearly a decade and a half. In the end it solved little but did much damage. Most importantly, it disrupted seriously the development of interdenominational trade unions. It discredited political Catholicism and Christian trade unions among a large number of Catholic workers and contributed to the growing strength of the SPD. Center politicians like Bachem and Trimborn had been keenly aware of the importance of Christian unions, not only for the organization of Catholic workers, but also for the party. While unionists were primarily fighting for the organizational integrity and the very existence of their unions, Center politicians realized that they too had a stake in the dispute. As Rudolf Brack has shown, Karl Bachem intervened in the *Gewerkschaftsstreit* in order to secure the help of the Christian trade unions during election campaigns, when they were seen to be a useful asset to fight liberals and Social Democrats alike.[50] Therefore it was in the interest of the Center to support them. "Christian trade unions," Bachem wrote in a memorandum to Rome in 1904, "dominate southern and western Germany, the very regions which are important for German Catholicism.... If the Center Party is to survive, and not be pushed out of the big cities and industrial regions, and limited to rural areas, it must also hope that Christian trade unions will prosper. Any damage to Christian unions will at the same time do damage to the interests of the Center."[51]

The controversy had a special significance for the Center, since its electoral success in industrial regions was tied to the existence or absence of interdenominational unions. Election results had provided unequivocal proof that the Center suffered greater losses in areas where the SPD was gaining disproportionate numbers of votes, especially

---

[50] Brack, "Bemühungen," pp. 217-8.
[51] K. Bachem, "Denkschrift nach Rom," HAStK Nl. Bachem 1006/215, quoted in Kiefer, *Bachem*, p. 136.

in areas where Catholic workers had joined Free Unions and where Christian trade unions were poorly represented or absent altogether.[52] Therefore, in order to defend its claim as a representative of Catholics from all classes and all walks of life, the Center was obliged to support Christian trade unions. Out of a similar concern for the isolation of the Center and the ability to attract voters and supporters grew the second large debate that buffeted the Center during the first decade of the twentieth century.

B. ZENTRUMSSTREIT

In the spring of 1906, while Centrists were still licking their wounds from the first rounds of the *Gewerkschaftsstreit*, the brief peace within the party was disturbed by the publication of Julius Bachem's article "*Wir müssen aus dem Turm heraus* [We Must Leave the Tower]." At first Julius Bachem's proposals seemed modest and uncontroversial. His cousin Karl thought them to be well within the bounds of traditional Center thinking. Just the title was unfortunate; Karl Bachem suggested: "*Es müssen in den Turm mehr Protestanten herein* [More Protestants Must Enter the Tower]."[53] In his monumental history of the Center, Karl Bachem dedicates over 130 pages to the sad story of this controversy. Bachem's jeremiad is a departure from the usually harmonious picture he draws of the Center. His bias in the controversy is obvious. His polemic against the "Roerenites" (see below) glows with contempt and indignation. They "lacked clear political ideas," and, Bachem charged, were driven by the backward, intransigent and dangerous notion of a purely Catholic Center.[54]

In retrospect, the *Zentrumsstreit* seems to have been a spurious argument, obscure to any but those intimately familiar with the ideological and personal rivalries within the Center Party. Even insiders found it confusing at times. What the *Zentrumsstreit* lacked in clarity, it made up handsomely in ferocity. It caused a rift in the party that not only intensified old rivalries but also destroyed long friendships. Politicians who had worked together for decades were unwilling to shake hands.[55] It was fought on several fronts with the sharp weapons of polemic, accusation, and innuendo. Yet despite its intensity the *Zentrumsstreit* has remained a very elusive issue. Contempo-

---

[52] Bierganz, "Cardauns," p. 263.
[53] K. Bachem to Jos. Dahlmann S. J., 1 June 1906, HAStK Nl. Bachem 1006/254b.
[54] KB, 7:177-8.
[55] K. Bachem to Roeren, 25 June 1909, HAStK Nl. Bachem 1006/284a.

raries and historians alike have had great difficulty in determining exactly what the Center was actually fighting about. This very vagueness, this proximity of opposing positions, was a major reason for the controversy's longevity. The *Zentrumsstreit* was aroused by different interpretations of Windthorst's political program and contradicting visions of the party's future. It pitted two factions against each other: the Cologne-Mönchengladbach group around the Bachems and the Berlin-Trier group whose most outspoken member was Hermann Roeren.

In Julius Bachem's view, the metaphor of the Center as an impregnable tower had outlived its usefulness. The tower had been built as a bulwark against Bismarck's Kulturkampf, and while attacks on Germany's Catholic minority had by no means ended (indeed as Bachem published his article they were intensifying again), different methods of responding to them were now called for. The political atmosphere in Berlin was growing ever more hostile toward Catholics: only the dependence of Prussia's leading statesmen on the Center in the Reichstag prevented outright attacks on the party. Anti-Catholic feelings had resurfaced during the heated election campaign. Without Protestant members, Bachem feared, the Center would soon "have no convincing argument to defend itself against the characterization [of it] as a purely...Catholic party."[56]

Therefore Julius Bachem argued for an interdenominational party. He encouraged the Center to field Protestant candidates not only in constituencies with Protestant majorities but also in those where Catholics were in the majority.[57] The Center, he argued, never *was* a confessional party: Windthorst had always insisted on the Center being a political, not a Catholic, party. Thus Bachem's proposal (at least in his view) did not deviate from party tradition. Indeed, the characterization of the Center as a confessional party was based entirely on prejudice and not fact.

Karl Bachem, too, saw an immediate and important need to attract Protestants into the party. He also insisted that the Center was not a confessional party, and tried to attract Protestants by appealing to common Christian principles. Part of this argument was clearly based on the conviction of the Cologne-Mönchengladbach wing that Catholics had to become part of the empire's dominant culture. The

---

[56]K. Bachem to Jos. Dahlmann S.J., 1 June 1906, HAStK Nl. Bachem 1006/254b.

[57] Julius Bachem, "Wir müssen aus dem Turm heraus," *Historisch-politische Blätter* no. 5, 1 March 1906, reprinted in Bergsträsser, *Katholizismus*, 2:332-41.

integration of the two confessions, Julius Bachem urged, "is the duty of anybody who loves his fatherland."[58] This duty had to be taken up "even if it meant far-reaching self-abnegation."[59] This is the crux of Julius Bachem's argument. Integration into German society was more important than the defence of the party's Catholic identity, and in order to prosper, the Center had to shed its Catholic attributes sufficiently to attract Protestant members. Not surprisingly, Bachem's assurance that Catholics would not have to "relinquish one iota [*ein Tüttelchen*] of their religious convictions,"[60] never assuaged his opponents.

Bachem's article stirred up immediate opposition, unleashing what seemed to be an endless, fractious controversy over the Center's character. Attempts of the Augustine League to create a united front among Catholic newspapers failed. Everywhere conservative Centrists were murmuring; nor did they restrain their pens. The first critical response to Julius Bachem's article, expressed in the fiercest language of polemic and antagonism, came from the *Essener Volkszeitung* and the *Saarbrücker Volkszeitung*.[61] Bachem was forced to elaborate on the arguments put forward in his article. In a response published in *Der Tag*, he defined a Catholic party as one which acts "solely in the interest of the Church in Rome, [and] is merely an organization in the Church's service." In that sense the Center was not a Catholic party. The fact that the overwhelming majority of Center voters and politicians were Catholic was irrelevant. The same could be said about the confessional composition of the Conservative Party, which was overwhelmingly Protestant. Those who claimed otherwise, whether enemies from outside or inside the party, would only "poison and burden the political life [of the Center] with their unproven and unprovable assertions."[62]

The Cologne wing, referring to tradition and to Windthorst's views on the matter, argued that the party was, of course, not a confessional party. The Berlin-Trier wing, also pointing to the party's tradition and the authority of its legendary leader, maintained the opposite. The opponents of Cologne argued that the only way the Center could survive was as a Catholic party: a party whose political principles were consistent with the Catholic *Weltanschauung*. Most "Roerenites" opposed interdenominational trade unions (although

---

[58] J. Bachem, "Turm," in Bergsträsser, *Katholizismus*, 2:339.
[59] Ibid.
[60] Ibid., p. 340.
[61] Kisky, *Augustinus-Verein*, pp. 179-81.
[62] J. Bachem, "Was ist das Zentrum?" *Der Tag* no. 254, 14 July 1908.

Matthias Erzberger is an important exception to this rule), viewing them as a further pollution of Catholic lay institutions. They demanded closer clerical supervision of all Catholic lay organizations, above all of the People's Association.

But the *Zentrumsstreit* was also a clash of different regional interpretations of the nature of the Center. It had been the experience of Centrists in the Rhineland and Westphalia that the party was struggling to maintain its support. They, more than Centrists in Bavaria or even Silesia, were confronted with the growing strength of the Socialist movement and the disappearance of small homogenous communities easily controlled by a parish priest.

Hermann Roeren, the most effective critic of the Cologne-Mönchengladbach group, had been a member of the Landtag since 1891. He was elected to the Reichstag two years later where he collaborated with Julius Bachem on the drafting of a commercial bill (*Gesetz gegen den unlauteren Wettbewerb*, 1896). He was a long-time personal friend of both Julius Bachem and his cousin Karl.[63] Roeren first gained national notoriety in 1906 by a campaign to expose colonial scandals and misadminstration, in which Matthias Erzberger was his main colleague.[64] Among Roeren's closest allies was Franz Bitter, a Kiel lawyer and a member of the Reichstag between 1907 and 1912. Bitter told an audience in Koblenz that he and men who thought like him were concerned that proclamations which "systematically tried to detach economic, political, and social questions from Catholic principles," were misguided attempts to present the Center as an interconfessional party.[65] Bitter maintained that the Center was "a political not a confessional party, whose program is based on Christianity, as interpreted by the Catholic Church."[66]

Matthias Erzberger had entered the Reichstag just three years before Julius Bachem published his contentious article. Yet he had already become a prominent, if not universally-appreciated member of the Center caucus. As one of the founders of the Christian trade

---

[63] Hugo Stehkämper, "Julius Bachem (1845-1918)," in *Zeitgeschichte in Lebensbildern. Aus dem deutschen Katholizismus des 20. Jahrhunderts*, ed. Rudolf Morsey (Mainz: Matthias-Grünewald-Verlag, 1973), p. 38.

[64] Klaus Epstein, "Erzberger's Position in the Zentrumsstreit before World War I," *Catholic Historical Review* 44 (1958), p. 7; K. Bachem to H. Roeren (copy), 25 June 1909, HAStK Nl. Bachem 1006/284a.

[65] Speech by Bitter, Koblenz 9 August 1909, reprinted in Bergsträsser, *Katholizismus*, 2:363.

[66] Athanasius [pseud. Adolf ten Hompel], *Das Cölner Osterdienstags-Protokoll* (Bonn: Carl Georgi, 1909), p. 11.

union movement, he had had a stake in the *Gewerkschaftsstreit*. In that dispute he was a champion of the interdenominational position, and belonged to the winning side. At the same time, he gained a reputation as an "aggressive and fearless [defender] of all Catholic concerns."[67] During the *Zentrumsstreit*, Erzberger argued vehemently against an interdenominational party and almost ruined his political career by initially backing the eventual losers. His identification with the Roerenites was the result of his reputation as a staunch defender of Catholic claims and his close personal ties to two of the main exponents of the Berlin faction.[68] His cooperation on colonial questions with Roeren, whom he resembled "both temperamentally and politically,"[69] had soured the relationship between the Center party and Chancellor von Bülow and was in part responsible for the dissolution of the Reichstag in 1906.[70] Erzberger's friendship with Count Hans von Oppersdorff, a Silesian land magnate and editor of *Klarheit und Wahrheit* (the main organ of the Roerenites), received its most public exposure when they collaborated in driving Martin Spahn out of public life in 1910. Eventually, however, Erzberger abandoned the Roerenites and became a champion of the Bachemite cause. Naturally Erzberger's political convictions were questioned and his timely defection to the winning side was never forgotten by either camp and became one of the accusations hurled at him in later years.[71]

The debate intensified when news leaked about a conference that had taken place in Cologne on Easter Tuesday 1909. The participants, among them the Center parliamentarians Roeren and Bitter, had signed a program condemning the interdenominational pollution of the Center, the People's Association and the trade unions. On Easter Tuesday, 13 April 1909, ten Catholic men met in Cologne to formulate a position for the Roerenites. Three of them (Roeren, Bitter, and Rev. Schopen) were Center politicians; four were Catholic journalists (P. Frick, U. Hommerich, Dr. Kaufmann, and Dr. Krückemeyer); one was a teacher (Professor Müller), one a university professor (Dr. Hüls), and one a landed factory owner (Underberg). All of them were concerned that the Center was losing its Catholic character. In addition to these participants, a number of Roerenites had indicated their support for the conference but could not, for one

[67] Epstein, "Erzberger's Position in the Zentrumsstreit," p. 3.
[68] Ibid., p. 9.
[69] Anderson, "Interdenominationalism," p. 359
[70] Klaus Epstein, *Matthias Erzberger and the Dilemma of German Democracy* (Princeton: Princeton University Press, 1959), pp. 73-75.
[71] Epstein, "Erzberger's Position in the Zentrumsstreit," p. 8.

reason or another, come to the meeting. The most prominent among these supporters were: Count Hans von Oppersdorff, Georg von Jochner (editor of the *Historisch-politische Blätter*), and two Rhenish Center parliamentarians, Quirin Peter Wallenborn (Bitburg) and Justizrat Müller (Koblenz). As Roeren and others would emphasize afterwards, this was a private meeting: the group represented no party body, had no official function, and did not aspire to such a role. Nevertheless, minutes were kept of the proceedings, which almost immediately were distributed, allegedly against the will of the participants. The minutes, known as the "Easter Tuesday Protocol," became the subject of a heated debate between the Roeren and the Bachem groups.

Rev. Schopen set the tone of the meeting, opening it by putting three maxims on the table which had been published by the *Historisch-politische Blätter*. The article had stipulated that the Center "was an interdenominational party." But in light of Julius Bachem's arguments, it was necessary to emphasize the party's traditional values as expressed by Ludwig Windthorst. "In the interest of a uniform and large worker's movement, a German Christian trade union with two independent headquarters" (one Protestant the other Catholic) should be formed. In view of the growing influence of the People's Association, it was also considered necessary "to create a closer organizational link to the episcopate."[72] Throughout the conference, the participants rejected the notion of an interconfessional party. They perceived Christian trade unions as a threat to the Center because they represented the special interests of workers; the People's Association posed a similar threat. Thus the Easter Tuesday Conference concurred with the view of the *Historisch-politische Blätter*. The conference ended with a resolution stating that the Center was a political party dedicated "to represent the interests of the entire people in all spheres of public life in accordance with the principles of the Catholic *Weltanschauung*."[73] Bitter declared at the conference that:

> The Center is a political party with an all-encompassing political program. This political party is based on a Christian *Weltanschauung* as it is perceived by Catholics and taught by the Catholic Church. The party is interdenominational in the sense that if a non-Catholic joins [our party], and if

[72] *Historisch-politische Blätter*, 143, no. 2, 16 Jan. 1909, quoted in Athanasius [pseud.], *Cölner*, p. 6.
[73] Athanasius, *Osterdienstags-Protokoll*, p. 12.

he subscribes to our program, he is welcomed with open arms. Our *Weltanschauung* is inseparable from all our practical work. Our entire culture grows out of the soil of religious dogmas, it is shaped by them. Our culture has a Christian soul. It is this Christian soul Modernists want to take away. The basic goal of Modernism is the exclusion of Catholicism from particular questions and aspects of life; it is a silent secularization.[74]

The Roerenites equated the interdenominational arguments of Julius Bachem and his followers with Modernism. Thus they labeled any follower a heretic after the Pope had indexed Schell's work, published an encyclical (1907) against such ideas and demanded the anti-Modernist oath (1910).[75] The integralist camp in the *Gewerkschaftsstreit* had used the very same language when they condemned Christian trade unions. Such links between theological and political questions had become rather blunt tools in times when the church hierarchy was losing ground to the Center Party in defining the ideology that held political Catholicism together. Roerenites also repeated the integralist mistake of demanding more clerical influence over the party and particularly over the People's Association. They believed that the "clergy must determine the direction the party was taking."[76]

Bitter's statement can be seen as a stirring and heartfelt reaffirmation of the strength of the Catholic milieu. Catholic dogma in his view had to be the exclusive source of Catholic political identity. To dilute it, to admit doubters and apostates, to concede that political behaviour is guided by principles other than those sanctioned by the Church—all this would constitute a step toward the disappearance of the very culture that provided the foundation of political Catholicism. Roerenites argued that political decisions, too, must be based on Catholic beliefs. Although this was one of the very arguments

[74] Ibid., p. 8.
[75] For a contemporary commentary by a liberal Catholic on the indexing of Schell's work see Franz Xavier Kraus, "Hermann Schell. Seine Reformschriften und seine Indizierung," in *Liberaler Katholizismus: Biographische und kirchenhistorische Essays von Franz Xaver Kraus*, ed. Christoph Weber (Tübingen: Max Niemeyer Verlag, 1983), pp. 214-54. On general reactions to the encyclical see Nipperdey, *Umbruch*, pp. 35-6; for an evaluation of Center responses to the anti- Modernist oath see August Hermann Leugers-Scherzberg, *Felix Porsch: 1853-1930. Politik für katholische Interessen in Kaiserreich und Republik* (Mainz: Matthias-Grünewald Verlag, 1990), pp. 160-4.
[76] Athanasius, *Osterdienstags-Protokoll*, p. 10.

that separated Roerenites from their opponents, they believed that insistence on a Catholic progam was also a means to unite the party. They argued that it was common Catholic ideology which could bridge the differences between the Right and Left of the party.[77] Despite these promises of the unifying effects of shared spiritual beliefs, differences of outlook were evident even within the Roeren group itself. Matthias Erzberger, for example, parted with Roeren because of the latter's belief that Catholic principles must guide all political acts. Erzberger "saw the folly of referring all party decisions to the arbitrament of specifically Catholic principles." For him Catholic precepts in the field of financial, military, and foreign policy simply did not exist.[78] Radical members of the Roeren group, such as Underberg, the owner of a manor and of a factory in Rheinberg (Düsseldorf district), looked upon Christian trade unions as "a danger to Center and Church." He warned that an "imprudent social education of workers [as advocated by the People's Association] can only lead them [the workers] into the arms of Social Democracy." Therefore it was necessary to bring the Association which lacked "authoritative leadership" under the control of the episcopate.[79] For Underberg, any cooperation with Protestants ("ninety-nine out of a hundred are not Christians anymore") was dangerous. He also saw no advantage in an alliance with the Conservatives. He was convinced that as soon as they no longer needed the Center they would discard the uncomfortable ally in any case. To be in opposition was better for the Center and the Catholics it represented.[80]

The Easter Tuesday Conference shared Underberg's dismay with the People's Association. It declared that, considering the Association's enormous influence over Catholic life, the organization needed to be more closely tied to the episcopate.[81] A few months later, Germany's bishops declared that the episcopate was confident the People's Association would "adhere to the principles contained in its statutes." The bishops also desired to be in constant touch with the Association's leadership with regard to the Association's property, and trusted that the hierarchy would be informed of all important matters and events.[82]

[77] Ibid., p. 9.
[78] Epstein, *Dilemma*, pp. 67-68.
[79] Athanasius, *Osterdienstags-Protokoll* , p. 12.
[80] Ibid.
[81] "Leitsätze der Osterdienstagskonferenz in Köln," 13 April 1909, reprinted in Bergsträsser, *Katholizismus*, 2:361.
[82] "Die Kölner Bischofskonferenz über den Volksverein für das katholische Deutschland," 6 August 1909, reprinted in Bergsträsser, *Katholizismus*, 2:362.

The events of Easter 1909, however, sharpened the distinctions between the various factions within the party, addressing not just questions concerned with the relationship between Church and party but also touching upon the way Catholics perceived their place within the empire. Margaret Anderson has argued that "the Roerenites differed from the Bachemites less in their stance toward labor or toward non-Catholics than in their attitude toward the social and political status quo." In her view, Roeren and Bitter "were critical of the government and the institutions of the Reich: of the high-handed and irresponsible administration of its colonies; of Prussia's plutocratic franchise; of the unfair treatment of its Polish minority; and of the absence of full autonomy for the churches."[83] The Cologne-Mönchengladbach group, on the other hand, the argument goes, embraced the empire more readily. Julius Bachem, for instance, reacted strongly to suggestions that the Center was "the father of all obstacles" in the way of a union between monarch and people.[84] Far from obstructing the Reichstag, the Center, when given a chance, had supported many important bills: the Civil Code, the navy bills and the tariff bills were only the most important examples. The very fact that the Center had played such a prominent role in past legislation invalidated the suggestion, believed Bachem, that it was a Catholic and not a purely political party.

In the beginning the *Zentrumsstreit* was a series of minor skirmishes and brief if virulent encounters between two conflicting party factions. After the Easter Tuesday Conference, however, it turned into a full-scale battle which did not end until one side had been defeated. Karl Bachem was among the first to receive a copy of the conference protocol. Almost immediately, he wrote a letter to Roeren demanding clarification and retraction "of the long list of the most stupid accusations" hurled against the Bachem group. Bachem was especially incensed about the branding of his cousin as a "liberal Catholic," whose ultimate goal was "to free German Catholic public life of the influence of episcopacy and orthodoxy." As heavily as accusations of "modernism" and "secularization" weighed with Karl Bachem, the sending of the protocol to German bishops outraged him more. Going behind the back of the Center leadership was a betrayal of party loyalty. Moreover, it was also a character assassina-

---

[83] Anderson, "Interdenominationalism," p. 363.
[84] J. Bachem, "Ist das Zentrum der 'Vater der Hindernisse'?," *Der Tag* no. 387, 17 Dec. 1908.

tion of Julius Bachem, "a man who for more than forty years has been in the thick of the struggle for Catholicism and the Center."[85] However, an apology from Hermann Roeren was not forthcoming. In a polite and calm letter, Roeren doubted the authenticity of the minutes, calling them "a mystification" of the actual meeting. He argued that far from attacking his friend Julius Bachem, he preferred an objective discussion, and that no protocol had been sent to the bishops. He carefully avoided addressing any of the specific questions Karl Bachem had put to him.[86]

After the Easter Tuesday Conference the Roerenites were clearly on the defensive. Their opponents painted the conference as an attempt to split the party. The rift between the two camps could not be bridged by polite correspondence and appeals to past friendship. As letters went back and forth between Roeren and Karl Bachem, the demands for an unambiguous stance and for recantation[87] were swept away by assurances that the whole protocol was nothing but a vicious fabrication and that Roeren was "willing to do everything to avoid a split in the party."[88] The unconvincing response from Bitter and Roeren was that their action had been aimed not at the party but merely at "the press and pamphlets which have tried to misrepresent the true character of the Center Party."[89] Their attempts to rally a public following to their cause largely failed. A rally in Koblenz, for example, though a stormy affair, was not even supported by the Trier Centrists. Although Trier had been the birthplace and center of the Roeren group, the district election committees of Trier-Stadt, Trier-Land, and Wittlich-Bernkastel did not support them and declined to participate in the Koblenz rally.[90]

The Roerenites knew that they lacked support among Center politicians. Bitter believed that too many Center parliamentarians were "ambitious office-hunters who lacked backbone." He also believed the Catholic people were behind him. But Roeren cautioned in 1909 that their group had not gathered enough support for an outright attack on the Bachemites. Hüls, too, thought that the public needed to be more informed about their position and suggested a

---

[85] K. Bachem to H. Roeren, 25 June 1909, HAStK Nl. Bachem 1006/284a.
[86] H. Roeren to K. Bachem, 27 June 1909, HAStK Nl. Bachem 1006/284a.
[87] K. Bachem to H. Roeren, 1 July 1909, HAStK Nl. Bachem 1006/284a.
[88] H. Roeren to K. Bachem, 3 July 1909, HAStK Nl. Bachem 1006/284a.
[89] Circular by Bitter, Juli 1909, quoted in Hermann Roeren, *Veränderte Lage des Zentrumstreits. Entgegnung auf die Kritik meiner Schrift Zentrum und Kölner Richtung* (Trier: Petrus-Verlag, 1914), pp. 29-30.
[90] J. Bachem, "Was geht vor?," *Der Tag* no. 187, 12 Aug. 1909.

press campaign in order to spread their viewpoint. Krückemeyer realized that their group could "do practically nothing about [support from] the trade unions." Financial support appears to have been small, too. At the meeting on Easter Tuesday the only mention of funds was 500 marks donated by Underberg.[91] The Roerenites lamented the lack of press support they could muster. The journalist Heinrich Krückemeyer told the participants of the Easter Tuesday Conference that in his view just a dozen Catholic papers were willing to support their cause. Some of the men present thought that even that small number was too high. Of the Rhenish Catholic papers only five supported the Roerenites: *Rheinischer Merkur* (Cologne), *Deutsche Reichszeitung* (Bonn), *Essener Volkszeitung, Echo der Gegenwart* (Aachen), and *Trierische Landeszeitung*.[92]

Most party leaders were offended by the Easter Tuesday Conference because it appeared to undermine the authority of the party organization. Rather than addressing their grievances through the proper channels, the Roerenites lacked party discipline. This group, Julius Bachem charged, had no business defining the character of the party. If such a definition were indeed needed, it was the responsibility of the party's Landtag and Reichstag factions to provide it. Bachem was incensed that Bitter, a member of the Reichstag for only one legislative period, had the audacity to ignore the authority of men such as von Hertling, Spahn, Herold, Fritzen, Hitze, Trimborn and others.[93] By the fall of 1909 the Center leadership had decided that firm action was needed to squash the Roeren campaign. If the party was seriously trying to win the battle of Catholic public opinion, it had to take a decisive authoritative stance.

On Sunday morning, 28 November 1909, the leadership of the Prussian Center and the directorate of the Reichstag caucus met in Berlin to resolve the matter of defining the Center Party.[94] Of the Roerenites, only Roeren himself was present; Bitter had been denied admission since he did not belong to any of the party committees present. Karl Trimborn and Julius Bachem had prepared a draft resolution which was the basis of the discussions. The debate, according to Karl Bachem, went smoothly and calmly, not least because Roeren maintained an objective disposition. Only Josef von Strombeck and

[91] Athanasius, *Osterdienstags-Protokoll*, pp. 14-6.
[92] Ibid., p. 13.
[93] J. Bachem, "Was geht vor?," *Der Tag* no. 187, 12 Aug. 1909.
[94] Only Spahn did not participate. This account is based on Karl Bachem's notes, "Landesausschußsitzung der Preussischen Centrumspartei," 28 Nov. 1909, HAStK Nl. Bachem 1006/285.

von Galen "made a very weak attempt to present his [Roeren's] point of view. Roeren himself said little, following the debate with a "depressed and bitter" expression on his face. Trimborn's resolution was judged too long and an editing committee (consisting of Porsch, Hertling, Trimborn, Gröber and Roeren) was charged with shortening the resolution and providing a draft on which the leaders could vote. Roeren, isolated and in a desperate minority of one, tried in vain to defend his point of view. In the end, he had little choice but to support the resolution of the committee which made no reference to Catholic *Weltanschauung*.

The *Zentrumsstreit* was like a bad family argument: vicious, petty, and incomprehensible to outsiders. Ironically, the opposing factions had more in common with each other than either had with any other German political group. They both professed to be the heirs to Windthorst's political philosophy. According to Epstein, the "common sense behind the Cologne position assured its triumph at all party meetings."[95] And, indeed, Roeren and his followers were condemned at a meeting of the combined Reich and Prussian party leaders on 28 November 1909. As Margaret Anderson has shown, on the other hand, the Roerenite argument was not as devoid of common sense as Epstein suggests. However, their chances of winning the controversy did not really depend on the strength of this argument. In January 1911 Julius Bachem decided that enough was enough. He wrote to Felix Porsch that he was not willing to discuss the question with Roeren further. Roeren's insulting charge that the *Kölnische Volkszeitung* was "heretical and had fallen from Catholic faith," and Roeren's superficial, manichean understanding of the issues, made more discussion fruitless.[96]

In the end, the Roerenites realized that they were outgunned. Their opponents controlled much of the Catholic press, occupied the key positions within the party, and had managed to marginalize them. Roeren and Count Oppersdorff were formally expelled from the party in 1912. Julius Bachem declared victory after those Centrists "who wanted to exclude non-Catholics" from the party either were not nominated in their ridings again for the 1912 Reichstag election or had resigned from the Center caucus.[97]

The fundamental difference between the Bachemites and the Roerenites was their opposing views on the role of the Center in

---

[95] Epstein, "Erzberger's Position in the Zentrumsstreit," p. 15.
[96] J. Bachem to Porsch, 12 Jan. 1911 (copy), BAK Nl. 176 Herold Nr. 4.
[97] Bachem, *Erinnerungen*, p. 180.

German politics. For the Bachemites, the Center was a political party with the desire to participate in government. To this end the Center had to pursue opportunistic policies, to make compromises even if they involved difficult concessions on many issues. Accordingly, Karl Bachem argued, the Center had voted for the Civil Code even though it contained marriage laws in contradiction with canon law. Like Erzberger, Julius and Karl Bachem saw no particularly Catholic component in tariff or navy bills. The Bachemites were also acutely aware of the need to address the problems of workers. Interdenominational Christian trade unions and the People's Association were the two most important institutions in securing working class support. This, of course, was an area of particular concern in the Rhineland, where industrialization and urbanization had affected the Catholic population more than anywhere else in Germany. It should come as no surprise, then, that a movement to incorporate these developments should originate and find its strongest support in such a region. It is also not surprising that some of the most ardent opposition to the Bachem group came from the rural areas adjacent to the Rhineland's expanding industrial areas.

Roeren and his followers, on the other hand, had little interest in the Center as a governing party. Their overriding concern was the preservation of a pure, undiluted Catholic subculture within an alien environment. To some of these men, participation in government was an outright danger to Catholicism: the Catholic integrity of the Center was more important than a share in political power. Here, it should perhaps be acknowledged that Roeren and his group were not unjustified in believing that compromises might lead to a weakening of the Center. After all, the Center had never been able to attract Protestants in any significant number; its political survival depended almost entirely on the support of Catholics. Could they not legitimately ask why Catholics should continue to vote for the Center if the party provided nothing more than the protection of economic interests?

With the *Zentrumsstreit* we can observe a paradox wherein the rhetoric of integralism and democracy threatened to destroy the very foundations on which the Center was built. The strength of the party was its ideological cohesion. Its supporters shared the belief that the principles of Roman Catholicism were the rock on which their communities—and ideally their state—should be built. Admission of a large number of Protestants or non-Christians would inevitably weaken this cohesion. Yet Julius Bachem and his followers believed that the only way the Center could continue to exist in imperial

Germany was to aggressively canvass the support of non-Catholics. In their minds, such efforts did nothing to weaken the link between the party and the Catholic identity of its members. Roeren and his followers believed the opposite: without cleaving to Catholic principles, the party would loose its *raison d'être*. The Center without Catholicism was about as relevant as the SPD without Marxism. Neither side ever questioned the assumption that religion had a place in politics. The idea of a secular Center was incomprehensible, although they both perceived the danger of a secular society and of *Kulturprotestantismus*.[98] There was no hope that the Center's political enemies would ever be convinced that the party was not acting in the interests of the Catholic Church. The discussions about the character of the Center elicited little more than "mild amusement" among non-Catholics. For in response to assurances from its leaders that the Center was not a confessional party, its opponents voiced only sarcastic disbelief. To opponents, liberal or conservative alike, Center assurances that it did not have a Catholic agenda were plain lies. In their eyes "the Center is and remains a confessional and political party."[99]

Margaret Anderson's argument that the Roerenites rather than the Bachemites had a more realistic grasp on political circumstances in the Germany of Bismarck and Wilhelm II, warrants close attention and general approval. Anderson convincingly argues that Roeren's interpretation of the Center's role within the Kaiserreich more closely reflected the existing position of Catholics in imperial Germany than that of Julius Bachem. To believe that there was room for an interdenominational party of the kind the Christian Democratic Union (CDU) would be after World War II is a fundamental misinterpretation of the realities of Wilhelmine Germany. The Center envisioned by Bachem would likely have suffered the fate the Roerenites predicted.

[98] Anderson, "Interdenominationalism," p. 375.
[99] "Konfessionelle Partei?," *Vossische Zeitung* no. 599, 22 Dec. 1909; "Lügen des Zentrums?," *Jungliberale Blätter* no. 3, 22 Jan. 1910.

VII.

THE RHENISH CENTER AND NATIONAL POLITICS

DURING THE LAST YEARS of the nineteenth century the Center emerged as the political party which held the balance of power in the Reichstag. Ludwig Bamberger likened the Center to "a lover courted by all parties of the empire." A Catholic publicist thought that the image of Don Juan was a more appropriate metaphor—obviously without considering the ruthless seducer's end.[1] Whatever image one prefers, the Center had become Germany's most influential party. In both the Reichstag and the Prussian Landtag the Center's stance toward the government had been transformed from ardent opposition to cautious cooperation. Under Lieber's leadership and with the encouragement of Caprivi (whose "conciliatory policy" toward the Center was initially surprisingly successful) the bourgeois (*bürgerlich*) forces within the Center gained the upper hand.[2] It became an active participant in the passing of social legislation, it supported the government's trade and tariff policies and it voted for army and navy bills. Repressive legislation such as the anti-revolution bill and the penitentiary bill (*Umsturz- und Zuchthausvorlage*), however, still did not receive Center backing. The party's support of army and navy bills, on the other hand, was explicit approval for Germany's *Weltpolitik* and its colonial claims. This kind of activity, Lieber hoped, would get German Catholics the "national rehabilitation" they were craving. As we shall see, Rhineland Centrists often opposed *Weltpolitik*, and favored social policies. They were not surprised that in the end Lieber failed in his efforts to make the Center an equal partner in government and instead the party was

---

[1] Felix Volkart, "Gestalten aus dem Reichstage," *Daheim*, vol. 37 (16 March 1901), p. 19.

[2] John C. G. Röhl, *Germany without Bismarck. The Crisis of Government in the Second Reich, 1890-1900* (London: B. T. Batsford, 1967), p. 75; Loth, *Katholiken*, p. 51.

tormented by serious inner tensions which had their roots in unresolved questions about its Catholic nature and its attitudes towards the growing working class.[3]

The reluctant cooperation between Caprivi and the Center was also detrimental to the chancellor and his government. Wilfried Loth has demonstrated how Caprivi's willingness to govern with Center support weakened his own position encouraging his opponents at court and in the Prussian government to intrigue against him.[4] Until 1894, however, attempts by his political enemies to remove him failed. Only in the wake of the Eulenburg crisis did the Kaiser dismiss Caprivi and appoint the Bavarian politician and diplomat Prince Chlodwig zu Hohenlohe-Schillingsfürst.[5] Hohenlohe who had no great love for Prussia and a great dislike for Junkers nevertheless had been an important supporter of Bismarck's unification. Bismarck, who appreciated Hohenlohe's talents, appointed him ambassador in Paris in the wake of the notorious Arnim affair and later governor of Alsace-Lorraine. The Bavarian statesman was the first Catholic to become Reich chancellor but he was no friend of the Center. This sentiment was reciprocated by many Catholics who deeply resented Hohenlohe's enthusiasm for the Kulturkampf, his opposition to the Vatican Council and his dislike of the *Societas Jesu*, whose activities he deemed "a declaration of war on the very foundations of our state."[6] The former minister president of Bavaria (1866-1870) was a Free Conservative member of the Reichstag since its beginning. He had the reputation of being a liberal conservative Catholic whose loyalty to the empire was unquestioned and whose social position was such that he was related to several of Europe's royal families and that Wilhelm II called him "Uncle" and addressed him with the familiar *Du*. When Hohenlohe became chancellor he was already seventy-five years old, his health was poor, he was hard of hearing, and suffered from a faulty memory. During the reign of most rulers these circumstances would have disqualified him from occupying Germany's most powerful political office, but to the Kaiser, who was merely looking for a figurehead, they appeared attractive. Hohenlohe's repu-

[3] K. Bachem notes, HAStK Nl. Bachem 1005/2, f. 174 quoted in Kiefer, B*achem*, p. 91.
[4] Loth, *Katholiken*, pp. 62-3.
[5] On the circumstances of Hohenlohe's appointment see Röhl, *Germany without Bismarck*, pp. 118-22. Unlike Caprivi, who sought a separation of Prussian and Reich offices, Hohenlohe occupied the Bismarckian triumpherate of Reich chancellor, Prussian minister president and Prussian foreign minister.
[6] Cited in KB, 5:368.

tation as a moderate conservative made him acceptable to large segments of the political spectrum. Despite their reservations about Hohenlohe, the "Center especially was anxious to keep him in office and frequently subdued its criticism of the government to this end."[7] This was in part due to the increased importance of the Reichstag in German politics. The Center politician Martin Spahn observed that during Hohenlohe's chancellorship (1894-1900), the Reichstag became the center of Germany's political life. While the government limited itself to the drafting of new legislation, it was the Reichstag that "determined the pace, the national value, the warmth and uniformity of national politics."[8] While overestimating the role of parliament in German politics, Spahn correctly observed a trend. The Reichstag was indeed playing a greater role than intended by Bismarck, although it never in the life of the Second Empire acquired the power of other European parliaments. Still, politics had become a full-time occupation. Parliamentarians, and in particular Socialists and Centrists but also others, abandoned their private careers. By the turn of the century, Berlin had become the hub of German political activities and the Reichstag could not just be ignored even by the Kaiser who detested it. Reichstag and Prussian Landtag, in which many parliamentarians had seats simultaneously, sat in parallel sessions, usually from November or December until May or June. During the summer, political life in the capital almost came to a standstill. Ministers and bureaucrats left for their vacations, the Kaiser went hunting and cruising and most parliamentarians returned to their homes. Yet political life did not come to a complete standstill. Parliamentary work was just one aspect of the life of modern politicians: party organization, fundraising and preparing election campaigns made demands on their time and energy.

A hallmark of Hohenlohe's transitional tenure as chancellor was the government's unending attacks on the Social Democratic Party. Despite its animosity toward Socialism and Socialists, the Center opposed attempts to restrict the right to assembly and association in Prussia (1895). Lieber was not willing to violate principles of the Rechtsstaat in order to limit the activities of a political opponent. Bachem, too, was determined to protect constitutional rights and the integrity of the Reichstag.[9] Not without justification did the Center fear that limits on Socialist activities were only the first step

---

[7] Röhl, *Germany without Bismarck*, p. 223.
[8] Spahn, *Zentrum*, p. 94.
[9] Loth, *Katholiken*, p. 63; KB, 5:389.

to general limitation of political activities. Thus the Center forced a lengthy debate of the proposed legislation and eventually the antisocialist bill was abandoned (October 1895). Ernst Matthias von Köller, the emperor's choice as Minister of the Interior, who had introduced the legislation, was dismissed in December 1895 after he had alienated his cabinet colleagues.[10] But however far such resistance to unconstitutional legislation went, it seemed unlikely to solve the basic problem. The German state, which never achieved an equilibrium of the claims to authority by the emperor, the Junkers, the military and civil administration on the one hand and political parties on the other, was in a permanent political crisis. Centrists and activists in the organizations of political Catholicism were forced to conclude that their political and social institutions were under constant threat and that they were rarely accepted as loyal subjects let alone equal partners in the political process.

In order to improve its precarious position, the Center, aided by its significant share of Reichstag seats which after 1893 gave it the deciding voice in all legislation of national importance, eagerly participated in shaping Imperial Germany. The legislation Centrists were most proud of was the introduction of a uniform civil code for Germany. Twenty-five years after the founding of the Second Reich, there was a general desire for an improved and uniform civil law. Until then German civil jurisdiction had been a patchwork of various regional codes: Bavaria adhered to the *Codex Maximilianeus Bavaricus* (1756), Prussian civil law was governed by the *Allgemeine preußische Landrecht* (1794) and the *Code Napoléon* (1804) was in force in Rheinhessen, Rheinpfalz, Baden, Alsace-Lorraine and the Rhineland. As well as creating a federal civil code, the new *Bürgerliches Gesetzbuch* (BGB) was seen as a further measure to unite Prussia and the states incorporated in the Reich in 1871 by the conformity of law and government. The Rhenish Center politician Victor Rintelen referred to the BGB as "a significant national undertaking" which the Center wholeheartedly supported.[11] However, Rintelen and his colleagues were not willing to accept the legislation in its original formulation.

The issue Catholics were most concerned about was that of civil marriage. The conflict was not new. It had been the impetus for the

---

[10] For details on the Köller affair see Röhl, *Germany without Bismarck*, pp. 142-6.

[11] Rintelen's address to the Reichstag, 3 February 1896, reprinted in Bergsträsser, *Katholizismus*, 2:285-301, this quotation on p. 285. Rintelen represented the Trier district from October 1884 to January 1907.

Cologne Troubles and Prussian legislation on civil marriage reached back to the Kulturkampf years. Civil marriage had already been introduced to the Rhineland during Napoleon's regime and in 1875 the Prussian law making civil marriage compulsory was extended to all of Germany. Although Catholic church leaders advised their flock to obey the state's laws, the clergy frequently protested against this perceived intrusion on ecclesiastical rights and Catholics in general opposed the state's interference.[12] During the drafting of the Civil Code, the issue was discussed by a twenty-one member Reichstag commission (to which Lieber, Spahn, Gröber and Karl Bachem belonged). The draft presented to the Reichstag included the very marriage law of 1875 which was incompatible with canon law but had been practiced for more than two decades.[13] Centrists were divided on the role their party should play in the incorporation of the marriage law into the Civil Code, some arguing that civil marriage should be voluntary, others denying the state any say in the administration of a sacrament. After failing to attract support for their compromise position from both the Conservatives and the National Liberals, Lieber agreed to the inclusion of obligatory civil marriage in the Civil Code in exchange for concessions on the property rights of women separated but not divorced from their husbands.[14]

Students of the Center Party have noted the difference between Lieber's attitude to the Civil Code and Windthorst's opposition to a uniform civil code as promoted by the National Liberal Party and based on "modern ideas" which, according to Windthorst, were a dangerous step toward "centralization and the striving for a uniform state."[15] In the end, Spahn wrote, the Center faction passed this "extraordinary test of [its] political character with flying colors."[16] Under Center leadership in parliamentary commissions and plenary sessions, and with its support in the final vote, the Reichstag eventually passed the Civil Code. Among the fruits the Center reaped for its support for the Civil Code were the recognition and praise of former political enemies. Karl Bachem cites with obvious pride the acknowledgment by the *Deutsche Reichspartei* parliamentarian Wilhelm von Kardorff, of the Center's part in the passing of important laws. This judgment, Bachem said, was particularly satisfying since von Kardorff had been "a fanatical opponent of the Center"

---

[12] KB, 5:428-9.
[13] Traut, *Lieber,* 135; KB, 5:433.
[14] Zeender, *Center Party,* pp. 59-60.
[15] Traut, *Lieber,* 134-5; KB, 5:424-
[16] Spahn, *Zentrum,* p. 102.

during the Kulturkampf.[17] This praise aside, other legislation passed with more difficulty than the Civil Code. The Courts Martial Bill was passed with Center votes, but Bavarian Centrists registered their opposition to the dissolution of the supreme military court of Bavaria (*oberster bayerischer Militärgerichtshof*) by voting against the new law. In the end a Bavarian chamber (*Senat*) was introduced to the central military court (*Reichsmilitärgericht*) in Berlin, and Bavarian Centrists agreed to the reform legislation.[18] Actions such as these, according to Karl Bachem, were one of the recurring problems the Reich and the Center Party had to deal with. The growing importance of the Reichstag and Berlin notwithstanding, particularism was not dead, regional rivalries still played an important role in Germany.

The question of social reform was an issue that divided the components of political Catholicism and brought to light the difficulties Centrists faced in a largely hostile political landscape. Unlike many other aspects of national politics, in the area of social policies there existed a particular Rhenish perspective. Many of the advocates of social reform among the Center ranks came from the Rhineland. More importantly, however, those organizations within political Catholicism most concerned with social reform and most directly involved with the question of integrating industrial workers into the fold of the Center Party were not only located in the Rhineland but were often led by Rhenish Catholics.

Social policies had been a noteworthy component of Center proclamations since the late 1870s. Concern for social reform and improved conditions for industrial workers grew during the 1890s. These were the years of the founding of the Peoples' Association, of Hitze's advocacy of Christian trade unions and workers' industrial councils, and of Wilhelm II's short-lived enthusiasm for social legislation. Pope Leo XIII's publication of the encyclical *Rerum Novarum* (15 May 1891) coincided with the ascendance of the Center's new leadership. Under the direction of Ernst Lieber and Franz Hitze, the Center, benefiting from the more benign climate after Bismarck's dismissal and the removal of the most ardent *Kulturkämpfer* from the Ministry of Ecclesiastical Affairs,[19] could pay more attention to the social question. The Pope's encyclical offered a Catholic response to the challenges and changes industrialization had brought to European soci-

---

[17] KB, 5:456.
[18] KB, 5:459.
[19] The full name was Ministry of Cults, Ecclesiastical Affairs, Education and Medicine.

eties. The pontiff's Christian social reforms did not offer concrete economic advice however. Indeed, the curia did not perceive the social question as primarily an economic or political problem at all. Instead, the Church argued that social ills must be cured by religious and moral remedies. The encyclical offered three principal vaccines against seduction by the false promises of Socialism: fraternity, charity, and faith. To counter Socialist efforts, Catholic workers should organize under close clerical supervision and guidance. A fraternity of Catholic workers, coming together under the umbrella of workers' clubs or trade unions, guided by notions of industrial harmony would provide the kind of protection against hardship and poverty workers needed in an industrial society. Those who fell on hard times could rely on the charity of the newly-created Catholic social institutions designed to alleviate the worst symptoms of rapid industrialization. Ultimately it was faith in Catholic morals and the Church, and the acceptance of Catholic values by the growing working class which provided spiritual immunization against the dangers of atheism and socialism.

The encyclical gave rather vague advice on how actually to formulate and organize a Catholic response to social change. The Center, never content to rely on clerical advice alone to work out its policies, drew up its own responses. Lieber's commitment to social reforms for Catholics workers was lukewarm. Always willing to make grandiose speeches about the value of trade unions, Lieber lacked "passionate conviction" for the cause.[20] Karl Trimborn, now chairman of the Rhineland Center, was passionate about social reform and carried this passion to Catholic workers in innumerable speeches he made on the subject and the organizational work he carried out for the Peoples' Association.[21] He took Franz Hitze's place as the party's expert on social legislation and together with Hitze and the general secretary of the Peoples' Association, August Pieper, he formed a formidable troika of Catholic social reformers. At the *Katholikentag* in Danzig (1891) Trimborn warned that Germany was in a deep economic and social crisis.[22] After the boom year of 1889, the Kaiserreich experienced its third and longest period of economic depression. Triggered by the collapse of the London Baring bank in early 1890, central Europe and with it Germany went through half a

[20] Zeender, *Center Party*, p. 76.
[21] Cardauns, *Trimborn*, pp. 70-1.
[22] Verhandlungen der 38. Generalversammlung der Katholiken Deutschlands zu Danzig vom 30. August bis 3. September 1891, quoted in Becker, "Enzyklika rerum novarum," p. 264.

decade of painful structural adjustment. Steel and iron production fell, the price for coal from the Ruhr declined and workers were laid off. Those who kept their jobs lost income, real wages could not keep pace with inflation, even the average income of the Ruhr region's well-paid miners decreased.[23] In this context, it is important to note the increased socio-political initiatives of the Center. Winfried Becker argues that this very activity indicates that the interpretation of the Center offered by David Blackbourn and Wilfried Loth has to be revised and expressed in less general terms. Rather than emphasizing the Center's embracing of mainstream Wilhelmian and Prussian society and state as well as the taking over by bourgeois Center leaders, Becker emphasizes the Center's new socio-political program based on *Rerum Novarum* and the efforts it made to secure working-class support.[24] The good showing of the Center in the 1893 Reichstag election, particularly in the Rhineland's industrial areas, seems to be proof of the efficacy of the Center's social policies. For the moment it appeared as if the advance of the Socialists had been brought to a halt.

The support of state legislation by Pope and Center was not without its pitfalls, given the Church's misgivings about state efforts to legislate an area which the clergy regarded as its prerogative. The state's claim to authority over these issues also threatened to take away one of the cornerstones of Center activity.[25] By the middle of the 1890s, the Kaiser was disillusioned with labor laws and the German working class. Reformers such as Hans von Berlepsch and Heinrich von Bötticher had lost the Kaiser's ear. Their place was taken by patriarchal industrialists such as Carl Ferdinand ("King") Stumm and Friedrich Krupp who treated their own workers well but violently opposed trade unions. Besides limiting work hours, Stumm and Krupp provided housing for workers and kindergartens and schools for the children of their employees. Not unlike the Catholic entrepreneur Franz Brandts, they believed that they had the right to determine political and social views of their employees. Stumm thought that in order to prosper an enterprise must be organized "in a military not a democratic fashion," Krupp advised his workers "to vote for the [candidates] suggested by men of trust," politics he said

---

[23] Hans-Ulrich Wehler, *Deutsche Gesellschaftsgeschichte* (Munich: Verlag C. H. Beck, 1987-), 3:577-9.
[24] Becker, "Enzyklika Rerum novarum," p. 273.
[25] Leo Haupts, "Wilhelm II., die deutschen Katholiken und die Anfänge der wilhelminischen Sozialpolitik," *Historisches Jahrbuch der Görres-Gesellschaft* 101, no. 1 (1981), p. 133.

is too complicated a subject for workers who lack "the leisure and understanding" to grasp political issues.[26] This patriarchical approach did "everything for the worker but allowed nothing to be done by the worker," as Karl Bachem put it.[27] The reversal of Wilhelm II's attitudes toward German workers and the abandonment of industrial social reform posed new problems for the Center. The substitution of Stumm and Krupp also displaced Hitze who had advised the government on labor policies. With Hitze's falling out of favor, the Center lost one of the few avenues for influencing government labor policies. According to one historian of the Center, Lieber regretted and relished this development at the same time. While the party leader mourned the decline of his party's influence on the government, his fears diminished that "a serious governmental commitment to social legislation would strengthen the position of the conservative wing of his party and enhance its efforts to create a Center-Conservative coalition which would identify itself with the ideals of a 'Christian social order and culture.'"[28] The divergent opinions among Center politicians on social reform add another layer of evidence to the argument that political Catholicism was a diverse movement which sometimes formed political ideas and strategies independent of the Roman Catholic Church and on occasion in opposition to it. As far as national politics were concerned the question of social reforms was soon eclipsed by Germany's ambition to play a leading role on the stage of Great Power politics.

A. The Center and Weltpolitik

Karl Bachem believed that nobody in the Center caucus was capable of "forming an independent judgment on…the difficulties and entanglements of international [affairs]."[29] Despite Bachem's self-effacing dictum it is worth examining how the Center Party dealt with foreign policies. Disputes among the Reichstag parties and between the Center and the government and the Kaiser became the main stage for their confrontation. The role of the Center in domestic politics was intricately tied to imperialism, anti-Socialism and naval

---

[26] Stumm and Krupp quoted in Peter Brandt, ed. *Preußen: Zur Sozialgeschichte eines Staates. Eine Darstellung in Quellen* (Reinbek bei Hamburg: Rowohlt, 1981), pp. 247-8.
[27] KB, 5:416.
[28] Zeender, *Center Party*, p. 75.
[29] KB, 5:382.

policies.[30] Although the Center's foreign policy positions were almost exclusively formulated by the Reichstag caucus and by their very nature often lack a regional perspective, it is worthwhile to investigate how the Center responded to calls for a more aggressive colonial policy and, above all, for a larger navy. As we will see, Rhenish Centrists figured importantly in debates of these questions. And while there is no "Rhenish foreign policy" *per se*, there are significant differences between the national Center position on *Weltpolitik* and that of Rhenish Centrists.

The debate of patriotic loyalty and political coalitions became part of a crucial discussion about German *Weltpolitik* which also involved the Center. Many Germans thought that the national destiny lay in a more deliberate overseas expansion. Their country had joined the ranks of world powers and was entitled to its "place in the sun."[31] Many merchants, the Cologne industrialist and liberal politician Gustav Mevissen among them,[32] were convinced of the commercial advantages of colonial possessions. Rhenish merchants and manufacturers founded the West German Association for Colonization and Export (1881). Strongly influenced by the ideas of the Protestant pastor and "father of the German colonial movement," Friedrich Fabri, the association's program set out to further German export, to support German emigrants, and to acquire agricultural lands overseas.[33] Although Catholics played only a minor role in such enterprises, Center politicians had to recognize or at least pay lip service to colonial enthusiasm. Ludwig Windthorst grudgingly agreed with Mevissen and Bismarck that German industrial products needed new

---

[30] Eckart Kehr, *Battleship Building and Party Politics in Germany, 1894-1901: A Cross-Section of the Political, Social and Ideological Preconditions of German Imperialism* (New York: Kraus Reprint, 1975), pp. 374-5.

[31] Speech to the Reichstag, Bernhard von Bülow, 6 December 1897, reprinted in Michael Behnen, ed. *Quellen zur deutschen Außenpolitik im Zeitalter des Imperialismus: 1890-1911* (Darmstadt: Wissenschaftliche Buchgesellschaft, 1977), pp. 165-6.

[32] On Mevissen's views on colonialism see Beate-Carola Padtberg, "Gustav (von) Mevissen, ein rheinischer Unternehmer zwischen Wirtschaftsleben und Politik (1815-1899)," in *Die Rheinlande und Preußen: Parlamentarismus, Parteien und Wirtschaft*, Landschaftsverband Rheinland (Cologne: Rheinland-Verlag, 1990), p. 136.

[33] The "Westdeutsche Verein für Kolonisation und Export" was founded as a chapter of the "Centralverein für Handelsgeographie und Förderung deutscher Interessen im Auslande." For details on the cicumstances of its establishment see Ulrich S. Soénius, *Koloniale Begeisterung im Rheinland während des Kaiserreiches* (Cologne: Rheinisch-Westfälisches Wirtschaftsarchiv zu Köln e. V., 1992), pp. 15, 21-5.

markets, the question of exports was at the "heart of German colonial expansion" added Viktor Rintelen.[34] Karl Bachem, too, supported colonial expansion primarily for economic reasons.[35] German industry required access to raw materials and only the possession of colonies, the argument went, would break Great Britain's monopoly on world markets. There were other motives for German colonialism. It was after all the Age of the Empire and empire building, now a genuinely global affair, became the ambition of virtually all European states; only an empire many believed would elevate the young Kaiserreich into the ranks of great powers.[36] German patriots enchanted with an empire endowed with grand, mystical meaning dreamed of colonial possessions and loudly demanded a stronger army and a larger navy.[37] Many Centrists joined the chorus of colonial enthusiasts and anglophobe right-wing patriotic associations when Bismarck agreed to accord government protection to German overseas business interests.[38] As so often in the history of the Center, the tone of its announcements and the tenor of its press, namely that of *Germania*, were manifestation of Catholic loyalty to Hohenzollern Germany. One such manifestation was dislike of England and the English. Even level-headed politicians such as Matthias Erzberger (who had never visited the British Isles nor knew much about its people) subscribed to the widespread dislike of Great Britain. In his view, British opposition to a strong German navy was just another "act of typical British arrogance."[39] More disturbing still, the aggressive stand of some Center politicians on colonies foreshadowed their ardor for German aggression during World War I. Peter Spahn and Adolf Gröber were early supporters of *Weltpolitik*.[40] Karl Bachem disliked England, favored colonies, and subscribed to a "militant nationalism" which made him an ardent supporter of annexations and unlimited submarine warfare; during World War I, the Vatican

---

[34] Hans-Ulrich Wehler, *Bismarck und der Imperialismus* (1969; reprint, Frankfurt a. M.: Suhrkamp, 1985), p. 171.
[35] Kiefer, B*achem*, p. 173n13.
[36] Of the significant European powers only Austria-Hungary had no imperial ambitions.
[37] Thomas Rohkrämer, *Der Militarismus der "kleinen Leute": Die Kriegervereine im Deutschen Kaiserreich, 1871-1914* (Munich: R. Oldenbourg Verlag, 1990), p. 238.
[38] Hans Pehl, *Die deutsche Kolonialpolitik und das Zentrum 1884-1914* (Limburg: Limburger Vereinsdruckerei, 1934), p. 14.
[39] Epstein, *Dilemma*, pp. 92-3.
[40] Loth, *Katholiken*, pp. 79-80.

would regard him as "an obstacle to peace [*friedliche Verständigung*]."⁴¹ Karl Trimborn, on the other hand, was remarkably immune to the idea of Germany as a world power.

The enthusiasm for *Weltpolitik* among Centrists and German Catholics was tempered by the question of how they fit into the national and political landscape of Germany; the wounds of the Kulturkampf had far from healed. A few Centrists realized the potential for the problems associated with colonial expansion. When August Reichensperger retired from parliamentary life, he warned his voters that navy expansion, the construction of ports and naval stations in Africa, and the ambition to become equal with sea powers such as France and England would cause "great costs and difficulties [*Verlegenheiten*]" for the country.⁴² The costs and risks associated with colonialism remained a concern for the Center. Two decades after Reichensperger, Matthias Erzberger exposed mismanagement and corruption in Germany's colonial administration.

In the eyes of navy supporters, colonial promoters and many conservative Germans, a Catholic's stance on colonial questions provided a shibboleth for allegiance to the new Germany. Catholics and their political representatives were judged by their attitudes towards colonies and the navy. They found it very difficult to give unmitigated support for colonial expansion yet any hesitancy was interpreted by their opponents as proof for their unpatriotic attitudes. Colonies, however, were not just about commercial opportunities, national rivalries, and loyalty to the state, they also had a religious component.

There were Protestants and Catholics who believed in the notion of a German empire as the instrument of the Christian duty to spread the faith and to abolish slavery.⁴³ Protestant missions were active earlier and more widespread than Catholic ones which were hampered by the prohibition of Catholic orders as part of Kulturkampf legislation and the absence of diplomatic relations with the Vatican until 1882. The struggle to gain government approval for German Catholic missionaries came to an end only in 1896. Catholic attitudes to colonial expansion and Christian mission were not just discussed in the context of a confrontation between German Catholics and the government but also generated dispute among clergy, Center politicians, and Catholic interest groups. Cardinal Kopp who saw

---

⁴¹ HAStK Nl. Trimborn 1256/178 f. 3-4; Loth, *Katholiken*, p. 287; Kiefer, B*achem*, pp. 178-9.

⁴² Pehl, *Kolonialpolitik und das Zentrum*, p. 16.

⁴³ See Langner, *Katholizismus*, esp. pp. 74-8.

himself as the leader of German Catholic hierarchy resented the Pope's appointment of the Archbishop of Cologne, Phillipp Krementz, as principal representative of the German episcopacy in matters concerning the missions. This dispute went beyond personal rivalries, German bishops were divided on the implications the erection of a German mission entailed. Some bishops opposed missions altogether, fearing that the already diminishing ranks of the Catholic priesthood would be further weakened by the sending off of priests to Africa and Asia. In this debate, the views of Cardinal Kopp and the bishops of south Germany prevailed. They believed that missions would help reverse the Prussian anti-Jesuit legislation, enhance the international standing of German Catholics, and bring financial benefits, eventually.[45] Mission provided the crucial motivation for Catholic and Center support for colonial and naval policies. It is Albrecht Langner's accomplishment to have pointed to the crucial connection between missions and naval policies of the Center. Political Catholicism, he argues, "turned out to be a solid pillar of imperial [*reichsdeutsch*] policies, as soon as Wilhelmine *Weltpolitik* seemed to correspond with truly Catholic [*christlich-katholisch*] ideas."[46]

The most important political force behind the promotion of Catholic missions was Prince Franz Ludwig von Arenberg.[47] A wealthy Rhenish Catholic aristocrat with estates in Belgium, France and Germany, Arenberg belonged to the extreme right wing of the Center Party. He incurred the anger of his more moderate party colleagues and much of the Catholic public when he supported Caprivi's Army Bill (1893), and again made enemies when he undermined the Center's position on the Civil Code by engaging in negotiations with the papacy behind Karl Bachem's back.[48] In 1894, at the Cologne *Katholikentag*, Arenberg made a passionate speech calling for Catholic participation in missions and colonial enterprises.[49] For more

---

[45] For an example of the rivalry between the French and German episcopacy see Karl J. Rivinius, "Interdependenz von Politik und Evangelisation in China," *Historisches Jahrbuch der Görres-Gesellschaft* 109 (1989), pp. 407-9; Horst Gründer, *Christliche Missionen und deutscher Imperialismus. Eine politische Geschichte ihrer Beziehungen während der deutschen Kolonialzeit (1884-1914) unter besonderer Berücksichtigung Afrikas und Chinas* (Paderborn: Ferdinand Schöningh, 1982), pp. 60-3.

[46] Gründer, "Nation," p. 76.

[47] He became a member of the Prussian Landtag in 1882 and represented the district of Aachen-Stadt in the Reichstag from 1890 until his death in 1907. In 1892 he became one of the vice chairmen of the *Deutsche Kolonialgesellschaft*.

[48] On the argument between Bachem and Arenberg see Kiefer, B*achem*, p. 103.

[49] Gründer, *Christliche Missionen*, p. 68.

than a decade, Arenberg remained the Center's most influential proponent of the party's cooperation with the government on colonial issues.⁵⁰ But colonial expansion and the support of Catholic missions overseas were also supported by bourgeois members of the Rhenish Center.⁵¹

Generally, the Center was willing to lend support to the government's colonial and naval policies, provided their concerns for the dispersion of Christian culture and Catholic missionaries and their political demands were taken into consideration. This attitude is one of the instances when the Center tied political and religious issues. Here it was much more successful in obtaining significant concessions from the government than it had been on domestic issues such as the new Civil Code. The government's colonial policies, however, became a serious point of tension when the young Center politician Matthias Erzberger criticized the deficiencies of German colonial administration.

Matthias Erzberger's rise to political prominence was untypical and meteoric and made him as many friends as enemies. He grew up in Buttenhausen, a village in Württemberg with a population half Jewish and half Protestant and a small Catholic minority. Thanks to the support of his school teacher and the parish priest, this gifted son of a tailor left the village to be trained as a teacher, a training which, according to Rudolf Morsey, might have been the source of Erzberger's priggishness (*Alles- und Besserwisserei*).⁵² Josef Eckard, editor of the *Deutsches Volksblatt* and president of the Christian trade union in Württemberg, discovered Erzberger's political talent. At Eckard's invitation, Erzberger joined the *Deutsches Volksblatt*, where he won his spurs as a journalist and earned the living which political work alone could not provide. Together with Eckard, Erzberger was also active in Württemberg's growing Catholic working class movement. He organized workers' clubs and journeymen's associations, gave lectures on social and economic questions, and provided thousands of workers with individual answers to their questions on health and accident insurance, and the rights vis-à-vis their employers and landlords.⁵³

---

⁵⁰ Pehl, *Kolonialpolitik und das Zentrum*, pp. 49-50.

⁵¹ K. Bachem, Entwurf eines Aufrufs zur Nationalspende zum Kaiserjubiläum zum Besten der christlichen Missionen in unseren Kolonien und Schutzgebieten, n. d. [1913], HAStK Nl. Bachem 1006/327.

⁵² Rudolf Morsey, "Matthias Erzberger (1875-1921)," in *Zeitgeschichte in Lebensbildern. Aus dem deutschen Katholizismus des 20. Jahrhunderts*, ed. idem (Mainz: Matthias-Grünewald-Verlag, 1973), 1:104.

⁵³ Morsey, "Matthias Erzberger," pp. 104-5; Epstein, *Dilemma*, pp. 24-5.

His energies were by no means exhausted by his work as a journalist and workers' advocate. In 1903, at the age of twenty-eight, the ambitious representative of the Swabian constituency of Biberach-Waldsee-Leutkirch-Wangen became the youngest member of the Reichstag. Between his entry into parliament and his assassination by two members of the extreme right-wing "*Germanenorden*" in 1921, lay an exceptional political career marked by courage, extraordinary achievements, and fundamental misjudgments which infuriated political friends and foes and eventually cost him his life. He held decided opinions on a large number of topics; he enunciated them in pamphlets, in newspaper articles, and in public speeches, with an impressive self-confidence. He often evoked strong responses, his biographer, Klaus Epstein, thought him the "most despised German of the past one hundred years."[54] Many older Centrists resented and envied the impulsive upshot's "self-confident and arrogant" demeanor and his penchant "for acting off his own bat."[55] Karl Bachem was among Erzberger's most outspoken critics within the party and thought him a "careless, rash" politician who had "become too big too soon." Bachem retired from active politics in part because of disagreements with his rival.[56] Erzberger was one of the few Centrists who stood for workers' rights and trade unions; however, he attained national notoriety as a relentless critic of the government's conduct in colonial affairs. His criticism was well-informed and biting. Erzberger exposed inefficiency and corruption in the colonial administration, for instance, he spoke out against the buying of black girls as wives or concubines by civil servants, and he condemned the selling of alcohol to Togo and other colonies.[57]

Initially, Centrists, particularly those in Bavaria and the Rhineland, vigorously opposed the building of a large navy. Even Lieber, among the Center's most ardent supporters of imperialistic naval policy and always eager to awake enthusiasm for fleet building, found it difficult to support such "extravagant" (*uferlose*) navy appropriations of fifty-seven million marks which were part of the 1897/98 budget.[58] The Center appeared to be determined to continue on

---

[54] Epstein, *Dilemma*, p. 10.
[55] K. Bachem to Spahn, 26 September 1906, HAStK Nl. Bachem 1006/257b.
[56] Kiefer, *Bachem*, pp. 171-3, 173n14.
[57] Matthias Erzberger, *Die Zentrumspolitik im Reichstage. Reichtagssession vom 19. Februar bis 14. Mai 1907* (Berlin: Verlag der Germania, 1907), pp. 36-8.
[58] KB, 5:460-1; Traut, *Lieber*, p. 137; Wilfired Loth has recently argued that Lieber's enthusiasm for *Flottenpolitik* has been exaggerated by Zeender and Gottwald, see Loth, *Katholiken*, p. 64.

the "middle course" which had characterized its attitude toward navy building during the 1880s and 1890s. The Rhineland Centrist Aloys Fritzen, a Center expert on navy policies, said in February 1892 that "naval affairs leave us rather cool."[59] Richard Müller-Fulda explained the party's moderate attitude: "My political friends ... want to maintain the German navy in able condition, therefore they have always approved of the necessary [appropriations] to keep it efficient and ready for battle."[60] Until the government increased propaganda for a larger fleet in 1895/96 the Center remained relatively united on the issue. Moreover, during these years, Herbert Gottwald, mirroring Karl Bachem's statement, argues that the Center was not very interested in foreign affairs.[61] The Center eventually voted for a reduced navy bill, despite the fact that a majority of its supporters opposed the Kaiser's expansionist naval policies. The party leadership hoped that parliamentary approval of the naval bill would prevent a *coup d'état* not only guaranteeing continued constitutional rule but also ensuring that the Center played a significant role in the Reichstag. On the other hand, rejection of the naval bill probably would have spelled the end of Center participation in shaping the nation's domestic and foreign policies.[62]

The most significant reason for the Center's cautious, often ambivalent attitudes to the government's naval ambitions was the opposition of the party grass roots to such programs. Catholics, especially in Bavaria, constituted a balance to pro-navy forces in the Center. Those in the Bavarian Center in favor of naval expansion shared the experience of the Bavarian chapters of the Naval League; they found it difficult to overcome the skepticism of the region's Catholic peasantry and had to be prepared to make concessions to the interests of a predominantly rural population.[63] Rhineland Catholics were divided on the question of the naval bill of 1900. The "loud agitation by the navy" had made a definite impression on the province's youth. Even many older Rhinelanders, who "look upon [such issues] without a critical evaluation and who are inclined to the politics of emotion," were swept away by navy slogans. In contrast, almost the entire political leadership of the Rhineland Center was strongly op-

[59] Fritzen, quoted in Gottwald, "Zentrum und Imperialismus," p. 163.
[60] Müller-Fulda, quoted in Gottwald, "Zentrum und Imperialismus," p. 163.
[61] Gottwald, "Zentrum und Imperialismus," p. 165.
[62] Hürten, *Geschichte*, p. 163.
[63] Geoff Eley, *Reshaping the German Right. Radical Nationalism and Political Change After Bismarck* (1980; reprint, Ann Arbor: University of Michigan Press, 1991), pp. 174-5.

posed to the bill. Rhenish Center leaders could have been swayed to support the government if more concessions had been made to Catholic concerns in the late 1880s. Instead the government had "provoked and plagued Catholics in the most petty ways that must enrage any thinking and self-confident man."[64] In the end, the Center supported the navy bill and it was passed by the Reichstag in April 1900.[65]

Ironically, the Liberal Friedrich Naumann observed, even Conservatives supported *Flottenpolitik*, though not because it directly served their interests but because it gave them the lever they needed to pry out concessions on other issues.[66] The Center approached *Flottenpolitik* in a similar fashion. Men such as Karl Bachem, Aloys Fritzen and Karl Trimborn hoped that by agreeing to the Navy Bill they would secure concessions for the Catholic minority; the revocation of anti-Jesuit legislation was foremost on their minds.

Center concern over navy expenditures grew when it was announced that the Kaiser, in contradiction to Admiral Tirpitz's earlier assurances that the navy would not be enlarged, had plans for an even more ambitious navy program whose cost would exceed 180 million marks by 1900/01.[67] In order to reduce Center resistance to the navy bill, Tirpitz recommended to the Kaiser concessions on the anti-Jesuit laws. Karl Bachem, Count Ballestrem as well as Cardinal Kopp had heard from "sources at court" of the emperor's willingness to make a deal. Eventually, the Centrists as well as Wilhelm and his government decided against a deal and the bill passed without such any concessions on the anti-Jesuit laws.[68] By this time Lieber was too ill to participate in the Reichstag debates on the navy bill. Gröber, Müller-Fulda and the Rhenish Centrists Aloys Fritzen, took up Lieber's work and the navy bill was approved with the votes of the Center.

The construction of a navy and the ambition to become a world power had repercussions on domestic politics. The notion of *Sammlungspolitik*, an attempt to rally all national forces into a parliamentary alliance, has played a central role in discussions about con-

---

[64] Fragment of a letter to Bülow, n.d. [Feb. 1900], BAK Nl. Bülow Nr. 22, f. 247.

[65] Gottwald interprets Center support for the Navy Bill as the crucial step in a long march toward the Center's going-over into the camp of German imperialism, "Zentrum und Imperialismus," 162.

[66] Naumann, *Demokratie*, p. 216.

[67] KB 5:461, 6:24-5.

[68] Tirpitz, *Erinnerungen* (Leipzig, 1919), pp. 108f, excerpted in Behnen, *Quellen zur Außenpolitik*, 243-4; KB, 6:28-9.

tinuities in German history. It has also been a key concept in debates about the character of Imperial Germany's political and economic structure and the consequences these structures had for the formulation and implementation of both domestic and foreign policy. The Center was an important part of these decisions and formed coalitions with the governing parties which enabled the government to pursue *Sammlungspolitik*.

The term was coined by the Prussian Minister of Finance Johannes von Miquel in a speech made in the Prussian Landtag on 23 July 1897. He had first outlined his program a week earlier in the Reichstag. "Our Prussia and Germany," he said, "was neither an industrial nor an agricultural nation, it was both." Farmers and industrialists were in a symbiotic relationship of producer and consumer.[69] From these common interests sprang a broad political coalition of conservative, liberal and eventually Center forces which, according to one school of thought, formed "the basis of government policy right up until 1918."[70] It was an extension of the "great conservative counter-revolution between 1848 and 1879," which "buttressed the monopoly of power enjoyed by...privileged minorities," namely Junker and industrialists.[71] Others, however, have criticized this view of Imperial politics. Geoff Eley, perhaps the most vehement critic of the so-called Kehrites, argues that the concept of *Sammlungspolitik* as presented by Kehr, Wehler and others is misconceived.

Among the arguments Eley has put forward is the view that the concept of "social imperialism" developed by the Kehrite school "has been loosely and uncritically applied to Miquel's *Sammlungspolitik*."[72] Miquel did not wish to incorporate naval expansion and the idea of *Weltpolitik* into his *Sammlungspolitik*. According to Eley, Miquel had two basic objections to Tirpitz's proposal to include *Sammlungspolitik* into the naval program. The opposition most feared by Miquel was that of the agrarians. An ambitious naval program necessitated open trade routes, accelerated industrial growth, and had no room for ag-

---

[69] Miquel's speech to the Landtag excerpted in Ritter, *Kaiserreich*, pp. 293-4.

[70] Hans-Ulrich Wehler, *The German Empire, 1871-1918*, trans. Kim Traynor (Leamington Spa: Berg Publishers, 1985), p. 95.

[71] Wehler, *Empire*, pp. 94-6; for a discussion of Sammlungspolitik and related historiographical problems see James N. Retallack, "Social History with a Vengeance? Some Reactions to H.-U. Wehler's 'Das deutsche Kaiserreich'," *German Studies Review* 7 (1984), pp. 423-50.

[72] Geoff Eley, "*Sammlungspolitik*, Social Imperialism and the Navy Law of 1898," in *From Unification to Nazism. Reinterpreting the German Past*, ed. idem. (Boston: Allen & Unwin, 1986), pp. 113-5.

ricultural tariffs. Such a policy would have played "straight into the hands of agrarian demagogues."[73]

The second objection—the more important for our purposes—concerns Miquel's evaluation of the Center's reaction to a large navy bill.[74] The Kaiser often made it very difficult for the Center to support his navy plans. According to Martin Spahn, the party's "inimical relationship" to the Kaiser was one of its great disadvantages.[75] In an incident that eventually became known as the "Lieber Affair," Wilhelm II publicly displayed his contempt for Catholics. He snubbed the Center leader during a court ball by refusing to talk to him, instead conversing with an anti-Catholic ex-Jesuit who was also present.[76] On the occasion of a dinner given by Miquel, the Kaiser told participants, among them Center deputies, of "the need to restore the old Kartell of the 'national' parties, so that we should no longer have to depend on the Center for fleet money." Shortly afterwards he threatened Center Party leaders with a *coup d'état* if they reduced the naval estimates.[77] Indeed, Wilhelm II was not willing to depend on *anybody* for approval of his naval plans and was quite prepared to go ahead with the naval construction plan even without parliamentary approval.[78]

The Kaiser was not alone in his animosity toward Catholics. Such sentiments pervaded court circles. The Kaiser's entourage "was virtually unanimous in considering Catholics a contemptible, untrustworthy, 'international,' and therefore treacherous bunch with whom one seldom dealt and upon whom one never relied."[79] Lieber was convinced that the Kaiser's advisers were to blame and was also suspicious of Bismarck's influence after 1893 when the ex-chancellor's relationship to Wilhelm improved again.[80] In the end the Kaiser remained essentially hostile to his Catholic subjects. Of course, such sentiments need not be damaging to government if a prudent monarch, capable of distinguishing between his personal sentiments and

---

[73] Ibid., p. 115.
[74] Ibid.
[75] Spahn, *Lieber*, p. 45.
[76] For a detailed treatment of the "Lieber Affair," see Röhl, *Germany without Bismarck*, pp. 132-6.
[77] Holstein to Bülow, quoted in Röhl, *Germany without Bismarck*, pp. 210-1, 215.
[78] Röhl, *Germany without Bismarck*, p. 214.
[79] Isabel V. Hull, *The Entourage of Kaiser Wilhelm II, 1888-1918* (Cambridge: Cambridge University Press, 1982), p. 94.
[80] Spahn, *Lieber*, pp. 45-6.

public policy, does not allow his dislikes and impulses to intrude on public discussion of policy. But Wilhelm II never managed to make this distinction.

In the spring of 1897, the Kaiser characterized the Reichstag majority that had refused to pass the government's navy bill in favor of a more modest one as "unpatriotic fellows." Centrists were "bitterly hurt" by the Kaiser's remarks, as fifty million marks, more than ever before, had just been approved by the Reichstag with the votes of the Center Party.[81] The strongest reaction among Center leaders to Wilhelm II's threats came from Julius Bachem. He proposed that the Center "seize this opportunity to put an end to Wilhelm's personal rule."[82] Bachem argued that the Center's call to make the Kaiser realize "the realities of political life...would earn for the Center Party an immeasurable increase in popular support.... If a crisis occurred now, the Center Party's position after new elections would be absolutely invincible."[83] The Center leaders decided against Julius Bachem's plan, as it would only increase the Kaiser's prejudice against the Catholics.[84] Within a year, however, the Kaiser had managed to calm Center outrage; he awarded the prestigious *Roter Adlerorden* to the Center politician Baron Rudolf von Buol-Berenberg and invited a delegation of Centrists to a royal reception.[85]

Bernhard von Bülow, then Secretary of Foreign Affairs, told the Reichstag that Germany could not stand by idly while England, France and Russia were "again carving up the world." Germany, he said, had no ambition to intrude on the affairs of other countries, yet it was necessary to stand up for German interests. An extension of the navy was needed to ensure that the Reich could pursue "a peaceful, honest and independent *Weltpolitik.*"[86] Karl Bachem remembered the uproar in the Reichstag over such plans and the fear that the Kaiser would dissolve parliament, alter the constitution and in fact carry out a *coup d'état*. The Kaiser's threat: "If the Reichstag will not approve my ships you shall have a fracas the likes of which you have not seen," was taken seriously by Lieber and Bachem.[87] Wilfried Loth,

[81] K. Bachem, note, 8 May 1898, Nl. Bachem 1006/081.
[82] Röhl, *Germany without Bismarck*, p. 216.
[83] J. Bachem, *KV*, 15 March 1897 quoted in Röhl, *Germany without Bismarck*, p. 216.
[84] Röhl, *Germany without Bismarck*, p. 216.
[85] K. Bachem, note, 8 May 1898, Nl. Bachem 1006/081.
[86] Bülow's speech to the Reichstag, 11 Dec. 1899, excerpted in Behnen, *Quellen zur Außenpolitik*, 230-4.
[87] KB, 5:462.

on the other hand, argues convincingly that the danger of a *coup d'état* was not as imminent as Center leaders thought it may have been a few years earlier. In 1900 the Kaiser probably did not have the necessary power to force his will upon parliament. Had Centrists remained cool, calm and collected, had they shown a better tactical understanding of the political situation, there would probably have been no need to support the government as they did.[88] That being said, there is no doubt that Center leaders believed the monarch's threats to be real. Moreover, the Center, always attacked as being more loyal to the Pope than to the Kaiser, was eager to demonstrate its patriotism and that of German Catholics. It was therefore willing to strike a deal with the government. The Conservatives and Centrists alike, and for similar reasons, eventually gave their reluctant support to the second navy bill.[89] After the Reichstag had passed the bill Lieber was invited to attend a court banquet, where he was to have an opportunity to meet and speak to the Kaiser. When Wilhelm approached the Center leader, saying that this was the first time they had met, Lieber quipped: "This has not been my fault, Your Majesty." The Kaiser, obviously displeased by Lieber's tone, immediately turned his back on Lieber, walked away, and never spoke to him again.[90]

This encounter was typical of the relationship between politicians, particularly Catholic ones, and Kaiser and court.[91] Occasionally they shared common interests and needed each other's support, but close contact was a painful affair because the disdain on the Kaiser's part and the growing disenchantment on the part of politicians with the willful, unpredictable monarch proved insurmountable. The clash of personalities as incompatible as those of Wilhelm II and Lieber was only an extreme manifestation of the unbridgable gap between the emperor and parliament. Even Catholic aristocrats, such as Georg von Hertling, were snubbed by the Kaiser. Indeed with the exception of the Silesian coal magnate von Ballestrem, no Center leader was granted an audience between Windthorst's death in 1891 and the outbreak of World War I.[92] The Center had provided reluctant sup-

[88] Loth, *Katholiken,* pp. 74.
[89] James N. Retallack, *Notables of the Right: The Conservative Party and Political Mobilization in Germany, 1876-1918* (Boston, Mass.: Allen & Unwin, 1988), p. 150.
[90] KB, 6:15-6.
[91] On Wilhelm II's violent rejection of the Centre see John C. G. Röhl, *Wilhelm II: Die Jugend des Kaisers 1859-1888* (Munich: Verlag C. H. Beck, 1993), pp. 619-20.
[92] KB, 6:16-7.

port for the navy bill hoping to be compensated for its loyalty; yet the rewards never came and the party had lost its ability to protest navy bills. The following ones in 1906, 1908 and even 1912 were approved without much of a fight. As Karl Bachem realized "the time to resist [such bills] was over."[93] In the Center some warned that *Weltpolitik* and *Weltmachtpolitik* had to be distinguished, the former appropriate for a relative newcomer to the world's powerful industrializing nations, the latter a dangerous ambition bound ultimately to harm the interests of Germany.[94]

A question of German *Weltpolitik* was also the immediate issue over which Hohenlohe resigned as chancellor. After years of subserviently following the Kaiser's lead, Hohenlohe reluctantly stepped down when his master sent a German expeditionary force to China to suppress the Boxer rebellion. Wilhelm II accepted the resignation of his eighty-one year old chancellor, and unlike Bismarck and Caprivi who had left office in disgrace, Hohenlohe was given all the honors.[95] The Center press commented on the resignation of the first Catholic chancellor in a conciliatory manner, although "he had never done anything for the Catholics...clinging to his liberal animosity to the church."[96] Prince Arenberg, who knew him well, said that Hohenlohe was driven by two fears: "To further or assist Catholicism, and to harm Liberalism."[97]

B. THE BÜLOW YEARS, 1900-1909

Bernhard von Bülow was neither a Prussian nor a Junker, he was the son of a Danish diplomat who descended from an old aristocratic family from Mecklenburg with achievements in many areas of German life. On his father's side was the conventional collection of government officials and officers but also the first-rate musician and first husband of Hans Guido von Bülow; his mother came from the more humble origins of a Hanseatic family of merchants. Bernhard von Bülow enjoyed the privileges and advantages of his class. He studied law at the universities of Lausanne, Leipzig and Berlin, interrupted his studies to volunteer for the Franco-Prussian war but resumed his judicial career on the insistence of his father when he returned from the excitements of the campaign. He eventually entered

[93] KB, 6:46.
[94] KB, 6:50.
[95] Cf. Röhl, *Germany without Bismarck*, pp. 268-9.
[96] KB, 6:87.
[97] KB, 6:87.

the Foreign Office in November 1873.[98] Wherever the suave Bülow went, he charmed courtiers and diplomats with his "exceptional and striking personality." An "aggressively insincere" man, as Friedrich von Holstein called him, he flattered and intrigued his way to the top.[99] A master of polite conversation and venomous innuendo, Bülow steadily rose in the diplomatic corps, occupying posts in several of Europe's most important capitals, London the only notable exception. The most important of Bülow's friends was Prince Philip von Eulenburg, the Kaiser's "best friend" and political adviser.[100] When he became Secretary of State for Foreign Affairs in 1897, the Kaiser wrote to Prince Eulenburg that Bülow was a superb fellow. Eulenburg used all his influence to convince the emperor that Bülow was the best choice as chancellor. In 1900 Bülow's long efforts to attain the highest office came to fruition. Wilhelm II was glad to see a "young chancellor," much closer to his age than von Hohenlohe had been and, at least during the early years, the two met almost daily.[101] Ironically, the chancellor's familiar intercourse with the emperor was also his undoing. His unashamed flattery of the Kaiser was a costly instrument of power. It made him utterly dependent on the goodwill of his imperial master; and once Wilhelm felt that his trust in Bülow had been betrayed, the chancellor's dismissal became a matter of time and opportunity. But dismissal was almost a decade away and the early years of Bülow's chancellorship were characterized by a series of successes.

When Bülow replaced Hohenlohe in October 1900, many Center politicians welcomed his appointment. Their hopes of integration into Germany's dominant culture and participation in government seemed to come to fruition. Bülow soon had a close relationship to the Center, and met often with Lieber, Gröber and Müller-Fulda. Besides the Kaiser's trust and his domination of the executive, Bülow's reliable working relationship with the Center was an impor-

[98] For an engaging introduction to Bülow's early political career see Katherine Anne Lerman, *The Chancellor as Courtier: Bernhard von Bülow and the Governance of Germany, 1900-1909* (New York: Cambridge University Press, 1990), pp. 10-29.
[99] Count Robert Zedlitz-Trützschler, *Twelve Years at the Imperial German Court*, trans. Alfred Kalisch (New York: George H. Doran, 1924), p. 27; Rich, *Holstein Papers*, p. 548.
[100] On Eulenburg and his influence on Wilhelm II. see John C. G. Röhl, *Kaiser, Hof und Staat: Wilhelm II. und die deutsche Politik* (Munich: C. H. Beck Verlag, 1988), ch. 2.
[101] Wilhelm II., *Ereignisse und Gestalten aus den Jahren 1878-1918* (Leipzig: Verlag von K. F. Koehler, 1922), pp. 81-2.

tant reason for the successful early years of his chancellorship.¹⁰² He regarded confessional peace as crucial and made a considerable effort to maintain it. He was proud of his conciliatory policies on religious issues and stressed their importance publicly, even his admiration of Bismarck did not diminish his criticism of the first chancellor's Kulturkampf. In his memoirs he speaks with admiration of his dealings with Bishop Korum of Trier and mentioned with satisfaction the fact that the Pope sent his greetings via Baron von Schauenburg, who during his honeymoon was granted a private audience at the Vatican.¹⁰³

In his private life, von Bülow experienced some of the difficulties Catholics encountered in Germany. He fell in love with Countess von Dönhoff (née Marie Beccadelli di Bologna) an Italian-born princess married to an official in the Foreign Ministry. Their attraction for each other caused her divorce. They married (9 January 1886) after they had been granted a papal annulment. This marriage had the potential to sour the relationship with the Bismarck family— Bülow had known the Bismarcks since childhood when his father was Otto von Bismarck's State Secretary—and of seriously harming Bülow's career. Although Bülow was an opportunist with few convictions, at least in this instance he followed his heart rather than his ambitions.¹⁰⁴ In the end, little harm was done to his career, but there was still a price to pay for marrying a Catholic. Enraged Protestants who objected to the liaison sent anonymous letters to Bülow when he favored the revoking of the anti-Jesuit Law. Envious rivals and prattling courtiers spread malicious gossip which on occasion reached von Bülow's ear. "The Chancellor," one lady of the court remarked "has a Catholic wife, a Catholic adjutant, the Prince von Salm, even his private secretary, Privy Councilor Schefer, is said to be Catholic. In any case, his intimate friend [*Hausfreund*], the Prince von Arenberg, is a zealous Catholic, who accompanies the Chancellor's wife to mass at Hedwigkirche every Sunday. Where shall all this end?"¹⁰⁵

There was, of course, more to Bülow's relation with the Center than his friendship with Franz von Arenberg. Since the 1898 Reichstag election there was no parliamentary majority possible without Center support. Thus in order to pass the budget Bülow had to gain their support. At the same time, Bülow had to steer the difficult course

---

¹⁰² Lerman, *Bülow*, p. 74.
¹⁰³ Bernhard Fürst von Bülow, *Denkwürdigkeiten* (Berlin: Verlag Ullstein, 1930-1931), 1:588-9; Lerman, *Bülow*, p. 20.
¹⁰⁴ Lerman, *Bülow*, pp. 15-17.
¹⁰⁵ Bülow, *Denkwürdigkeiten*, 2:13.

between parliamentary compromises and the Kaiser's disgust with the Reichstag and particularly with the Center. The first few months of his chancellorship were spectacularly successful. The transition from Hohenlohe's administration went remarkably smoothly, none of the ministers were dismissed. Bülow managed to retain the indispensable though disliked State Secretary of Interior Posadowsky whose position was endangered by the so-called 12,000 Mark affair. Friedrich von Holstein, whom Bülow viciously maligned in his memoirs, too, remained at his post in the Foreign Ministry. The year came to an end on a high note for Bülow. The Kaiser awarded him Prussia's highest order, the Order of the Black Eagle, to show his gratitude for the chancellor's deft handling of the Reichstag.[106]

Bülow's assumption of office was followed eighteen months later by an equally important leadership change for the Center. On 31 March 1902 Ernst Lieber died in Camberg, only sixty-three years old. His illness had severely limited his political activities for several years. Already in September 1899 he delivered a farewell address to the *Katholikentag* in Bonn. He spent much time in Italy to convalesce, and against the expectations of his political friends, he recovered from his illness enough to return to Berlin to give a speech on the 12,000 Mark affair and he spoke again at the *Katholikentag* in 1901 (Osnabrück).[107] During the last two years of his life, however, he tired quickly and hardly attended parliamentary sessions, the party was led by younger men.

By the turn of the century, Karl Trimborn had become one of the main Center actors on Berlin's political stage. Not all was well, however, with his party's leadership. He wrote to his wife that he felt the Center faction was in bad shape and much of the burden of political work in Berlin was resting on his shoulders. "Hitze is ill, thus I am burdened with the parliamentary commission on the Workers' Compensation Act (*Unfallkommission*). Gröber is sick, and he has not been here [in Berlin] at all. Karl Bachem is hardly able to work (*nur halb arbeitsfähig*). Fritzen is always sickly. And Lieber is at death's door."[108] Although the situation was not as bleak as Trimborn described it—there were indeed some able-bodied Centrists left to share parliamentary work— he became the undisputed Center expert in at

[106] Ibid., 1:492.
[107] K. Bachem note, Dec. 1900, HAStK Nl. Bachem 1006/90; Rudolf Morsey, "Ernst Lieber," in *Zeitgeschichte in Lebensbildern: Aus dem deutschen Katholizismus des 19. und 20, Jahrhunderts*, ed. Jürgen Aretz, Rudolf Morsey and Anton Rauscher (Mainz: Matthias-Grünewald-Verlag, 1980), pp. 76-7.
[108] Trimborn to his wife, 7 Feb. 1900, quoted in Cardauns, *Trimborn*, p. 113.

least one area. Through his experiences in his native Cologne, work in the People's Association and his friendship with Franz Hitze, Trimborn gained a reputation as a "decided social politician, a *bürgerlich* democrat."[109] He also was the chief spokesman of Julius Bachem in the Reichstag where Trimborn "counted heavily upon Posadowsky to initiate new legislation for the working classes and full rights of organization for unions, in particular those in the Christian trade union movement."[110]

It would be tempting—and not necessarily inaccurate—to describe Lieber's tenure as party leader in the crude and simple terms of democrat versus notables, of modern political movement versus traditional political élite. Certainly, Lieber maintained that the party must become more democratic. Bismarck's successor, Leo von Caprivi, warned Cardinal Kopp, who had close ties to both Berlin and Rome, that Lieber would change the "clerical and confessional" Center of old into a "political and democratic" party.[111] In the Reichstag, Caprivi called the new party leader a "*Klerikaldemokrat*," a label which Lieber vehemently rejected.[112] Karl Bachem thought it inopportune that Lieber called himself a democrat and a "Prussian by necessity [*Mußpreuße*]."[113] Lieber continued Windthorst's efforts to integrate Catholics into the Reich.[114] Indeed, he embraced the German state to a degree unimaginable in Windthorst's day. He was receptive to Caprivi's offer to promise concessions "in Prussian education policy and government backing for the party's program of social protective legislation, which had been for so long discouraged by Bismarck."[115]

Under Lieber's leadership the Center had moved closer to the government. He could do this because the composition of the Reichstag had changed and the Center had become a sought-after partner in parliament. As liberal electoral fortunes had declined and internal conflicts intensified, the Center, despite a significant erosion of the Catholic vote, managed to hold on to about 100 Reichstag

---

[109] Cardauns, *Trimborn*, p. 101.

[110] Zeender, *Center Party*, p. 95.

[111] Leo von Caprivi to Cardinal Kopp (draft), 19 June 1893, reprinted in Herbert Gottwald, "Zentrum und Imperialismus. Zur Geschichte der Wandlung des Zentrums beim Übergang zum Imperialismus" (Ph. D. diss., University of Jena, 1966), 135.

[112] "Zentrum und Heeresvorlage," Lieber's address to the Reichstag 13 July 1893, reprinted in Bergsträsser, *Katholizismus*, 2:27.

[113] KB, 5:241.

[114] Blackbourn, *Class*, p. 41; Rolf Kiefer, *Karl Bachem: 1858-1945; Politiker und Historiker des Zentrums* (Mainz: Matthias-Grünewald-Verlag, 1989), p. 91.

[115] Evans, *Center Party*, p. 119; Zeender, *Center Party*, pp. 18-9.

seats.[116] In the Prussian Landtag the liberals, too, had lost seats, while conservative parties, aided by the three-class suffrage which shielded them from the "democratic pressures which had transformed the Reichstag," could hold on to their mandates.[117] Thus in the Landtag, too, the Center won about one hundred seats in each of the elections without gaining a central position, however, since the two conservative parties had about twice as many seats, and the two liberal parties won about one hundred seats. As a consequence, the traditional coalitions remained unchanged in Prussia. In the Reichstag, on the other hand, where the Center had obtained a pivotal position, no legislation could be passed without its support. In 1899 Lieber told some 6,000 supporters in Mainz that during the last decade the Center had been transformed from a persecuted and politically impotent party to one with a decisive voice in parliament. Under Bismarck's successors, he said, life for Catholics had become more bearable, indeed, Germany "was a warmer place."[118] It had been Lieber's goal to strengthen the role of parliament and thus make it possible for the Center to participate in governing the country. Shortly after his death, Bachem critically evaluated Lieber's achievements and failures. Whereas Bachem supported Lieber's decision to follow Bismarck's advice—that a loyal and patriotic Center could achieve much more for its Catholic constituency than a party confined to the role of opposition—he implied that Lieber had steered this course much too long. Karl Bachem declared that Lieber's policy "failed completely."[119] Bachem suggested that the Center had to reconsider its attitude toward the government and "the loyal and patriotic" support of the government had to be reconsidered.[120] Frequently, the Center had supported the government even against its better judgment and, as it turned out, without adequate political compensation. Lieber's hope that in exchange the government would seriously address Catholic concerns was disappointed. During the first decade of the twentieth century the challenge to the Center did not so much come from government and Protestants but from ideological divisions within political Catholicism and the growing importance of the working class.

[116] Sheehan, *German Liberalism*, pp. 221, 259; the 1912 election resulted in the lowest number of Center seats (91) after 1874.

[117] Sheehan, *German Liberalism*, p. 222.

[118] "Dr. Lieber über die innenpolitische Lage," *Kölnische Zeitung* no. 754, 25 Sept. 1899; *KV* no. 895, 25 Sept. 1899.

[119] K. Bachem to Kopp, 8 Feb. 1900, HAStK Nl. Bachem 1006/112 quoted in Kiefer, *Bachem*, p. 91.

[120] K. Bachem, "Nach Lieber's Tod," n.d. HAStK Nl. 1006/154.

And as we have seen already (Chapter V) much of the Rhenish working class preferred the SPD to the Center. In the election of 1903 the Socialist scored another increase in votes and seats. Characteristically Bülow shifted responsibility. In his memoirs, he blamed, at least in part, Wilhelm II, for the Socialist success. The emperor's "speeches and gestures," he wrote, had contributed to the creation of a Socialist "avalanche." In a telegram to his chancellor, the Kaiser dismissed the election results in characteristic fashion, "it was of absolutely no consequence whether the monkeys jumping around in the Reichstag cage were black or yellow."[121] Bülow claimed that he felt the SPD was not an unstoppable "force of nature [*Naturereignis*];" and from then on he searched for an opportunity to dissolve parliament and gain a more favorable parliamentary position in a new election.[122] This opportunity came in the fall of 1906.

By then the relationship between Reich Chancellor von Bülow and the Center had lost any enchantment it might have held for either side. The chancellor was willing to take the risk of an election to rid himself of a partner he detested at heart. The Center, in turn, was highly suspicious of Bülow and feared a resurrection of the Kulturkampf. The navy and army appropriation bill of 1906 was the issue over which Bülow eventually decided to call a general Reichstag election eighteen months before its statutory term expired.[123] He had told the emperor that the situation was serious, since it was quite possible that the Reichstag would demand considerable cuts in the strength of German troops in Southwest Africa. Should that indeed occur, Bülow had suggested that the best course was the dissolution of parliament. On 13 December 1906, the chancellor dissolved the Reichstag and called for new elections because parliament had refused to vote for additional moneys to fight the Hottentot rebellion. The Kaiser concurred with his chancellor and authorized this "grave step," which led to the so-called Hottentot election in January 1907.[124] It was an election campaign during which the Center Party's loyalty (and by implication the loyalty of Catholics at large) to emperor and fatherland was put into question.

---

[121] Bülow, *Denkwürdigkeiten*, 2:7.

[122] Ibid., 2:7-8.

[123] The government insisted it needed twenty-nine million marks to suppress the Hottentot rebellion in South-West Africa.

[124] Bülow to Wilhelm II, Dec. 1906, reprinted in Behnen, *Quellen zur Außenpolitik*, p. 74.

Bülow's election slogan was demagogic and divisive: "For Honor and Welfare of the Nation—Against Socialists, Poles, Guelphs, and the Center."[125] He anticipated that an election fought on the question of patriotic loyalty would deliver a decisive defeat to the Socialists as well as eliminate the government's dependence on Center support in the Reichstag. In his memoirs Bülow's contempt for the Center is still tangible:

> The necessity [to create a parliamentary] majority to support national issues without the Center Party...had been brought about by the advantage the Center had taken of its position of indispensability in the execution of national tasks. Therefore it was an old problem which had to be solved in 1907...: [to create] a patriotic majority without the Center. Not a minority opposed to the Center, not a patriotic majority that permanently excluded the Center, but a patriotic majority, strong and loyal and self-sufficient, enough to do justice to the national cause even without the support of the Center.[126]

As Bülow was pondering ways to exclude the allegedly unpatriotic Center from political power, Center politicians professed their loyalty to Kaiser and nation. Far from being "an enemy of throne and government"—the Center politician Wilhelm Busch assured a party congress in Düren—the Center supported the monarchy as well as the rights of the people.[127] Karl Trimborn, who attended the same meeting, reiterated Busch's argument, adding that the "enormous responsibility of the Catholic population was not to build a denominational party, but a party that defended the Christian Weltanschauung."[128] To the audience, Karl Trimborn's remark was an obvious comment on the *Gewerkschaftsstreit*, but beyond this it was also a commitment to the religious aspects of Center meetings that so often accompanied comments on politics and policies.

Among the defenders of the Center's national honor was also the Catholic press. Responding to liberal allegations that the Center was an ultramontane "troublemaker" and "anti-national party," the

---

[125] Quoted in Bernhard Fürst von Bülow, *Deutsche Politik*, ed. Peter Winzen (Bonn: Bouvier Verlag, 1992), p. 57.
[126] Bülow, *Politik*, p. 253.
[127] "Zweiter Parteitag der Zentrumspartei für den Reg.-Bez. Aachen," *Dürener Zeitung* no. 98, 30 April 1906.
[128] Ibid.

Kölnische Volkszeitung assured its readers that the Center's loyalty to the nation was not only a matter of self-congratulation but also had been acknowledged by Bismarck, von Kardoff, and Bassermann. In the same breath, however, it accused the SPD of being unpatriotic in the very same language liberals had used to attack the Center.[129]

Catholics were not just concerned with their patriotic reputation in the sphere of national politics. Impelled by their desire to embrace national values, the Catholic bourgeoisie participated in public celebrations of national symbols in their own communities. One such demonstration of the Wilhelmine national spirit were the celebrations of the Kaiser's birthday (27 January) which in 1907 coincided with the Reichstag election campaign. The birthday celebrations of 1907 are significant here for two reasons. First, 1907 was a watershed for the form national celebrations took in imperial Germany.[130] Until the early years of the twentieth century, Germans had celebrated primarily the unification of Germany; the most important event was *Sedantag*, commemorating the defeat of France's armies in 1870. After the turn of the century, Germans replaced this essentially backward-looking remembrance of the achievements of the empire with a celebrations heralding Germany's potential as world power. To political parties and modern interest groups the Kaiser became a symbol of Germany's political and economic progress.[131]

For Catholics the celebration of Wilhelm II's birthday was more palatable than commemorating Bismarck's victories. During the early decades of the Kaiserreich, Catholics had rejected *Sedantag* celebrations, marking instead the election of Pius IX as Pope.[132] *Sedantag* reminded them of the bitter Kulturkampf years; celebrating the Kaiser's birthday, however, did not have these connotations. Thus Catholics participated in these festivities. In Essen, for example, a banquet honoring the Kaiser was organized by the city's civil servants and bourgeoisie (*Bürgerschaft*). It was attended by the mayor, representatives of the local civil service, the chamber of commerce, representatives of the Protestant and Catholic churches, the city council, representatives of industry (among them of, course, a representative

---

[129] "Die 'denkbar internationalste und anti-nationale Partei,'" *KV* no. 691, 12 August 1906.

[130] Monika Wienfort, "Kaisergeburtstagsfeiern am 27. Januar 1907. Bürgerliche Feste in den Städten des Deutschen Kaiserreichs," in *Bürgerliche Feste: Symbolische Formen politischen Handelns im 19. Jahrhundert*, ed. Manfred Hettling and Paul Nolte (Göttingen: Vandenhoeck & Ruprecht, 1993), pp. 160-1.

[131] Ibid., pp. 160-1.

[132] Sperber, *Popular Catholicism*, p. 225; Nipperdey, *Umbruch*, p. 49.

from Krupp). The banquet was chaired by Franz Arends (a local Center politician and member of a prominent Essen brewing family). The celebrations included representatives from all political parties—except the Socialists.[133]

In Cologne, the city's elite, too, fêted the Kaiser's birthday. The social composition of the participants was similar to that of Essen. Representatives of government, industry, the professions and political parties dominated the events. In Cologne, Cardinal Fischer and mayor Becker shared the chairmanship of the celebrations. They sat at the center of the head table, next to each of them were the garrison's two highest-ranking officers. This arrangement of the head table, "demonstrated the growing together of city and state. Together the élites celebrated Kaiser and empire, and thus also themselves."[134] Since unification—and with increased enthusiasm after Wilhelm II's ascension to the throne—Catholics had been anxious to be accepted as true patriots; but their efforts, however strenuous, had been hampered by anti-Catholic sentiments. While they achieved acceptance in some areas (after 1890, for example, Rhenish Catholic businessmen were more likely to be granted the titles of Commercial and Privy Councilors than their Protestant counterparts[135]), Catholics continued to be easy targets for charges of unpatriotic behavior and Bülow was convinced that such sentiments could be exploited for electoral purposes.

The chancellor was convinced victory was assured by a wave of anti-Center and anti-Socialist sentiment he had noticed during the public debate of the colonial scandals.[136] He expected the pro-government parties, namely the Conservatives and National Liberals, to gain mandates at the expense of the Center and the SPD. The political attack on the Center was like a pincer movement: attacking the right and the left wing at the same time. This attack was designed to expose the party's right wing as the "clerically dominated" organization it was, and its liberal wing, if it survived at all, would be shorn of

---

[133] Wienfort, "Kaisergeburtstagsfeiern," p. 160.

[134] Ibid., p. 163.

[135] Despite such gains, Catholics remained underrepresented among Rhenish businessmen, titled or not titled. Karin Kaudelka-Hanisch, "The titled businessman: Prussian Commercial Councillors in the Rhineland and Westphalia during the nineteenth century," in *The German Bourgeoisie: Essays on the social history of the German middle class from the late eighteenth to the early twentieth century*, ed. David Blackbourn and Richard J. Evans (New York: Routledge, 1991), pp. 96, 101.

[136] Ward, "Election of 1907," p. 190.

[137] Ibid., p. 189.

its tendency to make common cause with Socialists.[137] Liberals also hoped that Bülow would both "fight the SPD with iron resolution" and resurrect anti-Catholic measures.[138] To be sure not everybody in the government was convinced that Bülow's tactics guaranteed victory. Posadowsky, for instance, warned the chancellor that the Center, even if weakened, would still hold the balance of power in the new Reichstag. Defense, colonial and economic policies would still be impossible without Center support.[139] Despite such warnings, Bülow felt he needed the emperor's favor more than the Center Party's parliamentary support.

Guided by these notions and supported by right-wing parties and nationalist pressure groups, Bülow fought a bitter election campaign against the SPD and the Center. National Liberals, motivated by their anti-Catholic sentiments, joined Bülow's emotionally charged campaign full of Kulturkampf rhetoric. Although the Conservatives enthusiastically shared Bülow's anti-SPD sentiments, they had grave misgivings over attacking the Center. For some time, the two parties had worked together in the Prussian Landtag on a number of issues. Conservatives agreed with Center support for religious instruction in primary school and also favored the government's agrarian, fleet, and financial policies. Conservatives also thought renewed attacks would strengthen rather than weaken the Center, as the experience of the Kulturkampf had shown.[140]

Bülow was afraid that the Center, "mindful of its support in industrial districts and the radicals within the party enjoying the upper hand, ... would make electoral pacts [with the SPD], especially in South Germany, and that an oppositional majority would be returned."[141] This fear was alleviated as soon as the Center appealed to its voters not to support any Social Democratic candidates.[142] The Center was also determined to give no quarter to the National Liberals. In the past it might have been opportune to cooperate with them but, "given the recent events" (the anti-Catholic defamation by that party and their "disturbance of religious peace"), there was no common ground left.[143] The election campaign was made more difficult

---

[138] Lerman, *Bülow*, p. 167.
[139] Ibid.
[140] Ward, "Election of 1907," pp. 195-6.
[141] Lerman, *Bülow*, p. 167.
[142] "Die Stellung der Zentrumspartei zu den übrigen Parteien in dem bevorstehenden Wahlkampfe," *Kölnische Volkszeitung* no. 1092, 21 Dec. 1906. An exception was the Hessian Centre which entered a formal alliance with the SPD.
[143] Ibid.

for the Center because of the discord within its own ranks. The *Gewerkschaftsstreit* was still raging and the party was in the early stages of the *Zentrumsstreit*. As a consequence, the party was far from united. In the Rhineland the internal divisions were rife.

One reason was the dispute over Karl Bachem's draft of an election proclamation which had been toned down by the Center's directorate. Since little could be gained by an internal quarrel, Bachem decided quietly to close ranks with the rest of the leadership. Nevertheless, he was incensed by Erzberger's antagonistic colonial critique which had unnecessarily stirred up anti-Catholic feelings and given ammunition to the Evangelical League.[144]

Party unity was threatened also by the criticism leveled by Rhenish Catholic notables against Erzberger's attack on the government and by the party's uncritical response. They published a manifesto condemning the Center's unpatriotic attitude. The majority of the *Nationalkatholiken* (as the group became known) were Catholic noblemen. Among the thirty-nine Rhenish "dissenters" who published the manifesto in early January 1907 were Count Beissel von Gymnich, the counts Hoensbroech-Haag and Hoensbroech-Kellenberg, two members of the von Loë family, Prince Salm-Reifferscheidt and Count Alfred Wolff-Metternich. The *Nationalkatholiken* even fielded their own candidates in a number of ridings, but none of them could muster much support.[145] In the end, most Catholics and their representatives united in a common front. To a large degree, it was the Center's sudden pariah status which helped it paper over potentially disastrous internal differences of both strategy and tactics.

Refusing to fight Bülow on the question of patriotism, the Center press emphasized that the party was far from unpatriotic. It was not even opposed to German colonial ambitions in South-West Africa as long as policies were "prudent and moderate." Center newspapers emphasized that it was not patriotism that was at the heart of the election campaign, but rather the budgetary rights of the Reichstag and the attempt of the government to limit the universal franchise. The dissolution of parliament was an attack on "the freedom and independence" of the German people, on the "constitutional rights of the Reichstag."[146] In this sense the Center could not avoid making common cause with the other "pariah" party of 1907, the SPD. Karl

[144] K. Bachem note, 18 Dec. 1906, HAStK Nl. Bachem 1006/260.
[145] KB, 6:405-6.
[146] "Der Wahlaufruf der Zentrumsfraktion," *Niederrheinische Volkszeitung* no. 1009, 17 Dec. 1906; K. Bachem's draft of the election platform, n.d. [Dec. 1906], HAStK Nl. Bachem 1006/260.

Bachem and others realized that the Center could lose its influential parliamentary position not because of an erosion of its own support but because of conservative and liberal gains at the expense of the SPD.[147]

Despite all these efforts to present a united front, the election campaign brought to the fore deep divisions within the Center. Conservative Centrists feared that Bülow had torpedoed their attempts to achieve a *modus vivendi* between throne and altar. Cardinal Kopp chastised the "myopic leadership of the Center" for jeopardizing good relations with the government. Matthias Erzberger was singled out as one of the "untrained politicians" who lacked "bearing and political tact."[148] The "democratic" wing of the party, on the other hand, had its worst fears confirmed. The conflict they had seen coming for some time had materialized: Liberals, in enthusiastic conformity with the ruling class and blind to public opinion, had now made common front against workers and Catholics.[149] Center "democrats" (often supported by the lower clergy), in south and west Germany, responded by combining an appeal to Catholic sentiments with protestations of support for the interests of "ordinary Catholics."[150]

Part of this Catholic populism was the fielding of working-class candidates. There had been only two workers representing the Center in the Reichstag before 1907. Now, however, the Center, motivated in part by genuine conviction and in part by the need to pay lip service to demands for better representation of Catholic workers, nominated nineteen working-class candidates. This election was the first time that the Catholic workers' movement acquired independent parliamentary influence.[151] An offer by the SPD to form coalitions during run-off elections was dismissed out of hand by the Center. Although tempted by this opportunity to defeat Liberal candidates in a number of ridings, the party leadership believed that an alliance with Socialists entailed the danger of "confusing and demoralizing Center voters." Accepting the SPD offer would also have rendered "the struggle against atheist Socialist tendencies" much more difficult.[152]

---

[147] KB, 6:404.
[148] Kopp to Johannes Montel Edler von Treuenfest, 22 Dec. 1906, quoted in Loth, *Katholiken*, p. 122.
[149] Loth, *Katholiken*, p. 123.
[150] Ibid.
[151] Ibid., pp. 123-4.
[152] KB, 6:408.

The election forced by Bülow's "sharp break"[153] with the Center took place on 25 January 1907 (the run-off election was held on 5 February). The outcome surprised many. The parties of the old Kartell (German Conservatives, Free Conservatives, and National Liberals), combined with the Left Liberals, who fought on the government side for the first time, won 187 seats. The SPD's number of seats was almost halved (43 instead of 81). But the Center won 105 seats, five *more* than in the previous election. One of its Rhineland seats (Ottweiler, Trier district) was lost to the National Liberals. Despite the overall gain of five mandates the Center could not tip the scales in parliament anymore. Bülow managed to form a Conservative-Liberal coalition, the so-called Bülow Bloc, which drove the Center into opposition. Bülow was determined to prevent the Center from regaining the pivotal position in the Reichstag it had enjoyed in the preceding decade. Personal animosity rather than sound political judgment was the reason for Bülow's "hardening attitude toward the Center." Despite all the advice he received to the contrary, Bülow dissociated himself more and more from the Center and took advantage of the unexpected defeat of the SPD.[154] Centrists felt betrayed by the chancellor and were convinced that this "political abnormality"[155] would not last long. Some of Bülow's close advisers also cautioned him "not to alienate the Center Party permanently but if possible to draw it into the Bloc."[156] After the hard-fought campaign, however, the Center was not at all eager to enter into any form of cooperation with Bülow.

The first business of the new Reichstag was the reading of the budget for 1907. Martin Spahn used the debate as an opportunity to attack Bülow for his irresponsible defamation of the Center's character. The party's honor, he charged, had been insulted by the accusation that the Center was guilty of "unpatriotic arrogance." When Bülow refused to apologize for his remarks Centrists, in protest, defied parliamentary custom and did not send their calling cards to the chancellor, cutting not just political but also social ties with their old ally.[157] Spahn's protestations might have appealed to the hurt feelings of Catholic politicians and voters, but they could do nothing to prevent passage of the proposed budget. The government deliber-

---

[153] KB, 7:xiii.
[154] Lerman, *Bülow*, pp. 172-3.
[155] Erzberger, *Zentrumspolitik*, p. 15.
[156] KB, 7:1; Lerman, *Bülow*, p. 172.
[157] Erzberger, *Zentrumspolitik*, p. 19; KB, 7:3-4.

ately avoided introducing contentious legislation during the first session of the new Reichstag. Whereas the government could look back on the first five months of 1907 with some satisfaction as "not politically damaging," Matthias Erzberger attacked it for its "poor showing."[158]

Despite the loss of parliamentary leverage, some Centrists believed the election results boded well for the party's future. Matthias Erzberger, for instance, thought that the election of 1907 was "a political storm which had swept away much of the dead wood."[159] In the short term, however, the victory of Bülow's strategy had some uncomfortable consequences for the Center. Although the Center was the largest faction in parliament and thus expected that the president would be chosen from its ranks, Bülow broke with parliamentary tradition and intervened in favor of the conservative Udo zu Stolberg-Wernigerode. Peter Spahn, the Center candidate for the presidency, was defeated. The leadership of the Reichstag faction also changed; Count Hompesch became its leader, and Dr. Schädler, Peter Spahn, and Adolf Gröber became his deputies. Among the Center parliamentarians who left the directorate were two Rhineland members: Karl Bachem and Rintelen. Karl Trimborn and Aloys Fritzen joined the directorate for the first time.[160]

After the election, Adolf Gröber, in a speech that became legendary among Centrists, attacked Bülow and his Liberal allies for resurrecting Kulturkampf slogans in order to defame Catholics, as in the 1870s, as "enemies of emperor and empire."[161] Bülow's behavior had made any reconciliation impossible. Although Center leaders cautioned against personal attacks in the press for tactical reasons they encouraged Catholic newspapers to attack the Chancellor's policies without mercy.[162] Karl Bachem likened his party's position after the 1907 election to that brought about by the Reichstag election of 1887. Both Bismarck and Bülow had built a majority against the Center. The crucial difference between them was that Bülow's Bloc was built from "very heterogeneous elements" which in 1887

[158] Lerman, *Bülow*, p. 172.

[159] Matthias Erzberger, *Das deutsche Zentrum* (Amsterdam: Verlag der "Internationale Verlagsbuchhandlung: "Messis", 1910), p. 99.

[160] Matthias Erzberger, *Die Zentrumspolitik im Reichstage. Reichtagssession vom 19. Februar bis 14. Mai 1907* (Berlin: Verlag der Germania, 1907), pp. 13-4.

[161] Hermann Cardauns, *Adolf Gröber* (M. Gladbach: Volksvereins-Verlag, 1921), pp. 120-1; KB, 7:3.

[162] Protocol of a conference of Center parliamentarians and press representatives, 22-23 July 1907 (copy, dated 19 Aug. 1908), HAStK Nl. Bachem 1006/268b.

had viciously opposed each other.[163] Thus the Bülow Bloc was built on a rather shaky foundation, despite the chancellor's show of supreme confidence after the election.

Armed with a solid majority, Bülow achieved easy passage of colonial, army and navy bills—the legislation closest to the Kaiser's heart. At the end of March, parliament approved changes in the naval bill which allowed the replacement of ships of the line after twenty instead of twenty-five years; a change that, in fact, doubled German construction of battleships in the dreadnought class. Tirpitz realized that even supporters of the Bülow Bloc only reluctantly supported the increase in battleship construction. There was opposition from almost all political quarters to his ambitious expansion plans. Conservatives, Tirpitz said, were "cold toward the awful fleet." The Center, "dagger in hand," also opposed the bill, whereas only certain quarters of the National Liberals were swayed by the Navy League.[164] In the summer of 1907, Count Posadowsky, a fervent opponent of Bülow's dissolution of the Reichstag and early critic of the Bloc, was dismissed. The Center had lost one of the few allies in the government who for many years had closely worked with them.[165] Karl Bachem argued that Bülow whenever he thought it necessary catered to the Liberals, thus putting off the Conservatives more often than they in the long run would tolerate. This swinging back and forth between catering to the Liberals and alleviating Conservative dissatisfaction was eventually the undoing of the Bülow Bloc.[166] The Center understandably was not going "to idly stand by as the Bloc worked out the divergent interests of the governing parties."[167] Foreign policy was the only area in which the parties of the Bülow Bloc could see eye to eye; on domestic issues the chancellor's uneasy coalition never reached a consensus. Meanwhile, the Center was searching for ways to poison the marriage between the conservative and liberal Bloc parties. The Center faction tried to split the government coalition by siding with and supporting one or the other government party, depending on which side of a particular question the Center stood.[168] Such efforts, however, remained largely fruitless through 1907 and most of 1908. It was the extraordinary spectacle of the Daily Tele-

[163] KB, 6:419.
[164] Tirpitz to Müller, 5 Dec. 1907 reprinted in Behnen, *Quellen zur Außenpolitik*, p. 393.
[165] KB, 7:11.
[166] KB, 7:13-14.
[167] KB, 7:15.
[168] KB, 7:15-16.

graph Affair in November 1908 that caused the first serious—and as it turned out, irreparable—cracks in the Bloc and the Kaiser's enchantment with von Bülow. During a long conversation the Kaiser "spoke with impulsive and unusual frankness" to Colonel Edward Stuart-Wortley about the relationship between Germany and England. Wilhelm II complained that he was a much maligned and misunderstood friend of England. The English, he said, "made things difficult for me" and his friendship for England was shared by only "a minority of the best elements" in German society; the lower and middle classes, however, disliked England.[169] The publication of these and other statements about confidential German policy in the *Daily Telegraph* triggered the most damaging crisis of William II's reign. It is ironic that Wilhelm (for once) had observed proper form and sent the article to Bülow who was vacationing on the island of Norderney. The chancellor, however, had not recognized the highly explosive nature of the article, and had unwittingly passed it to a subordinate, who approved it for public release. The immediate result was a public outcry over the sovereign's irresponsible statements which "hurt Germany almost as much as a lost battle."[170] Karl Bachem summarized the reaction of the German public to the Kaiser's remarks:

> The impression the publication made in Germany was simply horrendous. Now the German people saw clearly what until then could have only been suspected: the superficiality, the carelessness, the lack of understanding, diplomatic subtlety or political tact shown by the Kaiser when he spoke to foreigners about Germany's international relations with foreign powers.[171]

When it became known that the text had crossed Bülow's desk, the affair became a government crisis.[172] Bülow, who later called the Kaiser's remarks the height of "thoughtlessness and indiscretion," worsened his position when he refused to admit this in the Reichstag. During the Reichstag debates on 10 and 11 November 1908, Bülow, facing unanimous criticism of all parties, did not accept personal

---

[169] *Daily Telegraph*, 28 Oct. 1908; Bülow's translation reprinted in Behnen, *Quellen zur Außenpolitik*, p. 412.
[170] von Gerlach, "Adieu Bülow!" *Die Welt am Montag* no. 44, 2 Nov. 1908.
[171] KB, 7:20.
[172] Amtliche Erklärung zum Artikel des "Daily Telegraph," *Reichsanzeiger*, 31 Oct. 1908, reprinted in Behnen, *Quellen zur Außenpolitik*, pp. 416-7.

responsibility and defended the Kaiser half-heartedly. Thus at the same time he alienated the Kaiser, who felt betrayed by his chancellor, and he showed a fatal weakness to the Reichstag, which the Center and the Conservatives immediately set out to exploit. By February 1909 Bülow's fall had become all but inevitable. Bachem expected it to happen sooner rather than later—as soon as the Kaiser found a successor. In the meantime, however, the Center had to bide its time. Instead of giving in to the understandable temptation of "recklessly attacking" the despised chancellor, Bachem believed the Center should tread carefully. If it were perceived as the party that caused the chancellor's fall, it would be that much more difficult to engage in fruitful discussion about cooperating in government with one or several of the Bloc parties.[173] Thus Bachem wanted to prolong the "situation of helplessness" in which the Bloc found itself during that spring.[174] He wanted to wait until the Bloc collapsed under its own weight. But others were not as careful as Bachem. Porsch, for instance, gave a speech in Düren which "[made] it official that the Center was engaged in a life or death struggle with Bülow and wanted to topple him." The Center had committed itself and could not turn back.[175] Almost twenty years after the event, Karl Bachem still could hardly hide his satisfaction in Bülow's resignation. The Center politician likened Bülow's Bloc to a heavily-laden cart pulled by a Conservative horse veering to the right, a Progressive horse pulling to the left and a National Liberal in the middle, too weak to keep the cart on a straight line. In the end, Bülow was outmaneuvered by the Center and the cart stumbled over the reform of imperial finances in July 1909.[176]

While the Center was preoccupied with the collapse of the Bülow Bloc and the *Zentrumsstreit*, it also dealt with the election of a new chairman of the Center Reichstag caucus. The candidacy of Karl Trimborn for the position is an example for flexibility of alliances within the party that survived these various internal and external pressures. Georg von Hertling was the front-runner from the beginning of the race, only Martin Spahn seriously challenged the Bavarian nobleman's candidacy.[177] However, by 1909 Spahn, who was favored by Franz Hitze and August Pieper, had made many an enemy in the party "because of his unpleasant personality," opposition

---

[173] K. Bachem note, 10 March 1909, HAStK Nl. Bachem 1006/283.
[174] K. Bachem to J. Bachem, 12 March 1909, HAStK Nl. Bachem 1006/283.
[175] K. Bachem note, 16 March 1909, HAStK Nl. Bachem 1006/283.
[176] KB, 7:xiii.
[177] K. Bachem note, 2 Feb. 1909, HAStK Nl. Bachem 1006/283.

against his candidacy was growing.[178] Gröber, who had "become a hermit and was so unfriendly toward his colleagues that nobody was even thinking of nominating him," as well as Herold, Karl Bachem's own choice, also had no chance of winning the position.[179]

Karl Trimborn was the dark horse in the race for the chairmanship. His candidacy was favored by those in the party who wanted to see a "determined social reformer" at the helm. Among those who worked for the candidacy of the Cologne politician were Müller-Fulda, Erzberger and Count Oppersdorff.[180] Oppersdorff, who was a strong supporter of Roeren and Bitter in the *Zentrumsstreit*, saw no contradiction in supporting Trimborn, who clearly was in the opposing camp. Karl Bachem, whose choice was Herold, felt that there was little support for Trimborn because he was "too young and his personality not suitable for the job."[181]

After the party had made its choice and elected Georg von Hertling as the new chairman of the Center caucus, Trimborn told Karl Bachem that Erzberger at one point believed that he had almost secured a majority for his candidacy. Trimborn, who was opposed by the "democratic Rhenish judges" such as de Witt, Wellstein and Schmidt (Marburg), was not at all convinced that Erzberger could muster sufficient support for him, and he remained coy about announcing his candidacy.[182] Again we see how difficult it is to label the political position of leading Center personalities and factions in an exclusive, categorical way. Here we have Trimborn, who usually is described as one of the "democratic" leaders of the Rhenish Center, being opposed by other "democrats." Bachem explained this strange behavior with the "old truth that the 'democrats' of the Right prefer to submit to an aristocrat than to one of their own.... This explains their opposition to Trimborn."[183]

C. Bethmann Hollweg and the Center Party

After the collapse of the Bülow Bloc and the chancellor's resignation in July 1909 the Center once again occupied a powerful position in the Reichstag and was looking for ways to influence the new chan-

---

[178] K. Bachem notes, 2 & 10 Feb. 1909, HAStK Nl. Bachem 1006/283.
[179] K. Bachem notes, 2 & 19 Feb. 1909, HAStK Nl. Bachem 1006/283.
[180] K. Bachem note, 28 Feb. 1909, HAStK Nl. Bachem 1006/283.
[181] K. Bachem notes, 2 & 13 Feb. 1909, HAStK Nl. Bachem 1006/283. Trimborn eventually was chairman from 1919 to 1921.
[182] K. Bachem note, 28 Feb. 1909, HAStK Nl. Bachem 1006/283.
[183] K. Bachem note, 10 Feb. 1909, HAStK Nl. Bachem 1006/283.

cellor. Unlike the cosmopolitan Bülow, Theobald von Bethmann Hollweg had spent little time abroad. He lacked the urbane flair and diplomatic charm of his effusive predecessor. True, Bethmann was admired for his "moral courage, scrupulousness, thorough education, idealistic enthusiasm, and critical mind."[184] But his quick rise from Landrat to Prussian Minister of the Interior and Chancellor of the Reich "owed just as much to his capacity to internalize [the Prussian bureaucracy's] administrative ethos, his lack of making mistakes during his official career, and his pragmatic opportunism."[185] An experienced, dedicated civil servant and ardent monarchist, Bethmann Hollweg would probably also have preferred to govern without a parliament. He certainly had a "preference for closely reasoned memoranda, expert opinions, and endless meetings over the heat of parliamentary debate."[186]

For our purposes it is more significant that he lacked any significant contact with Catholics. Thus, Karl Bachem complained that Bethmann Hollweg "had not learned anything about conditions in the south and the west—where Catholics were concentrated."[187] Bethmann Hollweg would probably have preferred to govern without Center support. None the less, Bethmann resigned himself to the inevitable and pursued a course entirely different from Bülow's.[188] Realizing that Bülow's attempt to govern without the Center's support had failed, he neither governed with the Center nor against it. The reform of imperial finances was eventually passed by the Center and Conservatives in tandem *against* the plans of the government. Ironically, Bethmann Hollweg's own disposition toward Catholics was, if we can believe Karl Bachem, much more hostile than that of his predecessor. He could hardly contain the contempt of Catholics so common among his colleagues.[189] Still, he realized that there was no alternative than to rely at least occasionally on Center support. During the first three years of his tenure, Bethmann Hollweg hardly ever needed the support of the Center, however. Karl Bachem referred to these years as the "Second Bloc," the Bülow-Reichstag without Bülow. Bethmann Hollweg, according to Bachem, inherited the Bloc from his predecessor and "had no desire to construct any funda-

---

[184] Octavio von Zedlitz und Neukirch, "Kanzlerpolitik," *Die Gegenwart* no. 30 (1909), quoted in Jarausch, *Enigmatic Chancellor*, p. 67.
[185] Jarausch, *Enigmatic Chancellor*, p. 67.
[186] Ibid., p. 42.
[187] KB, 7:92.
[188] KB, 7:xiv.
[189] KB, 7:91.

mentally new [coalition]....Initially, he was content with the politics of search and trial."[190] The conservative Centrist Count Hertling, too, preferred to keep some distance from the new chancellor. Conversely, the left wing of the Center, or "democrats" as some have labeled them, were concerned that the National Liberals would enter into a "coalition of the left" with the Progressives and the SPD. To counter the National Liberal move they preferred a "bloc of solidarity" (*Solidaritätsblock*) consisting of Conservatives, National Liberals and the Center.[191]

Wilfried Loth regards the summer of 1909 as one of ambivalence with a crisis looming just beyond the horizon. He argues that there were three possible ways for Germany to resolve the political crisis: an authoritarian solution, a bourgeois solution and revolution.[192] What actually occurred was determined by four groups. The government exercised an authoritarian influence. Industrialists, although unhappy with the government's conservative politics, were also in favor of an authoritarian solution which would contain the growing demands of the working class and the SPD. The middle classes, imbued with a modern strand of nationalism, were determined to remove the traditional conservatism, but were as concerned as the government and industrialists about socialism. The last group was the Center. Its support of the reform of imperial finances constituted the first step toward an alliance with the Conservatives. On social issues it was not in concert with conservative notions; nevertheless, there was a decided shift to the right (*Rechtsruck*) by the Center in 1909.[193]

Neither the Center "democrats" nor "bourgeois" Centrists could afford to criticize the decisions of the summer of 1909 if they wanted to avoid a split in the party. Therefore they defended the reform of Imperial finances with vigor. According to Loth, however, the Center found itself in a difficult position in regard to its economic policies. The Hansabund competed after 1910 with the Center for its middle-class vote by attacking the party for its agrarian demagoguery. At the same time, the SPD tried to make inroads into the Catholic working class vote by attacking the Center's support of the Conservatives in the Reichstag. The Center, Loth argues, "radicalized" its economic program, pushing out workers and the new middle-class in favor of an appeal to its rural supporters.[194]

[190] KB, 7:91, 93.
[191] Loth, *Katholiken*, p. 183.
[192] Ibid.
[193] Ibid., pp. 182-3.
[194] Ibid., pp. 183-5.

Any discussion of changes in the Center Party, and particularly in its Prussian branch, must take into account the continuity among its leadership, unparalleled by any other German party of the time. The Center in the Prussian Landtag had an easier time than its counterpart in the Reichstag. Like the Reichstag caucus the Landtag caucus was concerned that its leadership should always represent the various regions. Karl Bachem, who was skeptical of this kind of particularism, nevertheless believed that it fulfilled a useful function.[195] Thus we find Westfalian, Silesian and Rhenish Centrists among the Prussian leaders. Under the chairmanship of the Westfalian Baron von Heeremann, a Rhinelander (Aloys Fritzen) and a Silesian (Felix Porsch) were vice-chairmen of the caucus directorate. When Fritzen succeeded to the chairmanship in 1900, the East Prussian (Ermland) cathedral provost Franz Dittrich joined Porsch as a vice-chairman. The Silesian Porsch, in turn, became chairman when Fritzen retired in 1904, the Westfalian economist Herold and Roeren joined Dittrich as vice-chairmen. This almost hereditary succession of Prussian Center leaders continued in 1915. After Dittrich's death (1915) the careful regional balance was maintained by electing Herold first vice-chairman. This pattern even survived the collapse of the Kaiserreich at the end of World War I, in 1929 Porsch and Herold celebrated the twenty-fifth anniversary of their membership to the caucus directorate.[196] Karl Bachem attributes the relative stable development of the Center caucus in the Landtag not just to the more manageable problems of the Landtag, but also to a large degree to the consistent, authoritative leadership of Porsch who avoided ideological controversies and pursued a conservative policy of gradual reforms.[197]

Bachem's assessment of stability in the Center Landtag caucus might very well be correct, but his evaluation of the significance of particularism within his party is clouded by his Catholicism. One of the reasons Bachem was uneasy about particularism was the fact that it was difficult to bring it into accord with the universalism of Catholicism.[198] Bachem was aware that the Church—while not unsympathetic to regional differences in episcopal organization—put great emphasis on the universal application of its principles. A closely related problem was the need to unite all German Catholics under the umbrella of the Center to emphasize the common Catholic *Weltanschauung*, and at the same time to accommodate regional in-

---
[195] KB, 7:102.
[196] KB, 7:102-4.
[197] KB, 7:104; Leugers-Scherzberg, *Porsch*, pp. 284-7.
[198] For Bachem's discussion of this problem see KB, 7:104-5.

terests. Bachem argued that the "noblest task of politically active Catholics is and remains their concern for the freedom of the Church and its natural rights in the state."[199]

Remarks like these show the crucial importance Catholic belief played for Center politicians and their followers. It is hard to imagine that any other party would have named the maintenance of church rights as the party's "noblest task." All other German parties envisioned their existence primarily within a certain state (although it might not be the *existing* state, as in the case of the SPD). The Center was different, despite its representatives' frequent protestations to the contrary. This was one of the party's strengths, but also a potential weakness. Bachem argued that "only when all German Catholics, regardless of their regional ties, stand together...will they as a minority in the German fatherland be able to secure the freedom of the Church."[200] Yet the Center's enemies could claim that the party was "un-national" because its interests extended beyond the borders of Germany. If particular interests within the nation were secondary to the interests of Catholics at large, then German Catholics shared more with Catholics outside Germany than with their compatriots.

We find a similar attitude to religion in Bachem's assessment of Rudolf Nieberding (who died in 1912). As a young man, Nieberding had held to "true Catholic beliefs [*treuer katholischer Gesinnung*]," but after he entered the civil service he grew "indifferent to the practice of his religion."[201] In Bachem's view, his career was incompatible with the exercise of his Catholic beliefs. We can only speculate whether personal ambition or weakening convictions led to Nieberding's "lukewarm" Catholicism. In light of Karl Bachem's observation that Nieberding returned to the fold after his dismissal it seems more likely, however, that he was willing to mute his religious fervor in order to further his career. The important point is that Bachem clearly understood Nieberding's dilemma: he could not serve two masters at the same time. Hand in hand with Nieberding's neglect of his religious beliefs went a distant stance toward the Center. An "all too close connection" with the party or the Church was cause for suspicion in government circles. Here Bachem made no attempt to disguise the fact that loyalty to the Church and the party were intricately connected.[202] The case of Rudolf Nieberding and others like

---

[199] KB, 7:105.
[200] KB, 7:105.
[201] KB, 7:107. On Nieberding's role in the formulation of the BGB see Kiefer, *Bachem*, pp. 105-6.
[202] KB, 7:107.

him illustrates the difficulty German Catholics faced in combining their religious beliefs and their allegiance to the Wilhelmine state. This dichotomy was never resolved; indeed, this ambiguous position of one third of Imperial Germany's population toward the Hohenzollern state was one of its defining characteristics. The relationship between religion and state was, of course, only one of the many aspects of Imperial Germany that caused tension. Another great issue is that of democratization. In the context of the Center Party we have already talked about reform of the party organization which brought changes which can confidently be interpreted as democratization. Part of this reorganization was the replacement of Catholic notables and aristocrats with professional politicians who came primarily from the bourgeoisie but even included a few workers. An additional issue was the franchise reform. The Reichstag franchise was broad but that of Prussia was very limited.

As far as the franchise was concerned, Prussia was an anomaly in Germany. Only in Saxony-Altenburg did the three-class franchise also exist, but there the vote was secret.[203] After the Reichstag election of 1907 the Progressive Party persisted in its demand that von Bülow keep his promise of franchise reform in Prussia. Wilhelm II, too, promised such a reform in his throne speech of October 1908, but nothing was done. The Center, Johannes Giesberts argued, had suffered particularly under the provisions for public voting. The "harassment and terrorizing of dependent Catholic voters had never ceased."[204] The Kaiser repeated the promise when he opened the Landtag on 11 January 1910 and on 4 February Theodor von Bethmann Hollweg introduced to the Landtag a bill for the reform of the Prussian franchise.

The chancellor's proposal, reflecting liberal demands, offered direct voting (eliminating the intermediate election of delegates [*Vertrauensmänner*]), but still refused the secret ballot. In order to alleviate the grossest effects of the three-class voting system, taxes paid by a voter which exceeded 5,000 marks would not be taken into consideration to determine the classes of voters. Furthermore, a number of "bearers of culture" (*Kulturträger*) were to be admitted to the

---

[203] On the introduction of the three-class franchise in Saxony see James N. Retallack, "'What Is to Be Done?' The Red Specter, Franchise Questions, and the Crisis of Conservative Hegemony in Saxony, 1896-1909," *Central European History* 23 (1990), pp. 271-312.

[204] Johannes Giesberts, *Das Zentrum und die Wahlrechts-Reform in Preußen* (Essen-Ruhr: Fredebeul & Koenen, 1910), p. 6.

[205] KB, 7:117.

higher voting classes without having to meet tax requirements. Among those "bearers of culture" were those who had completed three years of university studies, civil servants who had distinguished themselves by their service to the state and reserve non-commissioned officers. The inclusion of retired soldiers, designed to balance the influence of liberal academics with conservative soldiers, was considered particularly outrageous by liberals.

With the exception of the Social Democrats, no German political party whole-heartedly supported the introduction of the Reichstag franchise for Prussia. The Conservatives were set against any reform because they believed it to be the end of their influence in the Landtag; the National Liberals remained cool toward it for the same reason as the Conservatives; and the government thought the three-class franchise quite useful to restrain the Socialists. The Left Liberals, according to Bachem, only supported reform now because they hoped to benefit from it at the polls; in the past they had never done so. They still opposed the introduction of universal franchise in the municipalities (*Gemeinden*) because they feared for their urban candidates.[205] The Center could point to Windthorst's demand of 1873 for the introduction of the Reichstag suffrage to Prussia.[206] However, the Center had not pursued the reform with any vigor because in the face of conservative opposition it had virtually no chance of success.[207] Bachem argued that for the Center, reform of the franchise was not a question of power and influence. His party had fared well under both the universal Reichstag franchise and the three-class franchise of Prussia. The Center was not interested in furthering its own parliamentary influence, Bachem claimed, but realized "the inevitable necessity of a far-reaching reform of the existing franchise."[208] Giesberts also claimed that the exclusion of the masses (*breite Volksschichten*) was an important reason for the widespread indifference to the Landtag and the demands for a reform of the franchise. The impetus for reform, he argued, was the growth of the working class movement and its blatant underrepresentation in the existing voting system.[209] And in fact it was the SPD rather than the Center that became the most ardent champion of franchise reform. Demanding the introduction of the Reichstag franchise for Prussian Landtag elections, the Socialists staged mass demonstrations in many German cities during the winter of 1909-10, the largest ones occurring

[206] KB, 3:282-3.
[207] KB, 7:116.
[208] KB, 7:118.
[209] Giesberts, *Wahlrechts-Reform*, p. 7.

in Berlin. Many Centrists resented the "revolutionary character" of such SPD tactics and found it impossible to make common cause with a party that, in their view, used "violence" to bring the Reichstag franchise to Prussia.[210] Among the Rhenish Centrists, there was some resistance to the introduction of the Reichstag franchise in Prussia; not only rural representatives but also men like Karl Bachem opposed the universal franchise for Prussia. As a group, however, the Rhineland Center did support meaningful reform.[211]

The government proposal satisfied nobody. The Center, fighting for what it called a "healthy reform," was particularly incensed by Bethmann's insistence on public voting. The *Kulturträger* clause, it argued, would not alleviate injustices, it would only worsen the existing system.[212] During the debates in the Prussian Landtag, Center parliamentarians such as Herold attacked Bethmann's bill, claiming that it did not satisfy Center demands. At the same time the Center took the position that the introduction of the Reichstag franchise was an unobtainable goal, pursued only by the demagogues among the Progressive and the Socialist parties. The Center blamed them for obstructing "a progressive electoral reform" with their unrealistic demands.[213]

The Landtag eventually passed a provision for the secret ballot, which Giesberts and Bachem as well as most Centrists saw as an important achievement. In order to gain this reform a compromise with the Conservatives was necessary.[214] Still, faced with the unwillingness of the majority to replace the franchise with a new system, the Center was willing to support the government's proposal.[215] Bethmann's proposal, however, found no majority in either the Prussian Herrenhaus or the Landtag, and so the chancellor withdrew it on 27 May 1910.

After the reform had failed, the Center tried to console itself and its supporters by arguing that "even if today's electoral reform had failed in the end, in future the government shall not be able to table a reform bill that does not contain the right to a secret ballot."[216] Loth sees the Center's actions during the debate of franchise reform as further evidence for the movement to the right of the party. Cen-

---

[210] KB, 7:120.
[211] Giesberts, *Wahlrechts-Reform*, pp. 13-4.
[212] Ibid., pp. 8, 10.
[213] Ibid., pp. 15, 17.
[214] Ibid., p. 19.
[215] KB, 7:119.
[216] Giesberts, *Wahlrechts-Reform*, p. 20.

ter "democrats" were prevented from waging a public campaign for a widening of the franchise by conservatives within the party. In the commissions the Center made common cause with Conservative representatives to limit and eventually reject the franchise demanded by the Socialists.[217] Here the Center seems to be similar to the liberal German bourgeoisie, who supported reform of Prussia's three-class franchise because they were "more interested in parliamentarization than in democracy."[218]

The Reichstag election of 1912, the last of the Kaiserreich, was a watershed for the Center Party.[219] Like most observers, Karl Bachem was struck by the electorate's "sudden move to the left [*Ruck nach links*]."[220] More than 4,200,000 Germans voted for the SPD, making it the largest party in the Reichstag with 110 seats. All other parties, including the Center, lost voters and mandates. From the outset of the election campaign the Center fought a rearguard action. Rather than aggressively wooing new voters, the party was primarily concerned with guarding the *status quo*. Its election program was a replay of past concerns. Rather than offering new ways and means of dealing with the political and economic changes of the last decade, the Center warned of a return of the liberal era and the Kulturkampf. Moreover, the Center was emphatically in the camp of the "state-supporting" parties. In almost forty ridings it withdrew its own candidate and urged its voters to support the Conservative Party instead. In the last election the Conservatives had urged their supporters to break away from the Center. The "very Conservatives who not so long ago mentioned the names of Giesberts in the same breath with the Socialists," now made common cause with the Center.[221] The election platform stressed the party's cooperation with the government and its legislative achievements. The country's "economic boom," the Center boasted, "began when Bismarck split with the liberals and [instead] relied on Center support for new economic policies."[222]

---

[217] Loth, *Katholiken*, p. 187.

[218] David Blackbourn and Geoff Eley, *The Peculiarities of German History. Bourgeois Society and Politics in Nineteenth-Century Germany* (Oxford: Oxford University Press, 1984), p. 19.

[219] The election took place on 12 January, run-off elections followed on 20, 22 and 25 January.

[220] KB, 7:378.

[221] "Wie die Konservativen 1907 über das Zentrum urteilten," *Berliner Tageblatt* no. 16, 10 January 1912.

[222] "Wahlaufruf 1912" reprinted in Bergsträsser, *Katholizismus*, 2:380-3.

Karl Bachem told an audience in Cologne that the Reichstag election was the decisive battle between Conservatives and Center on the one hand and Social Democracy and the liberal parties on the other.[223] Beyond a vague promise to pursue a course beneficial to the *Mittelstand*, the Center offered no commitment to any specific policies or reforms—this way the party's hands were not bound by election promises. The election program also addressed colonial policies. Two issues were at the forefront of the Center proclamation: the rights of the Reichstag in shaping the empire's colonial policies and the insistence on the importance of missionaries and the "conquest of these countries in the name of Christian faith and Christian culture."[224] The last section of the manifesto dealt with religious questions. "Germany's historical development has led to the coexistence of two great Christian communities. The welfare of the fatherland peremptorily demands that the two separate denominations live together peacefully."[225] Thus the emphasis of the election program lay on three points: arousing Catholic fears of the return of the Kulturkampf in order to mobilize support, assurances of Catholic loyalty to the fatherland and to national politics (implying continued cooperation with the Conservatives), and stressing of the Catholic principles that formed the foundation of the party. Election campaigns were still largely local affairs. Candidates were chosen by district committees. The issues of election propaganda, too, were decided locally, and often voters identified with their candidate because they believed he would fight for their special interests. Besides the local party organization it was the provincial executive that set the tone for election campaigns in the Rhineland. It accomplished this by publishing its own election program.

Parties used a variety of means and tactics to get their message to the voters. In Prussia the Center had two main sources for propaganda material: the People's Association in Mönchengladbach and the party's executive committee in Berlin. Spurred on by the success of Socialist campaigns, the People's Association copied the methods of its most dangerous rival. In cities the Association organized mass meetings featuring Center politicians or prominent members of the People's Association as speakers.[226] Besides the Catholic press, the

---

[223] K. Bachem, "Die Bedeutung der bevorstehenden Reichstagswahl," speech delivered in Cologne, 11 December 1911, HAStK Nl. Bachem 1006/318.

[224] "Wahlaufruf 1912," reprinted in Bergsträsser, *Katholizismus*, 2:381.

[225] Ibid., 2:382.

[226] This description of the Peoples' Associations activities during election campaigns is based on Ritter, *Bewegung*, 270-4.

People's Association was the most important source of written propaganda. Since 1906, the so-called *Agitations-Flugblätter* (pamphlets in quarto format two to four pages in length) were distributed with some forty-five different texts and in editions of more than 100,000 copies; some had editions of several million.[227] In addition, more comprehensive treatment was given to the issues of the day in inexpensive booklets (*Hefte*) which were distributed by the local chapters of the Peoples' Association and in church. Not until the Weimar Republic did the agitation of the Association cease to be a useful tool to attract the attention of Catholic workers.

A second source of propaganda material was, of course, the party itself. With its headquarters in Berlin, it attempted to centralize the election effort as much as possible. This was often done with a jealous glance toward the People's Association in Mönchengladbach, which was seen as a "competitor that might undermine the uniform leadership of the Center."[228] Provincial party organizations, too, distributed pamphlets to aid in the election campaign. The Rhineland Center, for instance, published a leaflet entitled "What is at Stake?" (*Was steht auf dem Spiel?*), of which about one million copies were handed out, mostly in the Rhineland but also in other parts of the country. In Cologne, where the Center fought a particularly hard campaign, it published fifty-four different leaflets amounting to a total of about one million copies.[229] Center efforts, however, paled beside those of the Socialists. In Cologne they countered Center efforts by distributing more than twice as many pamphlets (2,136,700) than the Center. The SPD, in fact, outdid all other German parties in their election propaganda. In 1911 they distributed over eighty million leaflets, calendars and brochures.[230]

In addition to pamphlets and brochures election meetings and rallies took place throughout the Rhineland. These meetings were organized by the local party committees. The Rhenish Center as well as the People's Association and the Windthorstbund trained public speakers who appeared at such gatherings.[231] To be able to address

---

[227] For example: "Die Reichsteuern" (1909-1911, 5,000,000); "Wer ist Schuld an der Teuerung?" (1911, 4,000,000); "Vorwärts in den roten Sumpf!" (1911, 1,500,000), in Ritter, *Bewegung*, p. 272.

[228] "Zur Organisation der Zentrumspartei," *Germania* no. 274, 29 December 1911.

[229] Jürgen Bertram, *Die Wahlen zum deutschen Reichstag vom Jahre 1912. Parteien und Verbände in der Innenpolitik des Wilhelminischen Reiches* (Düsseldorf: Droste Verlag, 1964), pp. 177, 179.

[230] Ibid., pp. 174, 179.

[231] Ibid., p. 183.

local circumstances, speakers were briefed by local Centrists or the local press. For a speech in Essen, for instance, Karl Bachem received a letter from the editor of the *Essener Volkszeitung*, providing details on the local National Liberal and SPD candidates and suggestions for topics to be touched upon in the speech. Mankamer asked Bachem to address foreign policy questions, in order to give a "positive appraisal of Center achievements." It was not necessary to dwell on the recent reform of imperial finances—that issue has been dealt with. More important was a proper assessment of the local candidate (in this case Giesberts), stressing his commitment to serve all classes.[232] The need to heal the wounds of the deeply divided Center in Essen was reiterated in a letter from Eberhard Wild, son of the former party leader in Essen. The party consisted of two antagonistic factions, representing the working class and the middle class respectively. Wild informed Bachem "in absolute confidence" that his father's successor, the apothecary Gregor Overkamm, "lacked the authority to quell opposition from within party ranks."[233]

Naturally, the most prominent and most accomplished speakers were difficult to attract to a small meeting or a safe riding. But wherever the competition was stiff, Center leaders would appear frequently. In beleaguered Cologne, Karl Trimborn urged his friend Karl Bachem to step into the fray.[234] Bachem obliged, delivering a speech in Cologne, praising the political achievements of Trimborn. Bachem addressed no local issues but concentrated on the national and foreign policy questions which had been mentioned in the election proclamation.[235] Local election committees often found it difficult, however, to attract speakers of the caliber of Karl Bachem. A commentator complained in *Germania* that local party leaders even in hotly-contested constituencies had a hard time attracting well-known speakers. "Dozens of letters and telegrams were sent, yet the answers were almost always rejections. If there happens to be no personal connection, one rarely finds a member of parliament who is available as a speaker."[236]

---

[232] Mankamer to K. Bachem, 18 November 1911, HAStK Nl. Bachem 1006/318.

[233] Eberhard Wild to K. Bachem, 19 November 1911, HAStK Nl. Bachem 1006/318.

[234] Bertram, *Wahlen*, p. 184.

[235] K. Bachem, "Die Bedeutung der bevorstehenden Reichstagswahl," speech delievered in Cologne, 11 December 1911, HAStK Nl. Bachem 1006/318.

[236] *Germania* no. 4, 6 January 1912, quoted in Bertram, *Wahlen*, p. 184.

In past elections, candidates in safe ridings often made only one appearance before their voters at the beginning of the campaign; some candidates did not even bother to do that much. By 1912 the changes in party organization and the competition between parties had made such complacency a thing of the past. On average, a Center candidate had to reckon on about thirty appearances. Giesberts, for instance, spoke at thirty-six of the seventy-eight campaign meetings in his Essen riding.[237] Jürgen Bertram has estimated that a campaign for a serious candidate cost between 10,000 and 15,000 marks; only in the most highly-contested constituencies would the parties spend more than 20,000 marks.[238] The basis of these estimates is the well-documented expenditure of the SPD. The Center, probably aided by tactical advantage, spent less on its candidates. In Moers-Rees (Düsseldorf district), where the Center candidate faced serious opposition from a liberal candidate, the party spent about 8,000 marks in 1912 (compared to 5,000 in 1907).[239]

Although women did not have the right to vote, they played an important role in Center election campaigns. Priests knew that women were their best allies in the parish. They therefore urged wives to persuade their husbands to vote for the Center, assuming that such women had more influence on the outcome than male voters themselves did. In this spirit a Bavarian priest admonished his parish during a sermon: "Everybody has a duty to Lord Jesus Christ, to fight and stand tall for his faith... Women, urge your husbands to vote only for the Center."[240] No doubt Rhenish priests employed the same tactics. Women teachers, too, were targeted by the Center "to fight the social and political indifference in our own camp."[241]

Women were not just the instruments of clerical propaganda for the Center. Since the new Association Law (*Vereinsgesetz*) of 1908 had given women the right to organize, all parties made some effort to recruit them for political activities. Again it was the Social Democrats who made the most of this new opportunity. The Center had long been aware of the great influence women had on the formation of political ideas within families. The party also realized the threat that Socialist efforts to recruit women for their task posed to the Center and particularly to Catholic workers. The social work of the

---

[237] Bertram, *Wahlen*, p. 185.
[238] Ibid., p. 190.
[239] Ibid., p. 192.
[240] Quoted in Bertram, *Wahlen*, p. 194.
[241] Josef Jörg [general secretary of Rhineland Centre] to provincial chapters of the Centre party, 20 December 1912, HAStK Nl. Trimborn 1256/117 f. 3.

Catholic Women's League (*Katholischer Frauenbund*) was not enough to curb the influence of the Social Democrats.[242] As a consequence the Center aggressively recruited women into the party. The Center women's organization of Düsseldorf was founded in May 1911. By the end of that year it had more than 2,000 members.[243]

Schemes to attract voters were taken to new heights during the 1912 election. All parties manipulated or threatened voters to make headway in difficult constituencies. The means employed ranged from the production and distribution of false leaflets to the denial of venues to competing parties, from raiding opponents' rallies to boycotting individual businessmen or whole towns. Public rallies offered also an opportunity for the opposition to show its strength; deliberate disturbances of rival rallies were part of every party's campaign repertoire. Karl Bachem, for example, was prevented from finishing an election speech in Mainz by disruptive Socialists who had occupied the gallery (presumably for acoustic considerations) long before Center supporters arrived at the hall. Bachem, incensed about "poor preparation" by local organizers, tried to ignore the heckling, but was ultimately forced to abandon his address because the "wild yelling and stomping" drowned out his speech.[244]

One way to win a hotly-contested riding was to distort the voters' list by adding the names of voters who worked but did not live there.[245] Socialists used this scheme in places such as Frankfurt, Stuttgart, Leipzig-Land, and Düsseldorf, but the Center was guilty of some of the worst such offenses. In order to frustrate the campaign of the leader of the National Liberals, Ernst Bassermann, Centrists added almost 3,000 names to the voters' list of Saarbrücken. This maneuver had the appearance of legality since on weekdays many of the workers' who were recruited for this scheme stayed in the Saarbrücken district where most of the factories were located; only on the weekend did they return to their homes in the neighboring districts of Saarlouis, Landkreis Trier, and Birkenfeld.[246] Not surprisingly, tempers were running high during the campaign. To vent their frustration after their defeat, Center supporters attacked a National Liberal parade celebrating Bassermann's victory.[247]

[242] "Katholische Frauen," pamphlet distributed by the People's Association, Dec. 1912, HAStK Nl. Trimborn 1256/123 f. 1.
[243] Bertram, *Wahlen*, p. 198.
[244] K. Bachem note, 11 November 1911, HAStK Nl. Bachem1006/319.
[245] Bertram, *Wahlen*, pp. 201-2.
[246] Ibid., pp. 202-3.
[247] Ibid., p. 203.

During the election campaign the Center presented itself as a Christian *Volkspartei* (people's party). The Center tried desperately to stay above the squabbles of various interest groups, claiming again and again that the common bond was their shared religious beliefs.[248] "It is self-evident," it claimed "that there cannot exist agreement on all political and economic questions among more than 2,000,000 voters." After the election, Karl Bachem played down his party's losses. He noted the Center's decision not to field candidates in some forty-five constituencies where the Conservatives had a good chance to win the seat without a run-off election. In order to avoid a split in the "blue-black" vote and thus support the despised coalition of National Liberals and Progressives, the Center urged its supporters to vote for the Conservatives. According to Bachem's calculations, some 200,000 Catholics followed this advice. This allegedly accounted for the decline of the Center vote between 1907 (2,179,800) and 1912 (1,996,800). Furthermore, Catholics in Silesia had voted for Polish instead of Center candidates, and some, Bachem conceded, were probably discouraged by the divisive *Zentrumsstreit*.[249] Still, even Bachem realized that Center losses in big cities and industrial regions were worrisome signs. The Center could not rely any longer on the support of Catholic workers. Despite the efforts of the People's Association and the workers' clubs, the Social Democrats "had made substantial inroads into the Catholic constituency."[250]

Although Bachem argued that the Center had not lost a substantial amount of support, the losses were painful and warranted diligence to ward off further erosion. The main danger the party faced was the "continuing indoctrination of the urban and industrial masses by Social Democratic propaganda."[251] Bachem also realized that any support for the Center by German Protestants had become very unlikely; the loss of all "caucus guests" (*Hospitanten*) was a clear sign of this. Where could new support come from under these circumstances?

In the run-off elections the Center again lent its support to the Conservatives, and thus secured nine more seats for the Conservatives. Conservative support for Center candidates, on the other hand, was disappointing. "The Protestant masses could just not be won for the [Center] cause."[252] The Center's assurance that no Protestant need fear anything from the party, and the promise that the Center "joy-

---

[248] "Für den Reichstagswahlkampf," *Zentrum* no. 50, 9 September 1911.
[249] KB, 7:378-79.
[250] KB, 7:379.
[251] KB, 7:384.
[252] KB, 7:380.

fully welcomes more Protestants into its ranks," found no echo among Protestant voters.[253] Indeed, after the election the Center also lost all *Hospitanten* in Hanover, losing even the faintest claim to be anything other than a Catholic party or (at best) a party that was attractive only to Catholics.

The Rhenish Center experienced some hurtful defeats. The riding of Düsseldorf, long a Center stronghold, had been lost to the SPD in a 1911 by-election. In 1912, the Socialist candidate, with the support of the left liberals, again defeated his Catholic opponent. Hamm-Soest was also lost to the Socialists because of their run-off coalition with the National Liberals. Giesberts defended his seat in Essen. The most surprising and humiliating defeat was that of Karl Trimborn in Cologne. After the elections, several Centrists offered their seats to Trimborn, and he eventually accepted that of Dr. Becker, who had been elected in the riding of Siegkreis-Waldbröl.

The party also underwent changes in the social composition of the caucus. Lawyers and clergy, who had dominated the Center caucus and its leadership in the past, lost ground during the election of 1912. The Center caucus also had fewer civil servants and fewer representatives of trade, commerce and industry. Agrarian Centrists were an exception to this trend; among the Center establishment they were the only group to maintain their strength and influence. Lawyers, journalists, teachers, white-collar workers, workers, craftsmen and *Privatbeamte*, on the other hand, increased their presence in the Center caucus.[254]

A comparison of the last Reichstag election of the Kaiserreich in 1912 with its first in 1871 sheds some light on the changes that took place in German party politics during these four decades. Participation in elections rose consistently. In the election to the first Reichstag about half of those eligible took advantage of the right to vote, at the time this was a comparatively high number which reflected the enthusiasm for the newly founded empire and the relatively extensive voting rights. The Kulturkampf mobilized voters, not just in the Rhineland and other regions with large Catholic populations but also their Protestant opponents who voted for the liberal parties and in particular for the National Liberals.[255]

---

[253] K. Bachem, "Die Bedeutung der bevorstehenden Reichstagswahl," speech delivered in Cologne, 11 December 1911, HAStK Nl. Bachem 1006/318.
[254] Bertram, *Wahlen*, p. 171.
[255] Alfred Milatz, "Die linksliberalen Parteien und Gruppen in den Reichstagswahlen von 1871-1912," *Archiv für Sozialgeschichte* 12 (1972), p. 274.

Karl Rohe has observed that the Center on the whole managed to retain its support at the polls. Although the Center lost about a third of its original share of votes, the percentage of eligible voters that gave their vote to the Center changed only slightly.[256] More important for the Center's ability to influence political developments was the fact that the number of Center seats in the Reichstag remained roughly the same—about a quarter of all seats. Parallel to this relative stability of the Center, the Socialists experienced a dramatic increase in voters and in Reichstag seats. This success has been explained by the Socialists' ability to mobilize eligible voters who did not vote in the past and by the changes in the social composition of the electorate during the Kaiserreich.

These changes explain why the Socialists made such strides and they also help us understand why Center politicians in the Rhineland made such great efforts to attract working-class voters to the party. During the four decades between 1871 and 1912 the number of Germans employed in industry and trade grew steadily, while the number of farmers declined. Equally important was the growth of Germany's urban population. In 1871 nearly two-thirds (63.9%) of Germany's population lived in municipalities with fewer than 2,000 inhabitants. By 1910 those living in small communities made up only two-fifths (40%) of the total population. Given the fact that the Center had little hope of recruiting Protestant voters and that their support of rural Catholics and the urban middle classes was saturated, the only area of possible growth was the Catholic working class. The future must indeed have looked bleak because, in the one segment of Catholic voters that could help regain the losses of the 1912 election, the Center was badly battered by the SPD's successful drive for support.

These two trends—changes in the composition of the party leadership and changes in its electorate—reveal the main weakness of the Center. Agrarians were able to cling to their mandates because of the disproportionate role that rural ridings played for the Center. Defense of its position in parliament, however, depended on the support of Catholic workers, and while there was a slight increase in the number of Center politicians with a working class background, this did not translate into a larger share of Catholic working-class votes. Given the fact that agrarian Centrists continued to play an important role in the party's parliamentary representation and its leader-

---

[256] 1874, 17.5 %; 1903, 14.9%; 1097, 16.3%; 1912, 13.5%; Rohe, *Wahlen*, p. 99.

ship, the Center may be said to have maneuvered itself into a corner. The *Zentrumsstreit* had convinced Protestants that the Center would cling doggedly to Catholic ideology, and this made the idea of a Christian, interdenominational party obsolete. The *Gewerkschaftsstreit* had convinced many Catholic workers that their economic interest would be better represented by the SPD. Thus they, too, found it more and more difficult to vote for the Center. The party, unable and unwilling to implement the changes suggested by Julius Bachem, had indeed reached a position where, of all the policy options it had considered over the previous decade, only one remained viable—to safeguard the status quo.

VIII.
CONCLUSION

THIS STUDY has tried to explore four central aspects of Rhenish Catholic political culture: namely the effects and significance of the reorganization of the Center Party during the 1890s, the relationship between the party, Christian trade unions, the People's Association and workers, the extent to which democratic structures were introduced, and the place of the Center Party in German party politics.

Earlier than most Centrists, Karl Trimborn realized that in order to be successful a modern political party needed a tight permanent organizational structure. The old electoral associations which were only active during election campaigns were not suited to maintaining the grassroots support, raising the funds, and coordinating the party press and the many associations tied to the Center, needed for the success of a political party. These structural changes began in the early 1890s; it took almost two decades before the reforms introduced in the Rhineland were accepted and copied by other regional chapters and the national Center. In addition to erecting a solid, permanent party organization, Karl Trimborn built strong connections between the Center press, the People's Association, and the Christian trade unions. Although most organizations had a life apart from the Center, only in conjunction with the party did they gain significant influence.

This reorganization was part of a larger restructuring of Wilhelmine party politics. In the context of the German right Geoff Eley has referred to this process as the "mobilization of subordinate classes."[1] In the case of the Center this meant the relative decline of the influence of clergy and aristocracy, accompanied by the emergence of bourgeois politicians. Nationally this shift was represented by Ernst Lieber. In the Rhineland the Bachems and Karl Trimborn represented this new guard. As the changes in organization, changes in the composition of the party leadership was a slow process. The new leadership did not represent a sharp departure from the old.

[1] Eley, *Reshaping*, p. 354.

More often than not they came from prominent Catholic families. Their fathers had played significant political roles in Germany's Catholic milieu. Aristocrats, of course, did not disappear from the party's inner circle, but moved from the first tier of party leadership to the second or third. Ordinary Center supporters benefited from Trimborn's reforms. Most notably they played an important role in the selection of candidates for Reichstag and Landtag elections.

Not only a new party leadership was created but the party also courted new voters. The Rhineland's industrialization, the growth of its cities and the influx of immigrants, meant that the Center in order to be successful needed to gain support from the working class. In the Rhineland, the Center was unable to retain the working-class vote, in large part because the Socialist message became more attractive to workers than the Center's efforts to respond to working-class concerns. Herbert Gottwald has pointed out that any study of political Catholicism after 1890 must not ignore the challenge Social Democracy posed.[2] As the SPD threatened to cut into the Catholic working-class vote, as the People's Association began its educational and social programs; as the Pope entered discussions of the social questions with the encyclical *Rerum Novarum*, the politics of the Center had to take into account the reactions of the working class. In the Rhineland, with its industrialized areas and growing urban population, this need was particularly pressing. Thus the policies of the Rhenish Center differed from those in Bavaria and Württemberg, for example.

While the SPD steadily increased its share of the popular vote, the Rhenish Center could hang on to its seats because of the three-class voting system in Landtag elections and constituency borders which favored a party with a rural following in Reichstag elections. Thomas Nipperdey has argued that during the 1880s the liberal parties were forced into the uncomfortable position of sitting between two fronts: the conservative state and conservative social groups on the one hand and the proletariat and the Socialist movement on the other.[3] The Rhineland Center Party found itself in a similar position. The pressure it felt, however, was not generated so much by rival parties as by rival visions of the future shape of political Catholicism within the Center itself. In the Rhineland the two fronts squeezing the Center were the traditional rural support, led by mem-

[2] Gottwald, "Zentrum und Imperialismus," pp. 229-30.
[3] Thomas Nipperdey, "Grundprobleme der deutschen Parteigeschichte im 19. Jahrhundert," in *Die deutschen Parteien vor 1918*, ed. Gerhard A. Ritter (Cologne: Kiepenheuer & Witsch, 1973), p. 50.

bers of the conservative Catholic aristocracy, and an alternative vision put forward by those in the party who believed that the Center could only survive in the long run if it adapted to the changes brought about by the industrial revolution. In fact, the particular interests of the various factions could be divisive or mutually contradictory, and even where there was general agreement on principles (such as the belief that the Center was guarding the interests of Catholics), nuances and differing priorities precluded any simple consensus. This conflict was not confined, of course, to the Rhineland. But the Rhineland Center played a critically important role in this controversy over the nature of political Catholicism. Many of the modernizing impulses had their origins in the Rhineland, and the battlelines of the *Zentrumsstreit* and the *Gewerkschaftsstreit* were drawn particularly sharply there.

The third focus of this book is closely related to the first. The extent to which the Center espoused democratic principles and to which it furthered democracy in German politics is related to the party's organizational reforms. The party—through its hierarchy, its leadership, and its selection of candidates—made considerable strides in modernizing the organization. In the process the party became internally more democratic. Indeed, as far as party democracy and the modernization of structures are concerned, the Rhineland Center went further than other regional chapters.

The larger dimension of the problem of democratization forces one to inquire why the Center failed to bring about a reform of the authoritarian rule and authoritarian structures in Imperial Germany. The answer to this question cannot be found by looking at the Center and other political parties alone, or even their striving (or opposition) to implement full parliamentary democracy. By isolating the parties from the environment in which they functioned, one would ignore the structural framework that to a considerable degree shaped the alternatives that parties had to consider: political parties are the product of particular social and political constellations rather than their creators. Thus, to answer this question we have to look at some of the fundamental features of Germany's political system. Political parties gained in significance as the functions and power of the Reichstag were expanded. Yet the political system was still marred in ways that foreshadowed the collapse of the Second Reich and eventually of the Weimar Republic. M. Rainer Lepsius has argued that the remarkable longevity and stability of Germany's party system was the result of social and political structures that preceded the Second Reich. These structures continued to exert a determining influence

CONCLUSION   237

on the development of party politics, surviving the war and perhaps even the Weimar Republic.[4]

What place did the Center Party occupy in the world of German party politics? The Center was part of the parliamentary spectrum of the Kaiserreich; any definition that implies that political Catholicism was by its very nature opposed to the Bismarckian state does not reflect the realities of the Second Empire. But the Center was also a special case; what needs to be answered is David Blackbourn's question: how special? The Center was peculiar because it combined features common to various German political parties; it is their specific *combination* that makes it distinct. The Center existed within a distinctive Catholic milieu. It shared this characteristic with the Social Democrats, from whom it borrowed many of its organizational tools. The Center differed significantly from the SPD because it represented the economic and social interests of not one class but of a religious group spanning all classes. Most important is the fact that the Center was fundamentally a Catholic party, and that Center politicians regarded it as such. "The character of the Center," Bachem once wrote to a friend, "is not only determined by its political program as interdenominational, but also by the fact that its political program has by and large been accepted only by Catholics. Catholics are the foundation of the Center."[5] On the whole, Center leaders resisted the calls of their more extreme supporters for an exclusively Catholic party with close and explicit ties to the Vatican. Thus they fought a constant battle with pro-Roman clerics such as Cardinal Kopp or the integralists in Trier and Berlin. To be sure, the loyalty of the bulk of Center voters to their party was a barrier to the Center's sliding into the political margins throughout the Kaiserreich. Nevertheless, behind the security of its standing in the Reichstag and Prussian Landtag, it faced the threat of losing its identity during the *Zentrumsstreit* and losing the support of the growing Catholic working class during the *Gewerkschaftsstreit*.

The Center, in this context, could not transcend the limitations imposed by three structural preconditions to its existence: the *confessional* conflict between Protestants and Catholics; the *political* antagonism between the Prussian state and Catholicism; and the *regional* disparities in the concentration and local influence of Catholics. It was ultimately the complex interplay between political, social, and economic forces that restricted the development of German de-

[4] Lepsius, "Parteiensystem," p. 61.
[5] K. Bachem to Jos. Dahlmann, S.J., 1 June 1906, HAStK Nl. Bachem 1006/254b.

mocracy before 1918. In this complicated environment, Center leaders saw no alternative to embracing the German nation state, confirming the Hohenzollern monarchy, and siding with conservatives and the government against the Socialists. This orientation worked well in rural regions dominated by farmers and the middle classes of small towns. But in industrial cities it failed. In places like Cologne, Essen and even Aachen, this dilemma became clearly visible by the turn of the century. Although it posed no immediate threat to the parliamentary strength of the Center, the party's more farsighted leaders realized that the time had come to adopt the party to changing circumstances.

Julius Bachem's impassioned call to arms, *Wir müssen aus dem Turm heraus*, was only the most celebrated of such demands for change. Karl Trimborn's wish to concentrate on the social question and secure the loyalty of Catholic workers, as well as his efforts to create an organization that could generate the infrastructure (and funds) needed to run modern election campaigns, is another example of such concern.

The image of a tower may provide a useful metaphor for the Center Party, but the complex history of political Catholicism is better served by a more elaborate image. The milieu of political Catholicism may be compared to the defenses of a great medieval city, with walls and gates. There are many towers guarding the safety of the inhabitants. One of these towers was the Roman Catholic Church—ancient, battleworn, manned by experienced defenders of the faith. The Center Party provided a more modern tower, as did the People's Association, and the many religious and social clubs founded in the course of the nineteenth century. Among the most recently-established defenses of this imaginary Catholic city were the workers' clubs and the Christian trade unions, designed to guard the interests of its newest inhabitants. These fortifications protected German Catholics well against the attacks from the state during the Kulturkampf, but the broad and rapid onslaught of industrialization and modernization forced a restructuring of the defenses. The old structures controlled by the clergy were augmented by new defenses. Political and economic organizations in many ways replaced priests and religious orders. The credo of political Catholicism was not preached from pulpits alone, especially as the Catholic press grew in size and influence. The party, voluntary associations and the Catholic press, not only the Church, defined political Catholicism, for Catholics as well as non-Catholics. These new structures and attitudes were largely formed in those regions of Catholic Germany that experienced industrialization first hand, and of these, the Rhineland was most prominent.

The position of the Center, however, was more difficult than that of the liberal parties. Catholics were isolated from dominant Protestant society in two ways. Politically, their loyalty to the nation state was always considered problematic. Socially, they remained a disadvantaged group with only limited access to the centers of power and influence. The parallels between the Center's position and that of the Socialist movement are obvious. Both groups had to demonstrate their national loyalty in many exalted and unnecessary ways. The Center, however, though ultimately *less* a social and political pariah than the SPD, paradoxically found it more difficult to retain mass support at the polls. It stagnated and then declined, because many Catholic workers, particularly after the Kulturkampf had subsided, were willing to trade economic and class interest for religious loyalties and cultural identity.

Ultimately, then, the Center failed in those spheres of politics that its leaders believed to be most important for its survival. After 1890 it fought essentially a rearguard battle. It was relegated to maintaining the allegiance of its supporters rather than expanding its electorate. Not only did it fail to attract Protestants in any significant way, it also lost part of its Catholic constituency. Most notably, the Center lost the struggle for the working-class vote.

Nevertheless, the most important reason for this failure was ideological. Catholic faith and its defenders prevented the party from becoming truly interdenominational, therefore the party could not effectively respond to the Socialist challenge. The Center was modern in the sense that it realized that practical political questions had to be solved without justification in theory or ideology. Karl Bachem, the most prominent of the Rhenish Center politicians, has frequently been portrayed as a pioneer of Christian democracy in the mold of the post-1945 CDU.[6] The lines of continuity between the two epochs, however, are not as straight and uninterrupted as partisan politicians and some historians believe them to be. On the one hand, Rudolf Morsey's judgment, written a quarter century ago, has lost none of its insight: "The founding of the CDU and the CSU was the lesson learned by the survivors of this generation of Christian politicians...from the history and collapse of political Catholicism."[7]

---

[6] The most recent attempt is Rolf Kiefer's biography of Karl Bachem.

[7] Rudolf Morsey, *Der Untergang des politischen Katholizismus. Die Zentrumspartei zwischen christlichem Selbstverständnis und "Nationaler Erhebung" 1932/1933* (Stuttgart: 1977), p. 160.

Yet on the other hand, the CDU/CSU was *not* the realization of a vision held by Center leaders in the Kaiserreich. What the Bachems, Trimborn, and many other leading Rhenish Centrists realized was that the Center had to adapt to the changes industrialization and urbanization had brought. There were two main areas in which their party had to adapt: first organizationally, to win election campaigns and to hold the "flock" together; and second pragmatically, to refashion its attitudes toward workers and the social question. Undoubtedly, the Rhenish Center scored some success on both counts. Trimborn's organization of the Rhenish Center became a model for other chapters throughout Germany. Rhenish Centrists also played a crucial role in the party's ideological redefinition during the first fifteen years of the twentieth century. During the *Gewerkschaftsstreit* and the *Zentrumsstreit*, they addressed exactly those questions that became crucial to the CDU/CSU after World War II. The answers they were prepared to give, however, were very different from those provided by a later generation of Christian Democrats.

TABLES & APPENDICES

Reichstag Elections
in the Prussian Rhine Province 1890-1912[1]

Wahlkreis	1890	1893	1898	1903	1907	1912
Stadt Köln	C	C	C	C	C	SPD
Landkreis Köln	C	C	C	C	C	C
Bergheim-Euskirchen	C	C	C	C	C	C
Rheinbach-Bonn	C	C	C	C	C	C
Siegkreis-Waldbroel	C	C	C	C	C	C
Mühlheim-Wipperführt-Gummersbach	C	C	C	C	C	C
Wetzlar-Altenkirchen	NL	NL	NL	NL	WV	WV*
Neuwied	C	C	C	C	C	C
Coblenz-St. Goar	C	C	C	C	C	C
Kreuznach-Simmern	NL	NL	NL	NL	NL	NL
Mayen-Ahrweiler	C	C	C	C	C	C
Adenau-Kochem-Zell	C	C	C	C	C	C
Daun-Prüm-Bitburg	C	C	C	C	C	C
Wittlich-Berncastel	C	C	C	C	C	C
Trier	C	C	C	C	C	C
Saarburg-Merzig-Saarlouis	C	C	C	C	C	C
Saarbrücken	NL	NL	NL	NL	NL	NL
Ottweiler-St. Wendel	DRP	DRP	DRP	C	NL	C
Lennep-Mettmann	FVP	FVP	FVP	SPD	DFrVp	SPD/USPD
Städte Elberfeld-Barmen	SPD	SPD	SPD	SPD	DRP	SPD
Solingen	SPD	SPD	U	SPD	SPD	SPD
Düsseldorf	C	C	C	C	C	C
Essen	C	DRP	C	C	C	C
Mühlheim a. d. Ruhr-Stadt Duisburg	NL	NL	NL	NL	SPD	NL
Mörs-Rees	C	DK	C	C	C	C
Kleve-Geldern	C	C	C	C	C	C
Kempen	C	C	C	C	C	C
Gladbach	C	C	C	C	C	C
Krefeld	C	C	C	C	C	C
Neuß-Grevenbroich	C	C	C	C	C	C
Schleiden-Malmedy-Montojie	C	C	C	C	C	C
Eupen-Aachen Land-Burtscheid	C	C	C	C	C	C
Stadt Aachen	C	C	C	C	C	C
Düren-Jülich	C	C	C	C	C	C
Geilenkirchen-Heinsberg-Erkelenz	C	C	C	C	C	C

C – Centre Party   FVP – Progressives   NL – National Liberals
U – Unaffiliated   DRP – Free Conservatives   SPD = Social Democrats
WV – Economic Union   DFrVp – German Progressive People's Party

[1] Schwarz, *MdR*, pp. 196-206.

CHAIRMEN OF THE CENTER IN THE GERMAN REICHSTAG

1871-1875 Karl Friedrich von Savigny
1875-1890 Georg Arbogast Baron von und zu Franckenstein
1890-1893 Franz Count von Ballestrem
1893-1900 Alfred Count von Hompesch
1909-1912 Georg Baron von Hertling
1912-1917 Peter Spahn
1917-1919 Adolf Gröber
1919-1921 Karl Trimborn

Rhenish Members of the Center Party's Reichstag Caucus, 1871-1918[2]

Election District	
Köln-Stadt	1871-1877 Grossmann, Nicola 1877-1881 Schenk, Eduard 1881-1884 Custodis, Karl 1884-1887 Röckerath, Peter 1887-1890 Braubach, Bernhard von 1890-1895 Greiss, Adolf (died) 1896-1912 Trimborn, Karl 1912-1918 SPD
Köln-Land	1871-1877 Grossmann, Friedrich 1877-1893 Menken, Clemens 1893-1907 Pingen, Johann 1907-1912 Hamecher, Cornelius 1912-1914 Kuckhoff, Joseph
Köln-Bergheim	1871-1897 Rudolphi, Wilhelm (died) 1897-1906 Breuer, Johann 1907-1918 Fassbender, Martin
Köln-Bonn	1871-1884 Kesseler, Eugen von 1884-1887 Fürth, Hermann von 1887-1890 Virnich, Karl (died) 1890-1917 Spahn, Peter 1917-1918 Henry, Johann
Köln-Siegkreis	1871-1901 Lingens, Josef (resigned) 1901-1912 Becker, Karl (resigned) 1912-1918 Trimborn, Karl
Köln-Mühlheim	1871-1874 Bürgers, Ignaz 1884-1887 Hamm, Konstantin 1881-1890 Moufang, Christoph 1890-1893 Boedicker, Adolf (died) 1893-1909 de Witt, Hermann (died) 1910-1918 Marx, Wilhelm
Koblenz-Wetzlar	The Center never won this riding.
Koblenz-Neuwied	1871-1874 National Liberals 1874-1878 zu Stolberg, Alfred 1878-1901 Bender, Hermann 1901-1903 Krupp, Wilhelm 1903-1912 Stupp, Karl 1912-1918 Krings, Michael
Koblenz-St. Goar	1871-1875 von Savigny, Karl 1875-1890 von Hertling, Georg

[2] Compiled from Schwarz, *MdR*, pp. 196-206.

Koblenz-Kreuznach	The Center never won this riding.
Koblenz-Mayen	1871-1874 Moufang, Christoph 1874-1895 Kochann, Friedrich 1896-1917 Wallenborn Quirin 1917-1918 Schmitz, Johannes
Koblenz-Adenau	1871-1903 von Grand-Ry, Andreas 1903-1909 Ruegenberg, Gottfried 1909-1918 Pauly, Jacob
Trier-Daun	1874 zu Stolberg, Cajus 1874-1877 von Hompesch, Ferdinand 1877-1879 von Forcade, Friedrich 1880-1884 von Schorlemer, Wilhelm 1884-1887 Mosler, Hermann 1887-1891 Limbourg, Johann 1891-1893 Nels Eduard 1893-1903 Broeckmann, Wilhelm 1903-1907 Dasbach, Georg 1907-1918 zu Löwenstein, Alois
Trier-Wittlich	1871-1874 Fier, Ernst 1874-1898 Dieden, Christian 1899-1903 Biesenbach, Gustav 1903-1912 von Wolff, Ferdinand 1912-1918 Astor, Jacob
Trier-Stadt	1871-1874 Thanitsch, Jakob 1874-1884 Majunke, Paul 1884-1907 Rintelen, Victor 1907-1912 Euler, Jacob 1912-1918 Hartrath, Medard
Trier-Saarburg	1871 Bellinger, Julius(resigned) 1871-1893 Haanen, Bartholomäus 1893-1912 Roeren, Hermann (resigned) 1912-1918 Werr, Joseph
Trier-Saarbrücken	The Center never won this riding.
Trier-Ottweiler	1871-1991 Free Conservative Party 1884 National Liberals 1887-1901 Free Conservative Party 1901-1903 National Liberals 1903-1907 Fuchs Eduard 1907-1912 National Liberals 1912-1918 Kossmann, Bartholomäus
Düsseldorf-Lennep	The National Liberals, Progressive Party and the SPD held this heavily contested riding.
Düsseldorf-Elberfeld	D. E. was usually won by the Socialists who, however, lost the seat several times to National Liberal and Free Conservative candidates.

Düsseldorf-Solingen	Since 1881 dominated by SPD. Philip Scheidemann's riding after 1903.
Düsseldorf-Stadt	1871-1882 Bernards, Joseph (resigned) 1882-1890 Lucius, August 1890-1898 Wenders, Carl 1898-1911 Kirsch, Theodor (died) 1911-1918 SPD
Düsseldorf-Essen	1871-1874 Krebs, Joseph 1874-1877 von Forcade, Friedrich 1877-1893 Stötzel, Gerhard 1893-1898 Free Conservative Party 1898-1905 Stötzel, Gerhard (died) 1905-1918 Giesbert, Johann
Düsseldorf-Duisburg	This riding was a National Liberal stronghold. The SPD briefly held it between 1907-1912.
Düsseldorf-Mörs	1871-1874 von Loe, Otto 1874-1884 Grütering, Heinrich 1884-1893 von Hoensbroech, Wilhelm 1893-1894 Gescher, Alfred (resigned) 1895-1912 Fritzen, Carl 1912-1918 Bell, Johann
Düsseldorf-Kleve	1871-1877 Ulrich, Theodor 1877-1892 Perger, Clemens (resigned) 1893-1918 Marcour, Eduard
Düsseldorf-Kempen	1871-1874 Pelzer, Ludwig 1874-1888 Pfafferott, Hugo (died) 1889-1912 Fritzen, Alois 1912-1918 Chrysant, Peter
Düsseldorf-Gladbach	1871 Kratz, Franz, independent candidate (resigned) 1871-1898 von Kehler, Friedrich 1898-1918 Hitze, Franz Düsseldorf-Krefeld 1871-1884 Reichensperger, August 1884-1889 Trimborn, Cornelius (died) 1889-1907 Bachem, Karl 1907-1918 Pieper, August
Düsseldorf-Neuß	1871-1878 von Thimus, Albert 1878-1893 Dalwigk, Franz 1893-1898 Weidenfeld, Franz 1898-1899 Rath, Balthasar (died) 1899-1918 Am Zehnthoff, Hugo
Aachen-Schleiden	1871-1874 Liberale Reichspartei/Liberal Conservatives 1874-1881 Franssen, Heinrich (died) 1881-1887 Fritzen, Alois 1887-1890 Fritzen, Karl

TABLES AND APPENDICES 247

	1887-1907 von Arenberg, Franz (died)
	1907-1918 Fervers, Adolf
Aachen-Eupen	1871-1898 Bock, Adam
	1898-1903 Dasbach, Georg
	1903-1918 Nacken Josef
Aachen-Stadt	1871-1874 von Spee, Leopold
	1871-1874 Baudri, Friedrich (died)
	1874-1878 von Biegeleben, Maximilian
	1878-1887 Gielen, Viktor (died)
	1887-1898 Mooren, Theodor
	1898-1900 Hille, Philip (resigned)
	1901-1918 Sittart, Hubert
Aachen-Jülich	1871-1873 Decker, Johann (died)
	1874 Leykam, Werner (resigned)
	1874-1909 von Hompesch, Alfred (died)
	1909-1918 zu Salm, Alfred
Aachen-Geilenkirchen	1871-1877 Lucius, Karl
	1877-1884 von Fürth, Hermann
	1884-1898 Hitze, Franz
	1898-1912 Opfergelt, Anton
	1912-1918 Stupp, Franz

BISHOPS OF THE DIOCESES IN THE RHINE PROVINCE

Archbishops of Cologne

1825-1835	Ferdinand August Count Spiegel
1836-1842/45	Klemens August Droste zu Vischering
1842/45-1864	Johannes von Geissel
1866-1885	Paulus Melchers
1885-1899	Philippus Krementz
1899-1902	Hubertus Simar
1903-1912	Antonius Fischer
1912-1919	Felix von Hartmann

Bishops of Trier

1824-1836	Joseph von Hommer
1842-1864	Wilhelm Arnoldi
1865-1867	Leopold Pelldram
1867-1876	Matthias Eberhard
1881-1921	Michael Felix Korum

GLOSSARY

Arbeiterverein	workers' club
Arbeiterfreund	Zeitschrift des Arbeitervereins zum hl. Paulus
Arbeiterwohl	Workers' Welfare, founded by Franz Brandts in 1880
Aufruf	proclamation
Deutsch-konservative Partei	Conservatives
Deutsche Fortschrittliche Volkspartei	People's Progressives; left-wing liberal party
Deutsche Freisinnige Partei	Freisinnige; left-wing liberal party
Deutsche Kolonialgesellschaft	German Colonial Society
Deutsche Reformpartei	German Reform; anti-semitic party
Deutsche Reichspartei	Imperial Party (in the Reich); Free Conservatives (in Prussia)
Fachabteilung	confessional trade sections; craft union under church patronage
Freisinnige Volkspartei	Progressive People's Party; left-wing liberal party
Generalversammlung der deutschen Katholiken (also Katholikentag)	annual meeting of German Catholics
Gesellenverein	journeymen's association
Gewerkschaftsstreit	controversy over Christian trade unions
Katholikentag	annual meeting of German Catholics
Kölner Richtung	Cologne wing of the Center Party; Karl and Julius Bachem and Karl Trimborn belonged to this faction of the party
Kulturkampf	literally, cultural struggle; persecution of the German Catholic Church
Landrat	local official of the Prussian government
Landtag	state parliament

Liberale Vereinigung	Liberal Union; left-wing liberal party
Nationalliberale Partei	National Liberals; right-wing liberal party
Osterdienstag	Easter Tuesday
Preußisches Abgeordnetenhaus	House of Deputies, lower chamber of the Prussian Landtag
Preußisches Herrenhaus	House of Lords, upper chamber of the Prussian Landtag
Verein	association, club
Vereinsleben	associational life
Volk	people
Volksverein für das katholische Deutschland	People's Association for Catholic Germany
Vorstand	directorate
Wahlverein	electoral association
Wirtschaftliche Vereinigung	Economic Union
Zeitung	newspaper
Zentrumspartei, Zentrum	Center Party
Zentrumsstreit	literally, quarrel over the Center; controversy over the future nature of the party

BIBLIOGRAPHY

Unpublished Sources

Bundesarchiv Koblenz (BAK)

    Nachlaß Bülow

    Nachlaß Herold

    Sammlung Fechenbach

    Zeitgeschichtliche Sammlung 1 (ZSg. 1)

    Zeitgeschichtliche Sammlung 2 (ZSg. 2)

    Kl. Erw. 478-1 (Cardauns)

    Kl. Erw. 478-2 (Cardauns)

Bundesarchiv, Abt. Potsdam (BAP)

    Volksvereinsarchiv Abt. 74 V O1

    Reichslandbund, Pressearchiv Abt. 61 Re 1

Historisches Archiv der Stadt Köln (HAStK)

    Nachlaß Karl Bachem

    Nachlaß Karl und Jeanne Trimborn

Hauptstaatsarchiv Düsseldorf (HStAD)

    Regierung Aachen, Präsidialbüro

    Regierung Düsseldorf

Stadtarchiv Mönchengladbach (StAMG)

    Nachlaß Hohn

    Nachlaß Heinen

Published Sources

Agócs, Sándor. "'*Germania Doceat!*' The *Volksverein*, the Model for Italian Catholic Action, 1905-1914." *Catholic Historical Review* 61, no. 1 (1975): 31-47.

Altenhöfer, Ludwig. *Stegerwald: Ein Leben für den kleinen Mann. Die Adam-Stegerwald-Story.* Bad Kissingen: Verlag für Politische Schriften, 1965.

Amelunxen, Rudolf. *Das Kölner Ereignis.* Essen: Ruhrländische Verlagsgesellschaft, 1952.

Anderson, Margaret Lavinia. *Windthorst: A Political Biography.* London: Oxford University Press, 1981.

Anderson, Margaret Lavinia. "The Kulturkampf and the Course of German History." *Central European History* 19, no. 1 (1986): 82-115.

Anderson, Margaret Lavinia. "Interdenominationalism, Clericalism, Pluralism: The *Zentrumsstreit* and the Dilemma of Catholicism in Wilhelmine Germany." *Central European History* 21, no. 4 (1988): 350-78.

Anderson, Margaret Lavinia. "Piety and Politics: Recent Work on German Catholicism." *Journal of Modern History* 63, no. 4 (1991): 681-716.

Anderson, Margaret Lavinia and Kenneth Barkin. "The Myth of the Puttkammer Purge and the Reality of the Kulturkampf: Some Reflections on the Historiography of Imperial Germany." *Journal of Modern History* 54, no. 4 (1982): 647-86.

Andre, Joseph. "Zentrum und Landwirtschaft. Stoff für Vorträge in Ortsversammlungen der württembergischen Zentrumspartei." *Politische Zeitfragen in Württemberg. Zwanglos erscheinende Hefte*, 26 (1918): 3-32.

Applegate, Celia. *A Nation of Provincials: The German Idea of Heimat.* Berkeley: University of California Press, 1990.

Aretz, Jürgen, Rudolf Morsey, and Anton Rauscher, eds. *Zeitgeschichte in Lebensbildern. Aus dem deutschen Katholizismus des 19. und 20. Jahrhunderts.* 6 vols. Mainz: Matthias-Grünewald-Verlag, 1979-1984.

Aretz, Jürgen. "Otto Müller (1870-1944)." In *Zeitgeschichte in Lebensbildern. Aus dem deutschen Katholizismus des 19. und 20. Jahrhunderts*, ed. Jürgen Aretz et al., 191-203. Mainz: Matthias-Grünewald-Verlag, 1979.

Aretz, Jürgen. "Katholische Arbeiterbewegung und christliche Gewerkschaften—Zur Geschichte der christlich-sozialen Bewegung." In *Der soziale und politische Katholizismus. Entwicklungslinien in Deutschland 1803-1963*, ed. Anton Rauscher, 159-214. Vol. 2. Munich: Günter Olzog

Verlag, 1982.Aschoff, Hans-Georg. *Kirchenfürst im Kaiserreich—Georg Kardinal Kopp*. Hildesheim: Bernward Verlag, 1987.

Augustine, Dolores L. *Patricians and Parvenus. Wealth and High Society in Wilhelmine Germany*. Oxford: Berg Publishers, 1994.

Bachem, Julius. *Erinnerungen eines alten Publizisten und Politikers*. Cologne: J. P. Bachem, 1913.

Bachem, Julius and Karl Bachem. *Die kirchenpolitischen Kämpfe in Preußen gegen die katholische Kirche insbesondere der "grosse Kulturkampf" der Jahre 1871-1887. Sonderabdruck der Artikel aus der dritten Auflage des Staatslexikons der Görres-Gesellschaft*. Freiburg i. Br.: Herdersche Verlagsbuchhandlung, 1910.

Bachem, Karl. *Josef Bachem, seine Familie und die Firma J. P. Bachem in Köln, die Rheinische und Deutsche Volkshalle, die Kölnischen Blätter und die Kölnische Volkszeitung: Zugleich ein Versuch der Geschichte der katholischen Presse und ein Beitrag zur Entwicklung der katholischen Bewegung in Deutschland*. 2 vols. Cologne: Verlag und Druck J. P. Bachem, 1912.

Bachem, Karl. *Vorgeschichte, Geschichte und Politik der deutschen Zentrumspartei*. 9 vols. Cologne: Verlag J. P. Bachem, 1927-1932.

Bär, Max. *Die Behördenverfassung der Rheinprovinz seit 1815*. Publikationen der Gesellschaft für Rheinische Geschichtskunde, vol. 35. Bonn: P. Hansteins Verlag, 1919.

Bauer, Clemens. *Deutscher Katholizismus. Entwicklungslinien und Profile*. Frankfurt a. M.: Josef Knecht, 1964.

Becker, Winfried. "Peter Reichensperger." In *Zeitgeschichte in Lebensbildern*, ed. Jürgen Aretz et al., 41-54. Mainz: Matthias-Grünewald Verlag, 1982.

Becker, Winfried. "Die Deutsche Zentrumspartei im Bismarckreich." In *Die Minderheit als Mitte—Die Deutsche Zentrumspartei in der Innenpolitik des Reiches 1871-1933*, ed. *idem*, 9-45. Paderborn: Ferdinand Schöningh, 1986.

Becker, Winfried, ed. *Die Minderheit als Mitte—Die Deutsche Zentrumspartei in der Innenpolitik des Reiches 1871-1933*. Beiträge zur Katholizismusforschung, B, Paderborn: Ferdinand Schöningh, 1986.

Becker, Winfried. "Die Zentrumspartei und die Enzyklika Rerum novarum. Zur Wirkungsgeschichte der Sozialenenzyklika auf den politischen Katholizismus in Deutschland." *Rheinische Vierteljahrsblätter* 56 (1992): 260-77.

Behnen, Michael, ed. *Quellen zur deutschen Außenpolitik im Zeitalter des Imperialismus: 1890-1911*. Ausgewählte Quellen zur deutschen Geschichte, vol. 26. Darmstadt: Wissenschaftliche Buchgesellschaft, 1977.

Bergsträsser, Ludwig, ed. *Der politische Katholizismus. Dokumente seiner Entwicklung*. 2 vols. 1921-1922. Reprint. Hildesheim: Georg Olms Verlag, 1976.

Bers, Günter, ed. *Arbeiterjugend im Rheinland: Erinnerungen von Wilhelm Reimes und Peter Trimborn*. Die Arbeiterbewegung in den Rheinlanden, vol. 8. Wentdorf b. Hamburg: Einhorn-Presse Verlag, 1978.

Bers, Günter. *Katholische Arbeitervereine im Raum Aachen 1903-1914. Aufbau und Organisation des Aachener Bezirksverbandes im Spiegel seiner Delegiertenversammlung*. Die Arbeiterbewegung in den Rheinlanden, vol. 12. Wentdorf: Einhorn-Presse Verlag, 1979.

Bertram, Jürgen. *Die Wahlen zum deutschen Reichstag vom Jahre 1912. Parteien und Verbände in der Innenpolitik des Wilhelminischen Reiches*. Beiträge zur Geschichte des Parlamentarismus und der politischen Parteien, vol. 28. Düsseldorf: Droste Verlag, 1964.

Bierganz, Manfred. "Hermann Cardauns (1847-1925). Politiker, Publizist und Wissenschaftler in den Spannungen des politischen und religiösen Katholizismus seiner Zeit." Ph. D. diss., Rheinisch-Westfälische Technische Hochschule Aachen, 1977.

Bismarck, Otto von. *Die gesammelten Werke*. 15 vols. 1972. Reprint. Berlin: 1924 ff.

Blackbourn, David. *Class, Religion, and Local Politics in Wilhelmine Germany. The Centre Party in Württemberg before 1914*. New Haven, Conn.: Yale University Press, 1980.

Blackbourn, David. *Populists and Patricians: Essays in Modern German History*. London: Allen & Unwin, 1987.

Blackbourn, David. *Marpingen: Apparitions of the Virgin Mary in Bismarckian Germany*. Oxford: Clarendon Press, 1993.

Blackbourn, David and Geoff Eley. *The Peculiarities of German History. Bourgeois Society and Politics in Nineteenth-Century Germany*. Oxford: Oxford University Press, 1984.

Blackbourn, David and Richard J. Evans, eds. *The German Bourgeoisie: Essays on the social history of the German middle class from the late eighteenth to the early twentieth century*. New York: Routledge, 1991.

Blessing, Werner K. "Reform, Restauration, Rezession. Kirchenreligion und Volksreligiosität zwischen Aufklärung und Industrialisierung." In

Volksreligiosität in der modernen Sozialgeschichte, ed. Wolfgang Schieder, 97-122. Göttingen: Vandenhoeck & Ruprecht, 1986.

Brack, Rudolf. "Die Bemühungen Karl Bachems und führender Zentrumspolitiker um eine Beilegung des Gewerkschaftsstreites im Jahre 1904." *Annalen des Historischen Vereins für den Niederrhein* 177 (1975): 217-31.

Brandt, Peter, ed. *Preußen: Zur Sozialgeschichte eines Staates. Eine Darstellung in Quellen*. Reinbek bei Hamburg: Rowohlt, 1981.

Braudel, Fernand. *The Wheels of Commerce*. Vol. 2, *Civilization & Capitalism, 15th-18th Century*. Translated by Siân Reynolds. New York: Harper & Row, 1982.

Brecher, August. "Oberpfarrer L. A. Nellessen (1783-1859) und der Aachener Priesterkreis." *Zeitschrift des Aachener Geschichtsvereins* 76 (1964): 45-205.

Broch, Ernst-Detlef. *Katholische Arbeitervereine in der Stadt Köln 1890-1901*. Wentorf/Hamburg: Einhorn-Presse Verlag, 1977.

Brose, Eric Dorn. *Christian Labor and the Politics of Frustration in Imperial Germany*. Washington, D.C.: Catholic University of America Press, 1985.

Brunn, Gerhard. "Zentrale und Provinz in der preußischen Geschichte vom Wiener Kongreß bis zur Revolution von 1848." In *Die Rheinlande und Preußen: Parlamentarismus, Parteien und Wirtschaft*, ed. Landschaftsverband Rheinland, 27-39. Cologne: Rheinland-Verlag, 1990.

Buchheim, Karl. *Geschichte der christlichen Parteien in Deutschland*. Munich: Kösel-Verlag, 1953.

Buchheim, Karl. *Ultramontanismus und Demokratie. Der Weg der deutschen Katholiken im 19. Jahrhundert*. Munich: Kösel-Verlag, 1963.

Bülow, Bernhard Fürst von. *Denkwürdigkeiten*. 4 vols. Berlin: Verlag Ullstein, 1930-1931.

Bülow, Bernhard Fürst von. *Deutsche Politik*. Edited with an Introduction by Peter Winzen. Bonn: Bouvier Verlag, 1992.

Cardauns, Hermann. *Fünfzig Jahre Kölnische Volkszeitung. Ein Rückblick zum goldenen Jubiläum der Zeitung am 1. April 1910*. Cologne: J. P. Bachem, 1910.

Cardauns, Hermann. *Adolf Gröber*. M. Gladbach: Volksvereins-Verlag, 1921.

Cardauns, Hermann. *Karl Trimborn*. M. Gladbach: Volksvereins-Verlag, 1922.

Cardauns, Hermann. *Ernst Lieber. Der Werdegang eines Politikers bis zu seinem Eintritt in das Parlament (1838-1871)*. Wiesbaden: Verlag Hermann Rauch, 1927.

Chadwick, Owen. *The Secularization of the European Mind in the Nineteenth Century*. 1975. Reprint. Cambridge University Press, 1990.

Craig, Gordon A. *Germany 1866 - 1945*. New York: Oxford University Press, 1978.

Deuerlein, Ernst. "Der Gewerkschaftsstreit." *Tübinger Theologische Quartalsschrift* 139 (1959): 40-81.

Dowe, Dieter. "Die erste sozialistische Tageszeitung in Deutschland. Der Weg der 'Trierschen Zeitung' vom Liberalismus über den 'wahren Sozialismus' zum Anarchismus (1840-1851)." *Archiv für Sozialgeschichte* 12 (1972): 55-107.

Dowe, Dieter. "Organisatorische Anfänge der Arbeiterbewegung in der Rheinprovinz und in Westfalen bis zum Sozialistengesetz." In *Arbeiterbewegung an Rhein und Ruhr. Beiträge zur Geschichte der Arbeiterbewegung in Rheinland-Westfalen*, ed. Jürgen Reulecke, 51-80. Wuppertal: Hammer, 1974.

Ebertz, Michael N. "Die Organisierung von Massenreligiosität im 19. Jahrhundert. Soziologische Aspekte zur Frömmigkeitsforschung." *Jahrbuch für Volkskunde* 2 (1979): 38-72.

Eley, Geoff. "*Sammlungspolitik,* Social Imperialism and the Navy Law of 1898." In *From Unification to Nazism. Reinterpreting the German Past*, ed. id., 110-54. First published in *Militärgeschichtliche Mitteilungen* 15, no. 1 (1974), pp. 29-63. Reprint. Boston: Allen & Unwin, 1986.

Eley, Geoff. *Reshaping the German Right. Radical Nationalism and Political Change After Bismarck*. 1980. Reprint. Ann Arbor: University of Michigan Press, 1991.

Epstein, Klaus. "Erzberger's Position in the Zentrumsstreit before World War I." *Catholic Historical Review* 44, no. 1 (1958): 1-16.

Epstein, Klaus. *Matthias Erzberger and the Dilemma of German Democracy*. Princeton: Princeton University Press, 1959.

Erzberger, Matthias. *Die Zentrumspolitik im Reichstage. Reichtagssession vom 19. Februar bis 14. Mai 1907*. Berlin: Verlag der Germania, 1907.

Erzberger, Matthias. *Das deutsche Zentrum*. Amsterdam: Verlag der "Internationale Verlagsbuchhandlung: "Messis", 1910.

Bibliography

Eßer, Albert. *Wilhelm Elfes, 1884-1969: Arbeiterführer und Politiker.* Veröffentlichungen der Kommission für Zeitgeschichte, vol. B 53. Mainz: Matthias-Grünewald-Verlag, 1990.

Evans, Richard J. "Religion and Society in Modern Germany." *European Studies Review* 12, no. 4 (1982): 249-88.

Evertz, Wilfried. "Das Zusammenwachsen des Klerus unter Erzbischof Spiegel im neugegründeten Erzbistum Köln 1825-1835." *Annalen des Historischen Vereins für den Niederrhein* 197 (1994): 147-58.

Faber, Karl-Georg. "Die kommunale Selbstverwaltung in der Rheinprovinz im 19. Jahrhundert." *Rheinische Vierteljahrsblätter* 30 (1965): 132-151.

Fechenbach-Laudenbach, Friedrich Carl Reichsfreiherr von. "Die Familie Bachem-Lieber." *Die Zukunft* 14 (1896): 155-7.

Feldenkirchen, Toni. "Die Bonner Deutsche Reichszeitung im Kulturkampf." Ph. D. diss., Ludwig-Maximilians-Universität, München, 1933.

Fenske, Hans, ed. *Im Bismarckschen Reich 1871-1890*. Quellen zum politischen Denken der Deutschen im 19. und 20. Jahrhundert. Freiherr vom Stein-Gedächtnisausgabe, vol. 6. Darmstadt: Wissenschaftliche Buchgesellschaft, 1978.

Fischer, Fritz. "Der deutsche Protestantismus und die Politk im 19. Jahrhundert." *Historische Zeitschrift* 171 (1951): 473-518.

Ford, Caroline. "Religion and Popular Culture in Modern Europe." *Journal of Modern History* 65, no. 1 (1993): 152-75.

Freytag, Gustav. *Gesammelte Werke.* Vol. 7, 1st series, *Politische Aufsätze*. Leipzig and Berlin-Grunewald: G. Hirzel und Verlagsanstalt für Literatur und Kunst Hermann Klemm, n. d.

Gall, Lothar. *Bismarck. Der weiße Revolutionär.* Frankfurt: Ullstein Verlag, 1980.

Gatz, Erwin. "Das erste Vatikanische Konzil und die soziale Frage." *Annarium Historiae Conciliorum* 3 (1971): 156-73.

Gatz, Erwin, ed. *Geschichte des kirchlichen Lebens in den deutschsprachigen Ländern seit dem Ende des 18. Jahrhunderts. Die Katholische Kirche.* Vol. 1, *Die Bistümer und ihre Pfarreien*. Freiburg/Br.: Herder, 1991.

Gerschler, Walter. "Aachen als Sitz staatlicher Verwaltungsbehörden in der Zeit vom Ende der freien Reichsstadt Aachen im Jahre 1794 bis zum Amtsantritt der Aachener Regierung am 22. April 1816." In *150 Jahre*

Regierung und Regierungsbezirk Aachen. Beiträge zu ihrer Geschichte, ed. Regierungspräsident, 1-14. Aachen: Regierungspräsident, 1967.

Giesberts, Johannes. *Das Zentrum und die Wahlrechts-Reform in Preußen.* Essen-Ruhr: Fredebeul & Koenen, 1910.

Gollwitzer, Heinz. *Ein Staatsmann des Vormärz: Karl von Abel 1788-1859. Beamtenaristokratie—Monarchisches Prinzip—politischer Katholizismus.* Göttingen: Vandenhoeck & Ruprecht, 1993.

Gründer, Horst. *Christliche Missionen und deutscher Imperialismus. Eine politische Geschichte ihrer Beziehungen während der deutschen Kolonialzeit (1884-1914) unter besonderer Berücksichtigung Afrikas und Chinas.* Paderborn: Ferdinand Schöningh, 1982.

Gründer, Horst. "Nation und Katholizismus im Kaiserreich." In *Katholizismus, nationaler Gedanke und Europa seit 1800,* ed. Albrecht Langner, 65-87. Beiträge zur Katholizismusforschung, Reihe B: Abhandlungen. Paderborn: Ferdinand Schöningh, 1985.

Hegel, Eduard. "Die katholische Kirche in den Rheinlanden 1815-1945." In *Wirtschaft und Kultur im 19. und 20. Jahrhundert,* ed. Franz Petri and Georg Droege, 329-412. Vol. 3, *Rheinische Geschichte.* Veröffentlichungen des Instituts für Geschichtliche Landeskunde der Rheinlande der Universität Bonn. Düsseldorf: Schwann, 1979.

Hegel, Eduard. *Geschichte des Erzbistums Köln.* Vol. 5, *Das Erzbistum Köln: Zwischen der Restauration des 19. Jahrhunderts und der Restauration des 20. Jahrhunderts 1815-1962.* Cologne: Verlag J. P. Bachem, 1987.

Hehl, Ulrich von. "Zum politischen Katholizismus in Rheinland-Westfalen 1890-1918." In *Rheinland-Westfalen im Industriezeitalter,* ed. Kurt Düwell and Wolfgang Köllmann, 56-71. Vol. 2, *Von der Reichsgründung bis zur Weimarer Republik.* Wuppertal: Peter Hammer Verlag, 1984.

Heinen, Ernst. *Staatliche Macht und Katholizismus in Deutschland.* 2 vols. Paderborn: Ferdinand Schöningh, 1969,1979.

Heitzer, Horstwalter. *Der Volksverein für das katholische Deutschland im Kaiserreich 1890-1918.* Mainz: Matthias-Grünewald-Verlag, 1979.

Hettling, Manfred and Paul Nolte, eds. *Bürgerliche Feste: Symbolische Formen politischen Handelns im 19. Jahrhundert.* Göttingen: Vandenhoeck & Ruprecht, 1993.

Höffner, Joseph. "Die Stellung des deutschen Katholizismus in den sozialen Entscheidungen des 19. Jahrhunderts." *Geschichte in Wissenschaft und Unterricht* 4 (1953): 601-16.

Hohmann, Friedrich. "Die Soester Konferenzen 1864-1866. Zur Vorgeschichte der Zentrumspartei in Westfalen." *Westfälische Zeitschrift* 114 (1967): 293-342.

Hull, Isabel V. *The Entourage of Kaiser Wilhelm II, 1888-1918.* Cambridge: Cambridge University Press, 1982.

Hunley, J. D. "The Working Classes, Religion and Social Democracy in the Düssseldorf Area, 1867-78." *Societas—a Review of Social History* 4, no. 2 (1974): 131-49.

Hürten, Heinz. *Kurze Geschichte des deutschen Katholizismus, 1800-1960.* Mainz: Matthias-Grünewald-Verlag, 1986.

Immelen, Hubert. *Der Piusverein zu Aachen, 1848-1898. Gedenkblatt.* Aachen: n. d. [1898].

Jörg, Josef. "Organisator Rhenaniae." *Mitteilungen der Zentralstelle der Rheinischen Zentrumspartei*, 4 (2 December 1914): 29-38.

Kaelble, Hartmut. "Der Mythos von der rapiden Industrialisierung in Deutschland." *Geschichte und Gesellschaft* 9, no. 1 (1983): 106-18.

Kaiser, Jochen-Christoph. "Sozialdemokratie und 'praktische' Religionskritik. Das Beispiel der Kirchenaustrittsbewegung 1878-1914." *Archiv für Sozialgeschichte* 22 (1982): 263-98.

Kall, Alfred. *Katholische Frauenbewegung in Deutschland: Eine Untersuchung zur Gründung katholischer Frauenvereine im 19. Jahrhundert.* Beiträge zur Katholizismusforschung, Reihe B: Abhandlungen. Paderborn: Ferdinand Schöning, 1983.

Kaudelka-Hanisch, Karin. "The titled businessman: Prussian Commercial Councillors in the Rhineland and Westphalia during the nineteenth century." In *The German Bourgeoisie: Essays on the social history of the German middle class from the late eighteenth to the early twentieth century*, ed. David Blackbourn and Richard J. Evans, 87-114. New York: Routledge, 1991.

Kehr, Eckart. *Battleship Building and Party Politics in Germany, 1894-1901.* New York: Kraus Reprint, 1975.

Kellenbenz, Hermann. "Wirtschafts- und Sozialentwicklung der nördlichen Rheinlande seit 1815." In *Wirtschaft und Kultur*, ed. Franz Petri and Georg Droege, 1-192. Vol. 3, *Rheinische Geschichte.* Veröffentlichungen des Instituts für Geschichtliche Landeskunde der Rheinlande der Universität Bonn. Düsseldorf: Schwann, 1979.

Kempkes, Heidemarie. *Der christliche Textilarbeiterverband in Krefeld.* Die Arbeiterbewegung in den Rheinlanden, vol. 10. Wentorf b. Hamburg: Einhorn-Presse Verlag, 1979.

Kiefer, Rolf. *Karl Bachem: 1858-1945; Politiker und Historiker des Zentrums.* Mainz: Matthias-Grünewald-Verlag, 1989.

Kisky, Wilhelm. *Der Augustinus-Verein zur Pflege der Katholischen Presse von 1878 bis 1928.* Düsseldorf: Verlag des Augustinusvereins, 1928.

Klein, Friedrich. "Reichsfinanzpolitik und 'Nationalisierung' des Zentrums unter Ernst Maria Lieber 1891-1900." *Historisches Jahrbuch der Görres-Gesellschaft* 108, no. 1 (1988): 114-56.

Klöcker, Michael. "Der politische Katholizismus. Versuch einer Neudefinierung." *Zeitschrift für Politik* 18 (1971): 124-30.

Kocka, Jürgen. *Arbeiter und Bürger im 19. Jahrhundert.* Schriften des Historischen Kollegs: Kolloquien, vol. 7. Munich: R. Oldenbourg Verlag, 1986.

Köllmann, Wolfgang. "Von Rheinisch-Westfälischer Wirtschaft." In *Rheinisch-Westfälische Rückblende*, ed. Walter Först, 127-71. Beiträge zur Neueren Landesgeschichte des Rheinlandes und Westfalens, vol. 1. Cologne: Grote, 1967.

Komonchak, Joseph A. "The Enlightenment and the Construction of Roman Catholicism." *Catholic Commission on Intellectual Affairs Annual* (1985): 31-59.

Korff, Gottfried. "Formierung der Frömmigkeit: Zur sozialpolitischen Intention der Trierer Rockwallfahrten 1891." *Geschichte und Gesellschaft* 3 (1977): 352-83.

Landes, David S. *The Unbound Prometheus: Technological change and industrial development in Western Europe from 1750 to the present.* 1969. Reprint. Cambridge: Cambridge University Press, 1987.

Landschaftsverband Rheinland. *Die Rheinlande und Preußen: Parlamentarismus, Parteien und Wirtschaft.* Cologne: Rheinland-Verlag, 1990.

Langner, Albrecht, ed. *Säkularisation und Säkulisierung im 19. Jahrhundert.* Beiträge zur Katholizismusforschung, Reihe B: Abhandlungen. Paderborn: Ferdinand Schöningh, 1978.

Langner, Albrecht, ed. *Katholizismus, nationaler Gedanke und Europa seit 1800.* Beiträge zur Katholizismusforschung, Reihe B: Abhandlungen. Paderborn: Ferdinand Schöningh, 1985.

Lenger, Friedrich. *Zwischen Kleinbürgertum und Proletariat. Studien zur Sozialgeschichte der Düsseldorfer Handwerker 1816-1878.* Göttingen: Vandenhoeck & Ruprecht, 1986.

Lepper, Herbert. "Kaplan Franz Eduard Cronenberg und die christlichsoziale Bewegung in Aachen 1868-1878." *Zeitschrift des Aachener Geschichtsvereins* 79 (1968): 57-148.

Lepper, Herbert. "Die Generalversammlung der Katholiken Deutschlands vom 8. bis 11. September 1879 in Aachen." *Zeitschrift des Aachener Geschichtsvereins* 80 (1970): 235-42.

Lepper, Herbert, ed. *Sozialer Katholizismus in Aachen. Quellen zur Geschichte des Arbeitervereins zum hl. Paulus für Aachen und Burtscheid 1869-1878 (88).* Veröffentlichungen des Bischöflichen Diözesanarchivs Aachen, vol. 36. Mönchengladbach: B. Kühlen Verlag, 1977.

Lepper, Herbert. "Vom Honoratiorenverein zur Parteiorganisation. Ein Beitrag zur 'Demokratisierung' des Zentrums im Rheinland 1898-1906." *Rheinische Vierteljahrsblätter* 46 (1984): 238-74.

Lepper, Herbert. "Peter Joseph Schings (1837-1876) und die 'Christlich-Socialen Blätter'." *Annalen des Historischen Vereins für den Niederrhein* 191 (1988): 31-114.

Lepsius, M. Rainer. "Parteiensystem und Sozialstruktur: zum Problem der Demokratisierung der deutschen Gesellschaft." In *Die deutschen Parteien vor 1918*, ed. Gerhard A. Ritter, 56-80. Neue Wissenschaftliche Bibliothek, vol. 61. Cologne: Kiepenheuer & Witsch, 1973.

Lerman, Katherine Anne. *The Chancellor as Courtier: Bernhard von Bülow and the Governance of Germany, 1900-1909.* New York: Cambridge University Press, 1990.

Leugers-Scherzberg, August Hermann. *Felix Porsch: 1853-1930. Politik für katholische Interessen in Kaiserreich und Republik.* Mainz: Matthias-Grünewald Verlag, 1990.

Lill, Rudolf. "Kirche und Revolution. Zu den Anfängen der katholischen Bewegung im Jahrzehnt vor 1848." *Archiv für Sozialgeschichte* 18 (1978): 565-575.

Lidtke, Vernon L. *The Alternative Culture: Socialist Labor in Imperial Germany.* New York: Oxford University Press, 1985.

Löhr, Wolfgang. "Die Fabrikordnung der Firma Franz Brandts in Mönchengladbach." *Annalen des Historischen Vereins für den Niederrhein* 178 (1976): 145-57.

Lönne, Karl Egon. *Politischer Katholizismus im 19. und 20. Jahrhundert.* Neue Historische Bibliothek, vol. 264. Frankfurt a. M.: Suhrkamp, 1986.

Loth, Wilfried. *Katholiken im Kaiserreich. Der politische Katholizismus in der Krise des wilhelmschen Deutschlands.* Beiträge zur Geschichte des

Parlamentarismus und der politischen Parteien, vol. 75. Düsseldorf: Droste Verlag, 1984.

Lüdtke, Alf. "Eisenbahnfahren und Eisenbahnbau." In *Bürgerliche Gesellschaft in Deutschland*, ed. Lutz Niethammer, 101-19. Frankfurt a. M.: Fischer Verlag, 1990.

Mallmann, Klaus-Michael. "'Aus des Tages Last machen sie ein Kreuz des Herrn...'? Bergarbeiter, Religion und sozialer Protest im Saarrevier des 19. Jahrhunderts." In *Volksreligiosität in der modernen Sozialgeschichte*, ed. Wolfgang Schieder, 152-84. Göttingen: Vandenhoeck & Ruprecht, 1986.

Martin, Hortense. "Soziale Anschauungen und Bemühungen der Gebrüder Reichensperger und des Freihern von Thimus um die Mitte des 19. Jahrhunderts." *Archiv für mittelrheinische Kirchengeschichte* 7 (1955): 219-34.

Meerfeld, Jean. *Die Deutsche Zentrumspartei*. Sozialwissenschaftliche Bibliothek, vol. 3. Berlin: Verlag für Sozialwissenschaft, 1918.

Milatz, Alfred. "Die linksliberalen Parteien und Gruppen in den Reichstagswahlen von 1871-1912." *Archiv für Sozialgeschichte* 12 (1972): 273-92.

Milkereit, Gertrud. "Wirtschafts- und Sozialentwicklung der südlichen Rheinlande seit 1815." In *Wirtschaft und Kultur*, ed. Franz Petri and Georg Droege, 1-192. Vol. 3, *Rheinische Geschichte*. Veröffentlichungen des Instituts für Geschichtliche Landeskunde der Rheinlande der Universität Bonn. Düsseldorf: Schwann, 1979.

Misner, Paul. *Social Catholicism in Europe: From the Onset of Industrialization to the First World War*. New York: Crossroads, 1991.

Mittmann, Ursula. *Fraktion und Partei: Ein Vergleich von Zentrum und Sozialdemokratie im Kaiserreich*. Beiträge zur Geschichte des Parlamentarismus und der politischen Parteien, vol. 59. Düsseldorf: Droste Verlag, 1976.

Mockenhaupt, Hubert. "Franz Hitze (1851-1921)." In *Zeitgeschichte in Lebensbildern. Aus dem deutschen Katholizismus des 20. Jahrhunderts*, ed. Rudolf Morsey, 53-64. Mainz: Matthias-Grünewald-Verlag, 1973.

Moeller, Robert G. *German Peasants and Agrarian Politics, 1914-1924: The Rhineland and Westphalia*. Chapel Hill, N.C.: The University of North Carolina Press, 1986.

Mommsen, Wolfgang J. and Hans-Gerhard Husung, eds. *The Development of Trade Unionism in Great Britain and Germany, 1880-1914*. London: George Allen & Unwin, 1985.

Mooser, Josef. "Arbeiter, Bürger und Priester in den konfessionellen Arbeitervereinen im deutschen Kaiserreich, 1880-1914." In *Arbeiter und Bürger im 19. Jahrhundert: Varianten ihres Verhältnisses im europäischen Vergleich*, ed. Jürgen Kocka, 79-105. Schriften des Historischen Kollegs, Kolloquien, vol. 7. Munich: R. Oldenbourg Verlag, 1986.

Morsey, Rudolf. *Die Deutsche Zentrumspartei 1917-1923*. Beiträge zur Geschichte des Parlamentarismus und der politischen Parteien, vol. 32. Düsseldorf: Droste Verlag, 1966.

Morsey, Rudolf. "Die Zentrumspartei in Rheinland und Westfalen." In *Politik und Landschaft*, ed. Walter Först, 11-50. Beiträge zur Neueren Landesgeschichte des Rheinlandes und Westfalens, vol. 3. Cologne: Grote, 1969.

Morsey, Rudolf. "Die deutschen Katholiken und der Nationalstaat zwischen Kulturkampf und Erstem Weltkrieg." In *Die deutschen Parteien vor 1918*, ed. Gerhard Ritter, 270-98. Cologne: Kiepenheuer & Witsch, 1973.

Morsey, Rudolf. "Matthias Erzberger (1875-1921)." In *Zeitgeschichte in Lebensbildern. Aus dem deutschen Katholizismus des 20. Jahrhunderts*, ed. idem, 1:103-12. Mainz: Matthias-Grünewald-Verlag, 1973.

Morsey, Rudolf, ed. *Zeitgeschichte in Lebensbildern. Aus dem deutschen Katholizismus des 20. Jahrhunderts*. 2 vols. Mainz: Matthias-Grünewald-Verlag, 1973-1976.

Morsey, Rudolf. *Der Untergang des politischen Katholizismus. Die Zentrumspartei zwischen christlichem Selbstverständnis und "Nationaler Erhebung" 1932/1933*. Stuttgart: 1977.

Müller, Klaus. "Zentrumspartei und agrarische Bewegung im Rheinland, 1882-1903." In *Spiegel der Geschichte; Festgabe für Max Braubach zum 10. April 1964*, ed. Konrad Repgen and Stephan Skalweit, 828-57. Münster: Verlag Aschendorff, 1964.

Niderberger, Leonz. *Der Sozialdemokrat*. M. Gladbach: A Riffarth, 1891.

Niethammer, Lutz and Franz Brüggemeier. "Wie wohnten Arbeiter im Kaiserreich?" *Archiv für Sozialgeschichte* 16 (1976): 61-134.

Nipperdey, Thomas. "Grundprobleme der deutschen Parteigeschichte im 19. Jahrhundert." In *Die deutschen Parteien vor 1918*, ed. Gerhard A. Ritter, 32-55. Neue Wissenschaftliche Bibliothek, vol. 61. Cologne: Kiepenheuer & Witsch, 1973.

Nipperdey, Thomas. *Deutsche Geschichte: 1800-1866*. Munich: C.H. Beck, 1983.

Nipperdey, Thomas. *Religion im Umbruch: Deutschland 1870 - 1918*. Beck'sche Reihe, vol. 363. Munich: Verlag C. H. Beck, 1988.

Nipperdey, Thomas. *Deutsche Geschichte 1866-1918*. 2 vols. Munich: Verlag C. H. Beck, 1990-1993.

Nolan, Mary Lee and Sidney Nolan. *Christian Pilgrimage in Modern Western Europe*. Studies in Religion. Chapel Hill: University of North Carolina Press, 1989.

Oberdörffer, Johann Peter. *Verzeichnis geeigneter Bücher und Bühnenstücke für katholische Vereins-Bibliotheken*. Cologne: J. P. Bachem, 1893.

Pabst, Klaus. "Neutral-Morsenet. Ein Dorf ohne Staatszugehörigkeit (1815-1915)." In *150 Jahre Regierung und Regierungsbezirk Aachen. Beiträge zu ihrer Geschichte*, ed. Regierungspräsident, 29-43. Aachen: Regierungspräsident, 1967.

Pastor, Ludwig. *August Reichensperger 1808-1895. Sein Leben und sein Wirken auf dem Gebiet der Politik, der Kunst und der Wissenschaft*. 2 vols. Freiburg i. Br.: Herder'sche Verlagsbuchhandlung, 1899.

Pehl, Hans. *Die deutsche Kolonialpolitik und das Zentrum 1884-1914*. Limburg: Limburger Vereinsdruckerei, 1934.

Petri, Franz and Georg Droege, eds. *Rheinische Geschichte*. 3 vols. Veröffentlichungen des Instituts für Geschichtliche Landeskunde der Rheinlande der Universität Bonn. Düsseldorf: Schwann, 1976-1979.

Pfülf, Otto. *M. Clara Fey vom armen Kinde Jesus und ihre Stiftung. 1815-1894*. Freiburg i. Br.: Herdersche Verlagsbuchhandlung, 1913.

Pichler, Franz S. "Centrum und Landwirtschaft." *Sociale und politische Zeitfragen*, (1898): 214-80.

Plum, Günter. *Gesellschaftsstruktur und politisches Bewußtsein in einer katholischen Region, 1928-1933. Untersuchung am Beispiel des Regierungsbezirks Aachen*. Studien zur Zeitgeschichte. Stuttgart: Deutsche Verlags-Anstalt, 1972.

Poll, Bernhard. "Preußen und die Rheinlande." *Zeitschrift des Aachener Geschichtsvereins* 76 (1964): 5-44.

Poll, Bernhard. "Das Hineinwachsen der Rheinländer in den Preußischen Staatsverband." In *150 Jahre Regierung und Regierungsbezirk Aachen. Beiträge zu ihrer Geschichte*, ed. Regierungspräsident, 15-28. Aachen: Regierungspräsident, 1967.

Poll, Bernhard. "Zur neueren Wirtschaftsgeschichte des Aachener Landes." In *150 Jahre Regierung und Regierungsbezirk Aachen. Beiträge zu ihrer*

Geschichte, ed. Regierungspräsident, 59-84. Aachen: Regierungspräsident, 1967.

Raab, Heribert. "Auswirkungen der Säkularisation auf Bildungswesen, Geistesleben und Kunst im katholischen Deutschland." In *Säkularisation und Säkulisierung im 19. Jahrhundert*, ed. Albrecht Langner, 63-95. Beiträge zur Katholizismusforschung, Reihe B: Abhandlungen. Paderborn: Ferdinand Schöningh, 1978.

Rauscher, Anton, ed. *Der soziale und politische Katholizismus. Entwicklungslinien in Deutschland 1803-1963*. Vol. 2. Geschichte und Staat Bd. 250-252. Munich: Günter Olzog Verlag, 1982.

Reichert, Franz Rudolf. "Das Trierer Priesterseminar im Kulturkampf (1873-1886)." *Archiv für mittelrheinische Kirchengeschichte* 25 (1973): 65-105.

Repgen, Konrad. "Entwicklungslinien von Kirche und Katholizismus in historischer Sicht." In *Entwicklungslinien des deutschen Katholizismus*, ed. Anton Rauscher, 11-30. Munich: Verlag Ferdinand Schöningh, 1973.

Retallack, James N. "Social History with a Vengeance? Some Reactions to H.-U. Wehler's 'Das deutsche Kaiserreich'." *German Studies Review* 7, no. 3 (1984): 423-50.

Retallack, James N. *Notables of the Right: The Conservative Party and Political Mobilization in Germany, 1876-1918*. Boston, Mass.: Allen & Unwin, 1988.

Retallack, James N. ""What Is to Be Done?" The Red Specter, Franchise Questions, and the Crisis of Conservative Hegemony in Saxony, 1896-1909." *Central European History* 23 (1990): 271-312.

Retallack, James N. "From Pariah to Professional? The Journalist in German Society and Politics, from the Late Enlightenment to the Rise of Hitler." *German Studies Review* 16, no. 2 (1993): 175-223.

Ritter, Emil. *Die katholisch-soziale Bewegung Deutschlands im neunzehnten Jahrhundert und der Volksverein*. Cologne: Verlag J. P. Bachem, 1954.

Ritter, Gerhard A. *Wahlgeschichtliches Arbeitsbuch: Materialien zur Statistik des Kaiserreichs 1871-1918*. Munich: Verlag C. H. Beck, 1980.

Ritter, Gerhard A., ed. *Das Deutsche Kaiserreich 1871 - 1914: Ein historisches Lesebuch*. 4th ed. Göttingen: Vandenhoeck & Ruprecht, 1981.

Rivinius, Karl J. "Interdependenz von Politik und Evangelisation in China." *Historisches Jahrbuch der Görres-Gesellschaft* 109, no. 2 (1989): 387-420.

Roeren, Hermann. *Veränderte Lage des Zentrumstreits. Entgegnung auf die Kritik meiner Schrift Zentrum und Kölner Richtung.* Trier: Petrus-Verlag, 1914.

Rohe, Karl, ed. *Elections, Parties and Political Traditions: Social Foundations of German Parties and Party Systems, 1867-1987.* German Historical Perspectives, vol. 4. New York: Berg Publishers, 1990.

Rohe, Karl. *Wahlen und Wählertraditionen in Deutschland. Kulturelle Grundlagen deutscher Parteien und Parteiensysteme im 19. und 20. Jahrhundert.* Frankfurt a. M.: Suhrkamp, 1992.

Rohkrämer, Thomas. *Der Militarismus der "kleinen Leute": Die Kriegervereine im Deutschen Kaiserreich, 1871-1914.* Beiträge zur Militärgeschichte, vol. 29. Munich: R. Oldenbourg Verlag, 1990.

Röhl, John C. G. *Germany without Bismarck. The Crisis of Government in the Second Reich, 1890-1900.* London: B. T. Batsford, 1967.

Röhl, John C. G. *Kaiser, Hof und Staat: Wilhelm II. und die deutsche Politik.* 3rd ed. Munich: C. H. Beck Verlag, 1988.

Röhl, John C. G. *Wilhelm II: Die Jugend des Kaisers 1859-1888.* Munich: Verlag C. H. Beck, 1993.

Ross, Ronald J. *Beleaguered Tower: The Dilemma of Political Catholicism in Wilhelmine Germany.* Notre Dame, Ind.: University of Notre Dame Press, 1976.

Ross, Ronald J. "Enforcing the Kulturkampf: The Bismarckian State and the Limits of Coercion in Imperial Germany." *Journal of Modern History* 56, no. 3 (1984): 456-482.

Roy, Margret de. "Die Kommunalverwaltung im Regierungsbezirk Aachen seit 1816." In *150 Jahre Regierung und Regierungsbezirk Aachen. Beiträge zu ihrer Geschichte,* ed. Regierungspräsident, 29-43. Aachen: Regierungspräsident, 1967.

Rüther, Günther, ed. *Geschichte der christlich-demokratischen und christlichsozialen Bewegungen in Deutschland.* Cologne: Verlag Wissenschaft und Politik, 1986.

Schauff, Johannes. *Das Wahlverhalten der deutschen Katholiken im Kaiserreich und in der Weimarer Republik: Untersuchungen aus dem Jahre 1928.* Edited with an Introduction by Rudolf Morsey. Veröffentlichungen der Kommission für Zeitgeschichte, Reihe A: Quellen, vol. 18. Mainz: Matthias-Grünewald-Verlag, 1975.

Schell, Herman. *Der Katholizismus als Princip des Fortschritts.* 2nd ed. Würzburg: Andreas Göbel's Verlagsbuchhandlung, 1897.

Schiffers, Heinrich. *Der Kulturkampf in Stadt und Regierungsbezirk Aachen.* Aachen: Verlag Kaatzers Erben, 1929.

Schmidt-Volkmar, Erich. *Der Kulturkampf in Deutschland 1871-1890.* Göttingen: Musterschmidt-Verlag, 1962.

Schmitz-Cliever, Egon. "Die Choleraepidemien in Alt-Aachen und Burtscheid." *Zeitschrift des Aachener Geschichtsvereins* 64/65 (1951/52): 120-67.

Schmolke, Michael. *Die schlechte Presse. Katholiken und Publizistik zwischen "Katholik" und "Publik" 1821-1968.* Münster: Verlag Regensberg, 1971.

Schneider, Michael. *Die christlichen Gewerkschaften 1894-1933.* Politik- und Gesellschaftsgeschichte, vol. 10. Bonn: Verlag Neue Gesellschaft, 1982.

Schneider, Michael. "Religion and Labour Organization: The Christian Trade Unions in the Wilhelmine Empire." *European Studies Review* 12 (1982): 345-69.

Schneider, Michael. "The Christian Trade Unions and Strike Activity." In *The Development of Trade Unionism in Great Britain and Germany, 1880-1914*, ed. Wolfgang J. Mommsen and Hàns-Gerhard Husung, 283-301. London: George Allen & Unwin, 1985.

Schorn, Karl. *Lebenserinnerungen. Ein Beitrag zur Geschichte des Rheinlandes im 19. Jahrhundert.* 2 vols. Bonn: Verlag von P. Hanstein, 1898.

Schrörs, Heinrich. "Die Geheimpolizei am Rhein zur Zeit der Kölner Wirren (1837-1838) mit besonderer Rücksicht auf Aachen." *Zeitschrift des Aachener Geschichtsvereins* 48/49 (1928): 24-60.

Schuckmann, Gunnar von. "Die politische Willensbildung in der Großstadt Köln seit der Reichsgründung im Jahre 1871." Ph. D. thesis, Universität Köln, 1965.

Schumacher, August. "Zur Familiengeschichte der Ordensgründerin Klara Fey." *Mitteilungen der Westdeutschen Gesellschaft für Familienkunde* 8, no. 2 (1934): 53-66.

Schütz, Rüdiger. "Ultramontanismus und preußische Verwaltungsreform: Die Auseinandersetzung um die westfälische und rheinische Kreis- und Provinzialordnung von 1886/87." In *Rheinland-Westfalen im Industriezeitalter*, ed. Kurt Düwell and Wolfgang Köllmann, 25-39. Vol. 2, *Von der Reichsgründung bis zur Weimarer Republik*. Wuppertal: Peter Hammer Verlag, 1984.

Soénius, Ulrich S. *Koloniale Begeisterung im Rheinland während des Kaiserreiches.* Schriften zur rheinisch-westfälischen Wirtschaftsgeschichte, vol. 37. Cologne: Rheinisch-Westfälisches Wirtschaftsarchiv zu Köln e. V., 1992.

Spael, Wilhelm. *Ludwig Windthorst. Bismarcks kleiner großer Gegner. Ein Lebensbild.* Osnabrück: Verlag A. Fromm, 1962.

Spael, Wilhelm. *Das katholische Deutschland im 20. Jahrhundert. Seine Pionier- und Krisenzeiten 1890-1945.* Würzburg: Echter-Verlag, 1964.

Spahn, Martin. *Ernst Lieber als Parlamentarier.* Gotha: Friedrich Andreas Perthes, 1906.

Spahn, Martin. *Das deutsche Zentrum.* 2nd ed. Mainz: Kirchheim'sche Verlagsbuchhandlung, 1907.

Spencer, Elaine G. *Police and the Social Order in German Cities: The Düsseldorf District, 1848-1914.* DeKalb: Northern Illinois University Press, 1992.

Sperber, Jonathan. *Popular Catholicism in Nineteenth-Century Germany.* Princeton, N.J.: Princeton University Press, 1984.

Sperber, Jonathan. *Rhineland Radicals: The Democratic Movement and the Revolutions of 1848-1849.* Princeton, N. J.: Princeton University Press, 1991.

Steitz, Walter, ed. *Quellen zur deutschen Wirtschafts- und Sozialgeschichte im 19. Jahrhundert bis zur Reichsgründung.* Ausgewählte Quellen zur deutschen Geschichte der Neuzeit, vol. 36. Darmstadt: Wissenschaftliche Buchgesellschaft, 1980.

Suval, Stanley. *Electoral Politics in Wilhelmine Germany.* Chapel Hill: University of North Carolina Press, 1985.

Tennstedt, Florian and Heidi Winter, eds. *Quellensammlung zur Geschichte der Deutschen Sozialpolitik 1867 bis 1914.* I. Abteilung. Von der Reichsgründung bis zur Kaiserlichen Sozialbotschaft (1867-1881). Vol. 2. Von der Haftpflichtgesetzgebung zur ersten Unfallversicherungsvorlage. Stuttgart: Gustav Fischer Verlag, 1993.

Thun, Alphons. "Industrie am Niederrhein und ihre Arbeiter. Die linksrheinische Textilindustrie." *Staats- und sozialwissenschaftliche Forschungen* 2, nos. 2 and 3 (1879): 1-217, 1-261.

Tipton, Frank B. Jr. *Regional Variations in the Economic Development of Germany During the Nineteenth Century.* Middletown, Conn.: Wesleyan University Press, 1976.

Traut, Michael. *Der Reichsregent. Ernst Liebers Weg vom Männer-Casino Camberg an das Ruder kaiserlicher Großmachtpolitik.* Bad Camberg: Camberger Verlag, 1984.

Vierhaus, Rudolf. "Preußen und die Rheinlande." *Rheinische Vierteljahrsblätter* 30 (1965): 152-175.

Volkart, Felix. "Gestalten aus dem Reichstage." *Daheim*, 37 (16 March 1901): 18-20.

Wachtling, Oswald. *Joseph Joos. Journalist, Arbeiterführer, Zentrumspolitiker. Politische Biographie 1878-1933.* Veröfentlichungen der Kommission für Zeitgeschichte, Reihe B: Forschungen, vol. 16. Mainz: Matthias-Grünewald-Verlag, 1974.

Weber, Christoph, ed. *Liberaler Katholizismus: Biographische und kirchenhistorische Essays von Franz Xaver Kraus.* Bibliothek des Deutschen Historischen Instituts in Rom, vol. 57. Tübingen: Max Niemeyer Verlag, 1983.

Wehler, Hans-Ulrich. *Bismarck und der Imperialismus.* 1969. Reprint. Frankfurt a. M.: Suhrkamp, 1985.

Wehler, Hans-Ulrich. *The German Empire, 1871-1918.* Translated by Kim Traynor. Leamington Spa: Berg Publishers, 1985.

Wehler, Hans-Ulrich. *Deutsche Gesellschaftsgeschichte.* Vol. 2, *Von der Reformära bis zur industriellen und politischen "Deutschen Doppelrevolution" 1815-1845/49.* 4 vols. Munich: Verlag C. H. Beck, 1987-.

Wessel, Horst A., ed. *Thyssen & Co. Mühlheim a. d. Ruhr. Die Geschichte einer Familie und ihrer Unternehmung.* Stuttgart: Franz Steiner Verlag, 1991.

Wienfort, Monika. "Kaisergeburtstagsfeiern am 27. Januar 1907. Bürgerliche Feste in den Städten des Deutschen Kaiserreichs." In *Bürgerliche Feste: Symbolische Formen politischen Handelns im 19. Jahrhundert*, ed. Manfred Hettling and Paul Nolte, 156-91. Göttingen: Vandenhoeck & Ruprecht, 1993.

Wilhelm II. *Ereignisse und Gestalten aus den Jahren 1878-1918.* Leipzig: Verlag von K. F. Koehler, 1922.

Wittling, Gernot. "Zum Verhältnis von früher Industrialisierung und Technologietransfer im Rheinland und Westfalen nach 1815." In *Die Rheinlande und Preußen: Parlamentarismus, Parteien und Wirtschaft*, ed. Landschaftsverband Rheinland, 82-102. Cologne: Rheinland-Verlag, 1990.

Wynands, Dieter P. J. "Die Aachenfahrt während der französischen Herrschaft im Rheinland (1792/94-1814). Ein Beitrag zur Auslagerung des Aachener Münsterschatzes nach Paderborn." *Annalen des Historischen Vereins für den Niederrhein* 197 (1994): 127-45.

Zedlitz-Trützschler, Count Robert. *Twelve Years at the Imperial German Court.* Translated by Alfred Kalisch. New York: George H. Doran, 1924.

Zeender, John K. *The German Center Party 1890-1906.* New Series, vol. 66, pt. 1. Philadelphia: Transactions of the American Philosophical Society, 1976.

INDEX

For emperors, kings, and popes, dates are those of reigns. Names of historians are italicized.

A

Aachen 8, 18-20, 22-28, 31, 33, 36-39, 48, 54-56, 61, 64, 72, 83-84, 86-87, 89, 94-95, 98, 111-15, 120-21, 124, 129, 137, 139-41, 156, 173, 189, 205, 238
  Center Party in 48, 83-84, 86-87, 114-15, 137, 139, 238
  diocese of 19-20, 36-38, 54-55
  economy of 22-28, 112-13
  People's Association in 61, 64
  See also Katholikentage
ADAV, *see Allgemeiner Deutscher Arbeitesverein*
Adenauer, Konrad (1876-1967) 130, 148
Agrarian League 75, 78, 136
Agriculture 26, 32, 77
Allgemeiner Deutscher Arbeiterverein (ADAV) 128-29. *See also* Ferdinand Lasalle
Altkatholiken 98
Amberg (1884) 118
Amery, Carl 45
Anderson, Margaret Lavinia 14-16, 45, 50-51, 53-54, 56-57, 68, 70-71, 105, 149-50, 167, 171, 174, 176
Anti-Protestant League 60, 65, 69
Aquinas, St. Thomas 154
Arbeiter-Zeitung 134-35
Arbeiterfreund 101, 117, 249
Arbeiterinnenvereine, see Catholic clubs for women workers
Arbeitervereine, see Catholic workers' clubs
Arbeiterwohl, see Workers' Welfare

Arenberg, Prince Franz Ludwig von (1849-1907) 68, 117, 123, 189-90, 198, 200, 247
  and Civil Code 189
Arends, Franz (Center politician in Essen) 207
Arkwright, Richard (1732-92) 23
Army Bill
  of 1892 74
  of 1893 73-74, 76-77, 104, 189
Arnim, Count Harry (1824-81) 178
Arnoldi, Wilhelm (1798-1864) 40, 248
Arnsberg 26
Association of Christian Miners, 121-22. *See also* August Brust
Augustine League 90, 92-93, 96-97, 102-4, 159, 165
  founding of 102-3
Augustinus-Verein, see Augustine League
Augustinusblatt 103. *See also* Augustine League
Austria 50, 55, 187

B

Bachem, Johann Peter (1785-1822)
Bachem, Joseph (1821-93) 94, 100
Bachem, Julius (1845-1918) 16, 34, 41, 57-58, 60-61, 65, 71-72, 82, 86, 92-93, 99, 100, 108, 136, 146-47, 150-52, 163-66, 168-69, 171-76, 196, 202, 233, 238, 249

and press 92-93, 99-100
and party organization 86
political career 71, 136
and struggle for party leadership 71-72
and trade unions 146-47, 150, 152, 168
and *Zentrumsstreit* 163-66, 171-76
Bachem, Karl (1858-1945) 11, 16, 34, 43, 54, 60, 69-70, 72-74, 76, 79, 85, 92, 94-95, 100-1, 108, 117, 133-35, 139, 149, 155-56, 158, 160-64, 171-73, 175, 181-82, 185, 187, 189, 191-93, 196, 198, 201-3, 209, 212-17, 219-20, 223-25, 227, 229-30, 239
and agrarian-conservative wing 73, 76, 79, 189
and Civil Code 181-82, 189
and elections 133-35, 139, 209, 212-17, 224-25, 227, 229-30
as historian 11
and Kulturkampf 54
and organization of Center Party 85, 92
and press 94-95, 100-1
and role of Catholics in German state 43-44, 220
and struggle for party leadership 69-70, 72-74, 201-3
and trade unions 108, 117, 155-56, 158, 160-64, 191
and *Weltpolitik* 187, 189, 191-93, 196, 198
and *Zentrumsstreit* 171-73, 175
Bachem, Lambert (1789-1854) 94
Ballestrem, Count Franz von (1834-1910) 29, 68-71, 73-74, 134, 147, 193, 197
and struggle for party leadership 68-71, 73-74
Bamberger, Ludwig (1823-99) 177

Barmen 133, 242
Bassermann, Ernst (1854-1917) 206, 229-30. *See also* National Liberals
Baudri, Friedrich (1808-74) 114-15, 247
Bavaria 8, 13, 50, 96, 118, 135, 166, 178, 180, 182, 191-92, 215, 228, 235
Bebel, August (1840-1913) 131, 143. *See also* Social Democratic Party
Becker, Friedrich Wilhelm Bernhard (1835-1924)
Becker, Karl Georg (1858-1914) 1012, 16, 28, 51, 143-46, 183-84, 207, 231, 244
Becker, Winfried 10-11, 16, 28, 51, 143, 184
Belgium 19, 38, 55, 108, 189
Bergmännischer Interessenverband, see Miner's Union
Berlepsch, Hans von (1843-1926) 184
Berlin 8, 21-22, 35, 70-71, 74, 91-92, 97, 101, 103, 117, 121, 123, 129, 152-53, 155, 158-59, 164-65, 167, 173, 179, 182, 198, 201-2, 223, 225-26, 237
Berliner Tageblatt 77, 224
Bernadette, Saint, *see* Soubirous, Bernadette
Bertram, Jürgen 226-29, 231
Bethmann-Hollweg, Theobald von (1856-1921) 5, 216-17, 221, 223
Bielefeld 121, 136
Bierganz, Manfred 16, 72, 75-76, 100, 163
Birkenfeld 229
Bischofskonferenz 50, 109, 158. *See also* Fulda
Bismarck-Schönhausen, Count (later Prince) Otto von (1815-98) 7, 10-11, 16, 30, 36,

Index

40, 49, 51, 53-54, 56-58, 72, 77, 89, 96, 98, 128, 130-31, 145, 164, 176-80, 182, 186-87, 192, 195-96, 198, 200, 202-3, 206, 212, 224
Catholic opinion of 7, 98, 145, 195, 206
and Center Party 10-11, 51, 72, 89, 131, 212, 224
and Kulturkampf 53-54, 56-58, 96, 164, 200
and unification of Germany 16, 30, 49, 178
Bitter, Franz (1865-1924) 166-69, 171-73, 216
Blackbourn, David 13-14, 16, 33, 40, 42, 67, 92, 105, 107, 184, 202, 207, 224, 237
Bodelschwingh-Velmede, Baron Ernst von (1794-1854) 38
Boffin, Werner (member of Paulus-Verein) 115
Bönickhausen, Alexandre Gustave. *(See* Eiffel, Gustave) 27
Bonn 21, 32, 54, 70, 77, 97-98, 155, 201, 242, 244
University of 21, 32, 35, 95, 155
Brack, Rudolf 158, 161-62, 255
Brandts, Franz (1834-1914) 60-63, 65, 92, 104, 117-18, 120, 157-58, 184, 249
and Center Party 92, 104
and industrialization 61-62
and People's Association 60-63, 65, 157-58
and Workers' Welfare 117-18, 120
Brentano, Clemens von (1778-1824) 37
Breslau 68, 95, 98, 157
Breuer, Johann Gregor (1820-97) 111, 244
Brückmann, Karl Heinrich (1828-75)
Brügelmann, Johann Gottfried (1750-1820) 23, 25
Brust, August (1862-1924) 121, 156
Buchheim, Karl 11, 12, 255
Bülow, Count (later Prince) Bernhard von (1849-1929) 104, 167, 186, 193, 195-96, 198-201, 204-5, 207-17, 221
Bülow, Countess (later Princess) Marie von 200
Bülow, Hans Guido von (1830-94) 198
Bund der Landwirte, see Agrarian League
Buol-Berenberg, Baron Rudolf von (1842-1902) 196
Burtscheid 24-25, 55, 64, 112-14, 140, 242
and Christian-social association 112-14
economy of 24-25
People's Association in 64
Busch, Wilhelm (1867-1923) 145, 205

C

Camberg 68-69, 201
Camphausen, Ludolf (1803-90) 27
Caprivi, Leo von (1831-99) 72, 177-78, 189, 198, 202
Cardauns, Hermann (1847-1925) 16, 38, 60-62, 70, 72-73, 75-76, 79, 82, 84-85, 89, 93-95, 99-100, 124, 129, 132, 134, 147, 151, 163, 183, 201-2, 212
and *Kölnische Volkszeitung* 70, 93, 99-100, 134
and struggle for party leadership 72, 75-76
Catholic clubs for women workers 38, 123, 229
Catholic education/school 20, 34
Catholic farmers 12, 75

Catholic milieu 14, 17, 31, 44-46, 92, 101, 146, 154, 169, 235, 237
Catholic People's Party 115
Catholic workers' clubs 62, 107-9, 111-12, 114-15, 117-21, 123-24, 130, 152-53, 155, 157, 161-63
  and Christian trade unions 121, 123-24, 152-53, 155, 157, 161-63
  founding of 107-9, 112, 117
  and Free Unions 130, 163
  organization of 118-20
  and People's Association 120, 157
Catholic Women's League 229
Catholicism, *see* Roman Catholic Church
CDU, *see* Christian Democratic Union
Center Party 7, 9-10, 12-14, 16-17, 31, 33, 36-37, 41, 43-46, 48-50, 52, 67-69, 71-72, 75-76, 79-83, 85, 95, 101, 105-6, 108-9, 114, 123, 126-36, 139-48, 150, 153, 156, 160-63, 165-66, 169, 172-74, 177, 179-82, 185-89, 191-93, 195-97, 201-2, 204-5, 208, 210-12, 216, 218-19, 221, 223-24, 227-29, 231-32, 234-35, 237-38, 240
  and Catholic Church 12, 14, 31, 36-37, 43, 47-48, 70-71, 92, 109, 123, 140, 144, 151, 161-62, 165, 168-69, 176, 183-84, 219-21, 235, 237
  and Catholic farmers 12, 218, 235
  and Catholic milieu 43-46, 83-85, 87, 92, 150, 168-69, 175, 235, 237-38
  and Catholic missions 189, 225
  and Catholic workers' clubs 107-26
  and colonies 167, 177, 186-90, 204, 208-9, 225
  and conservative-agrarian wing 72-73, 75-79, 231-32, 236
  founding of 36-37, 49-59
  and franchise reform 221-224
  and leadership of 7, 67-80, 191, 201-2, 209-10, 212, 215-16, 219, 236
  as mass party 8-9, 31, 204, 210, 222, 230
  and navy 191-198, 213
  and notables 60, 67-69, 84, 105-6, 109, 119-20, 209
  and organization of 82-92, 139, 141, 225-26, 228, 234, 239
  and People's Association 38, 43, 60-67, 225-26, 234, 238
  and press 38, 205-6, 225, 227
  relations with state 10-11, 13, 33, 36, 41, 44, 49-50, 52, 82-83, 180, 206-7, 220-21, 224, 238
  role of clergy in 14, 36-37, 43
  social policies of 146-47, 177, 182-85
  and Socialists 12-14, 59-61, 65, 84-85, 93, 102, 114-16, 120, 126-48, 179, 208-10, 222-23, 229-33, 235, 237-39
  and women 38, 228-29
  and workers 12, 80, 101, 109, 111-14, 118-19, 124, 126, 130, 133, 139, 144, 162, 175, 204, 210, 218, 221, 230, 232-35, 238
Centrums-Parlaments-Correspondenz (CPC) 103
Charlemagne (742-814) 39, 83
Christian Democratic Union

INDEX

(CDU) 17, 32, 148, 176, 239-40
Christian Social Party 114, 129
Christian trade unions 8, 43, 62, 107-9, 111, 118, 121-26, 146, 150-63, 168-70, 175, 182, 234, 238
 and Catholic Church 109-10, 146, 151-63, 168-70
 and Catholic workers' clubs 123-26, 152-56
 and Center Party 109, 126, 146, 150-63, 168-70
 founding of 111, 121-22
 and People's Association 157-59
Christian-Social associations 111-12, 114-15
Christlich-Soziale Blätter 110-11
Christlicher Arbeiterfreund 101
Clemens, Jakob (1815-62) 30, 34, 37, 244, 246
Cologne 11, 17-18, 21, 27, 33-35, 37, 43, 47, 50, 55, 57-58, 70-72, 76-78, 81-82, 85-86, 90, 93-95, 102-3, 108, 110, 114, 120, 125, 127-29, 134, 137-139, 146, 148, 150, 156-57, 165, 167, 174, 186, 189, 216, 225-26
 Archdiocese of 33-35, 37-38, 50, 55, 57, 70, 108, 189
 Center Party in 50, 58, 71-72, 76-78, 81-82, 85-86, 90, 102-3, 127, 129, 134, 137-39, 146, 150, 216, 226-27
 city council of 57, 71, 81
 People's Association in 58, 86, 120
Cologne Program 110
Cologne Troubles 33-38, 47, 70, 93, 181
 consequences of 36-38
Conservative Party 78, 133, 165, 197, 224, 245-46
Constantia 56, 83-84, 87, 114, 132
CPC, *see Centrums-Parlaments-Correspondenz*
Cronenberg, Franz Eduard (1836-97) 111-17, 130

D

Daily Telegraph Affair 214
Dasbach, Georg Friedrich (1846-1907) 88, 97, 101, 108, 147, 245, 247
Der Arbeiter 132
Deuerlein, Ernst 89, 149
Deutsche Reichszeitung 77, 96-99, 173
Deutsche Volkshalle 94, 95
Dietz, Hermann Josef (1782-1862) 37
Dingelstad, Hermann, Bishop of Münster
Dittrich, Franz (1839-1915) 117, 123, 219
Dönhoff, Countess Marie von (née Beccadelli di Bologna). See Bülow, Countess Marie von
Duisburg 101, 134, 135, 242, 246
Düren 98, 112, 124
Düsseldorf 8, 10, 19, 21, 24, 26, 31, 59, 72, 75, 82-83, 105, 108, 129-30, 132-33, 139, 170, 228-29, 231, 242, 245-46
 Center Party in 59, 72, 105, 139, 228-29, 231
Düsseldorfer Volksblatt 102

E

Eberhard, Matthias (1815-76) 55, 248
Echo der Gegenwart 87, 95, 114, 116, 173
Eckard, Josef (1865-1906) 190
Eiffel, Gustave (1832-1923) 27
Eisenbahnhandwerkerverband, see

railway workers' association
Elberfeld 24, 28, 108, 111,
130, 132-33, 242, 245
Elections 9, 48-50, 73-74,
83-85, 88-89, 91, 107,
114, 126-27, 129, 133-37,
139, 141, 146, 162, 179,
196, 203-4, 225, 228, 234,
210, 222, 224, 228, 230-
31, 235, 238, 240
Landtag, 1873 59, 114
Landtag, 1879 138
Landtag, 1882 189
Landtag, 1898 138
Landtag, 1903 138, 146
Landtag, 1908 138-40
Landtag, 1913 91, 138, 141
Reichstag, 1871 51-52, 59,
114, 127, 231-32
Reichstag, 1874 59, 115, 142
Reichstag, 1877 73
Reichstag, 1878 128-29
Reichstag, 1890 71,
131, 133, 142, 189,
Reichstag, 1893 74-77,
105, 130, 180, 184
Reichstag, 1898 133-37, 200
Reichstag, 1903 135-37
Reichstag, 1907 88, 104, 137,
142, 167, 204-6, 207-12,
230
Reichstag, 1012 127, 135,
137, 142, 174, 224-32
Electoral system 126-27
Eley, Geoff 13, 192, 194, 224,
234
Engels, Friedrich (1820-95)
112, 128, 131
England 23-24, 26, 122, 126,
187-88, 196, 214
Epstein, Klaus 66-67, 170, 174,
187, 190-91
Erfurt Program 132
Erkelenz 27, 242
Ermland 55, 219
Erzberger, Matthias (1875-1921)
97, 166-67, 170, 174-75,
187-88, 190-91, 209-12, 216
and colonies 187-88, 209
and Gewerkschaftsstreit 170
political career of 166-67, 190-
91, 210
and press 97
Eschweiler 64, 112
Essener Volkszeitung 98, 165,
173, 227
Eulenburg, Prince Philip von
(1847-1921) 178, 199
Euler, Jakob (leader of artisans'
movement) 77, 245
Evangelical League 60, 69, 209
Evangelical workers' clubs 133

F

Fabri, Friedrich (1824-91) 186
Factory Regulation 62
Fachabteilungen 123, 153, 157-
58, 161
Falk, Adalbert (1827-1900) 55-56
Fechenbach, Friedrich Carl
Reichsfreiherr von 69, 76
Fey, Andreas (1806-85) 36, 38
Fey, Klara (1815-94) 38, 54-55.
See also Sisterhood of the Poor
Child Jesus
Fey, Louis (1778-1820) 36
First World War, *see* World War I
Fischer, Antonius (1840-1912)
155, 158, 160-61, 207, 248
Förster, Albert (priest and journal-
ist) 96
Förster, Arnold (president of
Constantia) 56
Fortschrittspartei, see Progressive
Party
Fournelle 158
Fraktion des Zentrums (Katholische
Fraktion) 49
France 26, 29, 32, 188-89,
196, 206
Frankfurt 153, 229

Index

Frederick the Great. *See* Friedrich Wilhelm II
Free trade unions, *also* Free Unions 122, 130, 149, 163
Free Conservatives 9, 130, 133, 211, 242
Freiburg 20, 157
Freie Gewerkschaften, see Free trade unions
Freytag, Gustav (1816-95) 52-53, 257
Frick, Philip (1857-1935) 167
Friedrich Wilhelm II (1786-97) 21
Friedrich Wilhelm III (1797-1840) 34
Friedrich Wilhelm IV (1840-61)
Fritzen, Aloys (1840-61) 60, 72, 105, 117, 123, 173, 192-93, 201, 212, 219, 246
  and Center Party leadership 105, 173, 201, 212, 219
  and navy 192-93
Fuchs, Eduard (1844-1923) 81, 85, 245
Fulda 50, 109, 153, 158
  Bischofskonferenz 50, 109, 158

G

Galen, Count Ferdinand Heribert von (1831-1906) 145, 173
Geilenkirchen 27, 242, 247
Gemmenich 36
Generalversammlung der Katholischen Vereine Deutschlands 48, 103, 120, 143-44, 183, 249
Genossenschaft der Schwestern vom armen Kind Jesus Schleiden, see Sisterhood of the Poor Child Jesus
German Catholic Workers Association 118-19
Germania 41, 57, 67, 74, 79-80, 91, 97, 98, 101, 104, 117, 136-37, 145, 187, 191, 212, 226-27, 252, 256
Gesamtverband der Christlichen Gewerkschaften Deutschlands 121
Gesellenvereine, see Journeymen's associations
Gewerkschaftsstreit 5, 123, 147-52, 158, 161-63, 167, 205, 209, 233, 236-37, 240, 249
Gewerkverein Christlicher Arbeiter, *see* Association of Christian Miners
Giesberts, Johannes (1865-1938) 101-2, 159, 221-24, 227-28, 231, 246
  and franchise reform 221-24
  and press 101-2
Görres, Joseph (1776-1848) 35-37
Görres Society 71
Gottwald, Herbert 191-93, 202, 235
Graß, Barbara (d. 1939) 123
Great Britain, *see* England
Greiß, Adolf (1829-95) 134
Gröber, Adolf (1854-1919) 60, 104, 117, 123, 136, 144, 160-61, 174, 181, 187, 193, 199, 201, 212, 216, 243
  and Center Party leadership 201, 212, 216, 243
  and *Gewerkschaftsstreit* 160-=61
  and press 104
  and *Weltpolitik* 187, 193
Gymnich, Count Beissel von 209

H

Hagen 24
Hamm-Soest 231
Hanover 51, 91, 231
Hansemann, David (1790-1864) 22
Harm, Friedrich (1844-1905) 130
Hauptmann, Peter (1825-95) 77, 97
Heeremann, Baron Klemens von

(1832-1903) 105, 219
Heidelberg 70
Heinsberg 27, 56, 242
Helena (c. 255-330) 40
Henckel-Donersmarck 29
Herold, Karl (1848-1931) 63, 86, 90-91, 104, 173- 74, 216, 219, 223
Hertling, Count Georg von (1843-1919) 16, 32, 68-69, 71, 145, 173-74, 197, 215-16, 218, 243, 244
and Center Party leadership 68-69, 71, 215-16, 243
and *Zentrumsstreit* 173-74
Heß, Moses 128
Hesse, Grand Duchy of 91
Hesse-Nassau 91
Historisch-politische Blätter 50 78, 164, 168
Hitze, Franz (1851-1921) 45, 61-63, 65, 82, 104, 116-18, 120, 123, 144, 146-47, 152, 156-57, 160-61, 173, 182-83, 185, 201-2, 215, 246-47
and *Gewerkschaftsstreit*152, 156-57, 160-61
and People's Association 61-63, 65, 104
relation with Karl Trimborn 82, 202
and social question123, 144, 146-47, 182-83, 185
and *Verband Arbeiterwohl* 63, 117-18
and workers 116, 120
Hödel, Max (1857-78) 128
Hoensbroech, Count Wilhelm von (1849-1922) 76-77, 246
Hoensbroech-Haag, Count 209
Hoensbroech-Kellenberg, Count 209
Hoffmann, district governor of Aachen 129
Hoffmann, Fridolin (1828-86) 95, 99

Hohenlohe-Schillingfürst, Prince Chlodwig zu (1819-1901) 29, 178-79, 198
Hohn, Wilhelm (b. 1871) 60, 63, 66-67, 159
Holstein, Friedrich von (1837-1900) 195, 199, 201
Hommerich, U. (journalist) 167
Hompesch-Rurich, Count Alfred (1826-1909) 117, 123, 212, 243, 245, 247
Huene von Hoiningen, Baron Karl (1837-1900) 69, 71, 73, 77, 79
Hüls, Dr. (university professor) 167, 172
Hungary 55, 108, 187
Hunley, J. D. 59, 259
Hüsgens, Eduard (1848-1912) *see* Augustine League

I

Imbusch, Hermann (trade unionist from Essen) 140-41
Immelen, Hubert (1843-1907) 48, 156
Ingersleben, Baron von 21
Innere Mission, see Kolping, Adolph 28

J

Janssen, Landrat of Heinsberg 56
Jesuit Law of 1872 54
Jesuits 70, 97-98, 152, 178
Jochner, Georg Maria von (1860-1923) 168
Joos, Joseph (1878-1965) 101, 123
Jörg, Josef, headed provincial general-secretariat 81, 86, 90, 92-93, 228
Jörg, Joseph Edmund (1819-1901) 50
Journeymen's associations 28, 43, 108-9, 111, 116, 190

INDEX

founding of. *See also* Kolping,
    Adolph
Jülicher Kreisblatt 91

K

Kalk 120
Kanzelparagraph, see Pulpit Law
Kardorff, Wilhelm von (1828-
    1907) 181
Karl Theodor, Elector 23
Kartell 118, 131, 161, 195, 211
Katholikentag 48, 61, 67, 93,
    95, 103, 111, 118, 120, 145,
    160, 183, 189, 201, 249
  1856 in Linz
  1869 in Düsseldorf
  1879 in Aachen
  1884 in Amberg
  1899 in Bonn
  1891 in Dsnzig 183
  1901 in Osnabrück 201
  1903 in Cologne 103
  1906 in Essen
Katholische Volkspartei, see Catholic
    People's Party
Katholischer Volksverein
  founding of 58
Katholischer Frauenbund, see
    Catholic Women's League
Kaufmann, Dr. Karl Maria
    (journalist) 167
Kaufmann, Franz (1892-1920)
    140-41
Kehr, Eckart 14, 186, 194, 259
Ketteler, Wilhelm Emmanuel
    Baron von (1811-77) 50,
    109, 111
Kiefer, Rolf 16, 100, 149, 152,
    155-56, 161-62, 178, 187-
    89, 191, 202-3, 220, 239
Klausener, Alfons (mayor of
    Burtscheid) 140-41
Kleve 19, 24, 75, 242, 246
Klöckner, Peter (1863-1940) 29
Koblenz 19-21, 26, 33, 37,
    41, 88, 166, 168, 172
  economy of
Köller, Ernst Maria von (1841-
    1928) 180
Köln, *see* Cologne
Kölner Wirren, see Cologne
    Troubles
Kölnische Blätter, renamed
    Kölnische Volszeitung 94-95
Kölnische Volkszeitung 16, 57,
    70-72, 75, 79-80, 91, 93-
    95, 97-101, 104, 110, 120,
    134, 136, 174, 206, 208
Kolping, Adolph (1813-65) 28,
    43, 108-9, 111, 120
Kommission für Zeitgeschichte
    16, 257, 266, 269
Kopp, Georg von (1837-1914)
    68, 71, 124, 153-55, 159-
    60, 188-89, 193, 202-3,
    210, 237
  and Center Party 68, 71, 202-
    3, 237
  and Christian trade unions 124
  and *Gewerkschaftsstreit* 153-55,
    159-60
  and *Weltpolitik* 188-89, 193
Korum, Michael Felix (1840-
    1921) 60, 65, 154, 158-59,
    200, 248
  and *Gerwerkschaftsstreit* 154,
    158-59
Krefeld, Otto, chairman of
    Augustine League 92. *See also*
    Augustine League
Krefeld 8, 10, 23-24, 28, 59,
    73, 88, 92, 101, 103, 121-
    22, 124-25, 132, 242, 246
Krementz, Phillipp (1819-99)
    189, 248
Krückemeyer, Heinrich Maria
    (journalist) 167, 172-73
Krupp, Friedrich A. (1854-1902)
    130, 133, 184-85, 207
Kulm 50, 55
Kulturkampf 7, 11-12, 14-17,

34, 36, 41, 44-46, 52-60, 63, 68, 72-73, 78, 83-84, 93, 95, 97-100, 105, 107, 111, 115, 121, 129-30, 133, 145, 164, 178, 181-82, 188, 200, 204, 206, 208, 212, 224-25, 231, 238-39, 249

L

Laaf, Johannes (1832-1906) 114
Landtag 8, 10, 22, 41, 48-49, 59, 63, 70-72, 76, 79, 81-85, 88-89, 91-92, 97, 105, 114, 116, 126, 127, 137-40, 147, 166, 173, 177, 179, 189, 194, 203, 208, 219, 221-23, 235, 237, 249-50
Langenberg 133
Langner, Albrecht 20, 58, 188-89
Lasalle, Ferdinand (1825-64)
Laurent, Johann Theodor (1804-84) 36-37
Law on supervision of schools of 1872 (*Schulaufsichtgesetz*) 54
Leipzig 60, 128, 198, 229
Lendersdorf 112
Lennep 133, 138, 242, 245
Leo XIII (1878-1903) 72, 144, 152, 182
  and Septennat Bill 72
Lepper, Herbert 48, 87, 110-12, 114-16
Lepsius, Rainer M. 44-45, 236-37
Lieber, Ernst (1838-1903) 68-77, 80-81, 104-5, 124, 143, 146-47, 156, 177, 179, 181-83, 185, 191, 193, 195-97, 199, 201-3, 234
  and Civil Code 181-82
  as party leader 105-6, 124, 177-79, 182, 185, 201-3, 234
  and press 104
  and struggle for party leadership 68-77, 80-81

and *Weltpolitik* 191, 193, 196
  and workers 147, 156
"Lieber Affair" 195-97
Lieber, Moritz (1790-1860) 70
Liège 19
  diocese
Lingens, Joseph Peter (1818-1902) 48, 244
Linz 95
Loë-Terporten, Baron Felix von (1821-74), leader of *Rheinischer Bauernverein* 69, 75-79
  and People's Association 75
London 183, 199
Loth, Wilfried 12, 15, 63, 67, 69, 72, 79, 105, 177-79, 184, 187, 191, 196-97, 210, 218, 223-24
Lourdes 40. *See also* Soubirous, Bernadette
Löwenstein, Prince Karl zu (1834-1921) 69
Luxemburg 36-37, 55

M

Mähler, Abundius (1777-1853) 37
Mainz Congress 121
Mainz Program 121
Majunke, Paul (1842-99) 57, 97, 245
Mallinckrodt, Hermann von (1821-74) 50
Malmedy 87-88, 242
Mankamer (journalist) 227
Mark, county of 24
Marpingen 40-42, 254
Marx, Karl (1818-83) 112, 128
Marx, Wilhelm (1863-1946) 88
Matzner, Franz Leopold (1863-91) 98
May Laws of 1872 54-55. *See also* Kulturkampf
Melchers, Paul (1813-1895) 50, 55, 57, 115, 248
Mevissen, Gustav (1815-99) 186

Mexico 25
Minden 35
Miners Union 130
Miquel, Johannes von (1828-1901) 194-95
Mitteilungen des Gesamtverbandes der Christlichen Gewerkschaften Deutschlands 121
Mittmann, Ursula 13, 93, 101, 104
Möckl, Karl 13
Modernism; *also* Modernist 150-51, 169, 171
Moeller, Robert G. 75-76
Moers-Rees 228
Möller, Theodor 134
Molz (railway worker) 134
Mönchengladbach 24, 28-29, 60-62, 64-65, 102, 124-25, 146, 155-59, 161, 164, 166, 171, 225-26
    economy of 24, 28
    People's Association in 60-62, 64-65
    Verband der christlichen Textilarbeiter in 124-25
Monschau 24, 27, 87-88
    economy of
Montjoie, *see* Monschau
Morsey, Rudolf 12, 38, 51, 55, 58, 61-62, 84-85, 90-91, 105-6, 108, 142, 149, 156, 166, 190, 201, 239
Moufang, Christoph (1817-99) 109, 111, 244-45
Mühlheim 29, 120, 134-35, 242, 244
Müller (teacher) 167
Osterdienstagskonferenz 170
Müller, Justizrat (Koblenz), Rhenish parliamentarian 168, 176
Müller, Otto (1780-1944) 101, 118, 120
Müller-Fulda, Richard (1851-1931) 192-93, 199, 216
Munich 8, 70
Münster 19-20, 33-34, 37, 50, 118
    diocese of 19, 34, 50, 118
    University of 20, 37
Muth, Karl (1867-1944) 151

N

Napoleon Bonaparte (1769-1821) 19-20
National Liberals 10, 51, 53, 56, 59, 114, 129, 131-32, 134-35, 139, 181, 207-8, 211, 213, 218, 222, 229-32, 242, 244-45. *See also* Ernst Bassermann
    and Center Party 51, 59, 114, 129, 207-8, 218, 229-32
    and Civil Code 181
    and elections 131-32, 134-35, 207-8, 211, 229-32, 242
    and franchise reform 222
    and *Kulturkampf* 53, 56, 129
National Organization of the German Trade Unions 125
Naumann, Friedrich (1860-1919) 193
Nellessen, Leonhard Alois (1783-1859) 36-38, 115
Netherlands 18-19, 102
Neutral-Morsenet 18-19
Niberding, Rudolf (-1912)
Niderberger, Leonz (Catholic writer) 116
Niederrheinische Volkszeitung 103, 209
Niederrheinischer Weberverband 125
Nipperdey, Thomas 35, 39, 113, 143, 150-51, 169, 206, 235
Nippes 102, 120
Nobiling, Karl Eduard (1848-78) 128
Nörber, Thomas, Archbishop of Freiburg 155

Norderney 214
Norrenberg, Peter (1847-94) 62
North German Confederation 81

O

Oberdörffer, Johann Peter (1852-1925) 66, 77, 120
Oppersdorff, Count Hans von (1832-1887) 167-68, 174, 216
 expelled from party 174
 and *Zentrumsstreit* 167-68
Osnabrück 50, 93, 201
Otto, Heinrich (b. 1851) 103. *See also* Augustine League
Overkamm, Gregor 227

P

Paderborn 34, 39, 97, 118, 270
Papal Encyclical
 Rerum novarum 121, 143-46, 152, 159, 182-84, 235
Partei der christlichen Sozialisten, see Party of Christian Socialists
Partito populare 32
Party of Christian Socialists 114. *See also* Eduard Cronenberg
Paulusblatt 101
Paulus-Verein 57, 113
People's Association for Catholic Germany 9, 17, 38, 43, 60-67, 74-75, 80-81, 86, 88, 92, 102-4, 117-18, 120, 130, 135, 150-51, 153, 155-59, 161, 166-70, 175, 182, 202, 225-26, 229-30, 234-35, 238
 and Center Party 43, 60, 67, 74, 80-81, 88, 159, 175, 202, 225-26, 230, 234, 238
 and Christian trade unions 117-18, 120, 130, 135, 153, 155-59, 234
 and Church 9, 43, 60, 62, 151, 153, 155, 158-59, 166, 168-70

 at *Katholikentag* 67, 118
 organization of 64-65, 75, 81, 86, 225
 as part of Catholic milieu 17, 43, 117, 170, 238
 position in *Gewerkschaftsstreit* 155-59, 161
 position in *Zentrumsstreit* and press 103-4, 159, 225-26, 234
 and public relations 66-67, 170, 235
 and social question 38, 61-62, 117, 182
 and workers 62, 65-66, 86, 102, 117, 120, 130, 135, 170, 175, 225-26, 235
Pieper, August (1866-1942) 60-61, 63, 65-66, 101-4, 118, 124-25, 155, 157-60, 183, 215, 246
 as general secretary of the People's Association 63, 103
 and *Gewerkschaftsstreit* 155, 158-60
 and press 101-4
 and social question 183
 and struggle for party leadership 215-16
 and *Volksbildung* 66
 and West German Catholic Workers' Association 118
 and workers 118, 124-25
Pilgram, Friedrich (1819-90) 97
Pius VII (1800-23) 19
Pius IX (1846-78) 52, 57, 206
Pius X (1903-14) 67, 117, 151, 161
Pius-Verein 17, 48
Pleß, Louis (1825-1906) 77
Poland 25, 31, 54, 108
Population growth 25, 30, 142
Porsch, Felix (1853-1930) 16, 69, 91, 117, 123, 157, 160, 169, 174, 215, 219
 and Bülow government 215

Index

and *Gewerksstreit* 157
and party organization 91, 219
and struggle for party leadership 69
Posadowsky-Wehner, Count Arthur (1845-1932) 201-2, 208, 213
 and Bülow government 208, 213
 and Christian trade unions 202
 as State Secretary of Interior 201
Posen 21
Press 5, 57, 64-65, 74, 80, 82, 86, 90-91, 93-98, 100-5, 126, 135, 159, 172-74, 187, 198, 205, 209, 212, 226-27, 234, 238. See also individual newspapers and Augustine League
 attacks on Bülow 198, 209, 212
 and Center Party 86, 90-91, 95, 97, 100, 102-4, 135, 172, 205, 226-27, 234, 238
 early Catholic newspapers 96-97
 and fundraising 91
 during *Gewerkschaftsstreit* 159
 growth of 96-97
 during Kulturkampf 57, 82-83, 97-99
 organization of 93-98, 102-3
 as part of Catholic milieu 86, 101, 135, 238
 and Prussian franchise reform 101
 relationship with Church 103-4
 success of 105
 and *Weltpolitik* 187, 198
 during *Zentrumsstreit* 172-74
Progressive Party 129, 218, 221, 230, 242, 245
 in 1907 Reichstag election 221, 230
 and Center Party 218, 230
 and Kulturkampf 129
 and prussian franchise reform 221
Prussia 7-8, 10, 18-27, 29, 31-33, 35-36, 38, 40-41, 44, 47-56, 58-59, 63-64, 70-72, 76, 81-83, 85, 91, 94, 97, 105, 127, 132, 137, 139, 161, 171, 173-74, 177-81, 184, 189, 194, 203, 208, 217, 219, 221-25, 237, 242
 administration of 8, 18-19, 21, 32-33
 Catholics in 7-8, 10, 21-22, 28, 31-33, 35-36, 38, 57, 161
 Church in 19-20, 31-33, 40
 economy of 22-29, 184
 Kulturkampf in 41, 44, 53-59, 178, 189
 Landtag of 8, 10, 22, 48-49, 59, 63, 70-72, 76, 81-84, 105, 127, 137-39, 171, 177, 179, 189, 194, 203, 208, 219, 222-23, 237
Prussian Concordat 20
Prussian Rhine Province 8, 18-21, 25-26, 32-33, 35, 38, 48, 57, 80, 85, 88, 95, 113, 127, 138-39, 242, 248
 administration of 8, 32-33
 Catholics in 18-19, 31-43
 economy of 23-30
 integration into Prussia 18-22
Pulpit Law of 1871 (*Kanzelparagraph*) 54

R

Radevormwald 133
Radowitz, Josef Maria von (1797-1835) 33
Railway workers association 89
Rampolla del Tindaro, Mariano (1843-1913) 104
Reichenbach-Neurode 136

Reichensperger, August (1808-95) 37, 50-51, 94, 188
and *Deutsche Volkshalle* 94
and founding of Center Party 37, 50-51
retirement from politics 188
Reichensperger, Peter (1810-92) 28, 37, 47, 50-51, 110
author of Cologne Program 110
and founding of Center Party 37, 47, 50-51
on social question 28
Reichstag, *see also* elections 7-8, 13, 48, 51-52, 54, 59, 63, 67, 69-74, 76-78, 80-83, 85, 88-92, 97, 100, 107, 114-16, 126-39, 141-42, 145-47, 162, 164, 166-67, 171, 173-74, 177-82, 184-86, 189, 191-94, 196-97, 200-6, 208-19, 221-27, 230-32, 235-37, 242-44
Center Party in 7-8, 13, 52, 67, 70, 74, 77, 80, 100, 131, 134-35, 145-47, 164, 166, 171, 177-82, 185-86, 191-93, 196-97, 201-3, 205, 208-9, 211-13, 215-19, 236-37
franchise of 126-27, 221-23, 236
social composition of 69
Reimes, Wilhelm (1872-1942) 142-43
Repgen, Konrad 45, 47, 49, 73
Retallack, James 96-98, 194, 197, 221
Reusch, Franz Heinrich (1825-1900) 95
Rheinbrohl 41
Rheinisch-Westfälische Zeitung 74, 77
Rheinische Provinzialblätter 94
Rheinische Volksstimme 75-76, 79

Rheinische Volkszeitung 78
Rheinischer Bauernverein, see Rhenish Farmer's Association
Rhenish Farmer's Association (*Rheinischer Bauernverein*) 75-76, 78
Rheydt 24, 28-29
Rintelen, Victor (1826-1908) 139-40, 180, 187, 245
and Civil Code 180
and *Weltpolitik* 187
Roeren, Hermann (1844-1921) 164, 166-68, 170-74
expelled from party 174
Rohe, Karl 9, 45, 142, 232
Roman Catholic Church 7-9, 11-13, 15-17, 19-20, 28, 30-32, 35-37, 39, 41-49, 52, 57-59, 62-63, 67, 70, 80, 83, 96, 98-102, 104, 107, 115-16, 126, 143-44, 146, 148-51, 153, 155-57, 162, 169, 172, 175-76, 180-82, 185, 189, 198, 203, 206, 219-20, 235, 238
and Center Party 9, 12, 17, 42, 48, 50, 70, 100-1, 104, 146, 162, 175, 219-20, 238
ecclesiastical borders of 19-20
and religious revival 28, 37, 42
and secularization 20, 31, 39-40, 43, 96, 102, 143
and social question 28, 31, 37-38, 42, 50, 62-63
and state 7, 13, 31-32, 33-36, 41, 49, 144-45
Rome 19, 52, 104, 109, 158, 161-62, 165, 202
Ross, Ronald J. 4, 13, 21, 32-33, 57
Ruhr region 28, 29, 35, 59, 118, 122, 129, 184 127-28, 130, 184, 242, 252
Ruhrort 134-35

Index

S

Saarbrücken 229, 242, 245
Saarland 40, 130, 157
Saarlouis 88-89, 229, 242
Sack, Johann August (1764-1831) 21
Salm-Reifferscheidt, Prince von (1863-1924) 200, 209
Savigny, Franz von (1859-1917) 152-55, 160
Savigny, Karl von (1814-75) 50-51, 243-44
Saxony 18, 21, 130, 221, 265
Schaaffhausen, Abraham (1756-1834) 18
Schädler, Franz Xaver (1852-1913) 117, 123, 145, 212
Scharmitzel, Theodor, general secretary of Trier Center district, general secretary of Windthorstbunde 89
Schaueberg, Baron von
Schefer (Bülow's Privy Councilor) 200
Schell, Hermann (1850-1906) 151, 169
Schieder, Wolfgang 39-40, 42, 255, 262
Schings, Peter Joseph (1837-76) 110-11, 261
Schlesische Volkszeitung 95, 98
Schmidt (Marburg) 216, 229
Schmitz, Hermann Joseph (1841-99) 102
Schneider, Wilhelm, Bishop of Paderborn 155
Schneider, Michael 62, 122, 124-25, 156, 267
Scholl, Franz Xaver (1801-1860) 36
Schopen, Edmund (b. 1882) 167-68
Schorlemer-Alst, Baron Burghard von (1825-95) 68, 75, 77, 143
Schorlemer-Lieser, Klemens Baron von (1856-1922) 21, 32
Schorn, Karl (student) 35
Schreiner, Franz 75
Schrevier, Dr., *Geheimer Medizinalrat*
Schwäbig, Engelbert (Cologne farmer, leader of annual procession to Kevelaer) 57
Secularization 9, 20, 39, 63, 117, 143, 169, 171
Septennat Bill 72
Siegkreis-Waldbröl 231
Sigmaringen 33
Silesia 8, 16, 21, 29, 31, 54, 68-69, 91, 97-98, 130, 136, 157, 166-67, 197, 219, 230
  Center Party in 68-69, 91, 230
  economy of 29
  Kulturkampf in 54
Simar, Hubert (1835-1902) 155, 160-61, 248
Sisterhood of the Poor Child Jesus (*Genossenschaft der Schwestern vom armen Kind Jesus*) 38
Sittard, Hubert (1860-1942) 137, 140-41
Social Democratic Party (SPD); *also* Social Democracy, Social Democrat, Socialist 10, 12-13, 43-44, 59, 61, 79, 84, 87, 89-90, 102, 106-7, 115, 120, 125-36, 138-39, 141-42, 144, 146-48, 153, 156, 162, 176, 179, 184, 205-11, 218, 220, 222-24, 226-29, 231-33, 235, 237-39, 242, 244-46
  and Center Party 59, 79, 126-48, 208-10, 218, 230, 237
  and elections 59, 115, 117, 127-28, 130, 132-34, 136-39, 146, 163, 204-5, 208-11, 224-25, 227-33
  on franchise reform 222-23
  as model for Center organiza-

tion 84, 87, 89-90, 139
and Prussian Landtag 127
in the Reichstag 131, 136
and religion 59, 61, 116, 142-43, 146
and Tariff Bill 135-36
and trade unions 122-26, 130-31, 160, 162
Soest Program 110-11
Solingen 133, 138, 242, 246
Soubirous, Bernadette 40
Southwest Africa 204
Spahn, Martin (1875-1945) 36, 70, 135, 151, 167, 179, 195, 211, 215
　on Ernst Lieber 70
　forced out of public life 167
　and party leadership 215
　on Tariff Bill 135
Spahn, Peter (1846-1925) 73, 187, 212, 243
　and party leadership 212
　and *Weltpolitik* 187
SPD, *see* Social Democratic Party
Sperber, Jonathan 28, 47, 52
Spiegel, Ferdinand August Graf (1764-1835) 20, 34, 248
Stegerwald, Adam (1874-1835) 122, 125, 152
Stolberg-Wernigerode, Udo zu (1840-1910) 24, 212
Stölzel, Gerhard (1835-1905) 133
Straelen 102
Strikes 62, 122-23, 125, 129-30, 144, 154
Strombeck, Joseph von (d. 1915) 173
Stuart-Wortley, Edward 214
Stumm, Carl Ferdinand von (1836-1901) *See also* Partito populare184-85
Suval, Stanley 126-27, 268
Switzerland 108
Sybel, Heinrich von 10

T

Teutonia (Catholic fraternity) 60
Thissen, *Landgerichtsobersekretär* 56
Thun, Alphons 111-13, 115,
Thyssen, August (1842-1926) 29
Timmermanns, Leonhard (president of Aachen's *Pius-Verein*) 48
Tirpitz, Alfred von (1849-1930) 193-94, 213
Treitschke, Heinrich von 10, 21
Trier 8, 19-20, 26, 33-34, 36-37, 39-40, 42, 50, 55, 60, 65, 88-89, 97, 101, 128, 136, 150, 152-55, 158-59, 164-65, 172, 180, 200, 211, 229, 237, 242, 245, 248
　Holy Shroud of 40, 42
Triererische Volkszeitung 88
Trimborn, Jeanne 38, 62, 201
Trimborn, Karl (1854-1921) 16-17, 38, 60-65, 73, 76, 79, 81-82, 84-89, 91-93, 102, 104, 117, 123, 131-32, 134-35, 137, 139, 141, 144, 147, 152, 157-58, 161-62, 173-74, 183, 188, 193, 201-2, 205, 212, 215-16, 227-29, 231, 234, 238, 240, 243-44, 249
　and elections 131-32
　Farmers' Association 79
　and *Gewerkschaftsstreit* 152, 157-58, 161-62, 205
　as leader of People's Association 60-65, 183, 202, 234
　loss of Reichstag seat 231
　and Navy Bill 193
　as organizer of Rhenish Center 81-87, 91-92, 135, 139, 141, 234, 238, 240
　and party leadership 76
　personality of 60
　political career of 81-82, 134, 183, 201-2, 212, 215-16

as political journalist 93
and presss 93, 102, 104, 234
and social question 117, 147, 202, 238
and *Zentrumsstreit* 173-74

U

Ultramontanism 12, 22, 52, 255, 267
Underberg (factory owner) 167, 170, 173
Unfallkommission, see Workers' Compensation Act
Unitas (Catholic fraternity) 62
United States of America 26, 126

V

Verband Arbeiterwohl 63
Verband der christlichen Textilarbeiter 124
Verbandskatholizismus 49
Verband katholischer Arbeitervereine West- deutschlands, see German Catholic Workers' Association
Vienna, Congress of 18-19, 43
Virnich, Winand (1836-90) 98
Vohwinkel 133
Volksverein für das Katholische Deutschland, see People's Association for Catholic Germany

W

Wagner, Cosima (née Liszt, 1837-1930)
Wallenborn, Quirin Peter (1848-1917) 168, 245
Wamboldt von Umstadt, Baron Franz von (1829-1908) 69
Wehler, *Hans-Ulrich* 184, 187, 194
Weilbächer, Paul (journalist) 103
Wellstein, Georg (1849-1918) 216
Westdeutsche Arbeiterzeitung 101, 102, 123
Westfälischer Bauernverein see Westphalian Farmer's Association
Westphalia 8, 18-19, 22, 26, 29, 34, 49, 57, 72, 75-76, 91, 128-29, 131, 136, 146, 166, 207
Westphalian Farmer's Association (*Westfälischer Bauernverein*) 75
Wichern, Johann Hinrich (1808-81) 28
Wiedenbrück 136
Wild, Eberhard, Center politician 227
Wilhelm II (1888-1918); *also* Kaiser 7, 131, 176, 178, 182, 184-85, 195-99, 204, 206-7, 214, 221
attitude toward Center Party 195-97, 204
and Bismarck's resignation 131
and franchise reform 221
and social legislation 182, 185
Windthorst, Ludwig (1812-91) 7, 14-16, 36, 48, 50-51, 57, 60-61, 65, 68-69, 70-71, 73, 75, 105, 131, 164-65, 168, 174, 181, 186, 197, 202, 222
and founding of Center Party 50-51
and founding of People's Association 60-61, 65, 75
at *Katholikentag* 48
political career of 7, 14-15
political philosophy of 168, 174, 181
succession of 68-69, 73
and *Weltpolitik* 186-87
Windthorstbund 89-90, 226
Witt, Hermann Ludger de (1856-1909) 77, 216, 244

Wolff-Metternich, Count Alfred
   209
Women workers 123
Workers, *See also* strikes 7-
   9, 12, 17, 23, 25, 31, 39,
   41-43, 107-8, 111-12, 116-
   21, 123-26, 130, 152-55,
   157-58, 161, 190, 230,
   238, 249
Workers' clubs, *see* Catholic
   workers' clubs
Workers' Compensation Act
   146, 201
Workers' Welfare 63, 117-19,
   249
World War I 7, 13, 32, 102,
   161, 166, 187, 197, 219,
Wuppertal 24
   economy of
Würselen 112
Württemberg 8, 13, 79-80,
   105, 136, 190, 235
   Center Party of
   Landtag of 105
Würzburg 20, 62, 70, 151

Z

Zeender, John K. 13, 67-69, 71,
   80, 135, 146-47, 181, 183,
   185, 191, 202
Zehnhoff, Hugo am (1855-1930)
   77
Zentrumsstreit 41, 99, 147-
   52, 163-64, 166-67, 171,
   174-75, 209, 215-16, 230,
   233, 236-37, 240, 250